The American South in the Twentieth Century

The Atlanta History Center

The University of Georgia Press
Athens and London

The American South

edited by

Craig S. Pascoe

Karen Trahan Leathem

and

Andy Ambrose

in the Twentieth Century

© 2005 by The University of Georgia Press
Athens, Georgia 30602
Set in 10 on 13 New Caledonia by Bookcomp
Printed and bound by Maple-Vail
The paper in this book meets the guidelines for permanence
and durability of the Committee on Production Guidelines
for Book Longevity of the Council on Library Resources.

Printed in the United States of America
09 08 07 06 05 C 5 4 3 2 1
09 08 07 06 05 P 5 4 3 2 1

Library of Congress Cataloging-in-Publication Data
The American South in the twentieth century / edited by
Craig S. Pascoe, Karen Trahan Leathem, and Andy
Ambrose.
        p. cm.
Includes bibliographical references and index.
ISBN-13: 978-0-8203-2594-1 (hardcover : alk. paper)
ISBN-10: 0-8203-2594-5 (hardcover : alk. paper)
ISBN-13: 978-0-8203-2771-6 (pbk. : alk. paper)
ISBN-10: 0-8203-2771-9 (pbk. : alk. paper)
1. Southern States—History—20th century.
I. Pascoe, Craig S., 1952–   II. Leathem, Karen
Trahan.   III. Ambrose, Andy.
F216.A66 2005
975'.043—dc22
2005011899

British Library Cataloging-in-Publication Data available

Contents

Changing Power Structures and Relations

Photographs

CRAIG S. PASCOE
KAREN TRAHAN LEATHEM
ANDY AMBROSE

Preface

The American South in the Twentieth Century began as a special issue of *Atlanta History: A Journal of Georgia and the South*. The journal, based at the Atlanta History Center, has been published for more than seventy-five years. Over the years the Atlanta History Center has become more involved in state and regional topics, largely because of the importance of Atlanta as a regional urban center and because its archives, housed in the James G. Kenan Research Center, contain documents and images pertaining to the region as well as the city. The Atlanta History Center's deputy director Andy Ambrose and then–managing editor of the journal Craig S. Pascoe wanted to put together an issue that emphasized the History Center's position as a regional history center.

For the special issue we invited eight scholars in the fields of history, economics, sociology, and political science to write "thought pieces" on the twentieth-century South. How had the South changed—or not changed? Had the South as a distinct region disappeared? Or had the South absorbed outside investment, immigration, and new technology and still retained its distinctive cultural and social patterns? Those were some of the questions that we asked the authors to consider when writing their essays. We also asked them to write essays that would appeal to a broad audience—scholars, students, and the general public. Those were the only parameters that we gave.

The issue, originally published in the winter of 2001, was well received by the Atlanta History Center membership, journal subscribers, scholars of the South, and other readers. We discussed the possibility of turning the special issue into a book with the University of Georgia Press. The book allowed us to expand our scope with nine additional topics, including essays on music, sports, education, and agriculture.

Although the authors worked independently on different topics, many of them address similar themes and events. One example is the importance of the Supreme Court case *Brown v. Board of Education*. Of course James Anderson, who writes about black education in the South, highlights the importance of the ruling for southern education. In addition, Charles Bullock and Janna Deitz, who write about federal intervention; Grace Hale, who writes about race relations; Julia Kirk Blackwelder, who writes about southern women; and Pete Daniel, who writes about agriculture and the rural South, all touch on how the Supreme Court decision affected life beyond the schoolroom.

The common ground of the essays, however, extends beyond such pivotal events. Certain themes link the essays, providing an overarching way of viewing the South in the past century. A brief outline of these themes follows.

Change and continuity. Ever since C. Vann Woodward argued in *Origins of the New South* that the Civil War marked a watershed in southern history—that economic power, social relations, and many other aspects of life changed from that point on—historians have often pondered the extent of the region's transformation. Most agree that dramatic change has occurred—with regard to race and politics, for example—but maintain that the South has not gone far enough. Others argue that the South is still tied to the past, that it carries on the traditions of the Old South under the cloak of modern ways. Still others, like James C. Cobb and Martin Sosna, posit that the post–World War II second New South is much like the first, doling out benefits in grossly unequal amounts. And some of the authors in this collection point out that change is not always good or accepted willingly, especially in the realm of race relations.

Race. Race is often used to identify the South as a region, society, political system, and culture apart from mainstream America. Likewise, many argue that racism and patterns of racial discrimination throughout the twentieth century also differentiate the region from the rest of the nation. All of the contributors weave this theme through their essays, showing how race was an important element in everything from women's work to collegiate sports.

Segregation and the fall of Jim Crow. Although segregation is connected to race, it deserves greater scrutiny. We are only now beginning to understand the complexities of the daily workings and political underpinnings of the system called Jim Crow. From the enactment of laws that mandated separation of the races in public venues beginning in the late 1800s to the massive resistance to desegregation in the 1950s, white southerners constructed and fortified a political, economic, and social system that sheltered themselves and oppressed African Americans. Some of the authors in this collection describe the efforts to dismantle that system while others explore white opposition and black resistance. The modern civil rights movement occupies a central place in the history of the twentieth-century South, and many of our contributors explore the contours and consequences of the movement.

Ethnicity. During the colonial period, southern society was composed primarily of American Indians, European settlers, and enslaved Africans. After the majority of American Indians were expelled from the South in the first half of the nineteenth century, many came to view the South as a society divided between black and white. While such a conception of the South was accurate to a certain extent, there were other ethnic and racial groups present who contributed to a more complex demographic portrait. From Jews scattered throughout the South to Irish and Germans in urban areas and French-speaking Louisianians, southerners made up a diverse lot.

In the twentieth century, an increasing variety of people migrated to the South, defying notions of the stereotypical southerner—black or white. Today, such new groups as Mexicans, Colombians, Hondurans, Caribs, Vietnamese, Laotians, Koreans, and others bring with them new cultures, new ideas, and new religions. In addition, newcomers from other regions of the United States, sometimes jokingly referred to as "foreigners," are also affecting southern culture. As southern residents, they are changing the way we define southern identity. If a first-generation Korean American operating a Mexican restaurant in Chamblee, Georgia, or a factory worker from the Bronx transplanted to Spartanburg, South Carolina, considers himself or herself a southerner, it means that the old stereotypes have to be discarded, or at least amended. A Latina clerk in an Indian grocery store in Atlanta wearing a T-shirt proclaiming "I Love NASCAR" is just one example of the recent twists and turns in the evolution of southern identity.

Women. The story of the twentieth-century South cannot be told without putting the changes in women's lives front and center. Women's expanding public roles as well as their role in shaping the South from the workplace to the civil rights movement is reflected in their political activism and their leadership in education and arts and culture. Beyond Julia Kirk Blackwelder's essay, we see the imprint of women, for example, in Andy Doyle's essay on sports; in Fred Hobson's exploration of Zora Neale Hurston's take on black culture and Eudora Welty's social commentary; and in Grace Hale's account of the African American freedom struggle in which such women as Mamie Bradley, Jo Ann Robinson, and Diane Nash played a significant part.

Cultural distinctiveness and identity. Many people agree that there is a South with a distinct culture and that the region is different from the rest of the nation. Yet attempts to define or describe the region inevitably lead to differences of opinion. Where is the South geographically? What character-istics distinguish southerners from everyone else? After all the changes of the past century, does a South exist, and if so, just who is a southerner? Distinct social and cultural markers like segregation, rural life, literature, agriculture, whiteness, location, and foodways were more prominent before mass culture homogenized the nation. Now these categories are no longer foolproof ways to spot a southerner.

Modernization. Since Reconstruction, southern politicians, boosters, news-paper editors, and business leaders have championed modernization—pop-ulation growth, increased cultural and economic diversity, new technologies, and stronger connections to the national (and now global) economy. While the South has seen much change in these areas, many critics find the gains inadequate. And others argue that modernity and economic prosperity have occurred only in isolated urban pockets. Many areas of the South still await the benefits of high-paying jobs, good roads, adequate schools, and higher standards of living.

Education. Although James Anderson's and Thomas Dyer's essays address education specifically, many of the other essays touch on it. Education, or the lack of it, had a profound effect on the twentieth-century South. From the establishment of compulsory education to the civil rights movement's focus on schools, education stood at the center of pivotal changes in politics, the economy, and racial matters. The issue of the distribution of educational resources continues into the new century as states and school districts deal with the No Child Left Behind Act and the push for charter schools.

Impact of outside forces. Some argue that the South would have remained mired in the past if not for the influence of outside forces. Charles Bullock and Janna Deitz believe that the federal government was the only force that could "overcome the region's intransigence in the sphere of race relations and the magnitude of its economic deprivation." James Anderson emphasizes the importance of the federal government in bringing about equal access to educational opportunities. Often, the outside influence was not welcome, as in the case of southern farmers' distrust of federal rules about what they could or could not grow on their land.

In addition, national and international events that influenced southern life, especially World War II, hastened the migration of both African Americans and whites into urban areas. Another notable development was the advent of a national television culture, which played a key role in the civil rights movement by exposing the stark racism and violence to the rest of the country.

Urbanization. One of the major factors that has distinguished the South from other regions of the United States is its persistent poverty and rural composition. In the decades after the Civil War, the South began to experience urban growth. But it was not until well into the twentieth century that urbanization had a dramatic impact. Cities like Atlanta, Dallas, Charlotte, and Miami grew to become important regional urban hubs. The growth of cities and their economic influence changed the nature of the southern economy and thereby southern life. Urban places in the South have also contributed to the changing nature of the region's culture—sometimes creating an environment that is difficult to define as "southern." Yet, rural lifestyles and values have not been entirely lost and indeed persist in religion and popular culture.

Economic issues. One of the most important changes in the region in the last one hundred years is the transformation of its economy to one that is now connected to national and international marketplaces. In this volume, economic historian Gavin Wright takes on the task of describing how the southern economy matured in the twentieth century, but other historians join him in reflecting on the impact of economic issues. From Pete Daniel's consideration of agriculture and its relationship to big business to Julia Black-welder's documentation of women working outside the home, many of the authors emphasize the significance of economic issues.

One of the issues that the reader should consider when reading the essays in this collection is—where exactly is the twentieth-century South? There is no single, accepted geographic definition of the region or even consensus on how the South's borders may have changed over time. Instead, there are many different tools and methods used to define the South. Some point to the former Confederate States as constituting the true South, while others rely on economic, political, or religious characteristics to identify the region. And then there are those who look for cultural traits and practices that are considered "southern"—anything from restaurants that serve grits and sweet tea to the use of the word "Dixie" in the local Yellow Pages to the greatest concentration of churchgoing Baptists or NASCAR fans.

There are also, it should be noted, differences in how southerners and nonsoutherners define the South. In response to this, some have suggested that the best way to identify the boundaries of the region is to consult the residents themselves. If a large majority believes that they are southerners, then they are indeed part of the South. But as all these various measures indicate, and the essays in this book suggest, the twentieth-century South (and, in particular, the "modern" South) is neither as solid nor homogeneous as many assume.

For the purpose of visualizing the South as a distinct region, the editors suggest that the reader consider the eleven states that seceded from the Union—Alabama, Arkansas, Florida, Georgia, Louisiana, Mississippi, North Carolina, South Carolina, Tennessee, Texas, and Virginia. Other border or nearby states, such as Missouri, Kentucky, Oklahoma, Maryland, and West Virginia, should also be included insofar as they are affected by the specific forces and shaping influences discussed and described in these essays.

It is our hope that this collection will provide readers with a better understanding of the South as a region as well as its twentieth-century transformation. The authors of the essays explore the many facets and meanings of southern history, opening doors for further inquiry. From the birth of the Delta blues to today's sparkling new automobile plants, the South provides a fertile ground for contemplating the past century.

The American South in the Twentieth Century

JAMES C. COBB

From the First New South to the Second

The Southern Odyssey
through the Twentieth Century

With its rigid system of racial apartheid and its labor-intensive agricultural economy, the South straggled into the twentieth century looking more like the South of 1850 than the America of 1900. Yet, although it strode self-confidently into the twenty-first century as the nation's most racially integrated and economically dynamic region, the real story of the southern experience over the last hundred years is the transition, not from the Old South to the New South, but from one New South toward another.

Edwin M. Yoder Jr. once observed that there have been as many "'New Souths' as French constitutions and theories about the fall of Rome." In reality, there have actually been only two New Souths, although one of them, the second, has been proclaimed almost incessantly since World War II. In this latter, much-anticipated incarnation, the New South would be a much healthier society, but its lifespan would be relatively brief because its radically reformed racial, political, and economic institutions would pave the way for its rapid absorption into the mainstream of American life. The original New South, however, was built both to last and to stand on its own; its architects promised reintegration into the national economy without the sacrifice of the region's racial, cultural, or political continuity or autonomy. In effect, the first New South was to be "new," observed W. J. Cash, only in "that it would be so rich and powerful that it might rest serene in its ancient positions, forever impregnable."

In the 1880s when Henry Grady foresaw a New South of surging prosperity, he also envisioned a New South where racial separation was the rule "in every theatre" and in "railroads, schools and elsewhere." Indeed, segregation was "nothing less than an organic component of the New South Creed," as John Cell put it, because it promised to stabilize race relations in urban areas where the lure of jobs promised to bring large numbers of racially obsessed lower-class whites into close physical proximity with large numbers of blacks who threatened to become both their economic and social competitors. Thus, segregation was crucial to maintaining the rigidly controlled labor climate that potential investors intent on taking advantage of the South's cheap labor deemed essential. Meanwhile, disfranchisement ensured a similarly restrictive political climate by stripping the vote from the South's black voters and many of its lower-class white ones as well and paving the way for conservative New South Democrats to achieve political insularity while still pursuing economic assimilation. Democrats soon dominated southern politics from the county seat to Congress, where the region's perpetually reelected, seniority-buttressed representatives practiced political obstructionism to near perfection, blocking any legislative initiative that gave even the slightest hint of disrupting the white-supremacist framework that quickly became synonymous with the "southern way of life."

Behind its smokescreen of economic progress, industrial philanthropy, and benevolence lay the raw realities of brutal exploitation of the mass of men, women, and children of both races. Elsewhere in this volume Dana White argues convincingly that Tom Wolfe's *A Man in Full* captures the runaway greed and ruthlessness so characteristic of Atlanta at the end of the twentieth century. An equally critical treatment of Atlanta much earlier in the century appeared in another novel whose central character, the brassy daughter of an Irish immigrant who had clawed his way up to a prominent position within the antebellum slaveholding regime, replicates her papa's feat in the wake of that regime's demise. In Margaret Mitchell's *Gone with the Wind*, after Scarlett O'Hara rises, ravenous, from the soil of Tara and heads off to Atlanta to make good on her vow that she will never be hungry again, her experiences reveal the underside of the New South's so-called rise from the ashes. Scoffing at the attempts of postbellum Atlanta's stodgy society women to maintain their old pretensions to gentility despite their new circumstances of impoverishment, Scarlett snorts, "The silly fools don't realize that you can't be a lady without money." As the idealist-aristocrat Ashley Wilkes sinks into poverty and despair, Scarlett seizes the day, realizing that in the resurrection of Atlanta "there is plenty of money to be made by anyone who isn't afraid to work or to grab." Scarlett fears neither and, after floating a loan from wartime profiteer Rhett Butler, she is soon running her own lumber mill with the ruthlessness and rapacity of a robber baroness. Stooping even to leasing convict labor, she proves herself more than the equal of her male competitors, scoffing at the strict gender conventions that, as Julia Kirk Blackwelder shows, confronted any would-be new woman of the first New South.

The greed and materialism of the New South were hardly appealing, but the realities of its racial violence and repression were even more repugnant. Proponents had promised that segregation and disfranchisement would restore the "natural" harmony between black and white that had prevailed under slavery. As Grace Hale points out in her essay, however, neither the ubiquitous, round-the-clock regimen of segregation nor the gruesome recurrent ritual of lynching succeeded in forcing southern blacks to accept their inferiority or in convincing southern whites that this superiority was immune to challenge. The reality of what passed for racial harmony and stability in the New South comes through in the dark humor of an African American elevator operator who remarked to Richard Wright that "Ef it wuzn't for them polices 'n' them ol' lynch-mobs, there wouldn't be nothing but uproar down here."

With the invasion of the boll weevil threatening to extinguish their already dim economic prospects, the allure of the urban North with its promise of jobs and escape from the South's racial pressure cooker proved irresistible to many southern blacks who joined the Great Migration, which saw nearly a half-million African Americans leave the region between 1916 and 1920 alone and eventually reduced the South's share of the nation's black population from 89 percent in 1910 to 53 percent by 1970.

The beginning of the Great Migration opened what many historians now cite as the most critical period in the history of the post-Reconstruction South. On its heels came the Great Depression and the New Deal. Alexander P. Lamis observes in his discussion of the rise of a two-party system in the region that the one-party South's obstructionist presence in Congress served as a choke collar on the New Deal's potential to trigger meaningful social and economic reform. Not surprisingly, as Pete Daniel points out in his essay on the transformation of the rural South, white planters and local political nabobs benefited disproportionately from the acreage-reduction subsidies dispensed by the Agricultural Adjustment Administration, and they also manipulated the New Deal's various relief programs to shift some of the burden of sharecroppers' upkeep to the federal government. Still, the New Deal farm program's inducements to sharecropper displacement and agricultural mechanization set in motion both a revolution in southern agriculture and, as both David Carlton and Gavin Wright indicate in their essays, a greatly intensified effort to promote the region's industrial development.

Meanwhile, the always-improbable New Deal coalition of organized labor, southern whites, and northern blacks (whose ranks had been fed by the aforementioned exodus of huge numbers of African Americans from a region where they could not vote to one where they could) seemed on the verge of a stress fracture by the end of the 1930s. The decision to drop the two-thirds majority requirement for the Democratic Party's presidential nominee effectively stripped the white South of its veto power over any candidate who seemed the least bit squeamish about the region's racial arrangements. In addition, the symbolically charged selection of a black minister to deliver the invocation at one convention session did not sit well with Dixie's delegates, particularly South Carolina's Ellison D. "Cotton Ed" Smith, whose famous stem-winding "Philladelphy Speech" described his ostentatious exit from the session and its endorsement by the hovering spirit of John C. Calhoun. This speech served Cotton Ed well as he prevailed in 1938 against President Franklin D. Roosevelt's effort to purge the Democratic Party of Smith and several other southern Senators who, so Roosevelt believed, had opposed his most progressive New Deal initiatives. Like his abortive effort to "pack" the Supreme Court with more liberal justices, Roosevelt's ill-fated purge effort in 1938 seemed to reflect his desire to desouthernize the Democratic Party.

As Charles S. Bullock and Janna Deitz indicate in their analysis of the role of the federal government in reshaping the region, World War II ushered in an era of defense spending that energized the South's economy far beyond anything the New Deal had managed. In fact, defense and military spending in the region amounted to a third and much deeper-pocketed New Deal for Dixie. Total government expenditures during the entire New Deal were roughly equal to the payout on the ten largest defense contracts issued between 1940 and 1944, and defense and military spending alone pumped as much as nine billion dollars into the South, spurring job growth as manufacturing employment grew by 50 percent during the war. At the same time, war-induced prosperity made conservative southern political leaders far less dependent on Washington's largesse. In response, they gave full vent to their antagonism toward federal interference in their racial affairs and assailed any and all government programs that might benefit either blacks or organized labor in any way. They were also quick to condemn First Lady Eleanor Roosevelt's obvious sympathy for African Americans struggling against the oppression of the southern racial system.

The apprehensions of many southern whites mounted rapidly as they watched the war draw away their cheap farm labor, raising wage rates as it did so and giving southern blacks unprecedented freedom from the economic coercion that had been a key weapon in Jim Crow's defense arsenal. Again, these changes in black-white interaction were part of a larger economic and demographic transformation wrought by World War II. Annual wages rose significantly across the board as well, drawing large numbers of women into the work force for the first time. Between 1940 and 1950 the number of women employed in manufacturing rose by 60 percent in Mississippi alone.

Fuller employment at better wages (wages that still, however, were well below the national average) gave the post–World War II South the consumer spending potential to attract more upscale market-oriented manufacturers such as the automobile industry, whose move to the Atlanta area seemed to suggest that the first of the New South's promises of plenty would soon be fulfilled. In the wake of World War II, however, "New South" took on a different connotation as the old promise of economic transformation without social or political change gave way to an expanded and dramatically altered vision of progress in which economic, racial, and political change were wholly interdependent and inseparable. World War II had forced a great many white Americans to confront at last the Jim Crow system's backyard mockery of the very democratic ideals that the nation's soldiers had gone thousands of miles away to defend. The speedy transition to the cold war, in which the United States quickly became the undisputed leader of the so-called free world, only made southern racial practices even more embarrassing, especially as Africa emerged as a new continent ripe for Communist conquest.

Beginning in the late 1930s, the Supreme Court issued a series of rulings suggesting that a critical reappraisal of the separate-but-equal doctrine might soon be in the offing. It went on in 1944 to overturn the racially exclusionary Democratic "white primary" laws (*Smith v. Allwright*) and practices that prevented southern blacks from voting in the only elections that mattered in their states. At the same time, returning black veterans voiced their determination that their risks and sacrifices in defense of democracy abroad would not be mocked by continued adherence to Jim Crow at home. Moderate Mississippi congressman Frank E. Smith insisted that "more men came home from World War II with a sense of purpose than from any other venture," but it did not follow that they all returned with the same sense of purpose. For every Medgar Evers who threw himself into NAACP efforts to overthrow white supremacy, there was a Byron De La Beckwith who came home ready to kill anyone who challenged "the southern way of life." White veterans swelled the ranks of the Dixiecrats, the Ku Klux Klan, and the White Citizens' Councils as the NAACP's challenge to Jim Crow gained momentum in the courts and in the press. At the same time, however, more moderate (though still strictly segregationist) whites focused on the need to modernize state and local governments and economies in the South. From Little Rock to New Orleans to Augusta, returning veterans ousted entrenched political machines and committed themselves to more efficient government and more aggressive pursuit of new industrial investment.

Although they were hardly committed to racial integration, in the wake of the *Brown* decision and the perceived "lesson of Little Rock" (that racial unrest and violence were anathema to relocating industrialists), the South's new development-oriented leaders began to calculate the costs of racial conflict in their states and communities. When the sit-in movement and the Southern Christian Leadership Conference's campaign of nonviolent protests focused national attention on segregation and voting discrimination in southern cities on the make for new industry or beholden to branch facilities of major national corporations, the key to the community's response was the willingness of business and development leaders to counsel acquiescence to at least token desegregation of local schools and other facilities.

The Rev. Martin Luther King Jr.'s brilliant blend of philosophical depth, Baptist fervor, and public relations savvy made him a fearsome antagonist to image-conscious development advocates across the South. This was certainly true in Augusta, Georgia, where the threat of pre-Masters protests and boycotts led to the speedy integration of the city's downtown theaters in 1962, because, as the former mayor explained to me, "We didn't want 'em to bring in Martin Luther King." King won his most important strategic victories where less canny whites resisted doggedly, violently, and openly. This was surely the case with Birmingham, where Bull Connor's police dogs and fire hoses helped fan the national outrage that culminated in the Civil Rights Act of 1964, and Selma, where Sheriff Jim Clark's police dogs and billy clubs contributed to the passage of the Voting Rights Act a year later. Both of these measures brought dramatic changes to the South, but the political impact of the Voting Rights Act was both immediate and revolutionary as the percentage of registered, voting-age African Americans rose from 5 to 59 percent in Mississippi between 1960 and 1971 and more than doubled in Alabama, Georgia, and South Carolina. This explosion of new black voters seemed to trigger a sudden impulse among once obstinately segregationist white politicians to lock arms with black ministers and civil rights leaders and sing "We Shall Overcome." Along with several federal court rulings overturning malapportioned voting systems such as Georgia's outrageously antiurban county-unit system, urban blacks and metropolitan whites were soon pivotally positioned in post–civil rights movement southern politics. Unfortunately for the Democratic Party, the same presidential and congressional initiatives that brought thousands of southern blacks into its ranks provoked a countervailing response from a great many southern whites who broke from the ranks of the party of their ancestors and, without looking back, rallied to the long-hated Republicans, whose nominee made no secret of his opposition to the Civil Rights Act and his desire to capture the support of disenchanted southern whites.

Barry Goldwater represented yet another lost cause for southern whites in 1964, but his ability to carry five southern states and take many counties by roughly the same huge margins as they had given John F. Kennedy four years earlier foretold the partisan realignment that had been hovering over the South since the late 1930s. It would be twelve years before the Democrats would break the GOP's grip on the South, and even then, native son Jimmy Carter would fail to capture a majority of the white vote in the region.

Although Bill Clinton would also succeed in denying the Republicans a southern sweep in both of his campaigns, he garnered little more than one-third of the southern white vote. Meanwhile, Republican inroads in the South, with its surging population growth, led to the return to congressional power of a new Dixieland band playing a somewhat familiar tune, albeit under a new partisan banner. At the state and local levels, the Republican move "down the ticket" manifested itself first in metropolitan areas but spread gradually into the hinterlands where local Democratic incumbents began to discover that their ostentatious displays of yard signs and bumper stickers supporting the GOP presidential ticket did not always suffice in the face of organized and well-funded local Republican challenges.

If the lily-white politics of the first New South had amounted to allocating most of a very little to a very few—"Juleps for the few and pellagra for the crew," as C. Vann Woodward put it—an increasingly dynamic regional economy gave practitioners of the second New South's biracial politics a much bigger pie with the potential for a more equitable distribution of its slices. Coupled with a relatively high birth rate, the accelerating southward shift of people (white, black, and immigrant) continued to enhance the South's market appeal and began to entice the entrepreneurs, managers, professionals, and skilled workers so long conspicuous by their absence in Dixie. The region's new role as the economic cornerstone of the Sun Belt seemed to suggest that the South had, at long last, not just plunged into the nation's economic mainstream but claimed it as its own.

Unfortunately, however, the South's conquest of the economic mainstream had been facilitated by the southward drift of the mainstream itself. The southbound exodus of jobs and investment capital that turned the nation's long-dynamic manufacturing belt into a stagnant and decaying Rust Belt was actually part of the larger, long-term process of economic globalization. The transfer of capital to the South with its cheaper labor market and lower operating costs was in large measure a response to the increasingly competitive world economy. As globalization gained momentum, however, the economic gains enjoyed by the post–World War II South quickly stripped it of its low-wage advantage relative to the untapped labor markets of so-called third-world nations or developing regions. Yet, owing to its chronic underinvestment in education (to which both Carlton and Wright allude) and human resource development in general, the South became a high-wage region saddled, for the most part, with both a low-wage infrastructure and a surplus of workers who lacked the experience or skills required by high-wage employers.

As Carlton shows, while state economic developers seemed to echo the irrational exuberance of Henry Grady as they trumpeted the glorious message of cutting-edge, high-tech jobs, their local counterparts often faced the reality of work forces lacking even the minimal reading and math skills demanded by the fast-food industry. Thus, at the end of the twentieth century, the economic philosophy of the second New South still bore a disquieting resemblance to that of the first New South at the end of the nineteenth. Southern states wooed automobile plants for the relatively higher-paying jobs they promised, but the pursuit of these economic benefits came at significant social cost. Alabama, for example, enticed the German-owned Daimler-Benz (for whom higher-than-average wages in Alabama still meant considerable wage and benefits savings compared to Germany) with six-figure-per-job subsidies and tax exemptions offered at the expense of a public school system that had long been one of the nation's worst. Meanwhile, the fact that areas with relatively high concentrations of African Americans continued to struggle to provide even low-wage jobs for their residents only highlighted the unevenness of southern economic growth.

On the other hand, for all the dark spots in its supposedly "sunny" economy, the post–civil rights movement South was definitely the place to go for African Americans on the move. Some 4 million blacks left the region between 1910 and 1970, but since that time, the South has steadily attracted more African

The BMW plant in Spartanburg, South Carolina.
Courtesy of BMW Manufacturing Company.

Americans than it lost, with the 1990s alone registering net black in-migration of approximately 579,000 as part of an overall black population growth of 3.6 million during the decade. Demographers foresee no end to this trend as black migrants head to such economic hotspots as Atlanta, Dallas, and Charlotte. Even rural areas saw a net gain in black population, however, as some in-migrants sought the peace, quiet, and sense of belonging that the urban North simply could not provide. As literary scholar Thadious Davis observed, the return of African Americans to the South represented more than a response to economic opportunity or "flight from the hardships of urban life." It also amounted to "a laying claim to a culture and to a region that, though fraught with pain and difficulty, provides a major grounding for identity."

Davis's observation seemed to be affirmed by polling data showing that, as John Shelton Reed points out, in the wake of the civil rights movement, African Americans living in the South have been just about as likely to identify themselves as "southerners" as have their white counterparts in the region. Speaking of these white counterparts, as Reed argues here and elsewhere, once their long, arduous, and erratic journey toward the mainstream of American life finally led them to its banks, many of them chose, despite their Baptist proclivities, to resist total immersion. Instead, they often waded in up to wallet or purse depth and opted for a selective sprinkling of the remainder of their torsos. It had long been thought that although economic mainstreaming was the best prescription for curing most of what ailed the South, it would also amount to a death sentence for southern distinctiveness. Sure enough, as Reed argues, economic progress has done much to eradicate the overt racism, ignorance, and provincialism that once set the great mass of white southerners apart. On the other hand, however, economic gains have both enabled and encouraged white and black southerners to seek affirmation of their regional identities or "invent new ways of being southern." *Southern Living* magazine comes to mind here as do Anythingsouthern.com and a host of other South-oriented cyber sites. Like Andy Doyle and David Stricklin, respectively, Reed cites stock car racing and country music as examples of relatively new manifestations of southern identity that have been exported well beyond the boundaries not only of the South but of the United States as well. The problem here is that, given the well-established national and international appeal of both phenomena, we must ask whether at some point they will simply cease to represent anything peculiarly "southern."

Questions of southern distinctiveness have traditionally been presented in terms of the South's differences from the rest of the United States. As C. Vann Woodward pointed out nearly a half century ago, however, the southern experience seems far less peculiar than that of the rest of the nation when both are placed in a broader global context. We live in an age of rapid economic and cultural globalization, where even distinctions among nations seem to be fading by the day. Does it really make sense, therefore, to continue to talk so much about "southern distinctiveness," especially when much of what now passes for it is little more than the caricatured creation of the crafty folks who have found an economic bonanza in marketing a commodified version of southernness to those who feel they have lost sight of what being southern really means?

If the South's identity crisis provides a niche market within its new consumer economy, it also has not just cultural but political ramifications as well. Blacks and whites may call themselves southerners in relatively equal percentages, but they clearly differ significantly when it comes to what "southernness" actually means, or as the ongoing battles over state flags, Confederate monuments, and other historical symbols illustrate, how it should be represented.

Although the fact that many white southerners still cling to the Confederate flag may seem to suggest that perhaps the South has not changed all that much after all, the direct and widespread challenges to it by black southerners and the relative success those efforts have enjoyed would indicate otherwise. Clearly, the story that unfolds in this volume is hardly one of consistent and undiluted change. In fact, to some extent all the essays present change and continuity not so much in conflict as in an exceedingly complex and uneven process of mutual adaptation. David Stricklin makes this point expertly in his treatment of the evolution of southern music, which, regardless of its Delta, Piedmont, or "hillbilly" roots, remained constantly a work in progress as its cultural foundations encountered a succession of commercial influences and economic and demographic changes. Andy Doyle also places his discussion of southern sports in the context of a South in transition. Its martial and masculine traditions meshed with its boosterism and its lust for the trappings of modernity to make the organized spectacle of college football a quasi religion although, until relatively recently at least, its racial and gender conventions restricted participation in certain sports and at certain levels by both African Americans and women.

In tracing the evolution of southern literature in the twentieth century, Fred Hobson explores the changing historical circumstances behind the search for southern self-discovery that brought us the Southern Literary Renaissance and inspired many of the leading writers of the Harlem Renaissance as well. The civil rights revolution and the subsequent Sun Belt economic boom also brought major changes in the South's literature as many white novelists moved out of the shadow of William Faulkner and into the shadow of Walker Percy, spurning identification as "southern" writers and shunning specifically regional themes and settings in favor of more universalist treatments of modern life. Rather than destroying southern literature as a distinct genre, however, the breakthroughs of the civil rights era simply brought a new set of practitioners to the fore. Freed from the pressure or sense of obligation to utilize their work as a means of protesting southern racial practices, black writers like Alice Walker and Ernest J. Gaines could now more fully embrace their southern roots and more richly depict the southernness of the characters and contexts they created. As a result, Hobson wrote in 1991, African American writers may have become "the truest contemporary heirs to the southern literary tradition."

The theme of persistence through adaptation runs throughout Charles Wilson's essay on the continuing importance of religion as a fundamental factor in southern life. In 1900, Wilson points out, "an interdenominational, biracial, evangelical Protestant religion dominated the region as no other society in the western world." The same might well be said today despite—and, in some cases, even because of—urbanization, industrialization, in-migration, and a host of other supposedly secularizing influences. The Missionary Baptists may have lost some ground to the upwardly mobile megachurchers, and, in some upscale neighborhoods, Get Right with God signs have given way to People of Distinction Prefer Jesus bumper stickers, but in today's South, as in William Faulkner's, religion is still something that's "just there."

So, too, is segregation, suggests Grace Elizabeth Hale, who reminds us that despite the current tendency to laud the South as the nation's most racially reconciled region, there are actually two stories of the battle against Dixie's "violent and unworkable and immoral culture of segregation." Both are "true," but while one is positive, the other is not. Ultimately, Hale concludes that despite the destruction of Jim Crow's de jure underpinnings, segregation survives, not just as a legacy but as an emotional reality, because of its role in preserving racial identity and the way in which both blacks and whites interpret that identity and present it to others.

Both the legacy of de jure segregation and the reality of continuing de facto segregation are, of course, major concerns in James D. Anderson's exploration of reform in African American education. As Anderson shows, the most successful efforts to improve black education began at the grassroots level, while those that flowed from the top down generally wound up reaffirming the prevailing racial and class hierarchy. Anderson also points to the cultural costs of the destruction of formerly all-black schools and the displacement and dispersion of the black educators who served as critical leaders and role models within so many black communities.

Focusing on southern higher education in general, Thomas G. Dyer sounds a more positive note despite the enduring realities of a sometimes hostile and often indifferent political climate and the inadequate funding that plagued many of the region's colleges and universities throughout the twentieth century. Like so many contributors to this volume, Dyer demonstrates that the major changes he describes have come in the last half century. As late as 1965, he argues persuasively, it would have been utterly unthinkable to predict that forty years later seven southern state schools would place among the top twenty in an influential ranking of the nation's best public universities.

Meanwhile, David Goldfield's essay reminds those who continue to see all southern questions, historical or contemporary, in terms of black and white of the "changing boundaries of race and ethnicity in the modern South," a region that is fast becoming a truly multiethnic as well as multiracial society. Although across the region as a whole, the recent growth of the South's Latino population hardly threatens to put African Americans and Hispanics on anything approaching equal numerical footing anytime soon, tensions between black and Hispanic workers competing for the same or similar jobs has been mounting for some time. The recent effort by African American legislators in Georgia to exclude Hispanics from the provisions of a bill to assist minority contractors also suggests that, as Atlanta Journal-Constitution columnist Cynthia Tucker put it recently, the growth of the South's Latino population represents "a wake-up call for black folks." W. E. B. Du Bois correctly predicted that "the color line" would be "the problem of the twentieth century," and it may well be that, as Goldfield suggests, a major concern for the twenty-first-century South will be the matter of where that line actually runs.

On the economic front, David Carlton focuses on the origins and evolution of southern industrial development strategies and their role in shaping a regional economy whose persistent distinctiveness in the midst of sweeping changes that Gavin Wright both documents and dissects. Both Carlton and Wright anchor their analyses in the historical and cultural realities that confronted southern developers, and both stress the enduring importance of race as a component of continuity and change in shaping the South's economic past as well as its future.

Charles Bullock and Janna Deitz provide a wonderfully focused analysis of the influence of federal policy on the South, discussing the effect reform, regulation, and spending had on the South's racial, political, and economic systems. While the overall picture offered by Bullock and Deitz is positive, Pete Daniel's assessment of Washington's role in reshaping southern rural life is not exactly upbeat. Daniel's essay raises the concern that the recent emphasis on the growth of the South's metropolitan areas may have distracted us from the plight of the disinherited, displaced rural farm folk of both races whose battle with the forces of nature was compounded by a host of federal "assistance" and regulatory programs.

Alexander Lamis chronicles the once-unthinkable demise of the Democratic Party's grip on the "solid" South and the rise of a "two-party South," where by the end of the twentieth century Democrats were consistently thwarted by a white Republican majority in presidential elections, struggling to maintain a respectable foothold in congressional delegations, losing ground in state legislatures, and facing an expanding challenge in local politics. Lamis recognizes the "rich complexity of the southern partisan reality" at the end of the twentieth century. Yet, though its strength is greatly diminished, just as it was in the one-party era, race is still the single most significant influence on southern voting behavior and the ever-present "moose on the table" at all partisan strategy sessions. Lamis concludes that the rise of a two-party South has "advanced the cause of democracy for all its citizens," but he clearly sees the ability of the southern Democrats to sustain a black-white voter coalition as a "bulwark" against a "racially polarized party system" as the key to preserving and strengthening an open and competitive party system in the South.

In his essay, Dana White provides rich insights into the transformation of the majority of southerners from country people to town people or, more accurately, "metro people." The cities and suburbs to which southerners flocked were shaped, however, by many a poor country boy like Tom Wolfe's Charlie

Croker, who, like Scarlett O'Hara, realized that there was money to be made and power to be grabbed in the blinding explosion of growth in post–World War II Atlanta. The deferred timetable of southern urbanization gave it certain distinctive aspects. The timely arrival of the automobile meant that many of the twentieth-century South's emerging cities could largely bypass the traditional northern/European pattern of residential progression from center city to urban ring. This development not only discouraged the creation of adequate permanent transit systems, but it also helped to trigger the infamous "sprawl" so commonly associated with the cities of the Sun Belt South. White's essay makes it clear that southern urban and metropolitan leaders must choose between "unchecked 'sprawl'" and "some form of 'Smart Growth.'" His discussion gives us some cause to doubt whether they will make the right choice or, for that matter, whether they are even fully aware that such a choice exists.

Julia Kirk Blackwelder shows us how and why, over the course of the twentieth century, southern women moved beyond the severely restricted spheres of work, influence, and social activity that prevailed in 1900 to become both beneficiaries of and active participants in the transformation of southern life. World War II proved a watershed for many southern women, black and white, as it both expanded their opportunities and broadened their perspectives. The passage of various civil rights statutes, especially Title VII and the Civil Rights Act of 1964, barring discrimination by sex as well as race, helped to open doors for women at a time when economic opportunities were becoming more plentiful. Much of the South's early postwar industrial development had centered on the recruitment of apparel and textile firms employing large numbers of women, but despite the region's continuing dependence on low-wage employment southern women are nearing wage parity with other women outside the South. A number of women have also earned high-profile positions in the region's expanding corporate sector. The results for women in the public sphere have been mixed as well. Ten of the fifteen states that rejected the Equal Rights Amendment were in the South. Yet Texas and Kentucky chose women as governors, and women became a much more visible presence in state and county governments throughout the region. If many southern women still found more cultural constraints than women elsewhere in America at the end of the twentieth century, it was nonetheless clear that those constraints were loosening rapidly.

Most who have studied the South over the years have tended to conflate change with a loss of regional identity. Like all professional "southernologists" who know what's good for them, however, the contributors to this volume seem to see a region that has undergone too dramatic a transformation to be mistaken for the first New South but, for ill or good, continues to resist the ultimate capitulation to anonymous Americanism necessary to fulfill the promise of the second one. Measuring change is a profoundly arbitrary exercise, of course, because it obliges us to see history as a consistent linear progression and to select a "point-to-point" time frame over which our assessment is to be conducted. (One might well ask, for example, whether our essays would be much different had they covered only the last sixty years instead of the last hundred.) Suffice it to say, if they are to be guided by the events of the last century, those who will attempt to reconstruct the South's course through the next one should bear in mind that they are tracking a target moving constantly but often erratically, not necessarily forward or backward so much as simply, in the words of Robert Penn Warren, "out of history into history and the awful responsibility of time."

The Question of Race and Gender

DAVID GOLDFIELD

Unmelting the Ethnic South

Changing Boundaries of Race and Ethnicity
in the Modern South

At the beginning of the twentieth century the South was America's most interracial region. Although no statistics would corroborate that impression, all you
had to do was look around at the wide variety of hues, derived mainly from
black-white sexual relations, hardly ever discussed publicly but whispered
about in private—a legacy of slavery and Jim Crow and all the inequality that
had existed in the South for nearly three centuries. Southern states wrestled
with definitions of whiteness, ranging in tolerance from one-fourth to one
drop of black blood, as if science could somehow illuminate the murky past
of interracial intercourse.

But ethnicity was another matter. The great wave of immigration that

19

washed over the United States between 1890 and 1920 largely bypassed the South. Jewish philanthropist Jacob Schiff resettled some Jewish immigrants in such places as Galveston and New Orleans, a relatively small number of Italian and Chinese farmworkers arrived in the Mississippi Delta, and Italians settled in Birmingham and New Orleans in the late nineteenth century, but such settlements were minor ripples in the large tide of overseas migration to the United States. This demographic circumstance contrasted sharply with the population profile of the Old South, especially in cities, where European immigrants comprised as much as 40 percent of the white population. After the Civil War, however, the economic contrast between the North and South grew, and immigration to southern states and cities declined accordingly.

Southern leaders, well aware of the benefits of a cheap, malleable labor force, periodically sought to attract European immigrants both to augment the indigenous black population and to replace African Americans whom they hoped would migrate someplace else—the North or Africa—but preferably out of the South. A Norfolk editor likened European immigration then flowing into northern cities to "a human Nile. Wherever its waves flow fertility is established." In Atlanta, boosters issued this greeting in the 1890s: "Come whatever your political and religious creed; visit us, live with us." The city formed an immigration committee and sent representatives to Europe.

Atlanta managed to attract some Russian Jews and Greeks between 1890 and 1920, though the total Jewish population by the latter year was only 3 percent and Greeks only .3 percent. Jews were markedly successful in Atlanta, proving at least one claim of the city's boosters. In terms of property accumulation and occupational mobility, they outdistanced their northern brethren, and they were the most stable population element. There was, of course, some self-selection among Jews arriving in Atlanta or in any southern city. They already possessed some residential experience in America; they frequently arrived with capital and marketable skills; and they had less need for a relatively large community of coreligionists to provide support.

In most southern cities, despite the relative success of immigrants, the proportion of the population they represented declined through the late nineteenth and early twentieth centuries. This was true even in port cities like Houston and New Orleans. In the former, the immigrant portion of the population shrank from 16 percent in 1870 to 10.4 percent in 1900; in New Orleans, there was an absolute decline in the number of foreign-born Germans as that population fell to half of what it was in 1860, and the Irish population increased by only one-fifth, though a relatively substantial influx of Italian immigrants partially offset the losses.

Since immigration followed the same lines as commercial shipping, the continued decline of direct imports to southern ports indicated fewer possibilities for immigrants to enter the South. In addition, staple agriculture was an even more dominant aspect of the southern economy in the postwar years, whereas the so-called new immigration that began during the 1880s was attracted most by urban-industrial opportunities. The tenant and sharecropping system of southern farms would not be much different from the agricultural tenure systems of their homelands. Greater economic opportunities existed in northern cities, especially those in which industry was becoming a major economic force. Not only was it easier to migrate to these cities, but the presence of established ethnic communities, many dating from the antebellum days, made the transition to American life easier for new arrivals. In southern cities, the antebellum ethnic communities were small and, by the late nineteenth century, relatively assimilated into the larger southern urban society.

The biracial nature of society had some impact on the reluctance of immigrants to travel south. Rumors persisted that the large presence of black labor depressed wages for all workers. There was also a reluctance to compete with black labor, both from fear of racial conflict and from a concern that such competition could only result in the same miserable living conditions for the immigrant. In 1906 Jacob Schiff devised a plan for diverting Jewish immigrants from northern ports and dispersing them more evenly throughout the country. He was concerned that concentration in the industrial Northeast would generate prejudice and about decreasing economic and housing opportunities for Russian Jews. Dispersion would also help to reduce friction between the well-established German Jewish community and the newer arrivals from Russia as the Germans worried that higher concentrations of Jewish immigrants could generate anti-Semitism that would affect all Jews. His plan included the diversion of immigrant ships to Galveston—a plan that should have resulted in some Jewish migration to nearby southern cities. Schiff, however, opposed southern settlement for these Jewish newcomers and hoped they would find their way farther west or north: "I am afraid Jewish immigration into the South would to a very large extent be used to place it in competition with Negro labor, and to attempt . . . to diminish the black predominance." Schiff believed that this scenario would ultimately work to the economic disadvantage of the Jews. His scheme for "immigrant deflection" achieved only meager results, but Jewish newcomers' avoidance in general of southern cities suggests that other Jewish community leaders shared Schiff's concern about the economic impact of pitting Jews and blacks against each other.

It is probable that reports filtered back to northern immigrant communities indicating that, despite the expressed welcome for immigrants, hostility lay beneath the smiles and handshakes of southern urban boosters. White solidarity was crucial in a biracial society, and the introduction of diverse groups into a culturally homogeneous environment increased the threat of dissent. Though immigrants in southern cities generally supported Confederate efforts, most of them professed Unionist sentiments at the outset and were hardly bitter at the peace. The same Atlanta booster who invited immigrants to "live with us" also issued an italicized warning that would scarcely warm immigrant hearts toward southern cities: "*Mind your own business* . . . and have no fear of . . . K.K.'s, or anything else." In addition, the "new" immigrants of the 1880s comprised southern and eastern European Catholics and Jews and as such were very different from the evangelical Protestant rural migrants who composed the majority of the white southern urban population. New South publicist Richard H. Edmonds reiterated his hope for European immigration to southern cities but at the same time complained that the immigrants of the 1880s were "not composed of the character of people desired by the South."

Occasionally, these sentiments flared into more overt expressions of nativism. In March 1891 a mob stormed a New Orleans prison and lynched eleven Italian immigrants after a trial freed three Sicilians accused and acquitted of murdering the police superintendent. Not only the Italians in New Orleans but all immigrant groups in that city received coarse treatment from the press in the form of derogatory remarks and denigrating cartoons, especially during the 1890s. The Italians were confined to the worst sections of the city, even more wretched than some of the black quarters. One magazine writer reported after a tour in 1898 that he found "a ten-roomed, leaky-roofed tenement house where fifty families eat, sleep, and have their being; old hags, drunken men, pale-faced young mothers and ghastly, bold-eyed children huddled together in penury and filth. . . . A dozen rickety stairways lead up to as many unwholesome rooms, about whose upper galleries, out of reach of molding damp and hungry children, hang festoons of macaroni, peppers and garlic." The scene was perhaps not much different from that in New York City's Lower East Side exposed by Danish immigrant journalist Jacob Riis in *How the Other Half Lives* (1890). But, considering the alternatives available to immigrants of all nationalities, the southern city in the midst of an overwhelmingly agrarian region held little attraction.

The lynching of Leo Frank in Atlanta in 1915 sent shudders throughout the entire southern Jewish population. Some Atlanta Jews even went so far as to flee to Birmingham in the wake of strong anti-Jewish sentiment in the more radical white press. And Frank was not an immigrant. He was a Texas-born, Brooklyn-raised executive. Even more worrisome for the city's Jewish population, in its swift conviction of Frank the jury overlooked or chose to ignore evidence that pointed to a black janitor as the murderer of thirteen-year-old Mary Phagan. Southern Jews worked under the assumption that the dividing lines in the region lay between black and white and not among various white ethnicities. The Frank lynching implied otherwise.

If, as immigration historians contend, the process of becoming American involved the process of becoming white, then that imperative must have seemed even more compelling to immigrants in the South. The distinction in the early twentieth century between Italians and Jews and African Americans, a distinction important throughout the United States, but especially pertinent in the South, was problematical. The word "guinea," for example, which originally referred to African slaves, emerged as a derogatory epithet for Italians and occasionally Greeks, Jews, and Puerto Ricans. When the Louisiana legislature debated disfranchisement in 1898, a lawmaker explained that "according to the spirit of our meaning when we speak of 'white man's government,' Italians are as black as the blackest negro in existence."

Considering the debilitating legislation foisted on African Americans in the South after 1900 and the customary restrictions of racial etiquette, dark-skinned immigrants from southern and eastern Europe who ventured into the region would have done well to prove their loyalty, and loyalty meant racial solidarity. Ethnicity in the South has always involved a triangular relationship: the ethnic group, native-born whites, and African Americans. This is not to say that ethnic southerners outdid native-born whites in promoting white supremacy (though occasionally that occurred), but that any racial sympathies were likely to be very private.

The case of Jewish southerners during the early decades of the twentieth century illuminated this point quite well. While the South has not always been a promised land for the Jewish people, it has been a hospitable region for Jewish aspirations and security. Rarely composing more than 1 percent of the region's population at any given time, Jewish southerners have attained economic influence far beyond their meager numbers. This positive state of affairs resulted from three factors. First, because of their small numbers, Jews rarely appeared threatening to other southerners. Second, the behavior of southern Jews has tended to mute their differences from the host society: a strong religiosity in a religious region and a relatively low public profile. Finally, race mattered most in the South. Even if some southern Gentiles considered Jews not quite white, they were not black either, and this fact was their greatest advantage in adapting to the region.

Yet the prevailing atmosphere excluded Jews from full membership in the white southern brotherhood. Louis D. Rubin Jr. told of a recurring dream he had as a child in Charleston in which Confederate soldiers patrolled the gateway to Hampton Park. "The soldiers . . . did not bar my passage through the gate," he recalled, "but they were present, going about their business, unconcerned with who I was or what I might want. To get into the garden I should have to go through the confederate soldiers." Rubin never made the attempt in his dreams, but it symbolized the Rubins' place in Charleston. As Rubin noted, "We were part of [Charleston's] community life. But we were Jewish."

Part of this ambivalence resulted from the pervasiveness of evangelical Protestantism. During the 1920s the Ku Klux Klan was as much anti-Catholic and anti-Semitic as antiblack. And, in recent decades, the Southern Baptist Convention has passed resolutions authorizing funding for the conversion of Jews and other non-Christians. But there are also many examples of philo-Semitism in evangelical circles: the close cooperation and proximity of Jewish and evangelical religious institutions in many southern towns and cities; Gentile store owners closing on Saturday morning in early-twentieth-century Woodville, Mississippi, to hear the preaching of an itinerant rabbi; and, as historian Eli Evans narrated, eastern North Carolina farmers coming to his grandfather's store to be blessed in the "original Hebrew." A Methodist in Port Gibson, Mississippi, purchased and restored an old synagogue in 1988 simply because, as he explained, "The Jewish heritage is deep rooted here, and that's where we all come from, after all, back to Abraham." In the South, perhaps the most important thing about religion is to have it and practice it openly and with devotion, regardless of variances of faith. But another key may be that neither Jews nor Roman Catholics composed more than a small percentage of the South's religious population outside of New Orleans and Acadian Louisiana.

Blacks generally perceived Jews as whites but as different from Gentiles and, in some cases, even as a different race. African Americans found some spiritual connection with Jewish southerners through biblical stories, especially Exodus. Black writer Zora Neale Hurston, for example, took Old Testament stories as inspiration for some of her early works, especially *Moses, Man of the Mountain*, a takeoff on the Book of Exodus.

Black affinity for Jews reached into the southern secular world. Jewish merchants and black customers established a close relationship during the Jim Crow era, and most black neighborhoods in the urban South included at least one Jewish-owned store. Jewish merchants occasionally, and always quietly, extended courtesies to black customers that white Gentile businessmen rarely offered. They allowed black customers to try on clothing and referred to them by "Mr." or "Mrs." Alex Haley noted how Jewish storeowners in Henning, Tennessee, treated his parents with respect. Witnessing Jewish business acumen firsthand, blacks often cited Jews as positive examples for their own race. In 1926 a black editor in Norfolk summarized the Jewish example for his readers:

> In many ways the Jews show us how to succeed. The Jews have taught the Afro-American people how to organize and stand together; how to make money and how to save and wisely spend it, and how to conquer prejudices, obstacles, by mastering for themselves a place in all of the thought and efforts of our tremendous civilization. . . . How do they do it? They do it by sticking together; by taking a commanding part in the trade and finance of the world and by going into all of the intellectual fields where money and influence are possible to be made.

Although blacks acknowledged that Jewish southerners were different in some positive ways from other southern whites, the dividing lines of race, class, and culture tempered black perceptions. Black and white southern Gentiles shared a tradition of anti-Semitism that existed alongside a tradition of philo-Semitism. In some respects the origins of black anti-Semitism reflected the southern heritage of blacks more than their racial background; in others, it related directly to the Jewish response to blacks.

For the most part, Jewish southerners took a vow of silence with respect to race relations in the Jim Crow era. Eli Evans admitted that "the Jews in the South have internalized a deep lesson: that the best way to survive was to be quiet about their presence." During the civil rights era many Jewish southerners remained on the sidelines, even if privately they cheered black protest. In smaller towns in the Deep South, Jews rarely spoke out. As one Meridian, Mississippi, Jew put it in the 1950s, "We have to work quietly, secretly. We have to play ball." Jews were so successful in maintaining their silence that white Gentiles had few clues about Jewish views on race relations.

This is not to say that Jews failed to respond positively to black civil rights initiatives. Even before the civil rights era, prominent Jews moved to the liberal edge of community sentiment, especially in the larger cities of the South. Early in the century southern Jews played an important role in the Committee on Interracial Cooperation. Southern chapters of the National Council of Jewish Women supported Jessie Daniel Ames's Association of Southern Women for the Prevention of Lynching. When Jews served on southern school boards in the Jim Crow era, they frequently advocated upgrading black public schools. Occasionally, southern Jews participated in NAACP protests against housing discrimination. And when the civil rights movement got underway in the 1950s, some Jewish clerics joined their black brethren. But just as African

Americans had to mind their place in the South, so, too, Jewish southerners were highly attuned to their niche and carefully balanced overtures to the black community (often out of public view) with fealty to regional racial customs.

The story of black-Italian relations in the South has yet to be written. But, as with the Jews, there seems to have been the same bittersweet encounters in such places as Birmingham factories, labor unions, and neighborhoods. The historic pattern in the South has been the suppression of ethnic identity in favor of racial solidarity. The relatively low numbers of immigrants and the abiding racial divide promised an ethnic meltdown to a degree much greater than in larger northern cities. What would happen if a substantially larger ethnic presence emerged in the South?

The question is more than academic. Asians and Hispanics have moved into the South in unprecedented numbers since the early 1990s. The Vietnamese population, for example, doubled nationally between 1900 and 2000, with the majority of migrants landing in western and southern states. While Vietnamese in California represented 40 percent of that group's total population in the United States, Texas included a substantial Vietnamese presence accounting for 10 percent of the national total in 2000, with Houston and Dallas as the South's leading destinations for Vietnamese, followed by New Orleans, Tampa–St. Petersburg, Austin, Orlando, and Charlotte.

South Asians are having a significant impact in the South, far beyond what their modest numbers would indicate. In Georgia, for example, the South Asian population more than doubled during the 1990s, with Gwinnett County in suburban Atlanta holding the largest share of that population. The Atlanta metropolitan area counted one hundred thousand South Asian residents in 2000, the third-largest minority after African Americans and Hispanics. Some, including novelist Tom Wolfe in *A Man in Full*, refer to the Atlanta suburb of Chamblee as Chambodia because of the numerous South Asian residents there. By 2000 more than seven hundred immigrant-owned businesses lined Buford Highway.

The South Asian population includes highly educated young adults who are moving into legal, academic, and high-tech fields. Their economic power is substantial, growing from $1.1 million in 1990 in Georgia, to $5.1 million in 2002. By 2007, their collective buying power in the state will reach $9 million.

But it is the Hispanic population that dwarfs all other ethnic immigrants in the South, though their political influence remains underutilized and their economic power is hampered by poverty, a lack of documentation and consequent exploitation in certain areas, and the transfer of funds to their former homes in Central and South America. Still, Hispanic political and economic

A Vietnamese-Buddhist temple in Houston, Texas. Courtesy of the Greater
Houston Convention and Visitor's Bureau, www.visithoustontexas.com.

power will only grow in the South during the coming years, and, together with other recent immigrant groups, they represent a substantial challenge to the traditional black/white paradigm of the region.

The 2000 federal census revealed that Hispanics have virtually tied African Americans as the nation's largest ethnic group, comprising nearly 13 percent of the total population and growing faster than any other ethnic group. In Florida, Hispanics are now the largest ethnic minority, accounting for 16.8 percent of the state's residents after their numbers grew by 63 percent during the 1990s. Nor are they confined to south Florida; Hispanics have begun to move up the coast and into the interior of the state. And they are redefining the culture of the places where they settle. A Florida State University demographer noted, "In the 1970s, Miami was a Jewish retirement community. This is the exact same place that was little brown Jewish women laying in the sun. Today it is Hispanic women on roller blades."

Unlike the early-twentieth-century wave of immigration, the new, post-1965 migrant stream has had a major impact on selected southern metropolitan areas. In addition to an unsurprising growth in the Hispanic population in places like Florida and Texas, the concentration of Hispanics is also increasing in the so-called New Sun Belt, in such states as Georgia, North Carolina, and South Carolina, which have also been the destinations of middle-class whites migrating from larger metropolitan areas of the North and West. A University of Michigan demographer termed these states "little melting pots" owing to the increased ethnic diversity in a region once typically defined by black and white divisions. The impact of this migration on public policy, race relations, and southern culture has been significant if not very well understood. Nothing less than a new multiethnic dynamic may be emerging in the South to replace the traditional black/white culture. The ramifications for both native white and black southerners may be enriching but also threatening.

The political consequences of the new immigration are evident in some of the region's larger cities. In Houston, for example, African American and Hispanic voters tend to vote differently, with Hispanics favoring more conservative candidates and being more willing to cross over to the Republican Party. In 1991 Hispanic votes were crucial when they swung the mayoral election to moderate white businessman Bob Lanier against a liberal black state legislator.

Part of the distinction results from differing economic interests. In 1995 Hispanics had an unemployment rate of 9 percent compared to 13 percent for African Americans. Black Houstonians were three times as likely as Hispanics to work for the government, even though Hispanics outnumbered them in the workforce. Wide differences emerged in family status as well: 18 percent of

Hispanic residents of Houston enjoying lunch at an open-air concession.
Courtesy of the Greater Houston Convention and Visitor's Bureau,
www.visithoustontexas.com.

Hispanic households with children were headed by single mothers, compared to 48 percent among blacks. And more than twice as many African Americans received welfare than Hispanics. These distinctions appeared in public opinion polls as 62 percent of Hispanics in Texas opposed increasing benefits for mothers who have additional children while on welfare, and 61 percent believed that people on public assistance were there because "they don't want to work" rather than because "they can't get a job." The mayoral elections and the demographics indicated that, with rising affluence, Hispanic voters could be more receptive to Republican candidates, or to moderate candidates in general.

Hispanics, of course, are far from a unified group, even if analysts and the Anglo public lump all Latinos into one ethnic group. Migrants from Central America differ greatly from Cuban Americans who, in turn, are different from Caribbean migrants and Mexicans. But, just as Italian immigrants a century earlier rarely thought of themselves as Italian but rather as Sicilians or Calabrians, the fact that native-born Americans and, in particular, American officials referred to them as Italian, eventually led the immigrants to assume that identity as well. Perhaps this transformation of identity will occur in the Hispanic community with attendant political benefits.

Even in states where the Hispanic vote will be relatively small, such as in North Carolina, that group's presence is attracting interest and funding from Republicans and Democrats for the simple reason that, unlike the black vote, political leaders view the Hispanic vote as uncommitted or at least willing to listen to more conservative candidates. The Hispanic population in North Carolina jumped from 77,000 in 1990 to 379,000 in 2000, though they represent just 1 percent of the state's registered voters, and only 1 Hispanic sits among the state's 170 lawmakers in Raleigh. But now that Hispanics comprise 5 percent of the state's population, politicians are making an effort to reach out to potential new voters. House Speaker Jim Black, a Democrat, plans to add a Hispanic affairs position to his staff.

Hispanics in the South are not waiting for the parties to come to them; they are organizing voter registration drives, and the Congressional Hispanic Caucus has raised four million dollars to recruit Hispanic candidates. Democrats persuaded Texas multimillionaire Tony Sanchez to run for governor in 2002, a race he lost to Republican Rick Perry by a substantial margin (58 to 40 percent). Sanchez's defeat highlighted the difficulty of translating relatively large population figures into political power: the Hispanic turnout in the Texas gubernatorial race in 2002 exceeded the turnout in the 2000 presidential election by only 4 percentage points, and most of the increase occurred in Sanchez's home base of the Rio Grande Valley. The Hispanic turnout in Harris County (Houston) was, according to the *Houston Chronicle*, "anemic." The paper observed that "voters in Harris's conservative Republican suburbs went to the polls at triple the rate of voters in most of the older barrio precincts on Houston's east side." And, among those Hispanics who voted, the draw of a Hispanic at the head of the ticket did not impress everyone. Perry garnered 35 percent of the state's Hispanic vote; down from the 43 percent George W. Bush won in 2000, but still a very respectable showing. The Hispanic vote, in other words, is not necessarily tied to one party or to just Hispanic candidates. That can only enhance the political power of Hispanic voters as the parties battle for their votes.

While the outlines of Hispanic political power in the South are becoming clearer, the impact of Hispanic population growth on the traditional racial divide remains uncertain. Focusing on out-marriage trends, black sociologist Orlando Patterson has predicted that by the year 2050 the historical black/white dichotomy will have relevance only in the southeastern part of the United States as the rest of the nation will have experienced a genetic jumbling making race, if not irrelevant, then distinctly unimportant, in defining self and group. But Patterson does not address the political and cultural implications of an African American population thus isolated from a heterogeneous and multiracial society.

As Latinos filter through the South, their political and economic impact will be significant. Memphis provides an example of how a city of secondary migration (that is, of migrants who come from other parts of the United States rather than from their country of birth) is becoming a place for initial entry as well. The city experienced a modest influx of immigrants in the late nineteenth century, with several hundred Irish, Italian, and Jewish families settling in an area known as the Pinch, just north of downtown along the Mississippi River. Today, the Pyramid, a sports and concert arena, dominates the Pinch, its former residents having moved up and out of the district generations ago. But, in an area of the city called Midtown, a trendy conglomeration of restaurants, blues clubs, art shops, and relatively inexpensive dwellings, a new polyglot city is emerging. Census Tract 36 in Midtown is 28 percent white, 27 percent black, 25 percent Asian, and 17 percent Hispanic, a mixture of secondary migrants and, increasingly, newcomers from Latin America. The immigrant population of the city has grown to the extent that local government has formed an Office for Multicultural and Religious Affairs to ease the transition of these groups to urban life. A Spanish-language radio station has appeared, Hispanic and Asian foods now grace supermarket shelves in town, and concerts cater to Hispanic musical tastes. And still, they constitute barely 3 percent of the city's population.

Even though most Hispanics work at relatively low-paying jobs, their impact is significant. One study in 2001 estimated that Hispanic workers had an economic impact of more than one billion dollars in the Memphis area, generated from almost thirty-six thousand jobs, mainly in construction, distribution, and retail trade, on earnings of between seven and ten dollars per hour. Although most Hispanic workers earn less than twenty thousand dollars a year, they are fully within the mainstream of American immigration history in their pattern of ruthless underconsumption. They save almost one-third of their income, sending two-thirds of those savings to Mexico or another Latin American country. The study also revealed that, despite this rigorous pattern of savings, Latino workers poured $359 million into the Memphis-area economy in 2000.

But there are concerns that the positive economic impact may be offset by increasing public service costs, especially in public education, where the number of Hispanic children has climbed to nearly 2,600 in 2000 from a figure just below 600 in 1993. The expansion of the city bureaucracy to deal with special issues of immigrants, from hiring Spanish-speaking civil servants to expanding the school curriculum to provide for bilingual education, also gen-erates costs. And, as the national economy falters, friction between the new ethnics and the native-born over jobs has escalated. The number of new jobs in Memphis outpaced the growth in the work force between 1995 and 2000, though a perception exists that Hispanics are crowding black Memphians out of low-paying work. Jose Velasquez of the Latino-Memphis Connection, a social service agency, has noted, "There are some people who see the growth of the Latino community as a threat." Some in the city's black community "think we're going to take things from them without having to go through the same struggles." Resentment exists in Memphis that Latinos receive services and favors that African Americans never enjoyed. That specific issue has roiled Miami politics for the past three decades but now is emerging in other parts of the urban South.

Even more dramatic has been the influx of Hispanics into smaller south-ern towns, such as Siler City, North Carolina, and Dalton, Georgia. Hispanics comprise 40 percent of the population of both of these communities that, a decade ago, had scarcely any immigrant population. This influx has placed significant pressure on social and educational services in jurisdictions that are not especially well off to begin with. In Magnolia, North Carolina, in Duplin County, a depressed area in the eastern part of the state, school adminis-trators cannot find qualified people to teach English to Hispanic students. Immigrants, mostly Hispanic students, make up nearly a third of the stu-dents at Rose Hill–Magnolia Elementary School. The school is next door to a turkey-processing plant that employs numerous Hispanics. The children's presence in the school system and their parents' work in the factory have generated resentment among locals, even though almost all of the funds used for bilingual education come from federal sources.

Rural areas of the South have not reacted well to diversity in the past, and some of these areas, beholden to single industries or large landowners, reflect the social relationships of the Jim Crow era. Also, many of these districts have experienced economic strife as brighter young people move on to the region's cities and jobs are lost to overseas competition and new technologies. Com-petition over remaining jobs is likely to be fierce and that, coupled with the immigrants' different ethnic and religious traditions in a once-homogeneous town, as well as the fiscal burdens on county governments, has resulted in a growing nativist sentiment.

In Siler City, North Carolina, the Ku Klux Klan and Louisiana white supremacist David Duke have denounced the town's Hispanic population for taking away jobs from local residents. But the objections often are less race based than class based. Perhaps, at long last, the immigrant surge in the

South is creating class solidarity among black and white residents. Economic imperatives may overcome racial divisions, though the price of such unity would be the ascension of new divisions and antagonisms in southern society. During a break at a slaughterhouse in rural Robeson County, North Carolina, a black worker pointed to a group of Hispanics conversing in Spanish and screamed, "This is America and I want to start hearing some English now!" One Hispanic worker simply shrugged and responded, "Blacks don't want to work. They're lazy." A black worker confided to a reporter, "There's a day coming soon where the Mexicans are going to catch hell from the blacks, the way the blacks caught it from the whites."

Despite these sentiments, some whites view the current struggle over immigration more in racial than class terms. In August 2001 about 75 protesters in Newton, North Carolina, in Catawba County, brandished signs proclaiming, It's Our Borders, Stupid and Now Swim Back. Confederate battle flags mingled with the placards. As a machinist explained, "If you can hire a Mexican for five dollars an hour, you'll get rid of the good man over here who wants six dollars an hour. They can work for less because they live twenty to thirty in a house. We Americans live here and have some bills to pay." Catawba County's jobless growth rate led the nation in 2001. Another white resident condemned the "invasion of our own country by Mexicans and other nonwhites. We want a white nation in North Carolina." A Mexican woman, who had been living with her husband and three children in Newton since 1996, regretted the rally and explained in a refrain that has echoed among immigrant groups down through the centuries: "We're not here to steal anything. We're here to work hard and get a better life for our kids."

Some nativist groups have attempted to tie the September 11 tragedy to immigration. At an anti-immigrant rally in Morganton, North Carolina, in May 2002, a woman held up a sign declaring "Aliens killed 6,700 Americans on Sept. 11." Morganton is a town of seventeen thousand residents that included fifty-eight Hispanics in 1990; a decade later, the Hispanic population approached two thousand. As the economy cooled after 2000, so did community sentiment toward immigrants. One white native-born resident tied race, class, and ethnicity together: "The only reason we let foreigners in was greed. Why did they originally bring the blacks in? Because of greed."

Also at issue with the expanding Hispanic population in the South is how that diverse group will "fit" into southern society. "Fitting in" was an issue in the South that, through the first half of the twentieth century, required a significant amount of historical, religious, and racial orthodoxy in public speeches, commemorations, school textbooks, pulpits, newspapers, and politics. Fitting in has always been an issue for immigrants, of course, and the degree and speed with which immigrant groups have "assimilated" or "adjusted" to American society has spawned an extensive literature.

Cuban-born Harvard economist George Borjas has raised concerns about Hispanic immigrants and the extent to which they can and will become Americans as compared to previous immigrant groups. Borjas has noted that Hispanics seem less likely than earlier groups to obtain U.S. citizenship. By the late 1990s an estimated 25 percent of immigrants were citizens, down from 66 percent in 1970, a decline attributed primarily to the surge in Hispanic migration.

Borjas and others fear that the numbers of Hispanic immigrants, their concentration, their continuing ties to the homeland, and their reluctance to obtain citizenship augur ill for the future of American society. Urban scholar Peter Salins, in his book *Assimilation, American Style*, points out that becoming part of American life never meant a forcible divestiture of homeland culture. Adjusting to this country did not entail abandoning ethnic traditions and affections. But successful participation in American society required three conditions. First, immigrant families had to learn English; second, they had "to take pride in their American identity" and in the nation's democratic ideals; and, third, they had "to be self-reliant, hardworking and morally upright."

Critics argue that Hispanics, especially Mexicans, fail on all three counts. Because of their geographic concentration, their frequent returns to their homeland, and their reluctance to adopt American citizenship, their English language skills suffer, and consequently, their understanding of American democratic ideals is inchoate. Also, Hispanics' allegedly liberal sexual attitudes and dependence on government agencies is at odds with the self-sufficiency characteristic of earlier immigrant groups. These characteristics are especially highlighted in the South, a region unaccustomed to significant ethnic differences. The result is increased hostility toward new immigrants and increased financial strain on local and state budgets. In North Carolina, for example, the birth rate for Hispanic girls ages fifteen to nineteen was triple that of other North Carolina young women. Police statistics indicate that 50 percent of Hispanics stopped in that state have no license or no registration, and of the Charlotte-Mecklenburg police department's Ten Most Wanted Fugitives, five were Hispanics, four black, and one Asian, despite the fact that Hispanics comprise about 1 percent of the district's total population.

Part of the animosity toward Hispanics may derive from their Roman Catholicism, though increasing numbers of Latino immigrants are attending evangelical churches. A leader of Miami's Haitian community, for example, estimates that more than 40 percent of that city's Haitians adhere to Pentecostal faiths. Still, the Hispanic migration is part of a larger overseas and northern United States population flow that has brought religious diversity to a region where, as late as 1940, more than 90 percent of the population identified themselves as evangelical Protestants. By 2000, over 15 percent of southerners claimed Catholic identity, and, overall, 21 percent were affiliated with non-Protestant faiths. That percentage is likely to grow. Two of the four United States dioceses with the greatest percentage growth among Hispanic Catholics were in North Carolina (Charlotte and Raleigh). These figures imply a range of distinctions from the Protestant culture, including differences in observance of the Sabbath, political attitudes, religious holiday observances and customs, and views on school prayer.

Catholics and Jews have been part of the South since the early colonial era. But only now, with the benefit of numbers and the removal of race as the glue for white solidarity, have these groups become more open and public with their religion. Some rabbis, for example, have taken to advertising and utilizing evangelical business strategies to increase their congregations (and have secured some Gentile converts in the bargain). In Charlotte during the mid-1990s, three Jewish traditions—Reform, Conservative, and Orthodox— combined to create a campus around a nondenominational Jewish Community Center. Such a bold move to set Jews apart from the larger community, to create, in a sense, a religious ghetto, would never have occurred a generation earlier. However, with the growing confidence among Charlotte-area Jewish families, inspired by their increasing numbers, and the diversity and tolerance of the larger religious community, most leaders of other faiths and their congregants applauded and appreciated the move to consolidate and identify Jewish Charlotte.

Still, given the intimate connection between religion and culture in the South, especially in smaller communities, evangelical Protestants may feel threatened by the region's increasing religious and ethnic diversity. The conservative wing of the South's evangelical culture already perceives itself under siege, particularly with United States Supreme Court decisions on school prayer, abortion, the Ten Commandments, and sexual orientation. In 2000, when the Supreme Court struck down the practice of student-sponsored prayer prior to Friday night football games in Santa Fe, Texas, the fact that the two students who brought the suit were Mormon and Roman Catholic respectively was not lost on town residents. The boundaries between church and state in the South have been so permeable as to be nonexistent, particularly in small towns. The assumption is that everyone is reading from the same Bible or ought to be. When Laotian and Thai Buddhists wanted to transform an existing building into a new temple in McAdenville, North Carolina, the town of six hundred residents blocked those plans on the grounds of traffic and parking concerns. But scratch the surface and other motives turn up. One neighbor wondered what the "unfamiliar religion" of these newcomers "might bring into the neighborhood."

Nativist and religious concerns are factors that have altered traditional black-white relationships in southern society and that also have affected ethnic newcomers' adjustment to southern society. Of course, this has always been so in the United States: immigrants exchange, change, and adapt parts of their culture in relation to the host society and, in turn, the host society changes accordingly. But in the South, where a layer of southern identity shaped by the region's particular history is superimposed on the larger national culture, these issues may evolve differently from the way they have in other parts of the country and thus result in immigrants to the South adjusting to American life in new ways.

The end of official segregation in the South after 1964 generated interesting cultural issues for Native Americans, such as the Waccamaw Sioux of eastern North Carolina. To preserve the cultural vestiges of their heritage and avoid absorption into the larger society, they initiated the pan-Indian powwow. They hoped to convey their identity to the public and reinforce their own culture by donning Plains Indians' regalia, even though such adornments as feathers, beads, and breastplates were not part of the indigenous culture of the Waccamaw Sioux. Such conflation and compromise is not unusual in American ethnic history. Jews, Italians, and, more recently, Hispanics have subsumed provincial cultural distinctions under a more inclusive ethnic identity that both perpetuates their own culture and eases their integration into and understanding of the broader society. In the process, the host culture has accommodated and modified its own traditions.

The Fiesta San Antonio is a good example of this latter phenomenon. The Fiesta began in 1891 as a commemoration of independence from Mexico and featured the leading Anglo families of the city among its organizers. More than a century later, the ten-day festival is now most closely associated with the group whose defeat the founders celebrated. In the early decades of the twentieth century, the Fiesta had a decidedly Old South flavor to it, with male participants dubbed "cavaliers" and balls with Old South themes. Today, the Fiesta prides itself on a show of Anglo-Hispanic unity as Mexican and Texan foods and events mingle with a diverse crowd totally oblivious to the Old South origins of the festival and only vaguely aware of its initial purpose as a celebration of Texas independence.

As a counterpoint to the ethnic blending in San Antonio, the Scottish Highland games in the South reflect a distinctly southern, as opposed to distinctly

Scottish celebration, replete with barbecue stands, religious events, fiddling competitions, and Confederate reenactments where Rebel regalia blend with tartans. Highland games in the northern United States have different agendas, where the emphasis is put on "games," as opposed to heritage. In the South, the popularity of these events is an acknowledgment both of the growing ethnic diversity of the South and the increasing tenuousness of promoting a distinctive southern white heritage in a multicultural age. As Celeste Ray explains: "By attributing southern distinctiveness to Scottish roots, a post–civil rights movement celebration of southerness takes on an uncontroversial, multicultural dimension focused on ethnicity rather than race relations." The games are a mechanism to honor southern white heritage without the baggage of white supremacy. The Celt is just another ethnic group in the increasingly multiethnic South.

In one sense, this trend of ethnicizing the South, whether through the introduction of Hispanics into traditional Anglo commemorations or by re-fashioning Scottish history to suit a new southern ethnic consciousness, is a departure from the historical pattern. As historian George B. Tindall noted a generation ago, "Over the years, all those southerners with names like Kruttschnitt, Kolb, de Bardeleben, . . . Toledano, Moise . . . or Cheros got melted down then poured back out in the mold of good old boys and girls, if not of the gentry." Not any more.

The sheer size of the Hispanic migration and the ten million northerners who have migrated into the South since 1990, bringing their own ethnic mixes, food preferences, and holidays with them, have colorized southern society. No longer black and white, the South today is increasingly a mélange of races and ethnic groups. This trend will likely continue and may eventually dissolve the traditional black/white dichotomy in the South, perhaps to the detriment of the region's African American population, while at the same time also chal-lenging regional religious, culinary, and cultural traditions. Will immigration and migration mark the end of a distinctive region? If the adjustment patterns of various immigrant and religious groups are any indication, the answer is probably not, which is why the South remains a fascinating laboratory in which to study the interaction of cultures, races, and ethnicity.

Suggested Readings

Borjas, George. *Heaven's Door*. Princeton: Princeton University Press, 1999.

Evans, Eli. *The Lonely Days Were Sundays: Reflections of a Jewish Southerner*. Jack-son: University Press of Mississippi, 1993.

Goldfield, David. "Sense of Place: Blacks, Jews, and White Gentiles in the American South." *Southern Cultures* 3 (1997): 58–79.

Grenier, Guillermo J., and Alex Stepick III, eds. *Miami Now! Immigration, Ethnicity, and Social Change*. Gainesville: University Press of Florida, 1992.

Miller, Randall M., and George E. Pozzetta, eds. *Shades of the Sunbelt: Essays on Ethnicity, Race, and the Urban South*. Westport, Conn.: Greenwood Press, 1988.

Moore, Deborah Dash. *To the Golden Cities: Pursuing the American Jewish Dream in Miami and L.A.* New York: Free Press, 1994.

Ray, Celeste, ed. *Southern Heritage on Display: Public Ritual and Ethnic Diversity within Southern Regionalism*. Tuscaloosa: University of Alabama Press, 2003.

Suro, Roberto. *Strangers among Us: How Latino Immigration Is Transforming America*. New York: Alfred A. Knopf, 1998.

Tindall, George B. *Natives and Newcomers: Ethnic Southerners and Southern Ethnics*. Athens: University of Georgia Press, 1995.

Tobar, Hector. "The Newest South: A Lotta Cultures Goin' On." *Southern Changes* 23 (2001): 22–24.

Tweed, Thomas A. "Our Lady of Guadaloupe Visits the Confederate Memorial." *Southern Cultures* 8 (2002): 75–93.

Webb, Clive. *Fight against Fear: Southern Jews and Black Civil Rights*. Athens: University of Georgia Press, 2001.

JULIA KIRK BLACKWELDER

Women and Leadership

A Century of Change in the South

Today women in the South wield political influence, lead corporate enterprises, and enjoy a level of well-being that women of 1900 could scarcely have
imagined. Most southern women of 1900 worked from sunup to sundown to
keep food on the family table and clothes on the backs of their children.
The people of the region wrangled as the still-impoverished stepchildren of
a wealthy industrial nation, but the rumblings of discontent foretold the un-
folding of a new society in the South. During the last century, women remade
southern communities through humanitarian reform and political action. At
the same time, economic development turned the New South into the Sun
Belt and transformed the lives of ordinary women. As these changes occurred,
southern women moved gradually into the mainstream of American life and
came to share fully in the nation's most prosperous century. Most southern

women still work from sunup to sundown as they combine paid employment with housekeeping, but they choose their employment from among an array of occupations, and their labors provide more than mere subsistence. From World War II through the 1990s, the standard of living across the South rose steadily as women's participation in the labor force increased.

Although still overwhelmingly rural and agricultural in 1900, the region stood amid vast currents of change that threatened rural hegemony. By midcentury millions of men and women had left their small farms or tenant lands for labor in factories, commercial establishments, or private homes. Generations of southerners had by now been born and raised in towns and cities with only loose ties to the countryside of their grandparents. The civil rights movement and additional economic developments further reconstructed the South. By the end of the century the majority of the South's mills and factories had closed, replaced by warehouses, office parks, and high-tech industries. The journey to the twenty-first century was painful in many respects, but the fruits of change far outweighed their costs, and virtually all southerners benefited from the economic growth of the region.

In the early twentieth century poverty, endemic diseases of tuberculosis and pellagra, high fertility, high mortality, Jim Crow, poor schools, and marginal farms distinguished the South from the rest of the United States. For women these gloomy claims to regional distinctiveness meant short lives of abiding disquietude and continuous physical labor. Wives' frequent pregnancies barely interrupted their work in the home and in the field or factory. Black and white women worried from day to day about the prospects of shoes for the winter and the baby's nagging cough.

Racial segregation marked all aspects of southern social and economic relations and affected the most intimate aspects of African Americans' lives. Jim Crow offered African American women three choices: a life of field labor in service to white landowners, a life of service to white homemakers, or migration to the North. Virtually all African Americans were poor and uneducated, but the vast majority of whites were as well. Poor white women's racial entitlement meant different, but also dismal, life options of field labor as the wife of a sharecropper or sixty-hour weeks in the textile mill. Fewer whites than African Americans entertained the alternative of leaving the South, although they also would join the migration in increasing numbers during World War II and thereafter.

Jim Crow left African American women the nearly defenseless victims of white men's advances while it protected virtually all white women against the slightest discourtesy or imagined impropriety on the part of African American men. Segregation dictated that all African American women would be sub-

Women workers at the Payne Cotton Mill in Macon, Georgia (1909). Library of Congress, Prints & Photographs Division, Washington, D.C., reproduction number LC-USZ62-43683.

servient to white women, in theory if not in daily practice. White southerners imposed the region's lowest earning potential and a virtual absence of health care on African Americans of both sexes. Motherhood consequently proved a greater challenge to African American women than to their white neighbors as parents fought for physical survival in the face of grave economic challenges and the lingering fear of racial violence.

While the advantages of whiteness were vast, white women, too, suffered from many of the disabilities that distinguished the South from the rest of the United States. At the outset of America's greatest century, ordinary southern women, black or white, rarely earned a high school diploma, and the vast majority of rural children did not complete the elementary grades. Women of both races generally married while they were still girls and bore children once every two years until their childbearing years had ended. At least one of the seven or more children borne to most married women would not live to begin school. Most children suffered from untreated tooth decay, and many faced malnutrition, pellagra, gastroenteritis, or tuberculosis in addition to the rash of childhood diseases that threatened most Americans before the advent of modern pharmacology.

Women who lived to their fortieth year had reached old age not long after their last child had entered the world, and there would be little, if any, leisure in the average remaining fifteen years of their lives. The life story of Aliene Walser, a North Carolina textile worker, characterizes the experiences of millions of women of both races in the first half of the century. Walser dropped out of school at age fourteen and soon married. She bore her first child in her first year of marriage without understanding how she had become pregnant. Exhaustion was her constant companion as she balanced mill labor with the births of seven more babies before her thirty-third birthday. Aliene Walser was a grandmother before learning that fertility could be controlled. The dark picture of southern life glimpsed in Walser's life recollections gradually brightened as World War II brought an end to the Great Depression. The war years yielded higher employment in industry and agriculture across the South and raised living standards for women of both races. The postwar years delivered improvements in diet and medical care as well as advancements in public education. In the second half of the century economic change, the civil rights revolution, and a round of advances in women's rights empowered women beyond the ballot box and opened the doors to lives even the most privileged women of 1900 could not have contemplated. Women played major roles in transforming the South and in building the prosperous and open society of the Sun Belt.

Female leaders of both races had begun charting paths to a better society before the turn of the century. As the nineteenth century waned, women in the South organized to battle disease, civic disorder, and failing schools. In the region's major cities and smaller towns, African American and white women formed separate, but often parallel, associations that set about changing the world around them as well as gave new purpose to their lives outside of the familial circle. Charlotte, North Carolina, counted fewer than thirty thousand souls in 1900, but it boasted scores of racially segregated women's clubs ranging from church charity circles and the Young Women's Christian Association (YWCA) to the African American Young Ladies' Independent and the Married Ladies' Social Clubs to the white Young Married Ladies' Club. In Charlotte, as in most southern towns, the Woman's Christian Temperance Union and the Colored Woman's Temperance Union drew their leadership from among the most prominent women of the middle classes, who carried on fervent campaigns for prohibition from the 1880s through World War I. Organizations such as Atlanta's Neighborhood Union, founded by Lugenia Burns Hope in 1908, brought the social settlement movement to the South's African American communities and simultaneously nurtured female leaders. Within gendered clubs desire for improvements in the status of women remained largely inchoate, but in their actions club women of both races foreshadowed broader public roles for women and sowed the seeds for a revolution in gender roles and race relations. The National American Woman Suffrage Association held its annual convention in Atlanta in 1895, and the National Woman's Party organized chapters in the South on the eve of World War I.

Not all southern women of the early 1900s embraced the winds of progress. Legions of southern white women resisted change and looked backward. They saw the educational and health care reforms they pioneered as promoting a needed separation of the races. They led efforts to memorialize the Lost Cause and reinforce a provincial way of life that was already fading as the New South creed had begun to elevate commerce and industry over nineteenth-century rural values. The United Daughters of the Confederacy (UDC) was formed in 1894 to commemorate southern heroism in the Civil War and to provide relief to Confederate veterans and their families. In the first decade of the twentieth century the UDC reached a membership of more than twenty thousand and continued to grow rapidly until the 1920s, when its membership crested at seventy thousand, at which point it began a continuous decline. Southern white women joined the Ku Klux Klan in large numbers before World War II, although they played only minor roles in shaping Klan ideology. While images of the Old South commanded the respect of countless southern white women, most did not register their patriotism through membership in the UDC or the Ku Klux Klan.

A small share of middle-class southern whites glanced back occasionally at the Old South at the same time that they fixed their gaze on the challenges ahead. Caught between nostalgia for the Old South and a desire to embrace the New South stood Margaret Mitchell. While actively promoting an idealized notion of the past, urban women like Mitchell ventured onto new roads that led them away from the caste-based society they lauded. Margaret Mitchell, the journalist and novelist who put Atlanta on the map, romanticized the nobility and suffering of women in the nineteenth-century South. She created a fictional past that many white southerners, especially women, embraced as historical reality and the noblest of times even though Scarlett O'Hara's circumstances forced her into territories no lady would enter. Despite its setting, *Gone with the Wind* embraced white twentieth-century values that had little to do with the legacy of Georgia's plantations. Fine furnishings and grand social occasions belonged to the privileged members of the white commercial and industrial middle classes of the urban New South and were only rarely enjoyed by nineteenth-century southerners. Margaret Mitchell, born in 1900, imagined the plantation South even as she lived amid constant reminders that such a world was indeed a Lost Cause.

Margaret Mitchell's blockbuster tribute to the Confederacy grew partly out of her own battle with financial and personal hardships. As a young wife in the 1920s Mitchell faced the future wedded to an abusive alcoholic with no prospects of supporting himself. The *Atlanta Journal* was her salvation, an escape from everyday burdens and the source of a weekly check that kept her household going. A happier second marriage and her declining health led Mitchell to retire from journalism and turn her talents to writing fiction. Mitchell's own pluck and the lessons of her mother's active leadership in the woman suffrage campaign provided models for drafting the determined, independent Scarlett.

The Atlanta that nurtured Margaret Mitchell boasted the splendid upper-class residential suburbs of Inman Park and Ansley Park. The neighborhoods of the merely prosperous classes stretched east along Ponce de Leon Avenue and north along Peachtree Road while Morningside, West End, and Decatur contained the solid bungalows of the striving middle and working classes. Atlanta offered fine shops and a variety of social and cultural amenities, but grand homes, fancy clothes, and balls at the Piedmont Driving Club were indulgences of the privileged. After *Gone with the Wind* made Margaret Mitchell wealthy, she devoted much of her energy to ameliorating the misery of ordinary residents of the Gate City, a metropolis marked by the racial segregation and industrial poverty that characterized the urban South. The city that included Ansley Park and Inman Park also incorporated Buttermilk Bottoms and Factory Town (later known as Cabbagetown), two of the city's notable slums, the first housing African American service workers and the second Fulton Bag factory hands.

The occupational patterns of Gate City women, black and white, mirrored employment trends throughout the South. Southern women not only accepted employment in great numbers at the outset of the twentieth century, but they also led the nation in this regard. Only in New England, where textile mills with their large female labor forces had dominated the economy since the mid-nineteenth century, could women's work rates rival those of the South. White women generally left their jobs after marriage, but few African American women could afford to stay at home. Although most married white women of 1900 were not in the labor force, a significant minority of wives and mothers did work and the broad availability of low-wage domestic labor provided by African American domestic workers facilitated their employment. As textile mills expanded throughout the South in the first three decades of the century, more and more white women stayed on the job after their childbearing cycle began.

Atlanta in 1900 was a harbinger of the good and the bad that Margaret Mitchell would find in the emerging metropolis of her adult years. After the

Civil War, southerners began moving into the region's towns and cities, a trend that continued into the twentieth century as textile mills, garment factories, and tobacco plants rose from the landscape. Women predominated among the city's newcomers. Between 1900 and 1920 the number of single, white working women in the Gate City tripled and the number of single, African American working women grew as well. Few earned enough to be truly independent women, but they got by sharing living expenses with friends and family or living in the city's burgeoning boardinghouses. Most white women found jobs in factories, shops, or offices, while the fortunate few who had access to the appropriate training were able to enter the nursing or teaching professions. With these changes in women's work patterns, increasing proportions of white families came to depend on women's wages for all or part of their income.

In African American families also, women's wage-earning roles grew increasingly important. Most African American women accepted the only work open to them, domestic labor in private homes and service or laboring jobs in factories or commercial establishments. Jim Crow mandated that African American women earn less than white women and work separately from them. Segregation also demanded that African Americans teach and nurse their own, a circumstance that nurtured a core of black professional women despite their inferior earnings and poor working conditions. In addition, Jim Crow laws and customs made available to black women a range of urban occupational entrepreneurial options that required little capital and minimal special training. These economic pursuits freed thousands of African Americans from employment in white homes and white-owned businesses. Black boardinghouse keepers, café owners, and beauticians pursued independent lives in southern towns and cities of the twentieth century.

The beauty industry offered proportionally more opportunities to African American women than to women of other races. Throughout the region in the 1930s and the 1940s black-owned schools of cosmetology trained women of color to meet the needs of a racially defined market for beauty products and services. The vast majority of black beauticians worked out of small salons in their homes or in owner-operated shops in African American commercial districts. Linked together through groups such as the National Beauty Culturists League, black beauticians united to advance their economic well-being at the same time that they championed African American civil rights within and outside of the South.

World War II marked an important turning point in women's employment throughout the nation but especially in the South. Women's employment in agriculture and industry suddenly skyrocketed. Southern mills, hit hard

Women working at the Bell Bomber Plant in Marietta, Georgia, during World War II. Courtesy of the Kenan Research Center at the Atlanta History Center.

by the Great Depression, hummed at full capacity, and women replaced men in many skilled jobs and supervisory positions. Despite labor shortages, African American women failed to advance significantly in the textile industry. The story was different in newly established aircraft and munitions plants where black women, although disadvantaged by racist hiring practices, did find comparatively high-paying jobs. War needs also forced employers to lay aside their prejudices against the employment of married women, and wage earning among wives and mothers rose to an unprecedented high through 1944.

As the end of the war approached, factories began to discharge production workers, and married women were generally the first to go. The war, nevertheless, had been a turning point rather than an aberration. Economic expansion, the result in part of the emerging cold war, proceeded almost without interruption after World War II, and employers again began to recruit female workers. Hardly any of the working women, however, returned to jobs in heavy industry. Rather, businesses hired women to fill their traditional roles in light industries, offices, and stores. World War II also brought a fertility boom, a trend that accelerated at war's end. As the first wartime babies reached school age, the demand for teachers rose sharply. Cora Kay Blackwelder, a young white Atlanta mother who had worked as an industrial chemist before the war, was recruited as an elementary school teacher at the end of the 1940s and remained in the labor force until her retirement in 1995. Blackwelder represented a growing trend of lifelong employment among southern women as the number of married women employed rose among both races even though Jim Crow dictated separate and inferior positions for black women through the 1960s.

In Margaret Mitchell's lifetime, greater Atlanta was a microcosm of a region in transition, but still burdened by the legacies of slavery and plantation agriculture. The Georgia Institute of Technology, Morehouse and Spelman Colleges, Agnes Scott College, and Emory University signified that southerners had ambitious hopes to build a stronger future on the ashes of the Civil War and a devastating 1917 fire, but higher education throughout the South remained almost universally segregated by race and by gender into the 1950s. Georgia Tech and Emory did not welcome women or African Americans. White women might turn to Decatur's Agnes Scott College or attend the publicly funded Georgia College for Women in Milledgeville. These lines of segregation had serious curricular implications. Through much of the South women had access to only one public college and these state women's colleges prepared women only for careers in teaching or as homemakers. Poorly funded public institutions for African Americans accepted women as well as men, but their curricula emphasized practical agricultural, mechanical, and domestic skills alongside the liberal arts. Prairie View A&M College in Texas trained the first generation of African American engineers in the South, but women were not among these pioneers. While many private northern colleges were also segregated by gender, most public institutions were coeducational, and no public college or university refused admission to African Americans.

Early-twentieth-century colleges and universities, regardless of their racial restrictions, defined their mission in women's education as preparation for motherhood, the explicit destiny of the sex. When South Carolina's Winthrop Training School renamed itself the Winthrop Normal and Industrial College in 1892 it announced its mission to be the training of "white women in stenography, typewriting, telegraphy, and bookkeeping," but also in "drawing, art needlework, cooking, housekeeping, and other such industrial arts as may be suitable to their sex and conducive to their support and usefulness." As the twentieth century approached, South Carolina's leading white men accepted the reality that women of their race needed to acquire the skills to support themselves, but they were not ready to surrender the notion that white women's proper place was at home with their children. This riddle of convention characterized the views of white men throughout the region, but also generally described the worldview of white middle-class women. Black Americans could scarcely imagine a world in which African American mothers stayed at home, but through the first half of the century more and more African American families would know this luxury as the black middle class grew.

Despite social conventions that dictated that educated mothers should remain at home, women's colleges and a handful of coeducational institutions of the first half of the twentieth century turned out female leaders who carved out special places for themselves in politics and employment. In so doing southern women brought all American women closer to equality with men and propelled the South into the national mainstream. Racially separate southern colleges trained Mary McLeod Bethune, Jessie Daniel Ames, and Barbara Jordan. Bethune, the fifteenth of seventeen children, founded a Florida college for African Americans early in the century, served as president of the National Association of Colored Women's Clubs in the 1920s, and advised American presidents of both political parties until the time of her death in 1955. Jessie Daniel Ames worked for woman suffrage, helped run her family's business, and founded the Association of Southern Women for the Prevention of Lynching. Barbara Jordan grew up in inner-city Houston and graduated from Texas Southern University before earning her law degree at Boston University. After establishing a private law practice in Houston, Jordan broke race and gender barriers in winning election to the Texas Senate before moving to the U.S. Congress. In 1994, two years before her death, President Clinton awarded Jordan the Presidential Medal of Freedom in recognition of her lifelong campaign for civil rights.

Behind the accomplishments of these women stood equally important, if less well-known, contributions of generations of educated southern women whose lives continue to offer role models for girls. Camille Kelley was named the first female jurist in Tennessee in the 1930s after the state legislature passed a special amendment to allow the appointment of women to the bench, an initiative taken specifically to allow Kelley to preside over the juvenile court of Memphis. Leila Denmark opened her Atlanta pediatric practice before World War II and continued to minister to the needs of Georgia children past her one-hundredth year of life. One of twelve children born to a south Georgia farm couple, Denmark completed her medical training in 1928 and was the third female graduate of the Georgia College of Medicine. North Carolinian Bonnie Cone transformed a Charlotte night school into Charlotte

Representative Barbara Jordan giving the keynote address at the 1976
Democratic National Convention. Library of Congress, Prints & Photographs
Division, Washington, D.C., reproduction number LC-U9-32937-32A/33.

College and oversaw the legislative drive that turned Charlotte College into the University of North Carolina at Charlotte in 1965.

While we remember the contributions of female leaders in the South over the past one hundred years, southern women alone did not transform the region and its people. Federal leadership brought immense progress to the South, making the second half of the twentieth century appear almost discontinuous with the first half. Midcentury federal spending, which stemmed less from the economic initiatives of the New Deal than from the imperative to defeat totalitarianism, rescued the South from its distinctive poverty and paved the way for the rise of the Sun Belt. During and after World War II, white southerners in Congress, all men, led the way in fighting for home-district appropriations that would ultimately end southern life as they then knew it. World War II, partly by opening the South to outsiders, challenged the South's unique institution of racial separatism and facilitated African Americans' struggle to defeat Jim Crow. Soldiers and civilian employees from outside the South contested the color line that stretched even onto military bases. Anna Graves, the first African American civilian clerical worker hired at San Antonio's Kelly Field, worked alongside whites eight hours a day but could not take her lunch in the base cafeteria. Such practices could not long survive as the decades following the war would prove.

Contemporary southern women of all races owe their well-being in large measure to the economic and the political developments that followed on the heels of World War II and to the civil rights battles of the 1950s and the 1960s. Jim Crow had helped to suppress southern wages and discourage effective labor organizing. Poor educational levels and the caste system of the South had discouraged northern industrialists from moving south in the 1940s and 1950s, despite the attraction of low wages and weak labor organizations. The removal of the color line in education and employment encouraged the movement of private capital into the South. During the 1960s, despite African American urban protests and white backlash, investment in the South accelerated. Southerners, whose fortunes World War II had boosted, also invested in the region, and federal spending continued through the sixties. Thousands of southern women, black and white, who had fled the South in the 1940s and 1950s returned home after 1965. Women of both races made economic progress even though their earnings continued to fall behind the earnings of men and of women outside the region.

Southern women also slowly closed the gap in legal rights between themselves and northern women, although only four southern states (Arkansas, Kentucky, Tennessee, and Texas) approved the Nineteenth Amendment during the ratification process and southern legislatures played the major role in defeating the equal rights amendment (ERA). Southern recalcitrance had been enough to defeat the ERA but not sufficient to stem the tide of evolving public expectations that women merited equality with men in the body politic. The advance of women clearly rose on the successes of African Americans through the civil rights movement, and women played significant roles in these closely related revolutions.

At the end of World War II, African Americans returned from defending democracy abroad only to be reminded how thoroughly and routinely the Jim Crow South denied them the rights of citizenship spelled out in the Constitution. Having risked their lives and sacrificed their husbands, fathers, brothers, and sons for the nation, African Americans would no longer settle for discrimination and intimidation at home. President Harry S. Truman initiated a national change in race relations when he ordered the desegregation of the military services. Truman's executive order signaled a new era in which the federal government would no longer cooperate in the white South's efforts to keep Jim Crow alive amid the death rattles of the despised institution. African American women, long denied office in white women's associations, utilized their race-based associational and employment networks to organize demonstrations, boycotts, and voter registration drives that led to the advances of the 1950s and 1960s. Activist Septima Clark, among others, also protested the gender discrimination within the civil rights movement that prevented women from rising to high office in such bodies as the Southern Christian Leadership Conference.

After making considerable sacrifices and displaying strong leadership, southerners were brought closer to the norm of national race relations by the *Brown v. Board of Education* Supreme Court ruling of 1954 and the Civil Rights Act of 1964, which paved the way for the rise of the Sun Belt. Without these changes, southern men, black or white, and women of all races and within all regions would enjoy markedly less economic opportunity than they do today.

When the Senate passed the Civil Rights Act of 1964 in its final form, it contained language that set off a virtual revolution for women. Title VII of the 1964 legislation outlawed employment discrimination by religion, race, national origin, or sex. Howard Worth Smith, a Virginia legislator who fought tooth and nail against civil rights legislation, offered the amendment that inserted the word "sex" in the House of Representatives version of the bill. Historians continue to debate Smith's motivations in modifying the bill. Some have argued that Smith believed that conservative white legislators from the North would not accept equality for women and would therefore vote against the entire bill. Others have maintained that Smith recognized that the bill would become law and he did not wish to see African American men and women move forward without taking white women along with them. Regardless of Smith's intent, the Civil Rights Act of 1964 opened new opportunities for white women and African American women and men and signaled the advance of all southerners into the mainstream of employment and public service. Title IX of the Higher Education Act of 1972 opened additional doors to women as the federal government banned discrimination against women in colleges, universities, and professional schools. Through the interaction of economic growth and federal guidelines, southern women have nearly reached earning parity with women elsewhere in the nation, and southern women of all political persuasions have left their marks on southern politics and the life of the nation. Barbara Jordan and Kay Bailey Hutchison in Texas succeeded Lady Bird Johnson, who had worked behind the scenes to build the Johnson family fortune and assure the political rise of Lyndon Johnson. Other states show similar lines of female inheritance, and southern women lead the ranks of accomplishment in medicine, law, religion, and other pursuits.

Although female leaders emerged largely from among the educated middle class of both races, there were notable exceptions. Fannie Lou Hamer rose from the humble ranks of the laboring classes to lead a national political revolution. Hamer made the way straight for Barbara Jordan, whose political star transformed the horizon for all southern women regardless of race. The Old South, the place partly invented in the twentieth century by Margaret Mitchell and Joel Chandler Harris, has long since passed. The civil rights movement left a permanent legacy of female as well as male southern leadership that has carried over into the twenty-first century. Just as the civil rights movement paved the way for the election of Atlanta's mayor Maynard Jackson, the city's activist women of both races set the stage for Shirley Franklin's election as mayor of Atlanta in 2001.

In the battle to resist desegregation and equal rights for African Americans, conservative white women also found new causes and new avenues to pursue. Gender and race, never separable issues in the South, interacted to fuel southern resistance to the equal rights movement just as the wedded concerns had earlier propelled resistance to woman suffrage in the South. Women across the South mobilized after 1972 to defeat the ERA, and this successful campaign resulted in new leadership roles as women gained influence in conservative groups such as Eagle Forum and in the Republican Party. White women assisted in the party's southern ascendancy and helped send conservative women such as Charlotte's Sue Myrick to Congress.

Migration and immigration also transformed the South from a biracial, segregated region into a pluralistic society. Native-born whites and African

Americans constituted the vast majority of southerners in the early twentieth century, but this, too, changed after 1960. By the year 2000 millions of Latinos, lesser numbers of Asian Americans, and significant communities of immigrants from the Middle East, the Indian subcontinent, Africa, and Europe had transformed the sights and sounds of the South. Latinas have joined white and black women in state legislatures and in the ranks of successful business entrepreneurs. While the color line has softened and pluralism has further blurred facile distinctions between black and white women, not all racial lines have been erased by desegregation or demographic change. Social and religious institutions remain highly differentiated by race, a reality that characterizes the nation and not only the South. Through membership in distinctive African American and Latina cultural organizations, black and Latina women continue to build their communities and preserve their heritage, but the days of forced separation are gone for good and to the benefit of all women.

Over the course of the twentieth century each succeeding generation of southern women enjoyed longer, healthier lives than their mothers, and each beheld an ever-widening array of opportunities. In contrast to their forebears a century ago, young women entering the twenty-first century in the South will complete high school, and most will seek training beyond the secondary level. Today many fewer women stay at home through their childrearing years than in the past, a change in family lifestyles resulting from smaller families but also from rising divorce rates and increased economic opportunities for married women and single mothers. The range of careers from which women may choose is virtually boundless, and they may aspire to high public office or corporate leadership. Ordinary women, regardless of race, will reasonably expect that marriage will compete with but not replace full-time employment. A girl of the twenty-first century may expect to marry in her mid- to late twenties and raise two children without fear that illness will prevent them from reaching adulthood. Average adult life expectancy has increased by more than twenty years since 1900. Anglo-American women continue to enjoy broader opportunities and longer lives than other women, but the well-being of all groups improved through the last century.

If some would pause to say that a gentler and more civil lifestyle has been lost in the process of women's march toward equality, their views should not be dismissed out of hand. The past did seem more refined and pleasant for some southern families. Middle-class Atlanta housewives of 1920 had leisure time for participation in church and charity work, arguing the merits and dangers of exercising the franchise, and curing a child's skinned knees with a hug and a kiss. A few African American wives also had these opportunities. Middle-class women in the twenty-first century, balancing paid employment with their private lives, have difficulty finding sufficient time for nurturing their children or participating in leisure and civic activities, but some gendered characteristics and traditional regional values have persisted or blended with new attitudes. Mothers continue to raise children, but fathers now share in the pleasures of parenthood. A distinctly regional vein of evangelical religion continues to tout subservient roles for women. Some women have embraced patriarchal family life wholly, while others have shunned these directives, even as a third group of women has continued to defer to male authority even though they work outside the home to help maintain their families. Southern manners and fashions remain distinctive, but these claims of difference belie far more commonalities with women elsewhere than could be observed in 1900, partly through the "southernization" of the nation that has had peculiar benefits for women. For example, Mary Kay Ash achieved multimillionaire status by building an empire in cosmetics, a business that rested upon white Texans' love of face paint and big hair. By the end of the century, Mary Kay sales agents included women of all races who marketed their wares throughout the United States and beyond. For the most part, however, southern women have advanced with rather than separately from American women overall.

The changes that have brought southern women to the bright prospects they enjoy today emerged from a confluence of forces. Capital from outside the region, especially federal dollars that southern men in Congress helped procure, bred new capital within the region and precipitated social and po-litical changes that benefited people of both sexes. While some women led resistance movements against changes in gender and race relations, many other women led in the forces for change. Southern club women, many of whom affiliated themselves with national women's organizations, facilitated the dissolution of regional insularity. Backward-looking groups such as the United Daughters of the Confederacy persist as the feminine side of the memory of white southerners' tragic past, although they garner less allegiance from the culture and hold less significance for it and the values of the region than ever before.

The South today remains a region of political conservatism, distinctive religious values, and traditional foodways, but in most other respects the South mirrors the rest of the nation in being a postindustrial, high-technology democracy where some girls grow up to become bankers, computer scientists, or politicians as well as mothers and citizens. Jessie Daniel Ames, Leila Den-mark, Fannie Lou Hamer, and Barbara Jordan helped make a better world for all southerners, but much remains to be done. Despite the advances of the twentieth century, race and class continue to divide southerners in the new century.

Since 1980 the concentration of wealth in the South has increased and the job growth of the 1980s and 1990s has stagnated. For southern women, who have not yet entirely closed the wage gap between themselves and women of other regions, the shrinking of the resources of the middle and lower classes has inflicted heavy burdens. The persistence of poor schools, the intractable problem of spousal abuse, the absence of affordable health care, and the blight of urban pollution are today's everyday challenges, although they are the dilemmas of a nation as much as a region.

Suggested Readings

Blackwelder, Julia Kirk. *Now Hiring: The Feminization of Work in the United States, 1900–1995*. College Station: Texas A&M University Press, 1997.

———. *Styling Jim Crow: African American Beauty Training during Segregation*. College Station: Texas A&M University Press, 2003.

Blee, Kathleen M. *Women of the Klan: Racism and Gender in the 1920s*. Berkeley: University of California Press, 1991.

Byerly, Victoria. *Hard Times Cotton Mill Girls: Personal Histories of Womanhood and Poverty in the South*. Ithaca: ILR Press, 1986.

Gillespie, Michelle, and Catherine Clinton, eds. *Taking Off the White Gloves: Southern Women and Women Historians*. Columbia: University of Missouri Press, 1998.

Gilmore, Glenda Elizabeth. *Gender and Jim Crow: Women and the Politics of White Supremacy in North Carolina, 1896–1920*. Chapel Hill: University of North Carolina Press, 1996.

Mathews, Donald G., and Jane Sherron De Hart. *Sex, Gender, and the Politics of the ERA: A State and the Nation*. New York: Oxford University Press, 1990.

Olson, Lynne. *Freedom's Daughters: The Unsung Heroines of the Civil Rights Movement from 1830 to 1970*. New York: Scribner, 2001.

Walker, Melissa, Jeanette R. Dunn, and Joe B. Dunn, eds. *Southern Women at the Millennium: A Historical Perspective*. Columbia: University of Missouri Press, 2003.

Wheeler, Marjorie Spruill. *New Women of the New South: The Leaders of the Woman Suffrage Movement in the Southern States*. New York: Oxford University Press, 1993.

GRACE ELIZABETH HALE

Of the Meaning of Progress

A Century of Southern Race Relations

This is an impossible history to write. To tell the tale of a century of race relations in the South more generally implies that there is a structure that can hold the story and a voice that can speak for both blacks and whites. Assuming that an accounting can be taken means believing that either an old "color-blind" white public can still speak for the whole or that an integrated public exists and has found its voice. Neither a lie nor a dream is a very good vantage point from which to view the century. Knowing the risks and the impasse at which America stands on the question of race, I take the dream.

My title is drawn from W. E. B. Du Bois's essay "Of the Meaning of Progress" in *The Souls of Black Folk* (1903). I would like to thank Peter Dimock and Ed Ayers for their suggestions.

There is a story I can tell that some people will like. It is a narrative of rising, of uplift, of progress. It is true. This story says integration is possible.

Segregation was dismantled in this century. The African American freedom struggle—the effort to realize the full measure of black citizenship—began decades earlier, with emancipation. Its depth and width and the strength of its current may have varied, but this river, as the historian Vincent Harding has described it, flowed unbroken across the century. What was new in 1945 was the changed national and international context.

The civil rights movement, the widest and best-known part of the stream, spread out then over a political world transformed by black migration, southern economic change, and the emergence of television use at home and the cold war abroad. The regional economy began improving during and after the war as the federal government built or expanded military bases like Fort Benning, near Columbus, Georgia. The mechanical cotton picker and other farm machinery provoked another exodus from the countryside, especially in the Deep South. Many of these migrants left the South altogether, more whites in fact than blacks, settling in places like Los Angeles, Detroit, and Chicago, but many southerners moved within the region, crowding towns and cities like Atlanta and Birmingham. In some places, half a century of relative stability enabled middle-class blacks to build their own businesses, churches, and schools into strong community institutions. Atlanta University Center—Clark, Morehouse, Morris Brown, and Spelman—for example, made Atlanta the home of more black professionals than any other city in the nation.

Outside the region, African American voters in the North, in cities like Chicago, had become vital to Democratic victory in important states like Illinois. In the four-way 1948 election, for example, this key black vote was widely credited with giving Truman the presidency. Black voters, in turn, insisted that politicians at least give lip service to civil rights. Against a backdrop of African and Asian decolonization, the cold war made the rights of African Americans in the United States an international issue as well. The Soviet Union had long publicized the treatment of black southerners. How could Americans be taken seriously in their attempts to promote democracy and its dependence on capitalism abroad while African Americans living in the South faced lynchings, segregation, and disfranchisement at home? Finally, in 1946, manufacturers marketed the first television sets to the public. By 1955, 65 percent of American households had them. Television gave black southerners a new stage on which to demonstrate to the rest of the nation the brutality of the South's culture of segregation.

These changes came together in the mid-1950s to produce what we now call the civil rights movement. The NAACP's legal defense team, led by

Thurgood Marshall, won a series of court victories in the late 1940s and early 1950s—most notably in *Smith v. Allwright*, the 1948 Supreme Court decision that outlawed the whites-only primary. After *Smith*, and given that the Fifteenth Amendment already enshrined blacks' right to vote in the Constitution, NAACP lawyers shifted their focus to public education. States, they reasoned, employed more people and spent more dollars in this area than in any other. At first, NAACP lawyers attempted to use the threat of bankruptcy to persuade southern states into giving up segregation by forcing them to make separate school systems truly equal. With the Supreme Court's decision in *Brown v. Board of Education* in 1954, however, the NAACP succeeded in its most ambitious goal, the overturning of the 1896 *Plessy v. Ferguson* decision that declared "separate but equal" constitutional. *Brown* made public education a major front in the fight against segregation.

The uproar surrounding the death of Emmett Till in 1955 suggested another direction for the movement. Till was an adolescent boy from Chicago, visiting relatives in Mississippi. He was lynched because he had whistled, ogled, or maybe just looked at a white woman working in a small store in the tiny town of Money. What made the Till case more than just another lynching was the fact that Mamie Bradley, Till's mother, took her boy's body north and turned his funeral into a different kind of spectacle. Television cameras captured the thousands of mourners pouring into a South Side Chicago church to view Till's body and emerging shaken and grimly determined on the other side of the casket. Bradley even allowed *Jet* magazine to publish a close-up of Till's face, all the more disturbing for the morticians' efforts to turn the beaten flesh back into the boy. Here African Americans made their own spectacle of the South's culture of segregation, revealing the threat of violence that always lay below the surface and compelled southern blacks to follow the laws and conventions that made them less than citizens. All that remained was for blacks to figure out a way without waiting for another lynching to take their performance back down south. And with the Montgomery bus boycott that began when NAACP member Rosa Parks refused to give up her seat in December 1955, activists created this third current of the movement.

To understand why direct action was so effective in the photojournalism and television age, we need to understand, as civil rights activists did, exactly how segregation worked in the region. In the antebellum South, slavery made racial difference. By the late nineteenth century, some white southerners had settled on spatial separation or segregation to continue this process of racial making in the postemancipation world. Over time, they elaborated an entire social order around this process of linking place and identity. Whites could not make African Americans be inferior, so instead they made blacks take on inferior roles in all the thousands of ritualized everyday encounters of the segregated South, from waiting for service in a store to yielding the sidewalk to getting a drink of water. Whites could not make African Americans be inferior, so they made blacks occupy inferior spaces like the back of buses, the dirty smoking and Jim Crow cars on trains, and substandard waiting rooms, restrooms, and dining rooms all over the South. And whites preserved their segregated world by banishing African Americans from the one place that mattered most, the polls.

With direct mass action and a philosophy of nonviolence, African Americans and a few white activists rewrote the everyday performances that made segregation. In the Montgomery bus boycott, local blacks spent more than a year after Rosa Parks's arrest walking to work and carpooling. Since they made up the vast majority of riders, their actions threatened the very survival of the local transit system. White authorities harassed and tried to intimidate the boycotters but their remarkable organization, community wide and church based, held firm. Their efforts attracted a great deal of national media attention. African Americans in Montgomery succeeded in forcing the integration of that city's public transportation system. Out of this successful grassroots effort emerged the leadership of black ministers like Martin Luther King Jr. and

An African American using the colored entrance of a theater in Belzoni, Mississippi. Library of Congress, Prints & Photographs Division, Washington, D.C., reproduction number LC-USF33-030577-M2.

Ralph Abernathy and new organizations like the Southern Christian Leadership Conference.

Montgomery's 1955–56 boycott, however, also demonstrates how years of organizing and institution building supported widely publicized protests. E. D. Nixon had spent almost half his life—he was fifty-six—as president of the Alabama branch of the Brotherhood of Sleeping Car Porters. Led by A. Philip Randolph, Nixon's idol, the Brotherhood of Sleeping Car Porters was the first major black trade union in America, and Randolph, at midcentury, was one of the nation's most important black leaders. Over the years, Nixon became the man that Montgomery's African Americans in trouble went to for help mediating disputes with local white leaders, policemen, judges, and other government officials. He also dominated the local branch of the NAACP. Nixon and the white liberal lawyer and former New Dealer Clifford Durr, a Montgomery native, were looking for a case they could use to attack Alabama's segregation laws. African Americans, in fact, had been pressing test cases against the segregation of transportation since the 1880s. *Plessy v. Ferguson* (1896), the Supreme Court decision that declared "separate but equal" constitutional, originated as one of these cases. In Montgomery, two other women had been arrested in 1955 for violating bus segregation laws, but Nixon, Durr, and other activists believed they weren't likely to win their cases—one, for example, was an unwed teenage mother. Rosa Parks, however, was perfect. As historian Taylor Branch has argued, Parks bridged the class lines that separated Montgomery's black activists. "Of working-class station and middle-class demeanor," Parks spoke quietly, wrote well, and held herself above factionalism. She also worked as a seamstress and took in sewing on the side, actively participated in her church, and led the local NAACP Youth Council. After being released on bail, Parks talked with her family and agreed to let Nixon, Durr, and local black attorney Fred Gray press her case.

Hearing about Parks's arrest, the more middle-class and professional Women's Political Council led by members like Jo Ann Robinson, a professor of English at Alabama State, produced a letter of protest. "Another Negro woman has been arrested and thrown into jail because she refused to get up out of her seat on the bus and give it to a white woman. Until we do something to stop these arrests, they will continue. The next time it may be you or you or you." The Women's Political Council then called for a boycott of buses on Monday to protest Parks's trial, after which Nixon called together a group of local leaders, mainly ministers, who met and produced a second flyer endorsing the boycott and calling for a mass meeting that Monday night. At a second meeting, the group named themselves the Montgomery Improvement Association. Martin Luther King Jr., the new minister of Dexter Avenue Baptist

Martin Luther King Jr. (left) at the Vine City (Atlanta) rent demonstration in January 1966. Courtesy of the Kenan Research Center at the Atlanta History Center.

Church, was elected president, as much for his lack of enemies as for his talents as a leader. On Monday, Montgomery blacks stayed off the buses and attended the mass meeting by the thousands, where King awed the crowds: "There comes a time when people get tired of being trampled over by the iron feet of oppression. . . . We are here—we are here because we are tired now." The Montgomery Improvement Association decided to continue the boycott and in 1956 won the first direct-action victory against segregation.

Southern blacks, however, could not boycott services and businesses from which segregation excluded them. In 1960 a small group of black college students from North Carolina A&T resurrected another kind of direct action that the Congress of Racial Equality (CORE), a northern-based group founded in 1942 with ties to the pacifist movement and a strong investment in Ghandian nonviolence, had pioneered in the South in the late 1940s. On February 1, four freshmen at North Carolina A&T demanded service at the for-whites-only lunch counter of the Greensboro Woolworth's. Over the previous three years, activists had conducted little-noticed sit-ins in at least sixteen other cities. But somehow the Greensboro students' protest started a wave of direct action across the South in 1960 and 1961 and resulted in the formation of the Student Nonviolent Coordinating Committee to give the student protest movement an institutional form. The sit-in movement, like school desegregation efforts, generated violent white resistance and the consistent opposition of local politicians and business leaders. Activists were covered with condiments and insulted, pistol-whipped, and teargassed. But many of these efforts succeeded, particularly in places like Nashville, outside the Deep South.

In Atlanta, for example, waves of sit-ins began after student leaders from Atlanta University, inspired by the Greensboro students, placed full-page ads, paid for by Georgia author Lillian Smith, in the Atlanta papers on March 9, 1960. Entitled "An Appeal for Human Rights" and written by Morehouse student Julian Bond and Spelman student Rosalyn Pope, the appeal declared, "We do not intend to wait placidly for those rights which are already legally and morally ours to be meted out to us one at a time. Today's youth will not sit by submissively, while being denied all of the rights, privileges, and joys of life. We want to state clearly and unequivocally that we cannot tolerate, in a nation professing democracy and among people professing Christianity, the discriminatory conditions under which the Negro is living today in Atlanta, Georgia—supposedly one of the most progressive cities in the South." After outlining specific areas of discrimination, the appeal declared that "the time has come for the people of Atlanta and Georgia to take a good look at what is really happening in this country, and to stop believing those who tell us that everything is fine and equal, and that the Negro is happy and satisfied. . . . We must say in all candor that we plan to use every legal and non-violent means at our disposal to secure full citizenship rights as members of this great Democracy of ours." Shocked white Atlantans claimed that they had no idea African Americans were dissatisfied. Governor Ernest Vandiver announced that the "leftwing" statement, "calculated to breed dissatisfaction, discontent, discord and evil," could not have been written by black students or anyone else in America and must be the work of Communists.

On March 15, two hundred students led by Atlanta native, popular student leader, and military veteran Lonnie C. King began a well-rehearsed series of protests. They chose their targets carefully, singling out lunch counters operating in public or tax-supported buildings like the state capitol, the Fulton County courthouse, city hall, and office buildings occupied by federal government agencies. Negotiations with divided African American and white leaders and white merchants, demonstrations and sit-ins at downtown department stores like Rich's, and boycotts of chain-store groceries like Colonial in black neighborhoods alternated throughout the spring and summer.

By the fall of 1960, Lonnie King and Herschelle Sullivan, a senior at Spelman College, were cochairing the highly organized Atlanta Student Movement. Participants, mostly black but with an increasing number of white Emory and University of Georgia students mixed in, divided into groups that carried out pickets, sit-ins, and sit-and-runs. The groups were dispatched according to information provided each morning by intelligence collectors on foot, by short-wave-radio-outfitted cars, and at the "field headquarters" on the "ramparts," the steps of the post office annex across the street from Rich's. In this way, activists kept most lunch counters closed simply by showing up when one reopened and requesting service. Most participants sat down anyway, demanded their rights, and waited for arrest. The picketers kept activities like the ongoing boycott of Rich's and other downtown stores visible. Activists filed frequent reports, by telephone and radio, keeping headquarters informed about where to send people or transportation next. Captain Lenora Tait filed this example on November 26 at 11:05 a.m.: "Lunch counters at Rich's closed. Proceeded to alternative objective. Counters at Woolworth's also closed. Back to Rich's for picket duty. Ku Klux Klan circling Rich's in night gowns and dunce caps. Looking good!" By March 7, 1961, over half a year of this extremely well-coordinated activism had forced leaders like Dick Rich of Atlanta's Rich's department store to agree to desegregate their stores completely—lunch counters, restrooms, restaurants, and changing rooms— by the fall of 1961. In Atlanta, student activists had at last cracked the segregation of public and commercial facilities in the Deep South.

On May 4, 1961, the next wave of direct action, the Freedom Rides, began as a group of seven blacks and six whites, organized by CORE, left Washington, D.C., on two buses bound for the Deep South. They intended to test the transit system's compliance across the region with the United States Supreme Court rulings against segregation on public vehicles that travel between states by sitting together on the buses and ignoring the Colored Only and Whites Only signs often posted in terminals. The riders reached Atlanta safely and had dinner with Dr. King. But King's warning to a *Jet* magazine reporter along for the rides that "you will never make it through Alabama" almost came true. In Anniston and Birmingham, angry white mobs viciously attacked the integrated freedom riders. When student activists in Nashville learned that these original riders were abandoning the buses, they decided to organize a group to travel to Birmingham to continue the journey. Diane Nash called Birmingham civil rights activist and minister Fred Shuttlesworth to tell him that the Nashville students were coming. Shuttlesworth, already legendary for his own iron courage, replied, "Young lady, do you know that the Freedom Riders were almost killed here?" Nash answered "Yes. That is why the ride must not be stopped. If they stop us with violence, the movement is dead." Later, when groups of riders finally did reach Mississippi, with the protection of federal marshals sent in by President Kennedy, they were immediately arrested for violating state law. By the end of the summer, however, the Interstate Commerce Commission declared that interstate carriers must not only obey Supreme Court rulings but must also post signs that promised service regardless of race. Nonviolence, persistence, and student courage had broken through the violent resistance of the segregationists. In 1963, the Birmingham movement made this point even more clear as local high school students faced down police dogs and fire hoses on televisions and in newspapers across the country.

With boycotts, sit-ins, freedom rides, and demonstrations, civil rights activists succeeded in breaking the connection between inferior spaces—the back of the bus, a dirty restroom in the basement of Rich's, no place to eat at all—and their own black bodies. The 1964 Mississippi Freedom Summer Project, the Mississippi Freedom Democratic Party, voter registration efforts across the Deep South, and the 1965 Selma to Montgomery march broke the barriers that made the franchise, too, and political participation more generally, a white space as well.

Media coverage at last gave activists a larger national and international audience for their efforts to make white violence visible, and public outrage finally forced the federal government to come down on the side of the civil rights activists. The 1964 Civil Rights Act and the 1965 Voting Rights Act codified in law these victories in the streets. The civil rights movement, a flooding river of black resistance, destroyed the South's unique twentieth-century racial order, its culture of segregation.

This story is true. Many people like it because it highlights African American courage and resistance. "We" shall overcome. Other Americans like it because it places the civil rights struggle within a more circumspect but still triumphant narrative of American progress. Sure, this story admits that America has not always been a place of freedom and justice for all. But "we" ended slavery and then outlawed Jim Crow. "We," too, shall overcome.

The problem is that this story describes integration (the historical phe-nomenon) while encoding segregation (insofar as the African American "we" remains crucially and fundamentally distinct from the white "we"). It is inte-grated in its content but not in its form. For all the clearing, quite literally, of the ground of southern segregation, of the signs for colored and for whites, two different imagined communities, two different "we's" remain. Most whites welcoming integration imagine a world in which there will be peace and African Americans will essentially become white. African Americans working for integration imagine a somewhat different world, a place where they can keep their sense of distinctiveness and yet have the same rights and oppor-tunities, the same access to power, as whites. Both the obstacles that are thought necessary to overcome on the way and the emotional climate of the anticipated, eventual success are entirely different.

This story also starts too late and ends too soon. Its post–World War II beginning ignores the fact that the culture of segregation was created in this century. Its ending denies the fact that racial segregation—in neighborhoods, schools, and religious institutions—in places both abstract and everyday—is very much with us still. Its contours ignore the fact that the South is now a region with many more categories than black and white.

There is, of course, also the problem of perspective. My voice is not just some abstract presence behind the ink. I was born in Atlanta in the middle of this last century of southern race relations, in the middle of this story. 1964 may not have been the exact middle in terms of years, but it was the high point of the hope. I am white. How can I sing this song of progress? There is, of course, another way to write this history.

There is a story I can tell that some people will like. It is a static, unbroken narrative of oppression. It is true. This story says integration is impossible.

Segregation was created in this century, give or take a decade. White racial prejudice, in this account, has not diminished; it has simply flowed into other forms. The culture of segregation replaced the world of slavery and some modified form of segregation, a kind of "corporate" multiculturalism, has replaced the old Jim Crow. George W. Bush, after all, has managed to appoint a rainbow cabinet and still oppose affirmative action. Everyone is represented, every "culture" is respected, but everyone is not equally likely to be shot by police, electrocuted by the state, or tracked out of college prep. If anything, white racism has grown more subtle and insidious and thus more difficult to eradicate. Or, from the opposite perspective, black urban behavior has grown more pathological, nurtured by welfare dependency, absent fathers, and drug abuse. These prejudices, in turn, have nurtured new kinds of black racism, neo-Confederatism, and "color-blind" conservatism, deepening the differences between blacks and whites.

This century started earlier, in the aftermath of Reconstruction. Whites spent a decade or two trying to revive an old personalized racial power, vested in paternalism and patronage, outside the bonds of slavery. When blacks had the courage to vote for the candidates of their choice and even run for office themselves, whites countered by stuffing ballot boxes, forming the Ku Klux Klan and other terrorist organizations, and beating and even murdering these newest American citizens. Led by the example of the 1890 Mississippi Plan and the federal government's refusal to enforce the Fifteenth Amendment, white southern lawmakers "cleaned up" elections by rewriting state constitutions across the region. Poll taxes, literacy and understanding clauses, and strict registration requirements succeeded in preventing most African Americans from voting without ever mentioning the word "race." Grandfather clauses returned many of the white men caught in these rules back to the rolls. The franchise, then, was the first white space in the new racial order of segregation.

But violence was not just about voting. Racial violence was absolutely central to the creation and maintenance of this New South social order. As the historian Edward Ayers has argued, African Americans forced southern whites to systematize segregation and set it down in the law because they consistently refused, for example, to give up—when they could purchase the ticket—their right to ride first class on southern trains. Southern blacks resisted the creation of the new racial order of segregation throughout the 1880s and into the early twentieth century. But beginning in the late 1880s, an epidemic of lynchings and other violent attacks, as both actual events and perpetual possibility, forced southern blacks to accept the loss of their citizenship—not just the vote but the increasing restriction of every aspect of black southern life. Southern whites invented a new form of horror, the spectacle lynching. At these popular "events," festive crowds of whites watched and participated in the torture and murder of black people and afterward sought body parts, charred wood, chain links, and photographs as souvenirs. These lynching "parties," along with race riots, bombings, and other white acts of terrorism, were most effective because of their visibility, which generated the fear that made many African Americans comply with the segregated order. Without the presence of violence—in actual event, in representation, and as conjured through fear—there would have been no culture of segregation.

Yet lynchings played another, perhaps even more important, role in the culture of segregation. Separation, after all, was something that African Americans wanted in certain circumstances in the wake of emancipation—separate churches and schools and plots of land. Separation could provide a kind of limited autonomy. But spectacle lynchings said that no space, not even the individual space of the body, was safe, that no space, in the sense of a staging ground for agency, was black. These lynchings as entertainment were the ultimate creators of racial identity and racial meaning. African Americans, the spectacle lynchings demonstrated, were people who could be publicly and torturously killed for the enjoyment of others. Whites were people who could kill blacks or watch blacks being killed without penalty. And, it needs to be emphasized, with more than a little pleasure. Making a spectacle of lynching united people—those present and those who viewed the photographs, however they interpreted the horror—across divisions of gender, class, and locality into something called "whiteness." You were either a potential spectator or a future body on the pyre. Which side you identified with was who you were.

Atlanta, to consider an urban example, was not immune to this violence. One of the earliest spectacle lynchings, an event that through widespread newspaper coverage created a kind of script for future lynchers, was the murder of Sam Hose outside the city, in Newnan, Georgia, in 1899. White folks in nearby Palmetto believed that Hose, a local farm laborer, split open to the eyeballs the skull of his employer, the respected white farmer Alfred Cranford, and then attacked Cranford's children and raped his wife within sight of the bleeding corpse. It was the Atlanta papers, however, that stirred up white outrage across central Georgia. "Determined Mob after Hose; He Will Be Lynched If Caught," read the headline in the April 14, 1899, *Atlanta Constitution*. The best white men were in the mob, unmasked and proud of it, the cream of "a half dozen counties," "lawyers, doctors, merchant farmers, and every creed and class of men." They vowed "never to give up the chase." For ten days the papers described the pursuit and interviewed those lawyers or doctors or farmers who were part of the mob. One calmly told a reporter, "whatever death is most torturous, most horrifying to a brute, shall be meted out. . . . [L]et him burn slowly for hours." The papers advertised chartered trains that would leave as soon as the mob captured Hose and telegraphed the news. When the mob finally found Hose, they took him on the regular

Macon-to-Atlanta train as far as Griffin, where the railroad provided a special train to take the fast-growing crowd on to Palmetto. The Atlanta and West Point Railroad estimated that it sold one thousand tickets to Palmetto and that stowaways stole five hundred spaces more. Ironically, afraid that Hose would be killed by the growing crowd, the mob lynched him at Newnan, ten miles from Palmetto, on Sunday just after church let out. Soon afterward, an Atlanta grocery store on Mitchell Street displayed Hose's knuckles in a jar.

Atlanta had certainly not always been, as Mayor William Hartsfield famously announced as the 1960–61 sit-in movement peacefully desegregated downtown, a "city too busy to hate." In September 1906, Atlanta newspapers filled their pages with stories about alleged rapes, mobs hunting alleged criminals, and lynchings, fueling white fears of a Negro crime wave. On September 22, a riot began, and over four days a white mob killed twelve people and burned hundreds of buildings. In 1915, Leo Frank, the not-quite-white Jewish manager of a pencil factory, was lynched. And, much later, throughout the 1950s and 1960s, Atlanta developers waged war on black neighborhoods. "Urban renewal"—the tearing down of "slums," the building of highways and expansion of existing roads, and the building of public housing—overwhelming affected African American communities, which bore the brunt of these geographically violent improvements. In 1958, the Temple, the oldest Jewish synagogue in the city, was bombed by white extremists who, in a call claiming responsibility, declared all Jews and blacks "aliens." In 1960, amid the Atlanta sit-in movement, a bomb wrecked a black elementary school near the site of the previous day's mass prayer meeting. From 1979 through 1981, thirty black children were reported missing, and twenty-nine bodies were eventually found at sites in and around the city. While Wayne Williams was convicted of two of the murders, some Atlantans still do not believe he was responsible for all of them. Racial politics, they insist, railroaded a black suspect in an attempt to restore civic peace.

And this record of white violence extends across the region. Southern whites lynched and rioted in record numbers from the late 1880s through the first years of the twentieth century. After World War I, another wave of race riots broke out as black veterans returned home. Lynchings decreased in number in the late 1920s and 1930s but continued through World War II with notorious cases like that of the two black men in Duck Hill, Mississippi, who were burned to death with gasoline blowtorches in 1937. Other methods of violence, like bombs, replaced the lynch ropes in the postwar period. NAACP activist Harry T. Moore was killed along with his wife in Florida when his house was bombed in 1951. Four young black girls were murdered by another bomb in 1963 while they attended Sunday school in

Leo Frank was lynched in August 1915 after his death sentence was commuted by Georgia Governor John Slaton. Courtesy of the Kenan Research Center at the Atlanta History Center.

their Birmingham church. NAACP activist Medgar Evers was shot in the back in Jackson, Mississippi, in 1963. Andrew Goodman, James Chaney, and Michael Schwerner were murdered in 1964 near Philadelphia, Mississippi. In Jasper, Texas, James Bird was lynched in 1999.

In the 1990s, black churches across the South burned in often still-unsolved crimes that police suspected were racially motivated. Sure, the violence has been driven underground—modern-day lynchers do not pose smiling with the corpse for the town photographer, and church arsonists do not brag to the media. But still, today, African Americans in the South must fear the violence of the police as much as the white extremists. Unarmed black men are not shot just in New York City—they are also shot in Athens, Georgia, and in northern suburban Virginia. And race, for all the carefully sanitized language of the last two decades, still plays a tremendous role in American politics.

This story of eternal oppression says integration is impossible. White people will oppress black people. And their opposition to equality will range along a continuum from "peaceful" protest—voting for disfranchising amendments, opposing affirmative action, and talking about "states' rights" as a color-blind code word for a segregationist political agenda—to outright violence. This story is harder to write than the story of steady progress. The historians who have worked on it in the past, often African American, have been neglected, and new attention to the topic, especially to the origins of the New Right in segregationist resistance to the civil rights movement, is just beginning to bear fruit. But in this story *Brown* was more important in galvanizing segregationist resistance than in destroying segregation. Integrated shopping and commercial districts—the victories won by the sit-in movements, for example—were not signs of progress because they existed in the very same small southern towns across the first half of the twentieth century where lynchings occurred. And for civil rights activists, nonviolence was just a strategy, not a way of life. North Carolina's own Robert F. Williams, the infamous author of the 1962 book *Negroes with Guns*, stood out because he openly promoted African Americans' armed resistance to white violence. But other civil rights activists, including NAACP lawyer Thurgood Marshall and Martin Luther King Jr., made sure weapons were close at hand as they canvassed the back roads of the region. Local blacks in communities across Mississippi that hosted Freedom Summer volunteers, in another example, often quietly used guns to protect the Freedom Houses and community centers where activists lived, held meetings, and ran citizenship schools and literacy programs.

Most deadly for integration in Atlanta (and many other booming cities across the nation) has been the absolute perfection of a new racial order grounded in white flight. Once the city's commercial life moved to the suburbs, it did not matter much that downtown was integrated. Once whites left the city's public schools en masse, it did not matter much that Atlanta's school system had desegregated peacefully in the fall of 1961. The "city too busy to hate" had become the city too busy moving to hate. Whites who wanted segregation could find it by moving farther and farther out into the spreading rings of suburbs. African Americans, at least those with means, could also chose segregation or integration, although the mixed neighborhoods they moved into too often ended up sliding right out from under them. Poor African Americans in Atlanta, on the other hand, had few choices. In the metropolitan region as a whole, integrating a moving target proved impossible.

We may not know the names of many of the lynchers but we know the names of the politicians: Ben Tillman, Woodrow Wilson, George Wallace, Tom Watson, and Herman Talmadge. We know the names of the segregationists: Tom Brady, the author of "Black Monday," an anti-*Brown* manifesto, Birmingham sheriff Bull Connor, Atlanta Klan leader and defender of segregated neighborhoods Joe Wallace, and Mississippi Klan leader and mastermind of the triple murder of civil rights activists in 1964 Sam Bowers. In this story these people become the icons, the antiheroes, and to some even the heroes, the counterweights to Martin Luther King Jr., Fred Shuttlesworth, E. D. Nixon, Rosa Parks, Diane Nash, Lonnie King, Julian Bond, Thurgood Marshall, and Fannie Lou Hamer. In this story, the opponent is not a white-hooded redneck. The enemy is not some vague concept like consciousness or some feeling or condition in the human heart. The enemy is real. The opponents are people, flesh and blood, and more likely to be modern suburbanites than small-town survivalists. Or, from the other perspective, the enemies are welfare mothers, crack dealers, and by extension all poor African Americans, even all blacks. And these two sides to the "integration is impossible" story are themselves impossible to reconcile. Both paradoxically contribute to a politics of apathy, to doing little and less every day on the national and state level to combat violations of our democracy.

This story, too, is true. It is favored by many academics and activists and Afrocentrists, but the people in these overlapping categories like the story for sometimes strikingly different reasons. Some people want to acknowledge the historic oppression of blacks in America in slavery, segregation, and whatever we want to call the post–civil rights movement present and the damage it has caused. They want to acknowledge and yet also paradoxically cleanse themselves of any responsibility by staring at the horror of photographs of lynchings and television shots of fire hoses and police dogs attacking black children. Surely "we" are not as bad as that. Surely the fact that "we" feel bad proves that "we" are good. Some people like this "integration is impossible" story because it fuels so well a black politics of victimization. As the sociologist Orlando Patterson has pointed out, this politics, even though it is rooted in a very real history of oppression, makes equality impossible. This version of the story says that African Americans always have and always will suffer discrimination of some kind. For many whites, seeing blacks as eternal victims ensures their privileged position as the people whose activities matter. "We" are the subjects of American history, the people who make up American society. They are its objects. For many African Americans, seeing blacks as eternal victims may limit historical agency but the rewards are "oh so sweet." "We" are morally superior in our suffering. "We" are not equal but better than you. And from an opposite political perspective, the "integration is impossible" story contributes to the ongoing resurgence of conservative politics in America.

Perhaps the problem in part lies in the very concept of race relations. Young scholars like Michael R. West and Clayton McClure Brooks are questioning the very idea of race relations as itself a part of the culture and practice of segregation. As West brilliantly argues, Booker T. Washington invented the concept of race relations in a speech he gave in Atlanta in 1895 at the Cotton States and International Exposition. Washington urged African Americans to pursue economic and educational advancement in the South first: "Cast down your buckets where you are. . . . It is at the bottom of life we must begin, and not at the top. Nor should we permit our grievances to overshadow our opportunities." Of blacks and whites in the South, he argued, "in all things that are purely social we can be as separate as the fingers, yet one as the hand in all things essential to mutual progress." Washington became the white-acknowledged leader of black America in the early twentieth century precisely because he offered a way to manage the glaring problem of continued black oppression in our postslavery democracy. Trading black demands for political rights for some measure of protection from white violence, he set up a racial peace. And this peace held until King and others urged African Americans to break it with nonviolent direct action. The very idea of race relations and perhaps even of racialized "cultures" has been a way to forestall the fulfillment of American democracy.

The South's culture of segregation was violent and immoral and unworkable and it had to go. But traces of segregation remain in all our current accounts of the last century of southern race relations. And traces of segregation still order and divide and rank our world. Segregation—as spatial division, as the imagination of distance between human beings—is exactly what creates racial identity. Such systems are, of course, more formidable when codified in laws and enforced by governments, but a system of segregation once created can, as the post–civil rights era has proved, continue to exist in important ways without such weapons. We are all afraid to give up on segregation because we are afraid to give up on racial identity. It is too much a part of what we know. It is too much a part of who we are. This "we," the human beings who cannot give up on the category of race, may be the most integrated "we" of all.

Suggested Readings

Ayers, Edward. *The Promise of the New South: Life after Reconstruction*. New York: Oxford University Press, 1993.

Bayor, Ronald H. *Race and the Shaping of Twentieth-Century Atlanta*. Chapel Hill: University of North Carolina Press, 2000.

Birnbaum, Jonathan, and Clarence Taylor, eds. *Civil Rights since 1787: A Reader on the Black Struggle*. New York: New York University Press, 2000.

Branch, Taylor. *Parting the Waters: America in the King Years, 1954–1963*. New York: Simon and Schuster, 1989.

Carter, Dan. *The Politics of Rage: George Wallace, the Origins of the New Conservatism, and the Transformation of American Politics*. Baton Rouge: Louisiana State University Press, 1995.

Garrow, David, ed. *Atlanta, Georgia, 1960–1961: Sit-ins and Student Activism*. Brooklyn, N.Y.: Carlson Publishing, 1989.

Hale, Grace Elizabeth. *Making Whiteness: The Culture of Segregation in the South, 1890–1940*. New York: Pantheon, 1998.

Harding, Vincent. *There Is a River: The Black Freedom Struggle in America*. New York: Harcourt, 1981.

Jacoby, Tamar. *Someone Else's House: America's Unfinished Struggle for Integration*. New York: Free Press, 1998.

Kelley, Robin D. G. *Race Rebels: Culture, Politics, and the Black Working Class*. New York: Free Press, 1996.

Payne, Charles. *I've Got the Light of Freedom: The Organizing Tradition and the Mississippi Freedom Struggle*. Berkeley: University of California Press, 1995.

Williamson, Joel. *The Crucible of Race: Black/White Relations in the American South since Emancipation*. New York: Oxford University Press, 1984.

Mapping Out the Economic and Spatial South

GAVIN WRIGHT

Persisting Dixie

The South as an Economic Region

From colonial times, the regions of the American South were known to be
economically distinct from those to the north. The economy built on staple
crops, plantations, and slavery enjoyed something of a heyday in the antebellum era, but its regional legacy was nearly a century of backwardness, poverty,
and isolation from the American mainstream. As everyone knows, all this has
now changed. Since World War II, the South has persistently outpaced the
rest of the nation in growth of incomes, industry, jobs, commerce, construction, and education. The most spectacular transformation has occurred in the
South Atlantic section. Using the standard economic measure of income per
capita, the South Atlantic states were the poorest in the country at the end of
the nineteenth century; by the end of the twentieth, their income per capita
was the highest in the region and virtually equal to the U.S. average (figure 1).

FIGURE 1

Per Capita Income: South as percent of U.S., 1880–2000

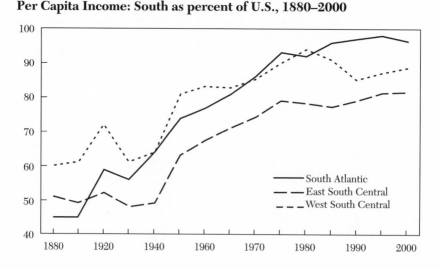

Figure 1 shows that although all parts of the South have gained on the national average, the three component census regions were at quite different positions at century's end. The contrast raises the question of whether the South as a whole still possesses any real cohesion as a regional economy. Writing on this subject in 1986, I had little hesitation in reporting that "the entity formerly known as the Southern economy no longer exists." Many others expressed similar views at the time. The late Mancur Olson, a lifelong student of the South, concluded his 1982 presidential address to the Southern Economic Association on this note:

> With a per capita income similar to the rest of the country, with institutional arrangements and racial policies much the same as those in the nation as a whole, and with rapid and inexpensive transportation linking it with the rest of the country, the South is losing its regional peculiarities. . . . [T]he South as an utterly distinctive region with its own sense of nationhood—the South of the old evils and the old romance—is already disappearing . . . and becoming one with the nation as a whole.

From the vantage point of the twenty-first century, this assessment seems premature, if not downright wrong. The South's particularity has proven surprisingly persistent, in economic as well as in cultural and political life. Because so much has changed, the challenge for the economic historian is to identify the new bases for regionalism in the economy of the New South.

But, in order to figure out where the South is now, we should first look back at where it has been.

Since the South was never *homogeneous* geographically or economically, one may ask whether a "southern economy" ever really existed. The answer is yes, it did. In the past, the various parts of the South functioned within a coherent, regionally oriented system, most notably in the labor market. Before World War I both African Americans and white southerners migrated primarily along east-west lines within the South. Immigrants from abroad avoided the South. At the peak of European immigration into the United States in 1910, less than 2 percent of the southern population was foreign-born. With respect to such basic ecodemographic indicators as average farm size and land-labor ratios, every single southern state moved in the same direction in every single decade between 1880 and 1930—toward smaller farm size and fewer acres per person—trends that were contrary to those prevailing in the rest of the country. This economic commonality reinforced the white political solidarity that derived from the race issue, giving the South a political unity unique among large American regions.

The southern labor market was both a reflection and a cause of the persistence of a distinctive southern regional culture documented by sociologists like John Shelton Reed. In itself, such regionalism doesn't necessarily imply economic backwardness. But taken together with the booming high-wage industrial economy of the northern states in the early part of the twentieth century, the South's regional isolation had adverse economic consequences for several reasons. First, high birth rates in rural areas produced more wage seekers than southern cities could absorb, putting steady downward pressure on regional wage rates. Second, the southern natural environment was sufficiently different from that of the rest of the country that the region had difficulty absorbing the benefits of technologies adapted to northern conditions. The problem of generating a regionally "appropriate technology" was not limited to resource-based activities but extended to manufacturing as well. Although "cheap labor" was the South's main source of competitive advantage in such industries as textiles, producers often had to choose between adopting highly mechanized laborsaving technologies from the North or retaining techniques that elsewhere had been discarded decades before. When a group of Georgians set out in the 1880s to establish a state school of technology, they had to rely on northern models, and the model chosen was the "shop culture" approach: highly practical "trade school" training, producing "graduates who could work as machinists or as shop foremen but who were not well prepared for engineering or original research." This choice may have been the only feasible one at that time.

Reliance on cheap labor does not in itself suggest social pathology or industrial stagnation—the wage gap after all was the vehicle through which southern industry could get a foot in the door of the national market. But cheap labor in the American setting did have a retrograde influence on southern economic *development*, because it undermined the incentive for employers to invest in education as a means of raising the standards of the labor force. This problem was most severe in the plantation belt, where planters regarded schooling for blacks as a threat rather than an opportunity. An Arkansas planter testified in 1900 that "my experience has been that when one of the youngster class gets so he can read and write and cipher, he wants to go to town. It is rare to find one who can read and write and cipher in the field at work." With attitudes like this, it is hardly surprising that spending on black schools in plantation areas was miserably low.

In the up-country, a process of "progressivism for whites only" was underway in the first half of the twentieth century. But the educational incentive problem also permeated the textile areas, where mill owners well understood that a high school diploma was as good as a ticket to leave the mill village. The lack of incentive to invest in education on the part of employers might not have mattered much, except for the broad failure of democracy in this era of southern history. Voting rates for whites were dragged down as a byproduct of the successful drive to disfranchise black voters at the end of the nineteenth century, leaving state policies in the hands of elites with a vested interest in maintaining regional isolation.

Between the 1930s and the 1950s, what economists call a "regime change" occurred in the South. The region's modern economic takeoff is often dated to World War II, but important changes were underway earlier. In part, postwar convergence in per capita income levels may be attributed to long-term trends brought about by advances in technology, including the falling cost of long-distance travel and communication. Science-based technologies relaxed many of the constraints that implicitly limited the geographic spread of modern practices to the temperate zone; one result has been a steady trend toward geographic dispersion in economic activity since World War II, to the western and southwestern parts of the country as well as to the southeast. In the South, however, the precipitate change in economic direction to a large extent reflected two major policy shifts: the imposition of national labor standards and the initiation of aggressive state programs of industrial recruitment.

The two were closely related. With the advent of the national minimum wage (and related labor regulations) in the 1930s, and the renewal and extension of these policies in the 1950s, it became clear to business leaders of the South that an Asian-style industrialization based on cheap labor within U.S.

The Rust cotton picker on the Clover Hill Plantation near Clarksdale, Mississippi. Library of Congress, Prints & Photographs Division, Washington, D.C., reproduction number LC-USF34-052474-D.

borders was not going to be feasible. Textiles and allied industries continued to loom large in the southern economy, but having moved into a laborsaving technological mode, they could no longer lead the way in terms of job creation. At roughly the same time, the end of the 1940s, full mechanization of cotton harvesting became technically feasible and was all but complete by 1960. Together, these developments tipped the political balance in southern states toward a policy whereby they would make vigorous efforts to attract business through tax breaks, municipal bonds for plant construction, industrial development corporations, research parks, and expenditures on publicity far beyond those of other regions. James C. Cobb calls it the "selling of the South." One still hears the claim that the South has not changed all that much, deep down. But on the economic policy front, the transformation was nearly total. As historian Numan Bartley puts it: "In 1940 the *raison d'être* of Southern state governments was the protection of white supremacy and social stability; thirty years later their central purpose was the promotion of business and industrial development."

As a case study in modernization, however, this episode was highly unusual in that the acceleration of economic growth coincided with massive out-migration from the region. Low-income, poorly educated southerners left the countryside for cities in both the North and South, while professionals and retirees began to move southward, into fast-growing cities and Sun Belt areas. One major structural change was racial: the African American share of the southern population fell sharply between 1910 and 1970; in the five states of the Deep South, blacks accounted for more than 50 percent of the total in 1910 but less than 30 percent in 1970. The reason is not difficult to identify: regional out-migration was racially as well as economically selective. Four million black southerners left the South between 1940 and 1970 because few of the region's newly emerging opportunities were open to them during that phase. Surplus labor conditions made it relatively easy for employers to reserve newly created job openings for whites only. For example, in South Carolina, which had been a black-majority state as late as 1920, 90 percent of new manufacturing jobs went to whites between 1940 and 1965.

During this first phase of the economic revolution, the South was trying to modernize economically while maintaining the entrenched traditions and institutions of racial segregation. As painful as it is to acknowledge, few of the region's political and economic leaders at the time questioned the viability of this strategy. This was true even in a city like Atlanta, proud of its tolerance and modernism. Founded on boosterism in the nineteenth century, Atlanta civic leaders were among the first to join the new southern bandwagon of courting conventions, tourism, and industry. From its earliest days, the city was thought to be "untypical" of the South, perhaps even "unsouthern" in its hectic lifestyle and openness to outside forces. But in its racial order, Atlanta remained thoroughly southern. Hotels and convention facilities were rigidly segregated. Black job opportunities were severely limited, and during the 1920s and 1930s, whites began to encroach even on what were formerly known as "black jobs." As late as the 1950s, many Atlanta jobs were closed to blacks in both the public and private sectors, such as firefighting, building inspection, truck driving, clerking, sales, and auto repair. Although in retrospect such policies seem not only indefensible but irrational from an economic standpoint, the hard lesson of this history is that purely economic forces were relatively ineffective in bringing about fundamental social change.

However, the forces of southern boosterism did come into collision with the demands of racial justice in the 1960s through the political mobilization of black political forces backed by the power of the federal government. The leverage of the civil rights movement came from the fact that southern leaders were no longer trying to protect a fortress; competition for outside capital required that they present their towns and cities as safe, civilized communities, with a labor force that was well behaved and eager for work. In city after city, turmoil over segregation in schools or other local facilities made industrial recruitment difficult or impossible. The most famous example was Little Rock, Arkansas, where a promising postwar development program came to a standstill when Orval Faubus called out the National Guard to block court-ordered school integration in 1957. Though the city had attracted eight new plants in 1957, not a single new plant came to Little Rock during the next four years. The case was widely discussed in the media and its lesson widely absorbed. A *Wall Street Journal* headline for May 26, 1961, read: "Business in Dixie: Many Southerners Say Racial Tension Slows Area's Economic Gains."

In her introduction to a systematic review of the role of southern businessmen in the desegregation crisis, Elizabeth Jacoway wrote: "In the 1950s and 1960s, white businessmen across the South found themselves pushed—by the federal government and civil rights forces as well as by their own economic interests—and values—into becoming reluctant advocates of a new departure in southern race relations." To be sure, more often than not these businessmen were pushing for mere tokenism and public relations "racial harmony." But as Jacoway went on to say: "The changes they accepted were the entering wedge for the much greater changes that have since taken place in southern life and race relations." Although few were willing to say so in public, many local leaders and business proprietors privately welcomed the federal civil rights legislation of the 1960s. These measures largely put an end to disputes over public accommodations and employment segregation, while providing managers the ready-made excuse that the matter was no longer in their hands.

As the quintessential New South city, Atlanta was in the forefront of these developments. Atlanta was the first southern city to negotiate a peaceful end to segregation in its tourist business in 1961. The city's chamber of commerce was the only major business group in the state openly in favor of desegregation, and Ivan Allen was the only mayor from the South to support the federal public accommodations bill. Although it was commonplace at the time to discount these gestures as self-interested and largely symbolic—as indeed they were— one cannot dismiss the long-term significance of the political changes they symbolized.

A series of studies coauthored by Nobel laureate James Heckman show persuasively that the civil rights revolution generated significant economic gains for African Americans in the South. The most dramatic breakthrough was the integration of the textiles industry, which had excluded blacks for a century. Here too, it often seemed that southern employers had to be coerced to act in their own self-interest! One mill executive wrote in 1968 that the Civil

Rights Act was "a blessing in disguise for us," because it allowed them to blame the federal government in justifying integration to resistant white workers. Timothy Minchin quotes another personnel manager: "The government gave us a nice way to facilitate it and if anybody wanted to complain about it, white people would say 'hey, why are you hiring all of these black people,' you'd say 'because the government forces us to do this,' you could place the blame on the government." Yet these employment breakthroughs were a genuine part of the civil rights revolution. Minchin's *Hiring the Black Worker* describes how, even with the backing of the federal government and the laws of supply and demand, the pioneer black textile workers had to cope with hostile reactions from whites and doubts about their competence on the part of supervisors. Contrary to expectations, company studies found no discernible racial difference in productivity.

Textiles was the most extreme case, but there were racial breakthroughs on many other economic fronts. In the paper industry, black representation in blue-collar jobs, including many of the higher-paying, machine-tending jobs they had previously been denied, increased from 15 to nearly 30 percent by the 1990s. In Atlanta and other cities across the South, "middle-class" jobs opened to blacks in significant numbers for the first time. This expansion of employment opportunity coincided with (and was complemented by) a sharp increase in the black high school graduation rate in the South, from 35 percent of the twenty–twenty-four-year-old population in 1960 to 57 percent in 1970 and to 71 percent by 1977. Black enrollment in higher education grew even more dramatically, from 84,000 in 1960 to 426,000 in 1976.

With the aid of hindsight, we can say that, however grudgingly they were offered, these changes have proven to be liberating for the southern economy in general, as well as for its African American citizens. Accommodating the civil rights revolution allowed the region to return to an agenda in which support for economic growth has been the highest priority. The hiatus in economic development from the mid-1950s to the early 1960s gave way to renewed rapid gains in the 1960s, as pursuit of the progrowth agenda succeeded in attracting capital, enterprise, and affluent migrants into the region over an extended period.

But this review leaves us with the question with which this essay began. If the isolation of the regional labor market came to an end, if the South opened its doors to inflows of outside capital and people from diverse backgrounds, and if the institutional structures of segregation were destroyed by a peaceful democratic revolution—why then should the South persist as a distinct regional entity? Cultural inertia is one obvious factor, but this cannot be the full explanation for regional *economic* distinctiveness. Not only have the policy expressions of regionalism changed over the years, but on close inspection, some of the most rabid southerners turn out to be born-again Yankees! Evidently there is a political-economic side to the matter, which deserves further attention. Without trying to preempt other possibilities, let me propose three elements of an answer to the question.

One image of the modern South is of a place with no regional economy. Instead, it is often said that there are two Souths, the burgeoning, prosperous metropolitan areas on the one hand, and on the other, poor, struggling rural backwaters that have been unable to connect to the productive networks of the "New Economy." True enough, in most southern states metropolitan areas have accounted for something between two-thirds and three-fourths of job growth in recent decades. But if we look beyond these tumultuous urban developments, we find a surprisingly persistent regionalism in some of the most robust southern industries.

One prominent example is the southern forest. When the cotton economy went into decline beginning in the 1920s, forest products seemed an unlikely basis for economic renewal. Some of the worst destruction of forest in the country occurred in the yellow pine area stretching from South Carolina to Texas: of an initial one hundred and fifteen million acres, less than twenty-four million acres of old growth pine timber remained in 1920. One government forester described it as "probably the most rapid and reckless destruction of forests known to history." When the first national forest survey was launched in 1928, however, the results indicated that the southern forest was capable of rapid regeneration and would produce a "second-growth forest." As new technologies for using younger resinous pine trees developed, the region's cost advantages in land, water, and labor became highly attractive to pulp and paper firms, for whom scale economies and fixed capital requirements dictated location close to the sources of raw material. Unlike the previous era, this new round of investment launched a concerted effort to create a sustainable basis for southern timber supply. By the 1980s, annual tree plantings in the South averaged two million acres per year, and timber had emerged as the region's number one cash crop.

Industrial forestry in the South was made possible by global scientific developments, but according to a recent study by William Boyd, successful application of these principles called for the mobilization of networks that were inherently regional. There were three major phases: (1) *rationalization*, creating a stable environment for long-term investment horizons, primarily through improved fire protection and management; (2) *regeneration*, developing the biological basis for reforestation of cut-over and marginal agricultural lands; and (3) *intensification*, accelerating biological productivity through advances in forest genetics and tree improvements. It was, in effect, an exercise in regional collective learning. Surprisingly, as the organizational and scientific knowledge base has evolved, its location-specific character has become more, rather than less, prominent. In the midst of fierce competition among firms and research organizations, regional foresters are said to have cultivated a cooperative professional culture of shared knowledge. Should we call it the Silicon Forest Phenomenon?

Some modern-era southern industries reflect regionalism through a combination of geography, labor markets, and political support systems. An example is poultry, which surpassed beef as the meat of choice in the American diet in the 1990s. In 1929, U.S. chicken production was scattered almost uniformly through the eastern half of the country. But in the wake of a revolution in the industry's technological and organizational base, its location shifted dramatically to the South. In the 1990s, the map of chicken production and sales almost traced out the boundaries of the Confederacy.

According to William Boyd and Michael Watts, the southernization of the broiler industry was facilitated by three key features of the rural South. First was the existence of a class of small marginal farmers looking for a means of viable livelihood from their farms. To them, broilers looked like "a good crop on bad land." Second was the established network of merchants and feed dealers extending credit to these farmers, which was readily adaptable to the contract grow-out arrangement that became prevalent in the 1950s. Third was the pool of surplus labor available to work in the processing plants. Together these conditions made the South irresistible as a production base for the integrated systems of emerging industry giants, of which the most famous is Tyson Foods of Arkansas. With its takeover of Lane Poultry and Holly Farms in the 1980s, this southern firm became the undisputed industry leader. The overwhelming national and international dominance of the South in broiler production points to an enduring regional dimension to the prominence of firms such as Tyson Foods. A close look reveals, however, that today's labor force in Tyson's processing plants includes a strong representation of immigrants to both region and country. This may be in some sense cheap labor, but if so, it is an outward-looking company policy, quite in contrast to the regional isolationism of former times.

A second source of persistent regionalism has been the political economy of industrial recruitment. Both before and after the civil rights revolution, the southern states differentiated themselves from the rest of the nation in the vigor of their recruitment activity. As of 1964, southern states held down nine of the top eleven positions in funds spent on print and advertising by state development programs. The effectiveness of southern state-sanctioned municipal bond programs was evident enough to prompt the U.S. Treasury to limit the federal tax-exempt status of such bonds in 1969. They were similarly dominant twenty years later in a 1986 ranking of state "business climate." A recent Stanford dissertation by Jonathan Rork confirms what many have alleged, that these policies have largely attracted firms engaged in relatively unskilled, labor-intensive production. When state manufacturing is ranked either by capital-labor ratios or by the share of employment that is skilled, the southern states persistently appear in the lowest percentiles, in the 1990s as in the 1950s.

In light of these effects, why have these policies had such staying power in the South? Quasi-conspiratorial explanations are not hard to find, but given the initial conditions ca. 1950—a large population of unskilled, poorly edu-cated, and underemployed workers—a labor-intensive orientation may have been both quite defensible and perhaps even unavoidable, as the only feasible way to provide in-state jobs quickly. As the decades proceeded, however, and as competitive recruiting forced them into low-revenue positions, southern states have in effect been locked into an equilibrium in which they are unable to finance the upgrading of their educational systems (and other forms of infrastructure) that would support the transition into higher-bracket activi-ties. Closely related to policies of active industrial recruitment is the South's status at the bottom of the "Green Index" ratings of 1991, summarizing 179 indicators of environmental conditions and 77 indicators of environmental policies. The southern states cluster at the low end, so much so that in nam-ing the lowest-ranked states, one would almost be listing the members of the Confederacy.

What seems to have occurred in the wake of the civil rights revolution and the demise of segregation is that a new political equilibrium in support of a particular brand of political economy has been established in each of the southern states. A cosmopolitan city like Atlanta may not feel that it is a party to this sort of southern politics, but on a wide range of policies, majorities at the state level are crucial, and key features of state politics have been remarkably similar across the region. Of course, these political realities have links to the older South. But their manifestation as the distinctive *regional* tendency is the outcome of a complex historical evolution, rather than the simple expression of preexisting economic interests. It is as though the South now derives its economic interests from its politics, whereas formerly it was the other way around.

The final leg on this proposed regional tripod is the African American presence. The South today is far more ethnically diverse than in the past, but African Americans still comprise the region's largest and most visible minority group. Locating regional identity in the southern black population may seem surprising and perhaps controversial. Surprising, because the term "southerner" in American usage has always meant "*white* southerner," and one can make a case that the main historical basis for this "pernicious abstraction" (in Jack Kirby's phrase) was a sense of white racial identity. And controversial because one often encounters disillusionment among blacks in the South despite the accomplishments of the civil rights era. Blacks are unquestionably overrepresented in the relatively poor rural population that has not shared much of the new regional prosperity. In *Dixie Rising*, Peter Applebome quotes Rose Sanders of Selma, Alabama: "Now for the majority of the people in the Black Belt, who are black and poor, their lives have not significantly changed." The overrepresentation of blacks among the urban southern poor is equally evident. On the political side, blacks do not constitute a majority in any southern state, and it would be hard to identify a state in which they are clearly "in power" as a full member of the dominant coalition. Perhaps as a consequence, Applebome reports that black nostalgia for the segregation era is "a common theme across the South."

Despite these disappointments, it seems to me that the African American presence is a distinctive feature of the South, in economic as well as political life. After the breakthroughs of the 1960s, net black out-migration from the region came to an end, and African Americans have been moving back ever since. Demographer William H. Frey shows that net black migration into the South totaled more than 579,000 between 1990 and 2000, whereas net black migration was negative for each of the other census regions. Although the southern black population is disproportionately poor and rural, regional black in-migrants are also well represented in the new professional and managerial jobs opening up in the booming metropolitan areas. Seven of the ten fastest growing counties for blacks are in the suburbs of Atlanta. Other areas of strong black population growth include Charlotte, Raleigh-Durham, and Greensboro in North Carolina; Norfolk and Richmond in Virginia; and Miami, Tampa, and Jacksonville in Florida. When African Americans self-identify as southerners, very likely it is because of the presence of a viable middle-class black community that they find attractive.

These communities offer economic opportunities as well as a sense of identity. Since 1977, the majority of the nation's black-owned businesses have been found in the South. The number of southern black-owned firms grew from less than 100,000 in 1972 to 435,000 in 1997. To be sure, the majority of these firms were small, not in themselves signs of affluence. But their numbers, size, and sales volume continued to expand throughout the 1990s, refuting the myth that African Americans are less business minded than other ethnic groups. Black-owned businesses undoubtedly did suffer in the wake of integration, as Robert E. Weems Jr. and others have argued. But it seems that subsequent migration patterns and economic advances have done much to reconstruct or replace the networks of earlier times.

Despite the frustrations of minority representation, the African American influence in southern politics is apparent. It is not that southern whites are necessarily more racially enlightened than American whites elsewhere. But the Voting Rights Act of 1965 almost immediately had the effect of eradicating the extreme racist rhetoric from southern politics that until that time had been its hallmark. Since then, the number of black officeholders in the South has steadily increased. Figure 2 reveals the perhaps surprising fact that since the early 1980s, black political representation in the South has greatly surpassed that in the rest of the nation. Even if they do not control any one state, this black political presence cannot be ignored. Political participation has had at least some positive effect on black access to government services: such things as street paving, garbage collection, recreation facilities, FHA loans and agricultural extension services, and state and municipal jobs. Inescapably, this political presence makes itself felt in economics.

Elections of black mayors often have a dramatic effect on the allocation of municipal contracts. The example of Atlanta and the H. J. Russell and Company, a construction and development firm, is a case in point. But there are many other less well-known examples, such as the black-owned investment

FIGURE 2

Black Elected Officials: South and Non-South, 1969–2000

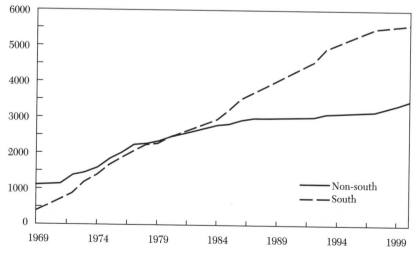

firm Daniels and Bell, whose business began with a public housing project in Bayou Mound, Mississippi, a town that had recently elected a black mayor.

Orlando Patterson calls this explicitly biracial politics the "Atlanta model" of race relations and believes it will become increasingly anachronistic as the nation at large moves toward generalized multiculturalism. To me it seems equally plausible that the African American presence will continue to be a distinguishing part of the fabric of life in the South, as persistent as other regional features. Having mistakenly predicted the demise of the South in the 1980s, I no longer believe that southern economic distinctiveness is on a path to disappearance.

Persistence of regional distinctiveness along political-economic lines does not, of course, mean that the South will never change. The era of low-wage, labor-intensive manufacturing may well have peaked, and political support for environmental values can be expected to rise with affluence, as it has elsewhere. The present stance of the region's representatives in national politics is by no means immutable and could change with relatively small shifts in voter sentiment. But the biracial quality of southern life seems deeply entrenched and unlikely to disappear in the near future.

Suggested Readings

Applebome, Peter. *Dixie Rising: How the South Is Shaping American Values, Politics, and Culture*. New York: Random House, 1996.

Cobb, James C. *The Selling of the South: The Southern Crusade for Industrial Development, 1936–1980*. 2nd ed. Urbana: University of Illinois Press, 1993.

Jacoway, Elizabeth, and David R. Colburn, eds. *Southern Businessmen and Desegregation*. Baton Rouge: Louisiana State University Press, 1982.

Scranton, Philip, ed. *The Second Wave: Southern Industrialization from the 1940s to the 1970s*. Athens: University of Georgia Press, 2001.

Wright, Gavin. *Old South, New South: Revolutions in the Southern Economy Since the Civil War*. Baton Rouge: Louisiana State University Press, 1996.

PETE DANIEL

Not Predestination

The Rural South and Twentieth-Century Transformation

Rural southerners suffered alarming demographic, social, and economic disruptions over the twentieth century. In 1900 the South's 2.4 million farm families, including about 750,000 African Americans families, were divided by legal segregation, a system that survived until midcentury. By the century's end, only 681,000 farms remained in the South, and 194,000 of those were in Texas. Only 18,000 black farms survived the turn of the twenty-first century. The families that had lived on those 1.7 million abandoned farms migrated across the country. They left when economic depression or low prices gave them no option, when dissatisfaction with poor schools or lack of opportunity pointed them elsewhere, when government policies defined them out of farming, or when machines and chemicals replaced them. Many rural communities that were fixated on agriculture either disappeared or were absorbed by agribusiness, suburbs, or corporations. A single Wal-Mart could erase a small-town business district.

At the turn of the twentieth century, residues of Civil War tension, bitterness from the Populist defeat, an exploitative sharecropping and crop lien system, and increasing racism poisoned southern society. Segregation, a modern solution to white fear of African Americans, dictated the social relations between African American and white farmers. While friendships sometimes crossed the color line in rural areas, in society at large legal segregation magnified tension along it. At midcentury, the civil rights movement eased discrimination and improved social relations. During that half century, farmers gradually moved away from labor-intensive farming practices and adopted tractors, picking machines, and chemicals. Increasing government intrusion into southern agriculture early in the century and the transformative power of the New Deal's Agricultural Adjustment Administration (AAA) empowered the rural elite, those farmers best able to grasp the significance of mechanization and government policy. The civil rights movement came too late for black farmers who had left the land, and machines and chemicals were beyond the reach of most small farmers. Millions of rural people left the land. In a world driven by science and technology, change was inevitable, yet such impersonal factors played only a minor role in the peculiar circumstances and timing of southern transformation. Policy, not predestination, shaped the rural South.

The federal government's involvement in agriculture began during the Civil War, when a newly created Department of Agriculture (USDA) haltingly began passing out seeds to farmers. Congress passed the Morrill Act in 1862, giving states public lands to endow (white) state universities that focused on a practical education in agriculture, homemaking, and the mechanic arts. In 1890 lawmakers authorized the creation of separate African American land-grant colleges, customarily designated as 1890 schools. Congress voted for the development of federal experiment stations in 1887 to encourage scientific farming. As the boll weevil paraded across the South in the 1890s, scientists focused on outwitting the insect by demonstrating to farmers how to interrupt its life cycle; such demonstrations also taught rural people the value of good advice. In 1914 the Smith-Lever Act institutionalized the federal extension service. The USDA approved each state's extension leader while land-grant universities organized and managed extension and home demonstration work. The Smith-Hughes Act in 1917 extended agricultural education to secondary schools. During World War I, government planning set a precedent that would blossom in the New Deal. By the end of World War I, then, state and federal programs had united to push for scientific farming.

Many farmers resented outside experts or any hint of government coercion, and, often justifiably, they scoffed at college-trained experts. Whatever the value of expert advice, African American farmers did not share equally the patronage of government programs, for black extension agents worked under the tight control of whites. Home demonstration agents preached the gospel of economy, nutrition, and sanitation, and, through community meetings and demonstrations, rescued many rural women from drudgery and privation. Yet men and women extension agents focused on middle-class and elite farmers, those who could invest in new implements, machines, stoves, irons, plumbing, and screens. In a sense, the extension service promoted consumer goods that not only would improve life but also urbanize rural tastes. In rural communities that contained sharecroppers, tenants, and planters, the extension service worked on the trickle-down principle.

Such urban-biased movements as the Country Life Commission viewed the rural South as deprived, backward, and dangerously uneducated in the ways of modernity. However, despite their reputation as mechanically challenged, many southerners operated and serviced steam engines, tractors, and cotton gins, and, as automobiles proliferated, tinkered obsessively with internal combustion engines. Even farmers who had no use for complex machinery tinkered with plows, harrows, wagons, churns, cream separators, and other gadgets. Either way, in the early twentieth century, rural people could survive and sometimes prosper with just the rudiments of book learning. Successful farming depended on an intense study of crops, weather, and the land, and such wisdom passed from generation to generation.

Rather than remaining in stagnant waters, the rural South moved into new channels of commerce in its search for sustenance. At the turn of the twentieth century, irrigated rice cultivation advanced into new growing areas west of the Mississippi River while flue-cured tobacco moved across the Carolinas into Georgia. In some areas of the South, one farmer would be taking advantage of advanced technology while his neighbor would still be using draft animals and engaging in intense labor. In the rice-growing prairies of Arkansas, for example, binders, steam engines, threshing machines, and rice mills became common early in the twentieth century, while across Crowley's Ridge in the Delta, cotton farmers used mules, plows, and hoes and picked cotton by hand. While cotton planting, cultivating, and picking were labor intensive and largely unmechanized, cotton gins dotted each Cotton Belt county and employed skilled craftsmen. Tobacco cultivation not only required heroic amounts of family labor but also skilled curers and graders and an infrastructure of warehouses to market the crop. Large sugar mills driven by steam power dominated the landscape of rural southern Louisiana.

The rural South at the turn of the twentieth century was often portrayed as static, conservative, intolerant, racist, poor, illiterate, and, by most measures used by social scientists to chart progress, hopelessly backward. Yet a part of the rural population was in constant motion—sharecroppers moved nearly every year, young people set out on their own, and musicians, tent shows, and carnivals visited small towns and crossroads. Such movement prevented isolation and educated country folks in the national culture. Illiteracy, poverty, lynching, peonage, segregation, and racism, some observers concluded, shorted out all signs of intelligence and originality. Yet violent and resentful sentiments existed side by side with hard work, generosity, religiosity, and dignity.

That many southerners did not travel widely suggests that they either did not have the opportunity or that they preferred to stay at home, but it does not mean that they were sheltered from the issues of state and nation. Crossroads stores and barbershops not only disseminated weather information, which all farmers sought, but also news of state and nation, providing a forum for analysis to boot. Peddlers brought commodities and news to rural women, musicians crisscrossed the South with information and songs, salesmen and extension agents pushed the latest goods, and the Sears, Roebuck catalog displayed fashion and technology.

Southern fiction, autobiography, and oral history provide compelling portraits of the rural South as it moved away from labor-intensive farming. William Faulkner's aspiring Snopeses supplanted the wealthy Varners and Compsons and then oozed over the Yoknapatawpha County landscape, polluting all they touched. In both "The Bear" and the other stories in *Big Woods*, Faulkner lamented the retreat of the Delta's cypress swamps before axes and plows, mixing in commentary on broken Indian treaties and environmental outrages. Ned Cobb understood not only *All God's Dangers* relating to race relations but also recalled the pride that came from owning a good team of mules (he had no use for tractors), boasted of his literate wife, keenly observed crop cycles, and fought for justice. By the 1930s, Erskine Caldwell's Jeeter Lester worried about getting furnished for just one more crop along *Tobacco Road*, while Ty Ty Bundren pondered the difference between those who tilled the earth or who tended spindles as he searched for *God's Little Acre*. Later, Harry Crews searched for his *Childhood* in Bacon County, Georgia, and reported fatalistic farmers waiting until disaster or hardship drove them to Jacksonville's Springfield section, where they were swallowed into factory work and the maw of conformity. Lurline Stokes Murray, as historian Lu

Ann Jones has recorded, "took work for granted." "Honey," she explained to Jones, "in our way of life, there ain't no banker's hours, and I don't find in the Bible there's no such thing as an eight-hour day." The witness of these southerners, and there are many more, suggests what the South was but does not explain what it became. The changes appearing in the form of tractors, picking machines, pesticides, and government policy play small roles in southern literature. One is left to imagine the transition from Varner's store to Wal-Mart, Ratliff's buggy to pickups, Mrs. Murray's flock of pecking chickens to Tyson's, sweating over a hot wood stove to Viking ranges, Black Draught and 666 to valium and pot, and square dances, womanless weddings, and tent shows to situation comedies.

Because farmers preferred their own counsel and distrusted frilly ideas, they were not easy targets for regimentation. For the rising cadre of agricultural engineers and managers, however, farming was too important to be left to farmers, and the South was surely too important to be left to southerners. Grimacing with distaste at the complex tenure arrangements in the rural South, the high illiteracy rate, and labor-intensive work, agricultural planners drew up blueprints that would rescue southern agriculture from its farmers. These ideas informed New Dealers, and the AAA became the expression of regulated production.

The growing currents of government policy, science, and technology converged in the 1930s. While the USDA, land-grant universities, experiment stations, and extension service were in place by World War I, the establishment of the AAA in 1933 moved the federal government into farmers' daily lives. It also empowered the USDA bureaucracy, extension agents, lobbyists, and county elites, the building blocks of agribusiness. Commodity programs favored landowners, and local agricultural oversight committees were invariably composed of the county elite that controlled acreage allotments and handled complaints. The AAA prevented most agricultural disputes from being heard by peers in county and state courts, placing them instead before county agricultural committees composed of the local elite. Taking on the local agricultural committee became a federal case. Indeed, although landlords disregarded AAA rules, took money intended for sharecroppers and tenants, and laid off unneeded workers, few of them were even reprimanded. When liberals within the USDA demanded the department support poorer farmers, they were purged.

Government intrusion decimated African American farmers who had made remarkable gains after slavery—accumulating property, achieving education, and building communities. Even during the years of segregation, black farmers survived and sometimes prospered. By 1910, nearly 132,000 black farmers owned land worth $165 million. After World War I, however, low prices, floods, and drought began to take a toll on black farm ownership. Indeed, economic forces pushed both black and white owners into tenancy and share-cropping. The New Deal hit all sharecroppers hard, but black croppers were crushed. Conservative USDA leaders idealized the Iowa blueprint of a farm-house and outbuildings nestled on a section or two of land. Sharecroppers in general, and black farmers in particular, did not fit into this scheme.

In theory the AAA offered a bold and democratic way to rid the country of surplus commodities that drove down prices. The AAA offered farmers an acreage-reduction plan, and farmers voted for or against it. In desperate depression years, few resisted the promise of higher commodity prices. Each county and farm received an acreage allotment based on former production. County agricultural committees, through the county agent and his staff, de-cided acreage for each farm. Most committees and USDA bureaucrats no doubt did workmanlike jobs, but, according to many complaints, a number of committee members gave into temptations to hoard extra acreage and assign it to relatives or themselves. Only landowners had allotments. "I do believe the laws are made with best intentions," Mrs. Homer L. Brown observed from Dixie, Georgia, in 1951, "but the local men have their favorites." It is a testament to unintended consequences of government programs that allotments, basically a right to grow a crop, became commodified and were bought, rented, and sold. More-educated farmers, who understood and could manipulate government programs, gained an advantage in the new system. The AAA propped up prices and added other incentives to encourage farm-ers to cooperate with federal programs and the successful ones invested in machinery and expanded their operations.

By empowering the elite, the AAA in essence shaped the emerging struc-ture of agribusiness. With government payments, landowners planned for the future. They bought tractors, laid off more workers, and, as allotments were cut, cultivated their best land. Government scientists found ways to farm the land more intensively, enabling farmers to raise more per acre, which in turn undermined the allotment policy. While the AAA's announced purpose was to stabilize farming, its unintended consequences drove off millions of farmers. Agribusiness visionaries saw no use for sharecroppers or farmers who were at the margins of a subsistence economy.

Such programs as the Farm Security Administration (FSA) offered some support for displaced farmers. The tens of thousands of photographs taken by FSA photographers remain one of the most important windows into rural America during the Depression. Yet struggling farmers were not high on the USDA agenda, and the advocates of large farmers resented programs that

View of a Farm Security Administration relocation project in Hazlehurst, Georgia. Library of Congress, Prints & Photographs Division, Washington, D.C., reproduction number LC-USF34-043711-D.

supported small farmers. During World War II, the Farm Bureau Federation, with the help of USDA supporters and friendly congressmen, eliminated the FSA. Shaken loose from the agricultural economy, millions of farmers were sucked into defense jobs or the military.

Despite acreage-reduction programs and a declining farm population, overproduction continued after World War II. As the USDA attempted to reconcile supply and demand by further cutting acreage or inventing other programs to reduce output, small farmers found it increasingly difficult to make a living. USDA bureaucrats, enjoying their power, often handled cases rudely, provoking outraged complaints. During the presidency of Dwight D. Eisenhower in the 1950s, Ezra Taft Benson headed the USDA. His policies unabashedly favored large farmers. During his administration, the USDA put an Orwellian twist on "saving the family farm," for Benson's policy was "get big or get out." Acreage cuts and the Soil Bank, which paid farmers to take land out of production, were no match for increased production enhanced by USDA research. Storage costs for Commodity Credit Corporation crops increased dramatically.

By the 1950s small farm owners were complaining vociferously, as they watched their acreage dwindle, that the government programs did not offer them much hope of survival. They criticized businessmen, doctors, and lawyers who bought farms to improve their tax status. They condemned feckless bureaucrats who seldom responded to their inquiries. They lashed out at local committees that they believed favored the county elite. They faced crucial decisions, for investing in machines and chemicals meant going into debt and running on the capital-intensive treadmill. But if they continued to rely upon the old ways, they might fail nonetheless. Many followed sharecroppers and tenants to towns and cities to seek another life, often blaming themselves for their failure to survive on the land. Between 1935 and 1959, some 1.8 million southern farmers left the land, a half million of them African Americans.

The Great Depression began a process of labor liquidation that AAA policies exacerbated and machines and chemicals completed. Few southern factory jobs were available to suck up the dispossessed rural workers who did not leave the South. They either settled into the new structure as tractor drivers, found local jobs, or relied on welfare. While pocketing sizeable subsidies from government programs, planters and successful farmers condemned the unemployed as no-accounts. Despite the fact that the use of herbicides and mechanical harvesting seemed likely to result in many lost jobs, no federal program was established to address this prospective problem.

Farmers' level of vulnerability often depended on the crops that they grew. The South's primary crops took different roads to agribusiness, for sugar, rice, tobacco, and cotton were at different stages of mechanization and organization. Cotton farmers, for example, were caught in a vise of depression, government programs, mechanization, and increasing pesticide use. During World War II, International Harvester, building on the work of the Rust Brothers, developed effective mechanical cotton pickers at the Hopson Plantation near Clarksdale, Mississippi. When the war ended, mechanical cotton harvesters quickly became available, and by 1964 machines harvested 81 percent of the Mississippi Delta's cotton.

During World War II, rice farmers turned to combines, enabling a farmer and a hired hand to harvest a two-hundred-fifty-acre field and deliver rice to the elevator. Using binders, it took two men to cut the rice and four to shock, and then fourteen men, eight teams and wagons, and two additional men to haul the crop to the elevator at threshing time. This structural change meant a major investment in machinery for farmers and driers for rice mills. Because rice farmers had always used machinery, the transition was easier than for many other farmers.

Tobacco farmers continued their labor-intensive practices into the 1960s. As flue-cured tobacco ripened, it was primed several leaves at a time for five to six weeks. Trucked from the fields by mule-drawn sleds, it was then tied to sticks, hung in barns for five or six days of curing, and packed away. In the autumn, women graded and tied it into hands for market. Government policy, more than mechanization, revolutionized tobacco culture. In the 1960s farmers were no longer required to grade each leaf, and so tobacco could be taken directly from the barn, tied into sheets, and taken to market. Rules changed to permit allotments to be transferred from farms, allowing larger producers to consolidate their operations. Larger fields set the stage for mechanization, although some farmers continued to prefer hand priming. By the end of the century, the sales warehouses that had provided so much pageantry (and so much wealth to the owners) closed as farmers began dealing directly with the tobacco factories.

Although the USDA despised and demeaned the southern rural working class, the last generation of sharecroppers possessed enormous talent and creativity. No matter where they settled, rural southerners carried their music and mischief. Rural music—blues, country, and gospel—was quintessentially American and became a driving force in the development of new genres of American music. This music reflected the everyday experiences of rural southerners. In part southern music goes back to European and African experiences, but it matured in the travail and triumph of rural life in the United States. Southerners were innovative in their musical offerings, and gospel singing wasn't just a part of Sunday services—there were also gospel sings and radio broadcasts. Country music provided not only pleasure in the hearing but also the cadence for square dancing. Blues evolved out of field hollers at the turn of the twentieth century, and, as sound recordings became available, quickly grew in popularity. When the Grand Ole Opry came on the air in 1925 on WSM, a large percentage of southern homes that could afford a radio tuned in. By the late 1940s, rhythm and blues gained widespread popularity, and its crossover to white audiences was helped by radio stations such as WDIA in Memphis, which used all-black announcers. When rural music collided with its urban counterpart, fresh interpretations led from rhythm and blues to rock 'n' roll and soul music. Urban America, as well as much of the world, is indebted to rhythms of the land.

Whatever the unique qualities of southern commodity cultures, after World War II, all relied upon synthetic chemicals. World War II gave birth both to the insecticide DDT and the herbicide 2,4-D. Both were regarded as miracle chemicals, both were marketed to the public in 1945, and the USDA proclaimed both no threat to human health. To some, synthetic chemicals took on a miraculous if not divine status. DDT and other chlorinated hydrocarbons killed insects and persisted for months or years while 2,4-D killed broad-leaved plants and spared such crops as rice and corn. During the war, Germans developed organophosphates, basically nerve gases, and such formulas as parathion and malathion arrived on the market by the early 1950s. In most cases these chemicals had no immediate discernible effect on humans, and the long-term effects would not be learned for years. Encouraged by USDA literature and advertisements that promised insect- and weed-free fields and yards, both farmers and homeowners embraced chemicals.

After World War II, synthetic chemicals spread rapidly, and their use ultimately led to health problems as well as to an assault on fish and wildlife. Herbicides quickly reshaped liability law, for they drifted from target fields and damaged other crops. Herbicides sprayed on rice fields, for example, could drift to cotton fields and cause extensive damage. As soon as 2,4-D went into use, suits began to be filed seeking damages, and the courts were confronted with the task of trying determine who was liable—the farmer who hired the spraying, the aerial applicator, or the manufacturer of the chemical. Aerial spraying had begun after World War I when a surplus of chemicals and airplanes led inventive people to put them together. Much of the early development work in the South took place at Tallulah, Louisiana, as farmers and scientists experimented with calcium arsenate sprayed from the air to kill boll weevils. In 1928 Delta Air Service emerged as the major power in the aerial spraying business. It later evolved into Delta Air Lines.

Farmers were often careless in applying pesticides and used far more than directions called for. There was often a macho attitude that caused users to disregard warnings on the labels, as if they were immune to the nerve gases they applied. Fortunately, in most cases there were no immediate symptoms, but chemicals could kill quickly. Children sometimes drank or ate pesticides, often with fatal results. Both parathion and malathion were extremely toxic, especially if they touched the skin. A young man who was doing inventory in a warehouse in South Carolina had a bag break and got 1 percent parathion on his skin. He washed it off as the label directed but died several hours later. Crop dusters, who were very attentive to chemical effects, sometimes were overcome in flight and crashed. Effects on people varied—some were sickened while others seemed to be fine. In many ways, in the 1950s and 1960s, people and animals were part of a large experiment on the health effects of synthetic chemicals.

The Agricultural Research Service (ARS), an arm of the USDA, embraced synthetic chemicals and insisted that farming could not survive without them. Research on biological control stopped after World War II, and the ARS

A Huff-Daland crop duster used by Delta Air Service.
Courtesy of Delta Air Lines, Inc.

mounted large and ill-considered spray campaigns across the country. The imported fire ant was just another southern pest that had little effect on crops (it actually ate boll weevils) until the ARS and eradication zealots transformed it into a major predator. Ultimately, the ARS sprayed millions of acres with highly toxic chlorinated hydrocarbons such as heptachlor and dieldrin to try to kill off the ant, whether farmers wanted it or not. This campaign proved deadly to fish and wildlife. In highly disingenuous testimony, the ARS claimed before Congress that it was the fire ants that had killed the quail and fish, not dieldrin or heptachlor. After three years of massive spraying, there were more fire ants than when the campaign began, a testimony both to the fire ant's reproductive and adaptive power and to the lack of research by the ARS.

In the late 1960s pressure mounted for another federal fire ant program using Mirex, which was projected to cost $150 million. It was halted only when scientists revealed that Mirex, a chlorinated hydrocarbon, was persistent and dangerous to fish and wildlife. Fire ants built up resistance to chemicals and evolved multiple queen colonies to ensure survival. The fire ant situation resembled a 1950s horror film: cunning fire ants trick the ARS into a vicious spray campaign that acts on them like steroids, kills off their enemies, and aids their conquest of the South. The USDA secured support for such dubious programs by mobilizing its vast network of county agents, land-grant university scientists, and farm lobby groups that pressured Congress. It did not matter that many entomologists insisted that the fire ant eradication campaign was foolish and sure to fail or that conservation organizations reported fish and wildlife deaths. In *Silent Spring*, Rachel Carson labeled it one of the worst of the chemical excesses of the 1950s.

While the fire ant campaign garnered both publicity and criticism, farmers continued to expand their use of chemicals. Pre- and postemergent herbicides controlled weeds, insecticides killed insects, and defoliants eliminated leaves to ensure cleaner mechanical picking in cotton culture. Tobacco farmers used herbicides to prevent suckers and insecticides to kill hornworms. Sugar farmers used endrin, which not only killed insects but also fish in nearby bayous. Chemicals were part of the post–World War II riddle of creation and destruction.

Pesticides became an integral part of farming, so much so that insects developed resistance, which then required farmers in the 1990s to use from two to five times more than they had twenty years earlier. Meanwhile, chemical residues showed up in water and endangered health. National Cancer Institute studies in the early 1990s suggested that farmers had an elevated risk of cancer because of pesticides. While scientists have promised to develop natural means of controlling pests, genetic engineering has offered several short-term "solutions." Roundup-Ready soybeans are engineered to resist massive doses of the herbicide. Genetically modified (GM) corn contains its own pesticide, BT, which kills insects (until they build up resistance) but that also spreads genetically modified pollen across the land. There are alarming implications of using genetic engineering, with no long-term studies of its possible dangers. Producers of GM products proclaim their absolute safety, and yet they refuse to label their products as GM. In 1995, the Texas Boll Weevil Eradication Foundation doused cotton crops with malathion to kill boll weevils, but the chemical also killed the natural enemies of the beet army worm that destroyed an estimated $140 million of the cotton crop. Outraged farmers voted in 1996 to discontinue the program, which was funded primarily from assessments on their acreage. Farmers can't get off the chemical treadmill, which offers only short-term solutions.

While legislation and court decisions reshaped social relations between blacks and whites in the South, USDA policies have decimated black farmers. In 1920, before the AAA, black farmers accounted for 14 percent of U.S.

farmers, but in 1997 they had fallen to less than 1 percent. Between 1978 and 1987, for example, the number of white-owned farms declined by 7 percent while black-owned farms declined by 23 percent.

In the 1960s, even as African American farmers gained more civil rights, the opportunity to farm became increasingly rare. The decline of black farmers was anything but accidental. Planters throughout the South allied with the USDA after the *Brown v. Board of Education* decision in 1954 and used federal programs to retaliate against blacks who signed petitions to integrate schools or who registered to vote. According to the 1965 U.S. Commission on Civil Rights report, *Equal Opportunity in Farm Programs*, in 1959 the median income for white farmers was $2,800 and for blacks $1,260. At the same time, 44 percent of white rural farm youth received twelve or more years of schooling compared to 16 percent of black youth.

In 1964, southern white land-grant colleges received $11.6 million in Cooperative State Research Service allotments; black colleges received no allotments. Blacks found it difficult to secure loans or to participate in Soil Conservation Service programs, and the segregated extension service discriminated against blacks. Significantly, by 1964 no African Americans held professional, clerical, or technical positions in 1,350 Agricultural Stabilization and Conservation Service (ASCS) offices in the South. Black ASCS employees consisted of seven part-time workers and one clerk. Despite the civil rights movement, the USDA has continued to discriminate against African American farmers.

In 1983 the USDA disbanded its civil rights investigative unit and consequently it stopped taking action on complaints. In the mid-1990s, it admitted that hundreds of black farmers had been denied loans simply because of their color. Local USDA personnel used computer errors, miscalculations, delays, and rudeness to mask discrimination. In one Virginia county in the mid-1990s, black farmers had to wait an average of 222 days for loan approval (56 percent approved) while white farmers waited 84 days (84 percent approved). In the decade between 1982 and 1992, the number of black farmers in the United States dropped from 33,250 to 18,816, a rate of decline five times that of white farmers. In the late 1990s, black farmers filed a three billion dollar lawsuit (*Pigford v. Glickman*) against the USDA. Even when they won the suit, they found it difficult to negotiate damages.

While black farmers fought entrenched racism within the USDA, white farmers also struggled to survive. By 1970 the rural South had been bled of sharecroppers and tenants, and science and technology had restructured farming operations. As farmers moved away, small towns collapsed, their structures undermined by lack of customers who instead flocked to malls and chain stores. Small farms and family farms struggled to survive, and many farmers worked off-farm to preserve their rural way of life. The logic of federal programs in agriculture supported larger farmers, those who produced the largest crops. The bottom tier of farmers, the logic dictates, was always at risk. The dream that planners had in the 1920s of efficient farms has turned into a nightmare, an endless treadmill of updated technology and more powerful chemicals.

Farming evolved into a race to keep up with the latest science and technology. Tractors grew larger and more powerful. Mechanical cotton harvesters went from a one-row to four-row capacity. Tractors grew to the size of the massive traction engines of the early twentieth century, dinosaurs that had given way to the nimble John Deeres and Farmalls that dominated midcentury agriculture. While farmers at the turn of the century learned from trial and error that some fields were more productive than others, in the 1990s farmers turned to computers, global positioning, and intense soil sampling to chart their fields. Each breakthrough in science and technology promised high returns, and many farmers embraced new technology in hope that it could ultimately keep them in business and not bankrupt them.

From the first AAA legislation in 1933 until the end of the century, farm policy constantly changed. Some farmers complained that they never knew what to expect, for every year the USDA had new programs and rules. Lobbyists attempted to secure advantages for their clients, and the competing interests created within the USDA a massive bureaucracy that resulted in conflicting programs. The attempt in the late 1990s to abolish support programs failed, and the next farm bill groaned under special-interest provisions.

Farmers who understood husbandry were deskilled and replaced by government programs, machines, and chemicals. Instead of husbandry, modern farms utilize formulaic planting, spraying, and harvesting. Instead of attempting to work in harmony with nature, modern agriculture has rejected nature as not good enough. Farmers accepted machines and chemicals and eagerly embraced genetically modified plants and animals. Not only has the structure of farming changed radically in the past hundred years but also farmers' regard for nature. During the last half of the twentieth century, southern farming came to resemble that in other parts of the country. Without sharecroppers and with but a handful of African American farmers left, the rural South appeared vastly different at the end of the century from the way it had at its turn.

The rural South thus lost much of its distinctiveness. Those who farm cotton, rice, tobacco, soybeans, catfish, and sugar rely on the same capital-intensive inputs as farming different crops elsewhere in the country. Still, the rural South has preserved some of the best—and worst—of its pre–civil rights movement heritage. The breakdown of legal segregation allowed blacks and whites to mix publicly, yet the residue of racism persists. In part the awkwardness is a result of the bitter fight for equal rights. Instead of just giving up the inequities of segregation and offering cooperation, whites had to be forced to change by courts and legislation. Resentment still smolders. That black farmers in the 1990s resorted to litigation to force the USDA to treat them equally was testimony to the legacy of segregation and discrimination. Still, the rural South at the turn of the twenty-first century was no longer segregated by law, and people are searching for ways to heal the wounds the legacy of segregation has inflicted, though the search is not being carried out by farmers so much as by rural people who work off-farm. They are searching for a new definition of what it means to be a rural southerner.

Suggested Readings

Daniel, Pete. *Breaking the Land: The Transformation of Cotton, Tobacco, and Rice Cultures since 1880.* Urbana: University of Illinois Press, 1985.

———. "The Transformation of the Rural South, 1930 to the Present." *Agricultural History* 55 (July 1981): 231–48.

Fite, Gilbert C. *Cotton Fields No More: Southern Agriculture, 1865–1980.* Lexington: University of Kentucky Press, 1984.

Hurt, R. Douglas, ed. *The Rural South since World War II.* Baton Rouge: Louisiana State University Press, 1998.

Kirby, Jack Temple. *Rural Worlds Lost: The American South, 1920–1960.* Baton Rouge: Louisiana State University Press, 1987.

DAVID L. CARLTON

Smokestack-Chasing and Its Discontents

Southern Development Strategy
in the Twentieth Century

On the surface, at least, the record of business enterprise and industrial development in the American South during the twentieth century was one of
striking success. The rate of industrial growth in the region outpaced that
of the nation as a whole and greatly contributed to the stunning economic
developments of the post–World War II era, when the per capita income
of the census Southeast (the Old Confederacy plus Kentucky and West Virginia but minus Texas) surged from 57 percent of national levels in 1940 to
85 percent in the early 1970s. (Texas, with its petrochemical, defense, and
technology complexes, follows a developmental path very different from the
one I am about to describe, and will not figure in the following account.)

Although the expansion of manufacturing built few great cities, it energized smaller cities and rural districts, affording alternative employment to small towners and to part-time farmers and their children, while providing those who remained on the farm with markets more stable and profitable than those for cotton. Further, as manufacturing expanded, it diversified, in the process raising wages, opening up new opportunities for skilled workers and stimulating state and local governments to provide training. Finally, at the apex of a newly sophisticated southern economy stood major metropolitan service centers such as Atlanta and (an overlapping category) budding high-tech growth poles such as North Carolina's Research Triangle. The latter, especially, forms a new and startling landscape of corporate campuses linked loosely together by a web of expressways, jogging trails, and fiber-optic cables.

But not all is currently well in the industrial South. Convergence on U.S. levels of income in the census Southeast has proceeded much more slowly since the early 1970s, reaching 91 percent of U.S. levels only in 1997 and then stalling. While Atlanta and other large cities have boomed and Deep South states have celebrated new auto "transplants," older industries have been shriveling. Apparel plants have been fleeing the region's small towns for decades and the textile industry, the old bellwether of the region's early industrialization, has been frantically "restructuring" for a generation. Major shifts in global trade in recent years have brought major segments of the textile industry to the verge of collapse, pulling down whole communities along with them. Some counties in the industrial heartland of the Carolina Piedmont now have per capita income levels on a par with Mississippi's, and local industrial recruiters and social services workers find themselves facing the daunting task of locating new jobs for industrial workers who lack the skills demanded by a modern economy. Other industries, such as light-assembly operations, move in and out of small-town and rural areas as exchange rates and increasingly volatile corporate strategies dictate. And large areas of the region—especially the old plantation belt and central Appalachia—remain economic basket cases. Not far from the towers of Charlotte or Birmingham, southerners continue to wrestle with problems bequeathed them by an older South—not, to be sure, the "Old South," but what is now an aging "New South"—that shaped the region fundamentally, for better or for worse, in the twentieth century.

To understand this long-in-the-tooth "New South" one needs to begin with the situation in which the region found itself at the nadir of its history, the immediate aftermath of the American Civil War. The year 1880 found the region mired in a deep slough of poverty, with per capita income at roughly half the national average, a dismal state in which the region and its people would persist for two succeeding generations. The downfall of the slave plantation had brought, first, chaos, and then a grim new agricultural regime hampered by inefficient, oppressive institutions like sharecropping and the crop lien. Cursed with stagnating markets for such dominant crops as cotton, and awash with superabundant, impoverished workers, the southern countryside was plagued by depressed living standards and stalling innovation. Southern farm folk lived on a treadmill, straining every muscle to go nowhere.

Intertwined with the plight of the agricultural sector was the sorry state of the manufacturing sector. The antebellum South had not exactly been bereft of manufacturing—in fact, by world standards an independent Confederacy would have been a quite respectable industrial power. But the plantation system, especially in the Cotton Belt, was not friendly to the factory. The lure of cotton profits siphoned off capital and entrepreneurial energies; overwhelmingly rural districts consumed fewer market goods than urban ones, and slave plantation districts fewer than small-farming districts such as the Midwest. Transportation and marketing systems geared toward moving crops across the Atlantic did little to develop internal markets for large-scale factory production. Much of the region's industry, in fact, survived on the natural protection offered by the isolation of much of the interior from outside competition. On the eve of secession the South accounted for only 10 percent of American manufacturing, putting it far behind the urbanizing Northeast. It even found itself slipping significantly behind the small-farming Midwest.

The heritage of the slave plantation regime was compounded by the circumstances and consequences of its demise. By the end of the war, southern factories were in a terrible state, though perhaps less from military assault than from disrepair. Following Appomattox, the manufacturing sector started to rebuild itself but was slow to recover—by 1880 less than 5 percent of American manufacturing could be found in the South. An abysmally poor rural society unused to spending much on store-bought wares did not clamor for factory-made goods. Conversely, the lack of a manufacturing sector deepened the dilemmas facing southern agriculture. Owing to the small number of industrial workers and the related scarcity of city dwellers, farmers were denied the sort of steady and diverse home markets that might have helped them break the cycle of dependence on inedible export crops and replace environmentally destructive staple-crop monoculture with soil-building, land-protecting mixed farming. Even more importantly, the lack of other employment kept rural southerners trapped on the agricultural treadmill.

Thus the South needed to industrialize—a point constantly hammered home by boosters of what the historian Howard Rabinowitz has termed the "first New South." Some were publicists like Atlanta's Henry W. Grady, dangling the economic promise of a forgiving and forgetting region before prospective (but still skittish) northern investors. Others were speculators, "boomers" in control of an actual or reputed natural asset—coal, iron, timber—whose value they hoped to inflate. Still others, perhaps a bit more sober, were small-town businessmen and editors who were seeking means of building their towns, providing them a basis for long-term growth that a stagnating agricultural hinterland could not offer.

But how to go about it? The model immediately before them was, of course, that of the vibrant industrial society to their north. The first American manufacturers had planted themselves within easy reach of prosperous small-farming regions full of buyers for a broad range of products; Philadelphia, the prototypical nineteenth-century workshop city, had built its industrial might through just such beneficial exchange with its hinterland. In the process, the Quaker City and its imitators, both in the Northeast and, later, the Midwest, had developed dense communities of workers and entrepreneurs, skilled in the cutting-edge technologies of the industrial revolution and eager to apply them to new products and processes. They had also constructed dense webs of informal relationships and formal institutions, which enabled them to spread out the inevitable risks of operating in a tumultuous marketplace and to develop human capital, disseminate information about markets and innovations, and assemble pools of savings to match with worthy enterprises. Over time these city-regions had knit their trading networks together and had begun to trade with each other as well as with their hinterlands; these expanded markets permitted industrial centers to specialize and capture economies of scale. By 1880 the combined efforts of myriad workers and entrepreneurs had created a vast manufacturing belt stretching from Boston to St. Louis, tied together by railway and communications networks channeling and combining vast flows of raw materials, products, people, capital, and ideas.

It was the dream of the New South promoters to replicate the success of the manufacturing belt and that older industrial power, Great Britain, even to challenge their supremacy. These ambitions could especially be seen in the new town promotions dotting the region. Cotton-mill villages in Piedmont counties such as Gaston County, North Carolina, took their names from Lowell, Massachusetts, and Mount Holly, New Jersey. Promoters touting the coal and iron resources of the Appalachian spine named their frequently overhyped settlements South Pittsburg, Tennessee; Middlesborough, Kentucky; Bessemer City, North Carolina; and (of course) Birmingham, Alabama. The latter, born in the 1870s of (said C. Vann Woodward) the union of a railroad and a land company, imagined itself not simply a purveyor of pig iron and cast-iron pipe, but a "workshop town" in which skilled mechanics produced a broad array of high-grade goods and a vibrant community of innovative entrepreneurs infused the city, and the region, with vitality.

Yet such ambitions proved difficult of consummation. First, as we have already seen, the South of 1880 lacked the home markets that had fueled the manufacturing belt's rise. Its people were impoverished, and its large black population was further held down by the grim heritage of slavery—landlessness, illiteracy—and by the ongoing determination of whites to keep them on the bottom rung of the economic ladder. A rural society sated with cheap labor likewise afforded a poor market for capital goods. It is telling that the most famous of all American farm machinery makers, Cyrus McCormick, found his greatest opportunities not in his home of Rockbridge County, Virginia, but in Chicago, from which he sold his equipment mainly to midwestern farmers.

Secondly, would-be southern industrialists faced frequently ruinous competition from a formidable community of experienced and increasingly efficient northern firms. The difficulties went far beyond those of breaking into new markets, for the years following Appomattox saw the South increasingly open to northern economic penetration. The incomplete antebellum railroad network was massively expanded and filled in, telegraph lines were strung along the new track, and efficiencies such as the through bill of lading were introduced to grease the flow of traffic. The numerous small roads of earlier times were integrated into giant systems operated out of the Northeast; these rail empires interconnected with northern lines, brought southern track gauges into conformity with the northern "standard gauge," and reoriented rail traffic along North-South lines.

This market integration, initially at least, allowed northern producers of basic goods, with their large-scale, low-cost production, to overwhelm southern markets. Local flour mills faded before the onslaught of Minneapolis. The hype about Birmingham and its imitators notwithstanding, the southern iron industry actually declined in the late nineteenth and early twentieth centuries, as backwoods forges and furnaces, which relied on small, low-grade local iron deposits and technologically obsolete, rapidly depleting charcoal fuel, gave way to low-cost Pittsburgh iron and steel made in giant furnaces charged with coked coal (much of it mined in Appalachia and shipped north) and rich, plentiful Mesabi ore. South Carolina, the early industrial historian Victor Clark remarked in 1916, offered the unique case of a state whose preexisting iron industry had completely vanished. Other southern states suffered similar, if lesser, declines.

Penetration of northern markets by southerners, on the other hand, proved more difficult. Specialty industries that required the ability to adjust quickly to customer demand, or producers of cutting-edge products needing customer feedback in their development, found that faster railroad and telegraph access to northern customers was no substitute for being where the action was. Regional disparities in freight rates—arguably justified by the higher and more evenly distributed volume of the traffic on northern lines—favored intraregional traffic in the manufacturing belt—a railroad district that the Interstate Commerce Commission formally recognized as "Official Territory." The dominant rail systems there, great east-west trunk lines such as the Pennsylvania or the New York Central, gave preference to long-haul traffic within the region over short-haul traffic introduced from the South.

Finally, the South suffered from abysmally underdeveloped human capital and institutions. Lack of prior industrialization meant a dearth of skilled workers and experienced entrepreneurs. In addition, the paucity of industrial cities inhibited the development of both the formal institutions and the informal networks northerners used to develop human capital, circulate technical and business knowledge, and raise capital. At that time, most manufacturing firms were risky, small-scale operations beneath the notice of Wall Street, and while numerous cities in the manufacturing belt operated stock exchanges serving local manufacturers, only Richmond and New Orleans in the region could boast such elaborate secondary capital markets. Banking was so poorly developed that at least one rural cotton manufacturer in North Carolina paid his hands with silver shipped from his Philadelphia selling agent.

Clearly it was a lot to overcome. But the South was not without its own resources, nor was its situation without its own opportunities. First, if the region generally lacked a diverse pool of skilled mechanics, it was well supplied with skilled businessmen. As a plantation society, it had long enjoyed close commercial ties to the outside world and had developed a merchant class to mediate between the Atlantic commercial and financial world and the farmers and planters of the countryside. After the Civil War, railroad and telegraphic penetration of the interior and fundamental changes in the financing and marketing of the great southern staple crops dramatically enlarged the southern business class. These postwar businessmen, with their allies in the professions and the media, formed the elites of the proliferating towns and filled the ranks of the postbellum promoters and boosters; indeed, they were the prototypes for the modern southern middle class. They developed skills in finance and accounting, along with a country-boy savvy at buying and selling, and began to forge informal networks of their own, networks that would aid them both in identifying opportunities and in acting successfully on them.

Equally importantly, the new relationship of the South to national markets opened up some new opportunities even as it was foreclosing others. For by the time the region was ready to industrialize, the industries that had led the first wave of the Industrial Revolution were maturing. To understand what this meant, consider the case of the cotton-textile industry. In its formative stages in eighteenth-century Britain and early-nineteenth-century New England, its pioneers had to solve a host of problems—they had to design machinery and factories, develop products, devise techniques for recruiting and managing workers, and organize purchasing and marketing networks that were continental or even global in scope. Early industrialists thus had to be mechanics and merchandisers themselves or had to have working relationships with mechanics and merchants close at hand. They also needed access to skilled workers who could operate machines that still required trained hands and eyes—workers available only in areas where the industry was already concentrated, or, in the case of those parts of the United States where it was not, areas that could attract skilled migrants from older industrial nations such as Britain.

By the 1870s, however, these basic problems had largely been solved, at least for those mills that concentrated on specialized bulk production of a small range of staple goods. The pace of technological change slowed, and a far-flung marketing system controlled from Boston, New York, and Philadelphia was now well established. Moreover, the marketers, mill architects, and machinery builders were now grouped in enterprises separate from the actual production of yarn and cloth. Their services were now available to anyone. Indeed, as the industry matured, its growth slowed, and its suppliers accordingly had to seek new business from customers outside the traditional textile centers of Britain and New England. Moreover, textile machinery had evolved in such a way as to make skilled labor less essential to its operation. Thus the textile industry became, in effect, portable. Indeed, for machine makers and marketers the best prospects for profit now came from exporting the industry to places brimming with poor people lacking industrial skills but willing to work for lower wages than were workers in the "core" regions. As a result, the late nineteenth century saw the export of textile technology, and the extension of textile marketing networks, to various parts of the "developing world," such as Brazil, India, and Japan.

Another such "developing country" was the American South. As noted earlier, native-born would-be southern industrialists were generally lacking in mechanical or technological skills, but they knew business quite well, and by virtue of the esteem they commanded in their communities could mobilize locally much of the investment capital needed to launch industrial enterprises. Often such mobilization entailed literally the collection of widows' mites from a host of small contributors; farmers took mill stock in payment for land or lumber. Once a project was germinated, prospective manufacturers would make contact with a New York or Philadelphia commission sales house—or these northern merchants would themselves come south to drum up new business from low-cost suppliers. The commission houses would offer short-term financing and marketing services but would also refer their prospects to mill architects and machinery builders who could design and equip a mill to the specifications needed for the product the mill would produce.

By and large, these products were the most commonly sold staple grades, the sorts of cloth used for basic sheeting, shirting, and dress wear. Specialty and high-fashion goods still were made in the North, for those who made such products required flexible, quick-response production techniques and ready access to market information and skilled labor. Bulk goods, on the other hand, could be produced by skill-saving machinery; spinning frames that used the so-called ring spindle could be operated by young girls standing on peach crates, and automatic looms—introduced in the 1890s and adopted in the South faster than in the North—likewise narrowed the productivity advantages of northern staple-goods producers over fresh-off-the-farm southern weavers.

Thus the new, portable technology of textiles allowed neophyte southern cotton-mill industrialists to substitute northern skill, as embodied in machinery and purchased services, for the community of skilled entrepreneurs and workers they lacked. Access to national markets likewise allowed them to substitute outside markets for poorly developed local ones. While some new southern industries, such as furniture making, relied on newly integrated regional markets for their sales, the typical industry of the New South built its strategy around exporting goods to the exploding continental markets of the new, urban-industrial United States. And the industries they chose were generally those in which skill and experience counted the least and in which low costs—specifically low labor costs—brought the biggest advantage. Southern cotton manufacturers could not easily compete with the fashion trades of Philadelphia, though they could provide the yarn to feed the Quaker City's specialty weave sheds and hosiery mills. In those branches of the industry in which price mattered most, though, southern textile producers could combine cheap, unskilled labor with skill-embodying machines to powerful effect. Similarly, Birmingham never became the "workshop city," the southern mecca for skilled metal tradesmen, of its promoters' dreams. Rather, it used its low "assembly costs" of raw material and masses of low-wage workers (many of them black, and many of its early miners leased convicts) to dominate national markets for such low-grade products as pig iron and cast-iron pipe.

Such a development strategy clearly had major implications for southern society as a whole. While southern manufacturers were able to expand their market shares in bulk-production, price-competitive industries, they generally continued to buy equipment and higher-level services from the more experienced businesses of the core industrial regions. Thus their weakness lay in failing to encourage the development of a diverse industrial base, particularly those industries that might engender a more highly skilled work force, new products, or cutting-edge technologies. A case in point is the southern experience with the automobile industry. Prior to World War I the American auto industry was not, as now, dominated by a handful of gigantic, vertically integrated firms but was highly decentralized, and the lengthy roster of automakers included a number of southern firms. However, for the most part these companies were little more than glorified body shops. Extensions of the local carriage and buggy works scattered throughout the nineteenth-century South, they constructed wonderful superstructures atop engines and chassis imported from midwestern producers. Standing outside the technological community that was laying the groundwork for the moving assembly line and the mass production of precision machinery (as late as 1915 there were virtually no southern machine tool manufacturers), southern producers were in no position to compete against such juggernauts as Ford, and virtually all were gone by the 1920s.

Moreover, the industrial labor force resulting from the southern industrial strategy was peculiarly disadvantaged. Migrating to the factories largely from the countryside, it came without modern industrial skills. The factories, for their part, offered their workers few opportunities to develop more than the most narrowly specialized proficiencies. Even if there had been opportunities for southern workers to acquire the mechanical knowledge that lay at the foundation of the industrial revolution, the industrial South offered few opportunities to exercise such skills. The common complaint of modern blue-collar southerners that retraining is worthless to them because "the jobs aren't there," and the equally common complaint of prospective employers that pools of skilled labor are lacking, is only the modern manifestation of a chronic catch-22 in southern economic life.

Furthermore, because the technology adopted by southern factories was so portable, and their business connections so easy to establish and maintain, factory siting was determined less by access to auxiliary services than by access to supplies of rural labor, lending southern industrialization a pronounced rural bias. Farm folk turned factory workers did not move all that far, geographically or culturally, from their rural origins. Cotton-mill managers hired whole families rather than individuals and relied on kinship networks to maintain a flow

South Carolina cotton mill family, ca. 1908. Library of Congress, Prints & Photographs Division, Washington, D.C., reproduction number LC-DIG-NCLC-01488.

of fresh recruits. Child labor thus was intrinsic to early industrial strategy. Not only was children's lack of skills not a serious problem for early industrialists, but employing them offered other advantages as well: hiring them helped anchor the family to the factory, allowed managers to use parental discipline to keep their workforce in line, and provided rural factories with an in-house pool of "spare hands." As they gained experience, workers learned to move about in search of fresh opportunities; nonetheless, the rural location of so many mills, and the resulting domination of so many communities by single employers, stifled the development of diverse opportunities for workers.

The industrial strategy pursued by southern developers also left southern workers with little power to improve their situation. Several generations of southern labor historians have thrown cold water on the notion that southern workers were "docile," but while white workers, at least, had some power to act on grievances as individuals, collective worker power under southern conditions was, for the most part, difficult or impossible to establish. Some have attributed the inability of southern workers to establish labor organizations to repression by manufacturers, whether by private means (blacklists, company goons, control of company towns) or through employer-friendly law enforcement and military power exerted by complaisant governments.

Yet violence and repression of this sort was hardly distinctive to the South; indeed, it was a common feature of American labor history in general, especially prior to the passage of the Wagner Act in 1935; furthermore, in time of labor conflict white southern workers, like their northern counterparts, frequently enjoyed the sympathy of the wider community and the support of such political champions as Olin D. Johnston, the "mill boy governor" of South Carolina.

What was distinctive about southern workers, rather, was the structural weakness of their position. They lived for the most part in dispersed communities rather than in cities. They lacked autonomous institutions, and their lack of skilled worker neighbors deprived them of critical alliances of the sort available to unskilled and semiskilled workers in the cities of the manufacturing belt. With a few exceptions, such as, notably, the cigarette industry, southern entrepreneurs built few large-scale enterprises; most firms were small businesses operating in highly competitive industries, selling generic, unbranded goods. Because they lacked market power and competed chiefly on price, resistance to unions was a high-stakes imperative for southern industrialists, more so than for the oligopolistic giants of the motor vehicle and steel industries, who could pass the costs of labor peace on to their customers. Nor was there much self-interest among southern elites, broadly defined, in expanding worker opportunity or purchasing power. Henry Ford's justification for his celebrated five-dollar day—that he was creating a market for his own products—made no sense to executives whose firms were built on their ability to undercut higher-wage producers in markets for competitive, mature products, and who lacked Ford's capacity to use a major technological innovation and a recognized brand to dominate a major growth market.

This, then, was the southern development strategy in place by the 1920s: attract or create industries with minimal requirements of skill and experience; acquire what one needed of technology and expertise from northerners willing to supply them; avoid competing on quality of goods or services (let alone innovation) and concentrate on price; and keep costs down even at the expense of a healthier development of a diverse industrial economy and society. By the 1920s this strategy was rapidly approaching its limits. The cotton-textile industry, as usual, was prototypical. After the Armistice, the industry became "sick"; New England mills entered into a catastrophic decline, and by 1930 the majority of bulk production had transferred to the South. The sectional victory, though, was Pyrrhic. Southern producers now controlled a mature, slow-growing industry and were now competing against each other—or, worse, against an even lower-cost upstart, Japan. Excepting cigarettes, which enjoyed booming sales, other southern industries faced similar problems in the interwar era—even before the Great Depression intensified the gloom.

Ill-equipped to compete except on price, southern cotton mills pushed to lower labor costs, chiefly by intensifying the work pace—a practice notoriously known as the "stretch-out." The result was a massive explosion of worker unrest. It reached a high point with the spectacular General Textile Strike of 1934, but the turmoil extended from the late 1920s through the 1930s and 1940s and only petered out in the early 1950s. Despite some sporadic successes in organizing, the relative weakness of southern workers relative to their counterparts in the great mass-production industries of smokestack America gave the upper hand to management. Indeed, the chief legacy of this period for workers was bitter division, as close-knit communities were torn apart.

However, while such "traditional" industries as cotton textiles struggled—in anticipation of their sharp decline in the last quarter of the twentieth century—new opportunities were beginning to appear, driven by major developments both inside and outside the South. First of all, with the erection of factories came the development of the South's infrastructure. Financial institutions, especially commercial banks, but other sorts as well, proliferated and elaborated. In North Carolina entities such as the Wachovia Bank and Trust Company developed extensive branch systems, paving the way for Charlotte to emerge as the nation's second largest banking center in the late 1990s. The "good roads" movement took shape in the early twentieth century, but received major boosts from the decision of the federal government in 1916 to aid in the construction of a nationwide highway system. The vogue of the automobile in the 1920s generated both demand for better roads and a means of financing them—massive issues of highway bonds underwritten by user taxes on vehicles and fuel. By the 1930s interstate trucking was becoming a competitive and flexible alternative to rail traffic. In the meantime, railroad unit costs in the South had converged on those in so-called "Official Territory," as southern traffic increased and northern facilities became congested. The North-South freight-rate differential persisted, but by the 1930s it had became both economically indefensible and politically vulnerable, and in the 1940s Georgia's Governor Ellis Arnall led a successful campaign to eliminate it. By the post–World War II period the southern transportation system was greatly enhanced in its flexibility, and southern manufacturers had gained greatly in access to markets—both in the nation at large and in the region's growing internal markets. Furthermore, highways, in particular, extended industrial viability to hitherto unindustrialized reaches of the rural South.

A similarly far-reaching development vastly expanded the availability of industrial power. The South, especially its Piedmont and Appalachian sub-regions, was well endowed with water-power resources, though they were frequently located at a distance from the archipelago of towns, cities, and industries offering the most lucrative markets for industrial power. By the 1920s, visionary engineers like South Carolina's William States Lee had teamed up with southern capitalists such as James Buchanan Duke—or more commonly with giant northern electric-industry corporations such as General Electric—to develop a regional power grid linking hydroelectric stations with industrial and urban users, a network that was in some respects among the most advanced in the world. The 1930s saw their efforts supplemented with federal involvement, through the creation of the Tennessee Valley Authority and other public power projects, and through the extension of electric service to rural areas by the Rural Electrification Administration.

Public power, like highway construction, was eagerly promoted by rural elites, for whom charges that such enterprises were "socialistic" weighed less than their potential to spread the benefits of industrialization. That such rural elites would *desire* the benefits of industrialization was itself a new development, primarily the product of an agricultural revolution that threatened to knock the props out from under the economy of the small-town South. As Gavin Wright notes elsewhere in this volume, a complex of changes that occurred from the 1930s through the 1950s effectively demolished the close relationship between southern agriculture and the maintenance of massive pools of cheap hand labor on plantations. The workings of federal farm price-maintenance programs, the availability of new and better sources of farm credit, the maturing fruits of a generation of agricultural innovation by federal and private agencies, the appearance of new crops and new markets, and the impact of the so-called "Great Migration" of blacks (and whites as well) out of the region all worked together to generate a self-reinforcing process of mechanization and diversification that in a mere twenty years cut the labor needs of southern plantations and farms to a small fraction of their traditional requirements.

Faced with the prospect of mass unemployment leading to a mass exodus, southern rural elites—many of them small-town merchants and landowners—became desperate for means of propping up their economies and keeping their customers at home. Accordingly, they became not only avid advocates of highways and public power, but began to leverage their traditional clout in state politics to turn the state governments themselves into industrial promoters. The result was the movement James C. Cobb has aptly termed "the selling of the South," or what others have termed the strategy of "smokestack chasing": the use of public inducements—publicly constructed infrastructure, capital and tax subsidies, and even direct payments—to lure outside enterprises to locate their operations in a receptive locality.

That the new "smokestacks" were transplants was a telling feature of the new strategy, one that reflected both the dearth of entrepreneurial skill in the more backward parts of the South and the increasingly portable, modular character of American business enterprise itself. As I suggested earlier, in the nineteenth century the process of industrialization was inseparable from the creation of industrial communities. Manufacturers clustered in cities, because as small businessmen they relied heavily on the support of their fellows, both in their own industries and in related ones. Furthermore, expanding urban markets drew many a manufacturer, native born and immigrant, to the city.

But by the twentieth century, the dependence of enterprises on the support services of a community were becoming attenuated, as transportation, communications, and electric power networks became more flexible and pervasive, and the sharp developmental distinctions between regions, and between city and country, began to blur. For many manufacturers, especially in competitive industries with relatively low-skill requirements, the costs of operating in the manufacturing belt—especially high prevailing wage rates and union pressures—were counterbalanced by fewer benefits than before, while the costs of moving to a more distant location were shrinking.

Southern rural and small-town elites began to exploit this opportunity as early as the 1920s. No longer did they have to organize their own manufacturing enterprises in order to industrialize, as did the leaders of the "first wave" of southern industrialization. They could, rather, mobilize local resources (notably public resources) to, in effect, purchase a complete package of preexisting entrepreneurial services. Luring a "runaway shop" to town was a fairly simple process, requiring no specialized institutions and involving no learning curve or complicated entrepreneurial problems to solve. The incoming owners brought their own skills, technology, and experience, along with their preexisting finance, supply, and marketing networks. The locality need only offer infrastructure and human capital of the most ubiquitous sort. What the cotton mill was for the "first wave," so the "cut-and-sew" operation was for the second; local government would throw up a simple structure financed with tax-advantaged industrial revenue bonds and offer a largely female work force accustomed to sewing, while the manufacturer would fill the building with equipment and contribute his preexisting know-how and outside business connections.

"Runaway shops" were typically small businesses, but other opportunities resulted from another major development in American enterprise, as the "core" industries leading the American industrial upsurge were being transformed into modern "big businesses." The new behemoths were vertically integrated firms embracing multiple processes of manufacturing under one corporate roof. Their size and market power gave them access to international capital markets, increasingly centered on Wall Street; their need to capture "throughput" economies through volume production led some to seek control of their raw materials and others to gain dominion over all or part of their marketing, whether through ownership of the distribution network or control of consumer demand via the instilling of brand loyalty. As industrial technology became more elaborate, it too became more the domain of the research-and-development organization and less of the garage inventor. By the 1920s whole industries had fallen under the sway of handfuls of firms, whose economies of scale and scope effectively blocked challenges from all but their fellow leviathans.

As the fate of the independent southern auto industry demonstrated, the rise of the modern "big business" confronted native entrepreneurs with new and daunting barriers to entry; in these sectors, the "grow your own" approach to industrialization, never easy for southerners, became almost prohibitively difficult. But, as with the "runaway shops," the rise of the modern corporation significantly increased the portability of modern manufacturing operations, if not of the enterprise itself. Operating on a national scale, such corporations had to develop internal organizations tying together multiple operations spread across space. Support services that traditional single-plant manufacturers had relied on other, locally based businesses to provide were now supplied from within the firm itself. Rather than being dependent on a community for its sustenance, the new corporation was in effect a virtual city, providing for its needs through its own structure. Its access to national and international capital markets rendered local capital mobilization beside the point; its technology, management, and market power was instantly available to any new community in which it chose to operate.

Thus, alongside the "runaway shop" spread the branch plant. For instance, by the 1920s independent southern automakers had been wiped out, but a "southern" auto industry continued nonetheless. Now, however, it was run from Detroit, as Ford and General Motors established plants in Atlanta, Dallas–Fort Worth, Charlotte, Memphis, and elsewhere. These plants, though, were basically assembly plants, where semiskilled workers combined technologically sophisticated parts designed and built in the Midwest with bodies constructed from local wood for sale to a regional market. The auto corporations and others siting branch plants benefited because they were able to minimize freight costs by shipping bulky products "knocked down"; localities benefited from the presence of relatively capital-intensive operations with payrolls that were high by southern standards. Even more did localities benefit from the ability to use branch plants to tap into the accumulated capital—physical, institutional, and intellectual—of a modern industrial society without having to actually create it from the ground up.

To be sure, unlike "runaway shops," branch plants were somewhat slower in coming to the region. Access to southern markets was a poor attraction when the South was still poor and rural; the Great Depression confronted the corporate giants with serious excess capacity at their existing production sites, leaving them loath to expand to new ones. With the post–World War II boom, however, capital expenditure budgets became flush again, and the branch plant joined the runaway shop as a cornerstone of the emerging southern development strategy. Indeed, over time southerners increasingly came to prefer branch plants; they often brought better paying jobs, and their larger capital investment made them more difficult to shut down or move.

Moreover, as private and public economic development operatives became more professionalized, the branch-plant strategy became more elaborate. Certain sorts of branch plants came to be seen as "growth poles," centers around which complexes of smaller enterprises might arise to supply important inputs. These industrial concentrations, it was hoped, might ultimately produce, through a process of intellectual spontaneous combustion, a genuine southern technological community, generating new ideas and new opportunities for entrepreneurs. Maturing by the 1970s, this version of the branch-plant strategy focused on—indeed became obsessed with—attracting primarily foreign-owned auto assembly plants—the so-called "transplants." A mere proposal from Toyota, BMW, or DaimlerChrysler would set off a mad scramble among state and local development officials, with governors pledging prospects significant chunks of their state budgets for infrastructure, worker training, and often out-and-out subsidies.

An even more sophisticated variant of this strategy involved attracting a complex of advanced corporate facilities to a single location where highly specialized services would be made available. The poster child for this strategy was North Carolina's Research Triangle Park. RTP was born in the 1950s, the brainchild of development-conscious officials and private developers, including the Tar Heel State's businessman governor Luther Hodges. Concerned about a continuing "brain drain" from the state and believing that it had an incipient "growth pole" in place in the form of a cluster of major universities—Duke, UNC–Chapel Hill, and North Carolina State—developers assembled a large tract of land within the triangle formed by the three schools, installed infrastructure, and began to peddle the park to high-technology firms. The success of this audacious scheme was long in coming, but by the late 1960s it began to attract production and research facilities in computers, telecommunications, and pharmaceuticals, and by the 1980s was a phenomenon of international renown—a southern locale transformed into a yuppie paradise in virtually a blink of an eye and a dazzling role model for numerous, and mostly less successful, imitators.

One final variant of the "branch plant" strategy that should be noted has been the attraction of government investment, especially in the form of military bases and the defense industry, to the region. The archipelago of installations strewn across the southern pine belt from Virginia to Texas and elsewhere in the region made use of otherwise desolate terrain, built up localities with little else to recommend them, and provided the men and women of the American military with a congenial environment within a larger nation that is ambivalent about its warriors and their way of life. Bases are, in a manner of speaking, the ultimate "branch plants," with some signal advantages over the privately owned variety. Development-oriented elites could attract them using fewer local inducements, and their connections with powerful southern congressmen have afforded these elites the sort of leverage over military decision making that they have lacked when dealing with absentee corporations. But military bases have not been engines of development; the civilian jobs they offer tend to be low-wage, and the technology they use is far too highly specialized to generate any local innovation. Military procurement spending has had greater developmental potential, both in itself and in its capacity for generating spin-off technology and enterprise. However, while procurement has favorably affected such areas as northern Virginia, central Florida, Huntsville, Alabama, and Dallas–Forth Worth, Texas, and has erected such monuments as the Newport News and Ingalls shipyards and the Lockheed-Georgia aircraft plant, the overall impact of defense procurement on the southern economy has, if anything, been less than the size of the region and its economy would warrant.

The strategy of "smokestack chasing"—drawing in outside entrepreneurs, whether as runaway shops or as branch plants, to substitute for the region's lacks in skills, technology, and institutions—has done much to transform the region, especially in the years since World War II. It has transformed small farmers into industrial workers, small cities into huge ones, and sleepy college towns into world-class research centers. Yet the successes of the new industrial strategy have hardly made up for the weaknesses of the old. Consider the case of the old bellwether, textiles. After World War II, though to a degree even before, the industry confronted ever-sharper challenges to its position in the low-end bulk segments from foreign producers—first the Japanese, then increasingly Latin American and other Asian producers. It responded

Production line at the Bell Bomber Plant in Marietta, Georgia, during World War II. Courtesy of the Kenan Research Center at the Atlanta History Center.

with massive improvements in productivity, trimming its labor requirements spectacularly. However, it failed to shake its historic dependence on technology imported from elsewhere. Indeed, "elsewhere" was now offshore, for the postwar American textile machinery industry, made stodgy by its poor growth prospects, was effectively vanquished by an invasion of revolutionary European machines replacing shuttles with air and water jets and collapsing several yarn preparation processes into a single "open end spinning" operation. These machines, furthermore, were available to competitors in other parts of the world as well. More fatefully, while one or two textile corporations, notably Spartanburg, South Carolina's Milliken and Company, broke with industry tradition and invested heavily in research, and others sought to combine the new technology with a flexible, "boutique" style of production not unlike the old Philadelphia shops, large segments of the industry continued to struggle in the bulk sectors, where they were vulnerable both to cheaper labor in the developing world and to the vagaries of floating exchange rates. With the Asian devaluations of 1997, much of the industry went into a devastating tailspin from which it will likely never recover.

Similar problems have appeared with the "cut-and-sew" shops and light-assembly operations that flocked to the small-town South following World War II. Not infrequently in my home state of Tennessee I will pick up my newspaper and find an account of some small town that had enticed an apparel manufacturer with a cinder-block building, tax breaks, and a pool of women eager for income. One Monday morning, the story would go, the women arrived for work, only to discover that the plant had been emptied out over the weekend, its owner having decided to try his luck even farther south. Local and state development officials would leap into action to fill the hole left, but if they could identify a new employer, it would be of the same sort: easy to lure, but ready to leave at a moment's notice. To a distressing degree, the industrial South still depends on factories that could be sited almost anywhere, and that increasingly can be better sited abroad.

Branch plants are frequently better rooted; many of them represent massive capital investments that are not easily moved, and furthermore many of them are drawn to the South by access to markets or natural resources. Paper mills are typically huge and well-paying employers, though as developers they are limited by the size of their "timber sheds." Likewise, the auto "transplants" are sited in the region in order to gain access to U.S. consumers and help their parent companies satisfy domestic-content laws. But branch plants have their own developmental limitations. Because they are components of giant enterprises that can satisfy many of their needs internally or can draw upon preexisting suppliers in other parts of the country or the world, they offer relatively few "backward linkages" of the sort that stimulate innovative enterprise. While the "growth pole" strategy has shown some success with auto plants, in the South it appears to have been more effective at providing opportunities for low-end suppliers than for cutting-edge, high-tech firms.

Branch plants can operate like enclaves in a community, largely separated from the rest of its economic life. A prime example is the early experience of the Miller Brewing Company facility in the old textile town of Eden, North Carolina, which when it began operations in the late 1970s found that few of the local industrial workers met its basic requirements of functional literacy; much of its own workforce commuted from nearby Greensboro. Similarly, the famous Saturn facility in Spring Hill, Tennessee, sits in magnificent isolation in the Middle Tennessee countryside, hidden behind massive berms, its work force largely recruited from other General Motors plants, resulting in sporadic displays of resentment from a community whose traditional major industry, phosphates, has been in decline. Even Research Triangle Park has not fully escaped these limitations. Rather than a roiling, spontaneously energetic high-tech powerhouse such as Silicon Valley, RTP is a collection of massive but self-enclosed corporate campuses, some the size of small universities, but spatially separated from each other by pine-forest buffers and gated access roads. While hope springs eternal that the concentration of highly educated specialists working in these enclaves might yet create a southern version of the garage innovators of the Valley, the joke persists around the Triangle that it has the heaviest concentration of Ph.D.s in the country—but they all work for somebody else.

Finally, in too many cases the branch-plant strategy shows signs of repeating the same old mistakes of relying heavily on mature industries. What the South ignores in its obsessive attention to auto assembly plants, for instance, is the reality that the world automotive industry is seriously overbuilt; far from being a growth industry for the future, the "transplants" are, like the cotton mills of old, battling for market share in a stagnant sector. By competing for and snaring these facilities, southern economic development officials may adorn the region's interstates with dazzling trophies of newfound industrial might, but it can be argued that in their development strategy, they are fighting the last war.

The southern industrial economy has indeed come a long way in the course of the twentieth century. The modern southerner's inner romantic antimodernist may complain of its fruits—eye pollution (and other sorts as well), urban sprawl, an increasingly rootless way of life—but few would gainsay the enormous benefits the region has garnered from casting its lot with the factory. But those gains are as yet incomplete; the South has embraced the factory, but has yet to create an economic life that can, on its own, generate innovation and a broad range of opportunity for its people. The "southern style" of industrialization has in many ways fit nicely into traditional ways of life. Small-town factories scattered over the nonmetropolitan South have offered southerners reasonable incomes without forcing them to break with old habits or break with the communities they have relied on for economic safety and emotional solace. But the plants have put down (so to speak) shallow roots and as a result are easily plucked up by the gales of globalization.

Some observers are increasingly arguing that the region needs to rethink its development philosophy; instead of chasing smokestacks, it should resort to "growing its own." More radically, some criticize the effort to take jobs to the people where they live; the only truly dynamic, self-generating industrial economy, they argue, requires concentrations of workers and entrepreneurs of the sort found in the cradles of the Industrial Revolution, or in present-day Silicon Valley. Whether southerners would *want* to live in a Silicon Valley, with its headlong pace and its well-documented social pathologies, could well be doubted. But slavish dependence on trailing-edge industries in the face of an ever-shrinking world may be leading much of the region into a developmental cul-de-sac. Can southerners make it to the leading edge of economic innovation and dynamic growth, and yet remain the sort of people we like to think we are? Maybe—but figuring out how is clearly a project for another century.

Suggested Readings

Carlton, David L., and Peter A. Coclanis. *The South, the Nation, and the World: Perspectives on Southern Economic Development.* Charlottesville: University of Virginia Press, 2003.

Cobb, James C. *Industrialization and Southern Society, 1877–1984.* Lexington: University Press of Kentucky, 1984.

———. *The Selling of the South: The Southern Crusade for Economic Development.* 2nd ed. Urbana: University of Illinois Press, 1993.

Leiter, Jeffrey, Michael D. Schulman, and Rhonda Zingraff, eds. *Hanging by a Thread: Social Change in Southern Textiles.* Ithaca, N.Y.: ILR Press, 1991.

Lewis, W. David. *Sloss Furnaces and the Rise of the Birmingham District: An Industrial Epic.* Tuscaloosa: University of Alabama Press, 1994.

Scranton, Philip, ed. *The Second Wave: Southern Industrialization from the 1940s to the 1970s.* Athens: University of Georgia Press, 2001.

Shulman, Bruce J. *From Cotton Belt to Sunbelt: Federal Policy, Economic Development, and the Transformation of the South, 1938–1980.* New York: Oxford University Press, 1991.

Wright, Gavin. *Old South, New South: Revolutions in the Southern Economy since the Civil War.* New York: Basic Books, 1986.

DANA F. WHITE

Cities in Full

The Urban South during the Final Century
of the Past Millennium

As John Bunyan's fictional hero Christian embarked on his allegorical journey
from the City of Destruction to the Heavenly Gates by way of Vanity Fair and
the Slough of Despond, Tom Wolfe's Charlie Croker ascended from Baker
County (near the lower end of what some Georgia writers ironically call the
"West Coast of Georgia") due north upstate to Cherokee County (at the
tail end of the Appalachian chain) by way of Buckhead and Spaghetti Junc-
tion. Bunyan would name his late-seventeenth-century protonovel *Pilgrim's
Progress*; Wolfe might have called his late-twentieth-century blockbuster
Peckerwood's Progress. Bunyan's is the story of early Protestantism while
Wolfe's is that of late-twentieth-century capitalism. Bunyan's triumphant

The Atlanta skyline. Courtesy of the Kenan Research Center at the
Atlanta History Center.

message promised salvation to the faithful; Wolfe's cautionary tale warned
of misfortune for the avaricious.

Wolfe's *A Man in Full* is an allegorical account of the modern South. The
biography of its fictional hero might also serve, in capsule form, as the biography of the region: Charlie Croker's roots were in the plantation South;
he made his mark in the Sun Belt South; and he acted as a force in the
overdevelopment of a sprawling South.

In the novel's prologue, we learn that "Cap'm Charlie" had "just turned
sixty." Given the book's contemporary setting and its November 1998 publication date, this would suggest he was born in 1937 or 1938. Still, given
that Wolfe provides this clue in the opening paragraph of a book more than
seven hundred pages long that took eleven years to complete and that, moreover, as late as ten weeks before its release a New York–based fact checker
called me to vet "the Bluff" and "English Avenue" as valid Atlanta locations,
it seems reasonable to assign an approximate, rather than precise birth date
for Wolfe's protagonist. Let's just say, then, that Charlie Croker was born

sometime during the mid-to-late 1930s. As to his purported place of birth, Baker County, precision is much more easily achieved.

"Yankees have been town people," urban historian Sam Bass Warner Jr. has written recently, "and so they remain today." Not so southerners: they are better described as "county people." Charles S. Johnson's *Statistical Atlas of Southern Counties*, which tabulated information on 1,104 such jurisdictions (circa 1930s), and that remains my favorite single source on the region, provides a useful freeze-frame of Charlie Croker's home county. Johnson's *Statistical Atlas* classified Baker County as A-2-8: that is, a "rural, non-industrial" "cotton" county whose farming was characterized by a "dual system" of "major crops" (cotton and corn in rotation). Its slightly more than 7,800 residents, over 60 percent of them "Negroes," had declined in number since the last count—with almost 6 percent of the total population and nearly 15 percent of African Americans on the move. Newton, with a shade over 500 residents, was the "largest town in [the] county"; nearby Albany, numbering some 14,500, was its "retail trade center." Some 84 percent of employed males were "in agriculture," and about 73 percent of them were "tenants." Almost 18 percent of county residents were illiterate, most of them African American. Between 1900 and 1931, four people had been lynched in Baker County—almost "five times the statewide lynching rate," according to the *Atlas*.

Charlie Croker's Baker County was not only poor, it was also in decline; still, it was hardly unique. Its poverty was mirrored in an east-to-west string of A-2-8 areas across the plantation South: Lowndes County, Alabama; Lamar County, Mississippi; West Feliciana Parish, Louisiana; Jackson County, Texas. Their seeming hopelessness inspired Franklin Delano Roosevelt's oft-quoted 1938 pronouncement: "It is my conviction that the South represents right now the Nation's No. 1 economic problem." Such hardscrabble places would remain a part of the problem throughout the rest of the century, but region-wide change, especially in its urban areas, would come quicker to the South than President Roosevelt could ever have anticipated in 1938—again, a likely natal year for Charlie Croker. And some of its key agents of change would be poor country boys, like Wolfe's Cap'm Charlie, who would shape a truly New South.

When the first significant scholarly analysis of southern cities, *The Urban South*, was published in 1954, high school fullback Charlie Croker would have been competing for the All-State recognition that would provide him with a ticket out of Baker County and into the larger world of big-time college football and, according to Tom Wolfe's scheme, on a powerhouse team in Georgia's capital city. In publishing the long overdue study of southern urban life, the University of North Carolina's Institute for Research in Social Science shifted its attention to southern "urbanization" from southern "regionalism" (on which it had a decades-old lock) and signaled scholarly recognition of a change in the urban-rural balance of the region. Why did it take so long to recognize the significance of an urban South?

From its beginnings, the South had always included numerous urban places—that is, towns and cities: Jamestown, Wilmington, Charleston, Savannah, St. Augustine, Mobile, New Orleans, Natchez, and San Antonio fanned out across the antebellum South. By 1900, a number of New South cities had mushroomed across the region: Nashville counted a population of more than 80,000; Atlanta, almost 90,000; and Memphis, just over the 100,000 mark. New Orleans, by far the largest city in the region and arguably its one true "major urban center" since its earliest days, numbered just over 287,000. Still, the Crescent City was unique to the region: it has always been to the urban South what Montreal has been to urban Canada—an anomaly.

In that same year of 1900, in contrast to its southern urban counterparts, America's "Second City" could claim a population of 1.7 million. "It is significant," sociologist T. Lynn Smith noted in *The Urban South*, "that the South contains a disproportionately large share of the smaller urban centers." Chicago, he neglected to note, had already established the accepted proportions for the American city. "Chicago is the *known* city," novelist Richard Wright would boast. "Especially has no other community in America been so intensely studied, has had brought to bear upon it so blinding a scrutiny." A "vast sociological laboratory," a founder of the Chicago School of Sociology, which would dominate that discipline into the 1950s, proclaimed it even before the opening of the twentieth century. This "city of the big shoulders," as the poet celebrated it, became—as had Manchester before it, and would Los Angeles after—noted British historian Asa Briggs declared, the "shock city" for its age. Chicago gave definition to the "modern city" as being polyglot, densely populated, heavily industrialized, commercially focused, horizontal in its expansion, and vertical in its reach—a city of towers, or "cloud scrapers" as they were sometimes called. Chicago, in other words, was all of the things that the scattering of southern towns and cities seemed not to be. They tended to be, instead, biracial in their makeup, with relatively low population densities, few heavy industries, defined-but-contained commercial cores, limited suburban rings, and modestly scaled office buildings.

Chicago, moreover, did not stand alone: it stood at the pinnacle of a marked hierarchy of urban places. In turn-of-the-century Ohio alone, a cluster of five cities surpassed the South's combined major urban centers in population with some 380,000 residents in Cleveland, 325,000 in Cincinnati, 130,000 in Toledo, 125,000 in Columbus, and 85,000 in Dayton. In the Midwest, this urban hierarchy was based on industrial production; in the turn-of-the-century South, by contrast, urban places largely remained agricultural entrepôts. As much of the nation became urban, the South still seemed rural.

As late as fifty years ago, the South was readily perceived as unchanging—a region fixed by its agricultural past and present. "It is my contention that no major changes occurred in the planting, cultivating, and harvesting of the staples—tobacco, cotton, corn, rice, and sugarcane—between 1612 and 1933," claimed historian Bennett H. Wall. "Hence, the basic pattern of rural life remained unchanged for 321 years—from John Rolfe to Franklin Roosevelt." As a lifelong resident of the region, Wall gave witness to its seeming timelessness: "In the world of my youth, which included both ex-slaves and Confederate veterans, staple crops were grown essentially as they had been for 160 years. Some of the machines and implements used actually had been passed down from what blacks and whites both termed 'slavery times.' Many buildings, including houses and cabins, gins and presses, still served the purpose for which they had been built more than a century earlier." From slavery times to modern times, the South seemed to remain the same, the nation's most distinctive region. Even today, it seems a virtual Ur-Region: in what other portion of these United States today, for example, would such an extensive analysis be devoted to a theme such as the one explored in these pages?

Little wonder then that the tone of *The Urban South* was less than celebratory. In its lead essay, "The Mainsprings of Southern Urbanization," sociologist Rudolph Heberle described the South as "one of the frontier provinces of the Euro-American economic system," with its essential function "resembling that of the Balkan and eastern European region in the other hemisphere. The similarities are striking," he noted:

Agricultural surplus production concentrated on large estates or plantations; crop specialization for export in vast areas . . . ; late development of secondary industries and these very largely limited to the extraction and first processing of products of such primary industries as lumber, steel milling, canning, paper, basic chemical and oil refining. Furthermore, in the South as in eastern Europe, until recently, one observes a predominance of low wage industries producing low grade consumer goods. . . . In both regions the result has been a sparsity of large cities, a predominance of small market towns, a high rate of fertility, and a strong tendency of migration to distant industrial areas.

These eastern European correspondences, Heberle concluded, demonstrated "that the so-called colonial character of the South's economy has retarded the urbanization of the region, although we find here some of the oldest cities in the United States." Ironically, as this unflattering, but once apt characterization appeared in print, the urban South, together with its agricultural hinterlands, was well under way in its transformation from an agricultural to an urban economy, from a traditional to a modern system. Southern cities, hitherto termed "colonial" or "provincial," would soon be celebrated as "Sun Belt."

During the late 1950s, Charlie Croker played fullback on offense, linebacker on defense, and was proclaimed Georgia Tech's ultimate "Sixty-Minute Man." His playing days at Georgia Tech spanned the transformation of the game from limited to free substitution and, to many, two-platoon football seemed practically a new game. Still, Tech football, big-time southern football, remained a white man's game; southern cities still functioned as white folks' preserves. As urban America became increasingly multiethnic, the urban South remained biracial, with the races in all ways separate but seldom equal.

From slavery times to modern times, southern towns and cities were marked by the separation of the races. "Side" thus became a standard demarcation in the geography of the urban South: larger municipalities usually had both a "white side" and a "black side." Public structures—office buildings, government centers, schools, libraries, theaters, restaurants, stadiums, hospitals—and often the facilities within them—entrances and exits, elevators, water fountains, restrooms, seating—were designated according to the race: White or Colored. Everyday behavior—forms of address, titles, dress codes—also came under this "etiquette" of race relations. "There is little thinking in the South," Charles S. Johnson observed in his classic survey, *Patterns of Negro Segregation*, "which the Negro does not in some way influence." In almost every imaginable way certainly, race marked the urban South: "separate but equal" and "the southern way of life" for white southerners; for African Americans, a "Jim Crow" system; and to outsiders, "segregation." Whatever it was called, it constituted apartheid, American-style, and its physical manifestations were compelling.

For instance, on alighting from my coach in Savannah, then the end of the line, after an all-night train ride from New York City during the mid-1950s, I was confronted with a choice of two water fountains—seemingly identical, except for the signage that read White and Colored. No real choice here for a first-time visitor on his way to a local (and integrated) military base who was "under orders," having received a predeparture "briefing" for incoming Yankees that boiled down to this: when in doubt, follow "local custom." On his first visit to the South toward the end of the decade, novelist-essayist James Baldwin even found himself prepared for "the racial setup. . . . It is the etiquette which is baffling, not the spirit." "Baffling" it might have seemed, but it was also purposeful.

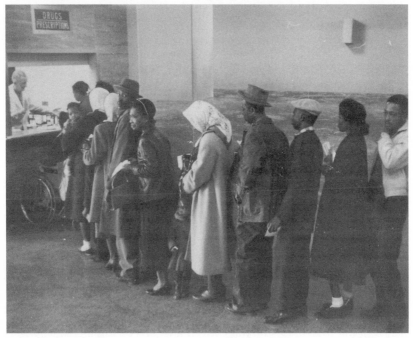

Segregated lines waiting for prescriptions at Atlanta's Grady Hospital. Courtesy of the Kenan Research Center at the Atlanta History Center.

During the decades following desegregation, the late Clarence Bacote, Atlanta University's senior historian, often reflected on the Jim Crow practices of the segregated Atlanta to which he had relocated in 1930. In a major downtown office building, he recalled, passenger elevators were reserved for whites, with African Americans relegated to freight elevators, on the way up. However, both blacks and whites could take passenger elevators down. Bacote offered two interpretations of these rules—one teasingly theological, the other pointedly psychological: whites and blacks might take different paths to heaven, Bacote would joke, but they took the same path to hell; or, alternatively, the very illogic of such practices, he professed, explained their true purpose. "Separate-but-equal" practices, in other words, purposefully defied logic—thereby serving as a form of psychological warfare. The official "rules"—the "etiquette"—were intended to keep those forced into segregated situations off-balance. "In their place" was the operative phrase, and the arbiters of the system determined when and how blacks would be put in it.

Ironically, the collapse of southern apartheid also witnessed the disappearance of much of its artifactual record. Few markers remain in today's urban landscape to indicate the pervasiveness of "separate but equal" in southern towns and cities during the first half of the twentieth century.

"Some decades ago—and I am deliberately vague about the date," Oscar Handlin suggested in 1963, "a significant change" took place in urban America. "To put it bluntly," he explained, "the urbanization of the whole society may be in process of destroying the distinctive role of the modern city." When the Harvard historian penned these words, Tom Wolfe's "Sixty-Minute Man" would have been peddling commercial real estate in downtown Atlanta; after all, his ex-wife explained, "that's what Georgia Tech graduates who aren't equipped to do anything but play football do." By the 1970s, however, Charlie Croker had extended himself beyond the downtown far out into the suburban outback and changed his occupation from realtor to developer. Once again, his personal history serves as an allegory of a changing South.

By the opening decades of the twentieth century, Handlin's heralded "urbanization of the whole society," which entailed a transformation in the relationship between central cities and their hinterlands, was under way nationwide—albeit less obvious in the urban South than in the urban Northeast and Midwest. Late-nineteenth-century suburbs had followed commuter rail lines and streetcar routes, whereas their twentieth-century counterparts were freed up by the free-ranging automobile. These new automotive suburbs crowded the spaces in between established railroad and trolley suburbs and, simultaneously, mushroomed ever outward, potentially without limits. Urbanization had given way to a suburbanization driven (literally) by automobility.

The Great Depression of the 1930s virtually halted construction throughout urban America; what is more, building supply shortages during World War II, as well as the postwar conversion from military to civilian production, resulted in continuing urban stasis during the 1940s. For two decades, consequently, urban America seemed virtually on hold. Then came what the editors of *Fortune* magazine broadcast as "The Exploding Metropolis" of the 1950s. Postwar planners advocated new dispersion patterns for urban Americans: the devastation inflicted on cities around the world by strategic bombing during the war, together with an escalating nuclear threat, their theory held, demonstrated that population concentrations in cities would be ready targets for the nation's cold war foes. Federal funds, therefore, would be devoted not to rebuilding downtown centers but, instead, to financing highways that would enable people to get out of them. During the early 1950s, the U.S. Department of Defense began financing the construction of the network of freeways, now designated the "Eisenhower Interstate System," that would—region to region, city to city—supplement and, indeed, supersede the nation-wide railroad system established during the nineteenth century.

Federal policies reshaped urban America nationwide. Liberalized mortgaging formulations facilitated expanded home building and ownership—mainly in the new suburbs—while slum clearance and urban renewal programs fostered commercial over residential development in central cities. In the South, especially, long-term forces of change that had been building since early in the century would affect postwar cities. Well before the Great Depression, an agricultural revolution had manifested itself, as traditional subsistence and single-crop farming ceased to dominate the region's economy. In the process, the work force that had serviced it, especially African Americans, abandoned the South in growing numbers. The so-called Great Migration out of the region, which began during World War I, would regain momentum during and after World War II. Wartime America, confronted by enemies across both oceans, massed its armed forces along its Atlantic and Pacific coasts, after having trained and mobilized a sizable proportion of them in the South. The magnitude of war thereby reconfigured the United States into a continental nation—not only in name, but also in action.

Postwar urban America was as mobile as it was affluent. Increasingly, Americans abandoned rural landscapes for metropolitan urbanscapes. They could travel from city to suburb, city to city, or region to region along the expanding grid of the Eisenhower Interstate System. Or, if distance was the determining factor, they could fly to their destinations along newly established continent-wide air routes. For airborne Americans, especially, distances seemed to diminish as faster planes—prop, turbo-prop, and then jet—cut travel days to travel hours and then further reduced those hours. Americans, always a people on the move, moved as never before but in unexpected directions.

As the nation expanded, it did so unevenly and in unanticipated ways. The growth line was marked by the 37th parallel: above it, a "Rust Belt"; below it, a "Sun Belt." During the second half of the twentieth century, the growth rate below that line was more than twice the growth rate above it. People flooded into a line of cities that stretched from Miami, Tampa–St. Petersburg, and Atlanta on the east; to Houston and Dallas–Fort Worth in the center; on out to Albuquerque, Phoenix, Los Angeles, and San Diego on the west. These Sun Belt cities, in contrast to the established industrial cities of the Northeast and Midwest—a New York or a Chicago, for example—were of a different order. It seemed almost as if they had jumped from being towns to metropolitan regions—without ever having become "citified" in the process. Low population densities, reliance on private over public transportation, the dominance of suburb over central core, a focus on commerce over industry, a surfeit of outlying land available for development: such were the defining marks of Sun Belt cities. Still, the concept itself was not without its critics.

What seemed unique to cities south of the 37th parallel was, it would be argued, not a regional but, instead, a national phenomenon. "Sun Belt," Joel Garreau charged, was a "spurious idea," even "a misleading confection." The concept failed to comprehend the "new urban agglomerations" variously described as "urban villages, technoburbs, suburban downtowns, . . . galactic city, pepperoni pizza cities, a city of realms, superburbia, disurb, service centers, perimeter centers, and even peripheral centers." The *Washington Post* feature writer offered his own entry in the name game—"edge city"—and it stuck. His specifications required that such a space had five million square feet or more of leasable office space; six hundred thousand square feet or more of leasable retail space; more jobs than bedrooms; was perceived by its population as "one place"; and was "nothing like 'city' as recently as thirty years ago." As of 1991, according to his reckoning, Atlanta had four edge cities, with three emerging; Houston, nine established and two emerging; Los Angeles, sixteen established and eight emerging; and greater New York, fifteen edge cities and three emerging. Garreau's "edge city" represented the most recent stage in the historical progression of urbanization nationwide.

For Tom Wolfe, Charlie Croker stands as "the inimitable Joel Garreau." For the novelist's fictive hero, who "wasn't much of a reader . . . a book called *Edge City*," all five hundred pages of it, had evoked "the *Aha!* phenomenon." Chapter three of *A Man in Full* offers developer Charlie Croker's airborne views, from the vantage point of his Gulfstream Five corporate jet, as well as his reflections on the booming edge cities along Atlanta's Northside. "How fabulous," he thought, "the building booms had been!"

As the novel opens, its hero owns his own edge city in Cherokee County, a twenty-nine-thousand-acre *latifundium* in his native Baker County, an English manor house in Buckhead, fleets of corporate jets and company limousines, and a "trophy wife" half his age: all markers of his own "fabulous" success. Yet all is at risk, for all rests on a builder's bubble. To begin with, his "Turpmtine Plantation" is no profitable agribusiness but, instead, a "show plantation," a weekend getaway for entertaining corporate clients. Baker County itself remains an economic disaster area, classified by the One-Georgia Authority as Tier 1, which comprises the poorest 71 of Georgia's 159 counties. Its population, which had numbered about 7,800 (and declining) in 1930, had plummeted to just over 3,600 inhabitants by 2001. "Croker Concourse" in Cherokee County, classified as Tier 4 (the top 18 counties statewide), is in the right sector, but the wrong location: development had yet to extend that far. Charlie Croker's two properties, then, reflect the problems of the "Two Georgias"—one stagnating, the other out of control.

As "conspicuous consumption" described the lifestyle created by the first wave of millionaire overachievers at the turn of the twentieth century, mainly in the Northeast and Midwest, "conspicuous construction" marked the ways of their successors a century later, largely in Sun Belt centers. The real estate pages of big-city newspapers and the glossy pages of regional "lifestyle" magazines regularly toted up the numbers of "million-dollar residences"— Crokeresque castles—both under construction or on the local market, and touted them as metropolitan success stories. Before the acronym ENRON ever became a widely recognized corporate logo, and later a national disgrace, it represented a Houston style-of-living: one much admired by many on the rise—especially some in the sprawling Sun Belt.

Tom Wolfe's "mighty king of the Crackers" personifies the situation of the modern urban South. Developer Charlie Croker is both a contributor to, and victim of, "sprawl"—the current term of choice in the urban name game. Sprawl, writes novelist Larry McMurtry, has "replaced the ozone hole as the worry of the week." Sprawl, more seriously, is emblematic of the course of urbanization in the twentieth-century South.

Before 1950, towns and cities had been scattered widely throughout the region's rural landscape. Over the following five decades, the spaces around and between them were filled in—roads and highways laid out; major airports and commuter air fields constructed; suburban subdivisions opened; regional shopping malls and local strip malls built; and, in all cases, the necessary infrastructure (heating, cooling, lighting, servicing, etc.) provided to support this largely unplanned, unchecked growth. By the close of the century, the price of progress along the nation's southern rim had become evident: an increasingly devastated landscape with fewer trees, polluted air, a shortage of water, and longer and more burdensome commutes. In a word, "sprawl"!

On the surface, today's sprawling megalopolitan regions scarcely resemble yesterday's scattered towns and cities; still, continuities persist. Always, and in all ways, economic disparities endure: the contrast between Georgia's Tier 1 ("dirt poor") and Tier 4 ("conspicuously constructing") counties is mirrored throughout the South. Race matters: suburbanization has taken jobs to the urban edges, but has left behind the in-town poor, many of them African Americans; what is more, waves of new immigrants (largely "people of color"—Asians, Latins, and Africans), rather than establishing "ghettos" of their own, often tend to locate between central cities (African American) and exurbs (white) to the interstices between them. All the same, everyday life in the urban South is still markedly "southern" in look, feel, texture, and experience.

At the three-quarter mark in the twentieth century, historian Blaine A. Brownell cautioned that although it might seem that "the principal differences between the cities of the South and those of the North" were only "differences of scale and dimension," such was a misperception:

> There are also peculiar features of southern urban life, only vaguely suggested in the statistics, that derive from regional customs, habits, and mores. Southern city dwellers [for example] tend to emphasize the institutions of church and family more than urban citizens elsewhere in the country. . . . To live in a southern city [then] . . . is to share an essentially urban experience with city dwellers everywhere. But a similar urban structure . . . and similar patterns of urban development do not suggest an identical response. If southern cities are different, these differences almost certainly lie primarily in those peculiar patterns of interpersonal relations that are deeply woven into the rich tapestry of southern cultural experience— patterns that continue in the southern metropolis.

Whatever these differences and similarities amount to, it can be said with some assurance that southern cities are neither carbon copies of their counterparts in other regions, nor are they unique forms of urban settlement.

The urban South of the twenty-first century, it may also be said with some assurance, is certain to be confronted with its own set of unique challenges, many of them unforeseeable at this point in 2005. All the same, it seems safe to predict that the first order of business for the new century will be to choose between continued unchecked "sprawl" and some version of "Smart Growth."

The alternative chosen—the how and the why of it—will likely engage "South watchers" for the rest of the present century. Either way, it is a choice that will have to be made.

Suggested Readings

Abbott, Carl. *The New Urban America: Growth and Politics in Sunbelt Cities*. Chapel Hill: University of North Carolina Press, 1981.

Brownwell, Blaine. *The Urban South in the Twentieth Century*. St. Charles, Mo.: Forum Press, 1974.

Cobb, James C. *The Selling of the South: The Southern Crusade for Industrial Development, 1938–1980*. Baton Rouge: Louisiana State University Press, 2000.

Crowther, Hal. *Cathedrals of the Kudzu: A Personal Landscape of the South*. Baton Rouge: Louisiana State University Press, 2000.

Goldfield, David R. *Cotton Fields and Skyscrapers: Southern City and Region, 1607–1980*. Baton Rouge: Louisiana State University Press, 1982.

Johnson, Charles S., ed. *Statistical Atlas of Southern Counties: Listing and Analysis of Socio-Economic Indices of 1104 Southern Counties*. Chapel Hill: University of North Carolina Press, 1941.

Vance, Rupert B., and Nicholas J. Demerath, eds. *The Urban South*. Chapel Hill: University of North Carolina Press, 1954.

Wolfe, Tom. *A Man in Full*. New York: Farrar, Straus and Giroux, 1998.

The Culture of the South:
What Makes a Southerner a Southerner?

JOHN SHELTON REED

Southern Culture

On the Skids?

If you had to choose one state to represent the entire South, which one would you choose? The answer is not obvious.

Not long ago Mississippi would have been a plausible choice, not because it was "typically" southern (whatever that might mean) but because it was *ultra*southern. For 150 years or more, most generalizations about the South went double for Mississippi. When the South was rich, Mississippi was richest; when it was poor, Mississippi was poorest. The South was mostly rural:

Portions of this essay are adapted from "Dixiology's False Dichotomies," in *Regional Images and Regional Realities*, edited by Lothar Hönnighausen, 183–91 (Tübingen: Stauffenburg Verlag, 2000). My title is ripped off from the Chapel Hill band whose latest CD is *Liquored Up and Lacquered Down*.

Mississippi was even more so. The South is biracial: Mississippi had and still has the highest percentage of African Americans in the country. White southerners were committed to white supremacy: eighteen of the forty martyrs commemorated on the Civil Rights Memorial in Montgomery were killed in Mississippi. And so on.

In short, for a long time Mississippi was the most southern of the southern states, and "southern" referred to the economic, cultural, political, and demographic legacy of plantation agriculture and slavery. Mississippi was at the core of Dixie, the land of cotton. It, with the other Deep South states, was where the sociologist Charles Johnson believed "the shadow of the plantation" fell darkest and lingered longest.

Dixie has had many lives. It was the Old South, the plantation South, the Cotton Kingdom—the South of both *Gone with the Wind* and *Uncle Tom's Cabin*. From 1861 to 1865 it was the Confederate States of America. For decades after the 1890s it was the "Solid South" in politics—solid for the Democrats, the party of states' rights and white supremacy. Well into the twentieth century it was, as Franklin Roosevelt saw it, "the Nation's No. 1 economic problem."

Only yesterday Dixie was still a powerful reality and perhaps an even more powerful myth. It still survives here and there, and the ongoing conflict over the Confederate battle flag suggests that old times there are not entirely forgotten. But if it is a little early to write Dixie's epitaph, that version of the South is clearly on its deathbed—and most southerners don't live there any more. Mississippi is no longer the most southern of the southern states because the South has changed. (So, for that matter, has Mississippi.)

Urbanization, industrialization, and the end of de jure segregation have produced what we can call (for reasons I'll get to) the "Southeast," a vibrant, dynamic, industrial region, a magnet for migration and investment from other parts of the nation and increasingly from abroad. The Southeast occupies much of the same territory as Dixie, but that should not blind us to the fact that it is an entirely new development—indeed, in many respects an entirely different region.

So what state is the most southern state now? Well, when a Southern Focus Poll conducted by the Odum Institute at the University of North Carolina in 1994 asked "If you had to say, what one state best captures your idea of the South?" the most frequent choice by far was Georgia, chosen by over a quarter of both southerners and nonsoutherners.

To be sure, Georgia was part of Dixie. Atlanta was the scene, after all, of the great Cotton States and International Exposition of 1895, the great race riot of 1906, the premiere of *Gone with the Wind* in 1939, and the funeral of

Martin Luther King Jr. in 1968. But I suspect that history is not the reason people these days say Georgia "captures the idea of the South." No, they choose it because Georgia's capital city has become the capital of the entire Southeast.

Consider: Atlanta is where regional trade associations have their annual conventions, where regional corporations are likely to be headquartered, where national corporations have their regional offices. It's where the television networks, wire services, and national publications have their southern bureaus. The *Wall Street Journal*'s Atlanta office now publishes a regional supplement, and the *Journal-Constitution* is the nearest thing the South has to a national newspaper. Atlanta is at the center of the South's transportation grid as well: its airport is, by some reckonings, the busiest in the United States, giving rise to the southern joke that even if you're going to hell you'll have to change planes in Atlanta.

The Southeast that Atlanta serves is the South of the future. It barely existed before World War II, but it's all around us now. And it seems to be unstoppable, as its booming economy and surging population are translated into political power (primarily through the medium of the Republican Party, Dixie's old adversary).

But there's a reason to call it the South*east*. We can see plainly now a development predicted fifty years ago by the sociologist Rupert Vance: the postagricultural South has split down the middle. Grant's work at Vicksburg has been completed: the Trans-Mississippi has been lost. More precisely, it has become a region in its own right—essentially greater Texas. Dallas and Houston don't report to Atlanta. The western South has its own regional institutions, its own magazines and corporate headquarters, even its own edition of the *Wall Street Journal*.

This distinction between Southeast and Southwest is increasingly evident in business and trade association names, and that's no accident, because these regions are primarily economic entities, not cultural ones. As Lew Powell was the first to observe, we speak of commercial activity in the Southeast, but not of southeastern religion, southeastern music, the southeastern gentleman, or southeastern fried chicken.

So we have Dixie—the old, agricultural South, rooted in the plantation economy and the institutions that grew out of that—fading fast and soon to be of interest primarily to historians. And we have this new metropolitan Southeast—a mere quadrant, culturally speaking, a region of interest primarily to economists and industrial recruiters. Is there anything left that is recognizably *the South*?

When Rupert Vance predicted the emergence of the Southeast and Southwest, he remarked that the South's continuing existence represented the triumph of history and culture over economics and geography, and it is to a shared culture that we must look if we are to find the South in the twenty-first century. Yet many argue that the South's culture has become virtually indistinguishable from that of the rest of the United States. Others argue that the South is so varied internally that it makes no sense to speak of it as a single entity. Some confused souls seem to accept both of these arguments, although it's not clear how Georgia and Kentucky can be greatly different from each other if they both look like Michigan.

Let's try to sort this mess out. Is there something we can call "southern culture"? If so, how is it different these days, if at all, from that elsewhere? If there are differences, are they disappearing?

The question of whether there is a single, dominant, widely shared southern culture has been on my mind of late, because I recently found myself coeditor of a journal called *Southern Cultures* (note the plural). I preferred *Southern Culture*, but my colleagues in this enterprise fought for the plural with a dogmatic zeal worthy of the Council of Chalcedon. For them, it was plainly not just a harmless gesture of political correctness but somehow a statement of objective truth.

And of course it is true that there are many cultures in the South. For starters, there are striking geographic differences. When Chapel Hill's Howard Odum compiled his encyclopedic survey in 1938, he called it *Southern Regions of the United States* (again, note the plural) and distinguished even then between the Southeast and the Southwest.

And of course there are subregions within subregions. You cannot understand the politics of any southern state without having a grasp of the differences between uplands and lowlands; mountains, piedmont, and coastal plain; sand hills, piney woods, and wiregrass. And each part of each state is a conglomeration of localities with more or less distinctive cultures, economies, societies, and interests, too.

Dwelling on these distinctions may be a southern trait, our notorious "sense of place," but it does keep cropping up. To take just one example, both John Hiatt's great song "Memphis in the Meantime" and Peter Taylor's lovely novel *Summons to Memphis* are basically about the difference between Nashville and Memphis.

If we hear less than we used to about geographic variation it is not because there is less of it, but because the new multiculturalism concerns itself with more fashionable diversities—those of race, class, gender, and so forth. But those, too, delineate different Souths. Although the South may have been a white man's country, the white man's story is not the only one that has played itself out in our parts.

But although there are many Souths, many cultures in *the* South, most of the many Souths do have something southern about them, and for some purposes that is what's interesting. Some students of the South want to document its diversity, but others want to examine the effects of the regional context on one or another of the diverse populations in it. For example, to summarize the results of one old article of mine, Jews in the South can be viewed as either southern Jews or Jewish southerners. In a southern context, they look culturally Jewish; in a Jewish context, they look culturally southern. Take your pick.

Similarly, we need to recognize the growing Asian and Hispanic presence in our region, but studies have found that Vietnamese immigrants in North Carolina and Mexican Americans in Texas differ from their compatriots in California in stereotypically "southern" ways. To make this observation is not to disregard or to disparage diversity. Quite the contrary, surely.

Even across the historic black-white divide, there has been an emerging, tentative recognition and exploration of the obvious fact that the two races have copied one another, shared with one another, stolen from one another, influenced one another to such an extent that we can speak in some respects of a biracial southern culture. If you doubt this, see Jimmy Lewis Franklin's recent presidential address to the Southern Historical Association, "Black Southerners, Shared Experience, and Place"—or, for that matter, just about any southern cookbook.

Those who have remarked about the southerness of black folk include Albert Murray, Ralph Ellison, and Martin Luther King Jr. a generation ago; Andrew Young, Randall Kenan, Alex Haley, Margaret Walker, Charlayne Hunter-Gault, Eddie Harris, Eugene Rivers, Glenn Loury, Anthony Walton, and a score of others more recently—to mention only *black* folk who've spoken to this point.

I think W. J. Cash got it just about right fifty years ago in *The Mind of the South*. "If it can be said there are many Souths," he wrote, "the fact remains that there is also one South." That there are many *kinds* of southerners is not the only truth about us. And, by the way, how is discussing the characteristics of southerners different from discussing those of Italian Americans or Hispanics or Asians—or, for that matter, African Americans or workers or women— rather than the many different kinds of each?

How you look at any social category depends on your purpose. Some of us are lumpers, others are sorters. What Cash thought southerners had in common was more relevant to his purposes than what divided them. Same for me, when I took Cash's observation as an epigraph for my book *One South*.

Cash also knew the argument that southerners are not "really" different from other Americans. He acknowledged those folks—"usually journalists

W. J. Cash, 1935.
Courtesy of the Cash
and Elkins families,
www.wjcash.org.

and professors," he said—who contended that the South is just "a figment of
the imagination." But he refused to take them seriously, and maybe that is
the right response. Certainly survey research suggests that most Americans
other than journalists and professors believe that southerners are a special
kind of American, and in some important respects they are right about that.
Southerners have been different from the run of the American mill in ways
that observers from Jefferson and Tocqueville to C. Vann Woodward, V. S.
Naipaul, and John Hope Franklin have identified.

Many of these folks have argued that the South is the least "American"
part of America. John Crowe Ransom, for instance, in *I'll Take My Stand*,
argued that the South was European in its disdain for the values of commerce
and industry. In "The Irony of Southern History," C. Vann Woodward put a
different spin on the same theme: the prosperity, success, and innocence of
the *nonsouthern* United States is (or was) what's unusual. Sheldon Hackney
has even written of the South as a "counterculture." On the other hand,

Howard Zinn, in his book *The Southern Mystique*, argued that the South is the *most* American part of America—and, writing from the perspective of the political left in 1964, he did not mean that as a compliment. Whatever the angle, though, the South has been used, again and again, to construct, in Woodward's phrase, an "American counterpoint."

Survey research can be used to measure some of these differences, and in many respects it *is* true what they say about Dixie. Southerners really do tend to be more religious, more conservative, more polite, more "touchy." They are more likely to hunt and fish, stop their cars for funeral processions, and eat black-eyed peas on New Year's Day. Whether these differences are big enough to signify is a judgment call, but the last time someone looked— Norval Glenn, over thirty years ago—he concluded that cultural differences between white southerners and white nonsoutherners were bigger than differences between blue-collar and white-collar workers, bigger than differences between the sexes or the generations, between high school graduates and those who had not completed high school, or between urban and rural folk. Regional differences among white Americans were about the same size, on the average, as cultural differences between black and white Americans. To be sure, Glenn looked at a rather arbitrary set of cultural indicators, but his results do suggest that if *any* cultural differences in the United States are important, regional ones are.

One interesting stream of research looks at the South as the Protestant, Anglophone, northern tip of a pan-American plantation region; leave that aside, however, and most really significant studies of the South have given at least implicit attention to how it differs from the rest of the United States. There's a good reason for that. The South is a complex, modern society; setting out to study it differs only quantitatively from setting out to study the world. As David Potter observed some time ago, focusing on those differences provides, if nothing else, a principle of selection.

But just as an emphasis on the many southern cultures ignores what they have in common as *southern* cultures, focusing on how southerners and non-southerners differ ignores what we have in common as Americans. Those who question the significance of regional differences in the United States do have a point: some countries much smaller than the United States show a regionalism even more vigorous, and an interesting question for research, or at least speculation, is why a continental nation like ours does not have even *more* differences, and larger ones. But my point is that sometimes it is useful to focus on differences, sometimes on similarities, and we need to keep in mind that there are plenty of both.

Another perennial question is this: Are the cultural differences between

South and non-South going away? This question is often confounded with the question of the relative importance of continuity and change in southern culture, but we have to untangle the two.

Perhaps because I once wrote a book called *The Enduring South*, I usually find myself put in the continuitarian camp, especially by people who have heard of the book but have not actually read it. At a symposium in Memphis some years back, I had the disconcerting experience of hearing myself congratulated by a sociologist from Mississippi State for having shown that there had been no important changes in the South, that the fundamental realities of racism and class hegemony were much the same as ever. When it came my turn to speak I couldn't resist observing that one thing at least has changed: you didn't use to run into Marxists from Mississippi State.

Ironically, one constant in southern history has been the experience of change—I started to say "never more rapid than in the past few decades" but no doubt historians would remind me of the dynamism of the early nineteenth century, not to mention some rather abrupt changes in the 1860s. Anyway, economic, demographic, and political changes both produce and reflect cultural change. So, of course there has been change in southern culture, W. J. Cash and my Mississippi State friend to the contrary notwithstanding.

But to allow that southern culture has changed, is changing, does not mean that it is disappearing as a variant on the American norm (whatever *that* might be). It is difficult to summarize the facts of southern cultural difference, however, because nearly every logical possibility of what *could* be happening *is* happening.

For example, most of the recent economic and demographic change in the South has been a matter of the South's converging on nonsouthern patterns (and the same could be said, in general, about changes in race relations), so those "southern" characteristics that were, in fact, the characteristics of poor, rural, poorly educated folks are plainly on the wane. But other longstanding cultural differences are hanging in there. For instance, attitudes toward the role of women have been changing everywhere, but the South remains relatively conservative on this score.

Some regional differences are even getting larger: the South is more Baptist now than it was a century ago, for instance; regional differences in churchgoing are larger than they used to be; southerners are now more economically conservative than they were a generation ago. And they're more likely to say "fixing to" and "might could."

In still other respects, the rest of the country is starting to look like the South. That is true for homicide rates, for the lack of a distinction between "pin" and "pen" in speech, for tastes in music and sports and some aspects of diet. Younger nonsoutherners are even starting to say "y'all." This isn't exactly the model of regional convergence most reformers have had in mind.

But that's not all. Some old regional differences have disappeared altogether, only to reemerge as differences in the opposite direction. Birthrates and support for the national Democratic Party were once both higher in the South than elsewhere. Now both are lower. And to complicate matters even further, new technology and new affluence mean that southerners keep inventing new and unpredictable ways to be different. We need to remind ourselves that country music, stock-car racing, and competitive bass fishing, for instance, are all twentieth-century innovations.

We can be sure that the culture of the twenty-first-century South will be different from that of the last century, just as the twentieth-century South differed from the nineteenth. Like other living organisms, cultures change as they age. But there is no reason to suppose that the change will produce a culture identical to that elsewhere in the United States.

One reason it will not is that the South is inhabited by people who identify with it, to the extent of calling themselves "southerners," and they won't let it. Southerners sometimes do things in "southern" ways because those things link them to their community and their heritage. In this, they are no different from the many other identity groups that make up our increasingly multicultural society.

That fact suggests that we might want to turn our attention from the specifics of cultural difference to the mechanisms that sustain group identity. In particular, we might want to look at the workings of what might be called the "southern culture industry"—magazines, associations, journals, conferences, academic programs, and the like that nourish regional identity, whether by studying it explicitly or simply by assuming that it is somehow a fact of nature. When we go looking for such institutions, we see that whatever the current state of southern culture may be, the *study* of it has never been in better shape. Maybe this is just a result of overproduction of Ph.D.s in the humanities and social sciences. Or perhaps, as George Tindall once suggested, it is the cultural equivalent of having your life pass before you as you are drowning—drowning, in this case, in the American mainstream. But, for whatever reason, the southern culture industry is booming. Witness the collection of essays that you hold in your hands.

Let me close by giving my own answer to the question I started with. If I had to choose one state to represent the entire South, I would pick Tennessee, not just because I grew up there (although I did) but because it displays both the legacy and the inventiveness of southern culture. Start with Bristol, in the eastern mountains, where Ralph Peer recorded Jimmie Rodgers and the

Elvis Presley's home Graceland and his pink Cadillac. Used by permission of Elvis Presley Enterprises, Inc.

Carter Family in 1927 and the Bristol Motor Speedway now hosts NASCAR's Sharpie® 500. Go west to Nashville, Athens to Atlanta's Rome, home of the Grand Ole Opry, the Vanderbilt Agrarian authors of *I'll Take My Stand*, and the Vatican of the Southern Baptist Convention (insofar as that fractious and decentralized body has one). Wind up in Memphis, a city of shrines: Beale Street, embalming Dixie's heritage of the blues; the National Civil Rights Museum in the Lorraine Motel; Mason Temple and the headquarters of the eight-million-member Church of God in Christ; and—one word—Graceland. Need I say more?

Suggested Readings

Cash, W. J. *The Mind of the South*. New York: Alfred A. Knopf, 1941.

Cobb, James C. *Redefining Southern Culture: Mind and Identity in the Modern South*. Athens: University of Georgia Press, 1999.

Couch, W. T., ed. *Culture in the South*. Chapel Hill: University of North Carolina Press, 1934.

Eagles, Charles W., ed. *The Mind of the South: Fifty Years Later*. Jackson: University Press of Mississippi, 1992.

Joyner, Charles W. *Shared Traditions: Southern History and Folk Culture*. Urbana: University of Illinois Press, 1999.

Reed, John Shelton. *The Enduring South: Subcultural Persistence in Mass Society*. Rev. ed. Chapel Hill: University of North Carolina Press, 1986.

Reed, John Shelton, and Dale Volberg Reed. *1001 Things Everyone Should Know About the South*. New York: Doubleday, 1996.

Twelve Southerners. *I'll Take My Stand: The South and the Agrarian Tradition*. New York: Harper, 1930.

Wilson, Charles Reagan. *Judgment and Grace in Dixie: Southern Faiths from Faulkner to Elvis*. Athens: University of Georgia Press, 1995.

Wilson, Charles Reagan, and William Ferris, eds. *The Encyclopedia of Southern Culture*. Chapel Hill: University of North Carolina Press, 1989.

FRED HOBSON

"To talk, to tell"

Southern Literature in the Twentieth Century

We need to talk, to tell, since oratory is our heritage. We seem to try in the single furious breathing (or writing) span of the individual to draw a savage indictment of the contemporary scene or to escape from it into a make-believe region of swords and magnolias and mockingbirds which perhaps never existed anywhere.

WILLIAM FAULKNER, unpublished manuscript (1933)

"Alas! for the South. Her books have grown fewer. She never was much given to literature." So proclaimed, at the brink of the twentieth century, J. Gordon Coogler, designated by H. L. Mencken as the "Last Bard of Dixie" and quoted by Mencken at the beginning of his own explosive essay "The Sahara of the Bozart" (1920). What Coogler suggested—and what Mencken contended, at greater length, in his essay—was that the state of letters in the American South

154

was indeed dismal at the beginning of the twentieth century. It was not as if the South had been at the center of the nation's literature in the nineteenth century: only Edgar Allan Poe and Mark Twain (one born in Boston, the other in Missouri, and thus both only arguably southerners) could compete with Emerson, Thoreau, Hawthorne, Melville, Whitman, Dickinson, and other members of the American literary pantheon. But at the end of the nineteenth century, the situation seemed especially dismal.

That was Mencken's take on the South in any case: Dixie was a "Sahara," a desert of literature, of the arts of any sort, "a gargantuan paradise of the fourth-rate," which contained no novelist of note (except perhaps James Branch Cabell of Virginia), no historians, philosophers, "critics, musical composers, painters, sculptors, architects [,] . . . not even a bad one between the Potomac mud-flats and the Gulf." In all those fields the South was "an awe-inspiring blank—a brother to Portugal, Serbia and Esthonia [sic]." In truth, of course, it was not quite that bad, as Mencken himself well knew. He admired the novels of Virginia's Ellen Glasgow, who had begun to write in the 1890s; he probably did not know of *The Awakening* and other stories of Kate Chopin, which had appeared in the late 1890s. And he, like other American critics North and South, still saw "southern literature" as white only, and thus would not have included Charles W. Chesnutt, James Weldon Johnson, and other southern African Americans who were writing at and just after the turn of the century (not to mention earlier writers such as Frederick Douglass and other authors of slave narratives, some of the most important American writing of the nineteenth century). So Mencken was wrong in the particulars, but, in a broader sense, he was correct: at the turn of the twentieth century the "Late Confederacy" (as he was fond of calling it) produced distinctly second-rate work in the realm of letters. At the time the rest of the nation could claim Henry James, Edith Wharton, William Dean Howells, Stephen Crane, Theodore Dreiser, and other realists and naturalists, of whom did the South boast? Largely, Thomas Nelson Page, Thomas Dixon, and other defenders of the earlier South, devotees of the Lost Cause.

And such would remain the case for the first quarter of the twentieth century. Although Cabell, Glasgow, James Weldon Johnson, and a very few others were producing work of distinction, in general the South continued to be if not an "awe-inspiring" blank, as Mencken charged, as least a distinctly inferior province. The prevailing view, one that has been current for more than half a century now, is that all that began to change in the 1920s: in that decade the Southern Literary Renaissance began, and it is said to have begun largely in Nashville, the home of a group of young poets associated with Vanderbilt University. The early leader of the so-called "Fugitive poets" (so called because of the title of their poetry magazine and their vow to flee "from nothing faster than from the high-caste Brahmins of the Old South") was John Crowe Ransom; his younger associates included Donald Davidson, Allen Tate, and Robert Penn Warren. These writers would go on to distinguish themselves not only as poets, novelists, and critics but also, in 1930, as contributors to *I'll Take My Stand*, a volume of twelve essays that sought to defend the southern, or "agrarian," way of life against the encroaching "industrial" way. In some respects—in its critique of industrial capitalism, its primary question, "Progress toward what?"—*I'll Take My Stand* was a prophetic volume, sharing certain philosophical concerns with works such as Thoreau's *Walden*. And it seemed particularly prophetic since it appeared at the beginning of the Great Depression, seen by some at the time as the death knell of industrial capitalism. But in other respects—particularly in its defense of the southern status quo in matters of race—*I'll Take My Stand* was hopelessly benighted, even for its own time and place.

In any case, the Fugitive-Agrarians have long been regarded as the first significant figures in what would come to be known as the Southern Literary Renaissance, although in fact other writers might have a clearer right to that distinction. Not only were Glasgow and Cabell already producing excellent fiction when Mencken published his "Sahara" in 1920, but just after that time—at the same time the Fugitive-Agrarians were beginning to publish modernist verse—Frances Newman of Georgia and Evelyn Scott of Tennessee were writing and publishing modernist fiction and a Kentuckian, Elizabeth Madox Roberts, produced in *The Time of Man* (1925) a novel that depicted southern agrarian life far more accurately and compellingly than did the poets in Nashville. Indeed, before any of them, two African American writers, Johnson in 1912 in *Autobiography of an Ex-Coloured Man* and Jean Toomer in 1923 in *Cane* (another work that provides an earlier and a truer picture of agrarianism than that of the Fugitive-Agrarians), produced books that should be regarded as central works in the Southern Renaissance but generally have not been. Accompanying these works of fiction and poetry—and another often neglected part of the Southern Renaissance—were the iconoclastic essays of southern social critics, particularly Gerald W. Johnson and W. J. Cash of North Carolina, both of whom challenged traditional southern ways of thought and emboldened young southern writers to look on Dixie in a different manner.

In the 1920s itself, though hardly afterward, the Southern Renaissance was defined as a movement, characterized largely by realism and satire, that had a great deal in common with mainstream American literature of that decade. T. S. Stribling of Tennessee, author of novels dealing with small-town life in

Tennessee and northern Alabama, was called the southern Sinclair Lewis. Cabell, Glasgow (when she chose), Frances Newman, and others also wrote satire, though of a more elegant variety than Stribling. Paul Green of North Carolina was acclaimed for his plays of hard-bitten rural realism, and the iconoclastic journalists seemed to be southern versions of Mencken. Even the Fugitives of Nashville, before 1925, called for harsh criticism of the southern status quo.

But all that is very different from the manner in which the Southern Renaissance is generally perceived today. Several things, some of them extraliterary, played a part in the change from the southern critical realism and satire of the 1920s to something quite different in the 1930s. One of those things was the Scopes evolution trial in Dayton, Tennessee, in July 1925—an event that, more than anything else, changed the minds of the Nashville writers about the modern critical spirit and southern manifestations of it. Ransom, Tate, and Davidson in particular responded to the trial—and even more to the ridicule heaped upon the South from outsiders—by retreating from their own earlier iconoclasm and launching a defense of the South. That defense, as I suggested earlier, would find its most notable outlet in their essays in *I'll Take My Stand*, but in fact their so-called Agrarianism became a movement that most of the Fugitive-Agrarians advocated throughout much of the 1930s. They found their adversaries in the new southern critical thinkers—Green, Johnson, Cash, and, most of all, sociologist Howard W. Odum—in North Carolina, those whose primary purpose was not to defend the South but to reform it, to flee (as the Fugitive-Agrarians themselves had vowed at first) from the Old South. It is impossible to separate southern literature of the 1930s from this battle, fought in part on an academic level but broadening into a debate waged in national magazines and widely reviewed books. Ransom, Tate, Davidson, Warren, and their followers were in the Agrarian camp; Green, Cash, Johnson, and the young Thomas Wolfe were generally placed in the camp of the "Southern Regionalists" of North Carolina.

Donald Davidson, for example, once wrote of Wolfe, a native of Asheville, that he would have been a vastly different writer if he had gone west to Vanderbilt for college rather than east to Chapel Hill. At the University of North Carolina, Davidson charged, Wolfe had fallen under the "social program" of Odum and the southern critics. Davidson was a little off in his timing—in fact, Odum had not yet arrived in Chapel Hill when Wolfe graduated in 1920— but his point was that Wolfe, the much acclaimed author of *Look Homeward, Angel* (1929), held a negative view of the South that he had learned in Chapel Hill and that his protagonist and alter ego Eugene Gant were made to express that view frequently in Wolfe's novel. In fact, it was not principally Chapel

Hill that made Wolfe what he was but rather a romantic imagination, the sensibility of the lonely artist who wanted out of what he felt to be his provincial, benighted environment—and he felt that way before he arrived in Chapel Hill. In the end, Wolfe transcended the Agrarian-Regionalist debate of the 1920s and 1930s—in fact, for most of the 1930s, he was coming closer to the Agrarian point of view—but the Agrarians never quite realized that. Wolfe was that unlikely combination, a nineteenth-century romantic *and* an early twentieth-century modernist, but if he was a self-conscious critic of the South in his early writing (the satirical plays as well as *Look Homeward, Angel*), the impulse to criticize had largely fled by the time of his early death in 1938.

A writer who, much more than Wolfe, transcended the southern debate of the 1920s and 1930s—whose first major novel was published within a month or two of *Look Homeward, Angel* but who received far less attention than Wolfe in the beginning—is William Faulkner. It might be difficult to believe today—when one reads of the Faulkner Industry, the Dixie Limited, and all the other terms suggesting Faulkner's prominence—just how little regarded he was in the beginning, and continued to be for a couple of decades. Reviewers and critics simply did not know how to approach him at first. With his harrowing tales of southern racial violence and his depictions of southern poor and plain whites, he was often placed in the company of Erskine Caldwell, the Georgia-born author of *Tobacco Road*, *God's Little Acre*, and other tales that combined social realism with cruel satire. Or Faulkner—with his early novels covering a broad sweep of southern history of the nineteenth and early twentieth centuries—was seen as a sort of southern social chronicler. Others saw him, correctly, as a modernist, but still did not fathom the extent to which the meaning of his fiction transcended the American South.

Faulkner's great period is generally conceded to have been between 1929 and 1936, the span in which appeared his four great tragedies, *The Sound and the Fury* (1929), *As I Lay Dying* (1930), *Light in August* (1932), and *Absalom, Absalom!* (1936). In three of the four novels Faulkner tells the story of a southern family, first the aristocratic Compsons of *The Sound and the Fury*, then the poor white Bundrens of *As I Lay Dying* and the emergent Sutpens of *Absalom, Absalom!* In all three of these works, in the liberties he takes with conventional chronology and his use of stream of consciousness, Faulkner the modernist is clearly on display. *The Sound and the Fury* has three narrators—Benjy, the mentally deficient son of a proud family; Jason, the money-grubbing son; and Quentin, the sensitive son with a love-hate relationship with his homeland—in addition to a fourth section told through the point of view of Dilsey, the black family servant who struggles, in the absence of strong Compson parents, to keep the family together. *The Sound*

William Faulkner, 1954. Library of Congress, Prints & Photographs Division, Washington, D.C., reproduction number LC-USZC2-6403.

and the Fury is both a family tragedy and a commentary on a changing South, the decline and fall of the old order. It is also a novel that transcends the American South in its meaning and artistry, a drama based in Mississippi (and, in Quentin's case, Massachusetts) but worthy of the Greek tragedians.

Absalom, Absalom!, set in nineteenth-century Mississippi but narrated in the early twentieth century, tells the story of one of Faulkner's great creations, Thomas Sutpen, the son of poor whites from the Virginia mountains who goes to Haiti and then to Mississippi in search of his own version of the American dream. Having been turned away from the front door of a plantation home in Tidewater Virginia, Sutpen vows to become the man who can own such a home and turn others away. His "design," as he calls it, fails because—despite hard work, determination, strength, and shrewdness—he does not in the end regard other human beings, white or black, as human beings. The story of Sutpen is narrated first by Rosa Coldfield, one of those whom Sutpen has used and rejected, and then by Quentin Compson, his father, and (in the latter half of the book) his roommate at Harvard. It is, finally, a story about the telling of a story, a commentary on the elusive nature of historical truth.

What *did* happen in Mississippi in the mid-nineteenth century and why? The reader becomes, in some sense, the fifth narrator, the final arbiter of truth.

Faulkner's prominence in twentieth-century American fiction is not based solely, however, on his tragic works; indeed, he brings together those often disparate strains in American fiction, the tragic and the comic, more successfully than any other American writer of the century. If the tragic sense is most prominent in the four early novels, the comic genius is seen largely in his later trilogy, *The Hamlet* (1940), *The Town* (1957), and *The Mansion* (1959), all dealing with the Snopes family, Faulkner's ascendant poor whites. In the "Spotted Horses" episode of *The Hamlet*, in which Faulkner describes the chaos that ensues when a group of men buy and then try to break wild horses, one is reminded of Mark Twain and the earlier Southwest Humorists. Certain of Faulkner's Snopeses are superb comic creations, but Flem Snopes, rapacious, predatory, is Faulkner's amoral man, on his way up but bound by no codes of ethics or honor. Flem and his spiritual brothers, Faulkner suggests, were gaining control in the South in the late nineteenth century.

Though he published novels now widely regarded as classics, Faulkner did not achieve a particularly lofty eminence in American letters until Malcolm Cowley's *The Portable Faulkner* appeared in 1946, with Cowley's introduction making a case for this provincial Mississippian as a writer of international importance. Four years after Cowley's book, Faulkner was awarded the Nobel Prize in literature, and one traces the beginnings of the Faulkner industry from that point. The manner in which he has been read since that time has depended in large part on *when* he has been read. In the 1950s and 1960s, an era during which English departments of American universities were still dominated by the New Criticism and its close readings of texts, Faulkner was regarded as the literary master par excellence and his novels were mined for their structural and stylistic complexity. In the 1970s and 1980s, critical theorists such as Andre Bleikasten, Donald Kartiganer, and John T. Matthews, while viewing Faulkner with something other than the reverence of the previous two decades, nonetheless focused on his artistry, the play of his language. Beginning in the mid-1980s with Eric Sundquist's *Faulkner: The House Divided*, scholars began increasingly to place Faulkner more fully in a historical and cultural context, focusing closely on issues of race, class, and gender. At the end of the century Faulkner emerged not unscathed but still intact as the most prominent southern, indeed American, novelist of his century.

He was the most prominent but he was hardly the only southerner to achieve greatness on the national stage in the last half of the twentieth century. Robert Penn Warren, having atoned for his racial sins in *I'll Take My Stand*, emerged in his mid- and later years as perhaps the nation's leading (or, in any case, most versatile) literary figure: Pulitzer Prize–winning novelist and poet as well as playwright, biographer, critic, social commentator, and Consultant in Poetry of the Library of Congress. Warren became best known for his novel *All the King's Men* (1944), a study of conscience and power, means and ends, as well as another exploration of the burden of southern history, but in fact long before his death in 1989, Warren's reputation was higher as poet than as novelist. His fellow Fugitives did not succeed so spectacularly as he after they left the southern for the national stage, but Ransom did achieve eminence as editor and critic and Tate as poet, critic, and—in *The Fathers*, another treatment of family and history—novelist. Davidson, who never came up from segregation, remained physically and spiritually in Dixie.

Other, more liberal voices emerged from the 1930s South as well, although—so strong was the influence of the Agrarians and of conservative southerners in general in not only interpreting but defining the South—these were voices often not accepted as "southern" at the time. Faulkner was hardly the only Mississippian to emerge from what one commentator in the 1920s called America's "Heart of Darkness": Richard Wright, born in 1908, poor and black, into a world controlled completely by Jim Crow—that is, in some measure, born at the worst possible time (at least, postbellum) in the worst possible place—emerged from a world of racial savagery to write a number of stories drawing on his Mississippi past, as well as the revolutionary novel *Native Son* (1940) and a classic of American autobiography, *Black Boy* (1945). Finding himself out of step from the beginning, not only with white society but also with genteel black society and much of his own family, Wright never successfully learned to live Jim Crow. Indeed, as he demonstrates in *Black Boy*, he succeeded largely *because* of his inability to live Jim Crow: he was determined to leave the South and to use words as a "weapon" in the service of personal liberation.

Wright's success was of a different variety from that of perhaps his primary rival among African American writers in the 1930s and 1940s, Zora Neale Hurston. Wright saw life as battle, not only with the white but also with much of the black community: he found little in African American culture—certainly not that traditional solace found in religion, place, humor, and a strong folk tradition—to sustain him, and thus he struck out largely on his own. Hurston reveled in the rich black folk culture that she described in her novel *Their Eyes Were Watching God* (1937) and her autobiography *Dust Tracks on a Road* (1942), and in *Dust Tracks* she describes a far more hospitable South than that depicted by Wright. Her portraits of whites she knew in her childhood in north Florida are so favorable, indeed, that one wonders whom

Richard Wright, 1943.
Library of Congress,
Prints & Photographs
Division, Washington,
D.C., reproduction
number LC-USW3-
030278-D.

she is trying to please—white patrons, reviewers, readers? She and Wright took diametrically different approaches to the matter of race in America: all writing to Wright, in some measure, was protest, but to Hurston it seemed largely celebratory—a celebration of the richness of black culture, of "how it feels [as she writes] to be colored me."

Wright and Hurston were hardly the only southerners departing from the Agrarian ideal of "southern" in the 1930s and 1940s; the white South, too, at least in terms of literature, was not as monolithic as it might sometimes seem. Lillian Smith of Georgia was the boldest, most outspoken of white southerners on the matter of race in the first half of the century. In her novel *Strange Fruit* (1944) and her autobiographical work of social commentary *Killers of the Dream* (1949) she probed the depths of the white southern psyche, tying together race and sexuality as few if any of her contemporaries would. For a time Smith edited a revolutionary southern magazine, *South Today*, for which she enlisted as a contributor W. J. Cash of North Carolina, another white southerner who departed (though not so fully as Smith) from

Zora Neale Hurston,
between 1925 and 1943.
Library of Congress,
Prints & Photographs
Division, Washington,
D.C., reproduction
number
LC-USZ62-62394.

the Agrarian ideal of the South and who, like Smith, felt the Agrarians' scorn. Cash's sole book, *The Mind of the South* (1941), is rightly adjudged by contemporary historians to have many flaws and limitations: it focuses on the Carolina textile belt to the exclusion of the Deep South, the Protestant upper South rather than the Catholic Gulf Coast, and the white male southerner to the exclusion of women and African Americans (except as women and African Americans affect the white male). Further, the author sets forth not so much the South's "mind" as its temper. Nonetheless, Cash's book is still, more than six decades after its publication, perhaps the best guide to the world of the plain white southerner and it is written with a flourish that is the literary equivalent of a Confederate cavalry charge. Appearing the same year as Cash's masterpiece was James Agee's *Let Us Now Praise Famous Men*, another semiautobiographical work that attempts to understand the plain white—or in Agee's case, the poor white—southerner. Descended from humble Tennessee roots on one side, a more prominent family on the other, educated at Harvard, and making his living in New York, Agee had written *Famous Men* after he returned south to write an article on sharecropping and sharecroppers for *Fortune*. What resulted was instead a lengthy book, a tour de force, part poetry, part sociology, in which Agee, sometimes self-indulgently, tries to identify with the subjects.

The 1940s, in fact, was a golden age for southern autobiography—in addition to Agee's work and Hurston's, Wright's, and Lillian Smith's autobiographies, there was also William Alexander Percy's *Lanterns on the Levee* (published the same year as Cash's book, and by the same publisher, Knopf, but as different in its interpretation of the South, particularly in regard to class, as it could be), Ben Robertson's unsung classic about the South Carolina up-country, *Red Hills and Cotton* (1942), and Katharine Du Pre Lumpkin's *The Making of a Southerner* (1947), another racial conversion narrative similar to Smith's. Despite the quality of these works, autobiography until recently was the neglected (which is to say, uncanonized) child of southern literature, although that situation is finally changing.

It is often taken as a tenet of revisionist southern literary history that women writers were excluded from the twentieth-century southern canon; in fact, only certain categories of women—most notably African Americans but also iconoclasts such as Lillian Smith—were excluded. Such writers as Eudora Welty, Katherine Anne Porter, Flannery O'Connor, and Caroline Gordon— all apparent cultural conservatives, several of whom had close ties to the Agrarians—have in fact been fixtures in the southern canon for some time. In the cases of those who *were* included, however, as Patricia Yaeger has demonstrated in her groundbreaking study *Dirt and Desire* (2000), they were often read in the wrong way—which is to say, were not always read fully for what lay beneath their often smooth surfaces—and thus (with the exception of O'Connor) were often seen as chroniclers of a largely conventional southern life, very much within a southern genteel tradition. Welty, second only to Faulkner perhaps as the most celebrated of twentieth-century southern fiction writers, is a case in point. The author of that apparent plantation idyll *Delta Wedding* (1946) as well as a number of other novels and stories often labeled comic, Welty is generally assumed to be an apolitical writer, one who depicts southern life—usually white, middle-class life—as she finds it, without challenging in any serious way the southern status quo. One might find a few quirky characters in her fictional world, but in general her fiction has been taken to represent a sort of charming, if sometimes eccentric, normalcy. On the contrary, Yaeger contends, Welty's work is "freak-obsessed and fiercely disturbing," and Yaeger draws from several Welty stories to prove her point. As far as Welty's alleged apolitical stance goes, one might say that *overt* political statement violates her fictional creed (as set out in her famous essay "Must the Writer Crusade?"). But in fact, Harriet Pollack and Suzanne Marrs suggest in their recent book, *Eudora Welty and Politics: Did the Writer Crusade?*, the extent to which much of Welty's fiction—and not only the rare racially charged, topical story such as "Where Is the Voice Coming From?" but much other work as well—includes incisive, if often sly, social commentary on her own time and place. She did not crusade, but she was very much aware of the inequities of race and gender in the world around her.

Certain other southern women writers have always been described as producers of loaded fiction. Both O'Connor and Carson McCullers have long been labeled practitioners of southern Gothic, portraying a haunted, backward South and populating their fictional worlds with a multitude of lonely, driven figures—those whom Sherwood Anderson, in his earlier work of midwestern gothic, *Winesburg, Ohio*, would have called "grotesques." O'Connor's depiction of benighted backwoods southerners, however, was usually in the larger service of an essentially conservative theological agenda: she believed modern readers, spiritually blind and complacent, needed to be shocked into an awareness of the sinfulness of the contemporary world. She was one of a number of Catholic writers—Caroline Gordon, Allen Tate, and Walker Percy (all through conversion) were others—who trained their eyes on an overwhelmingly Protestant South.

But the rural, traditional Dixie of O'Connor, Gordon, and Tate, not to mention Faulkner, Warren, and Welty, was not the South one increasingly witnessed as the southern states entered the last third of the twentieth century and attempted a metamorphosis from the old benighted Dixie into the Sun Belt. That transition hardly came easily. In many ways, in fact, the decade of the 1960s might be seen as pivotal in southern life and letters in much the same way the 1920s had been: it was a time of great intellectual ferment, of notable attention from without, of great social change. The sites this time were not Dayton, Tennessee, and a series of southern textile towns but rather Birmingham and Selma and Philadelphia, Mississippi. The effect, however, was the same: southern barbarities were exposed, traditions and customs were challenged, the South changed, a watershed in southern thought resulted— and, in some ways, a new literature emerged. The new set of assumptions had something to do with the fact that after the 1960s it appeared that the South had endured its crisis, had triumphed over itself, had in fact come through. According to its self-congratulators, the South had thrown off the old albatross of racism, and with that gone, it was no longer what it had long been: defeated, poor, guilt ridden, backward looking. So said its public relations advocates, in any case. What that change in perception did to southern writers—white writers, at least—is intriguing: Faulkner and the most prominent writers of the Southern Renaissance had written with the assumption that the South *was* the defeated, guilt-ridden, backward-looking, even tragic part of the United States. It was spectacle, almost too much to comprehend—"better than *Ben Hur*," as Faulkner's Shreve says in *Absalom, Absalom!* Much of the power of their fiction came from that assumption. What was the new southern chronicler of a land labeled, blandly, the Sun Belt to do with what was touted as a suddenly superior South—optimistic, forward looking, more virtuous, and now threatening to become more prosperous than the rest of the country? (Never mind that image did not always reflect reality.) Success would require a new voice—and less reliance on the models of the past.

But that voice did not emerge all at once, was in fact rarely heard before the 1970s. Many writers of the sixties, it seems to me, still found themselves in the shadow of Faulkner. William Styron, one of the most significant southern writers of the past half century, could not seem to escape, perhaps did not want to escape, the influence of Faulkner and Thomas Wolfe. Louis D. Rubin Jr. and others have pointed out the many resemblances, structural, stylistic, and thematic, between Styron's first novel *Lie Down in Darkness* (1951) and *The Sound and the Fury* (1929). *The Confessions of Nat Turner* (1967)—in part its construction but even more its subject, the racial burden of southern history—had to remind Styron's readers of Faulkner's world as well. Other writers of the 1960s—Reynolds Price and his first novel, *A Long and Happy Life* (1962), come to mind—were also obviously conscious of Faulkner. And not only in the realm of fiction. Numerous real-life Quentin Compsons emerged, most prominently Willie Morris, another cerebral Mississippian who left home for the urban Northeast, agonizing over a love-hate relationship with his homeland.

Ralph Ellison, arguably southern (if not by virtue of birth, in Oklahoma, then by ancestry and a formative college experience at Tuskegee), also dealt with the burden of race in his 1952 classic *Invisible Man*, but his treatment, by necessity, was vastly different from that of Faulkner and his white contemporaries. The relationship of the African American writer to the South is too complex a topic to investigate fully here, or even the relationship of the black writer to the southern literary canon: having been excluded from it for so long, it would be understandable if the black writer now hardly *wanted* inclusion in it. Yet Ellison, in many ways, saw himself as indisputably southern, and the mark of the South—from segregation to yams—is all over *Invisible Man*. In the realm of African American letters, in which the anxiety of influence is fully as pervasive as in the white literary community, Ellison would seem in many respects to have more in common with Zora Neale Hurston than with Richard Wright, the African American writer whose mantle he is often thought to have inherited. Like Hurston, Ellison immersed himself in the black folk culture; like Hurston, he had no desire to write protest fiction as such. In *Invisible Man*, however, he produced something of an amalgam—one of the two or three most significant American novels of the latter half of the twentieth century and a novel that transcends race, but also a work that has become, despite itself, an eloquent social document.

If most southern writers of the fifties and sixties, white and black, could not escape race—how could they, given its centrality in their world?—and could not escape the southern past, one among them did immerse himself in the present, became in fact a sort of protochronicler of the Sun Belt. At first, Walker Percy would seem to have had more reason than most to look backward. He had grown up partly in the Greenville, Mississippi, home of his kinsman William Alexander Percy, author of that most nostalgic of southern memoirs, *Lanterns on the Levee*. The Percys of Mississippi—for more than a century, powerful, cultivated, possessed of the habit of command, the closest one came to true aristocrats in a land of fraudulent ones—were in many respects right out of Faulkner's fictional world. But Will Percy had sent Walker out of the Deep South for his education—to Chapel Hill, that center of southern progressivism abhorred by the Agrarians, and then to New York for medical training—and the younger Percy, who had more reason than most to be burdened, in fact seemed far less burdened by southern history than most of his contemporaries. Indeed, his early novels, *The Moviegoer* (1961) and *The Last Gentleman* (1967), played lightly with the idea of southerness, satirizing it or at least satirizing the seriousness with which others took it (all the while, in certain dark moments of *The Last Gentleman*, being unable to escape it himself). Setting his fiction in what was then the newest of New Souths—suburbs, golf courses, country clubs—Percy looked ahead, and subsequent writers such as Barry Hannah, Richard Ford (at least in *The Sportswriter*), Josephine Humphreys, and Padgett Powell demonstrate his influence, whether they acknowledge it or not. Indeed, if there has been any shadow cast over southern fiction for the past three decades, it is not the shadow of Faulkner but rather that of Percy (along with, perhaps, Welty and O'Connor), and that influence has seemed in general a more benign one.

The world of contemporary southern fiction is too multifaceted to explore here in any detail, and I will make only a brief foray into the great debate, "Is there anything southern left about southern fiction?" One answer that has been given to that question is "yes," and that something is said to be "voice." That is true of the writing of a number of present southern writers: certainly, the fiction of Lee Smith, Clyde Edgerton, Jill McCorkle, and Kaye Gibbons, among other writers, is distinguished by a distinctive voice that can still be called "southern." But the same answer hardly applies for a number of other southern writers, white and black. Barry Hannah has a distinctive southern voice—irreverent, a little bizarre—that is very different from any of the writers mentioned above. So does Josephine Humphreys, and so do Ernest Gaines and Fred Chappell. Richard Ford (more than any writer I know) has a number of voices: the narrative voice of his first novel, *A Piece of My Heart* (1976), is vastly different from that of *The Sportswriter* (1986), which in turn differs from the voices of his collection of stories, *Rock Springs* (1987).

What is certain is that the old verities—or what the Agrarians took to be the verities—of southern writing have broken down: a sense of place and community, an overwhelming awareness of the past in the present, a deeper religious sense, a preference for the concrete over the abstract, and so forth. In fact, those qualities never were as absolutely southern as their proponents suggested: Vermonters had as deep a devotion to place as Mississippians, and the spirit of community was at least as deeply felt in a Connecticut village as in a Georgia one. (Indeed, the value of community should be reevaluated in any case: that organic spirit that embraces can also exclude, that quality that ensures a sense of place can also keep people *in* their places.) The much vaunted southern rage against abstraction might be the greatest myth of all: there was no greater abstraction than the antebellum South's commitment to "states' rights," not to mention a devotion to honor and chivalry and to the *idea*—though often not the reality—of woman. And what more monstrous abstraction than segregation, the classification of human beings by race—by color even in those cases in which there was really little or no difference in color.

If contemporary writers have moved beyond those assumptions about the southern mind and temper, that is altogether for the best—although one cannot say, in all cases, they have absolutely moved beyond them. Rather, in many instances, postmodern southern writers remark on those assumptions in a distinctly postmodern way. Bobbie Ann Mason, for example, is as postmodern in her worldview as one can be. She values popular culture fully as much as high culture, and she has no high regard for the eminence of family or the glory of "Southern History" (which generally meant the Civil War and its century-long aftermath, the racial burden of the southern past) or traditional ideas about place. Yet, in her finest novel, *In Country* (1985),

Mason is keenly aware of place, although place to her is more real in a series of interchangeable Howard Johnson motel rooms than on an ancestral family farm. Similarly, "community," even "family," can be constituted by those who watch, each week at the same time, the same television program—or who, every night, watch Johnny Carson. And Mason's protagonist, Sam Hughes, is very much aware of "the war," its casualties and its legacy, except the war in this case is Vietnam, and the dead include her own father. The burden of history is at least as great; it is just that the source of pain lies a decade, not a century, in the past. Mason is very much aware that she is playing off those stock southern assumptions and themes.

So is Richard Ford in *The Sportswriter*, a work set principally in New Jersey that would seem to have nothing to do with the South. But the continued insistence of Ford's southern expatriate protagonist Frank Bascombe that he has no interest in place and history and ancestral family suggests that he can't get these things off his mind. "Does it seem strange that I do not have a long and storied family history? . . . Or a list of problems and hatreds to brood about?" he asks at one point. "Whose history can ever reveal very much?" he asks elsewhere. Near the end of the novel he visits some newly discovered relatives in a south Florida stucco bungalow, and reflects:

> And truthfully, when I drive back up Highway 24 just as the light is falling beyond my condo, behind its wide avenue of date palms and lampposts, I am usually (if only momentarily) glad to have a past, even an imputed and remote one. . . . There is something to that. It is not a burden, though I've always thought of it as one. I cannot say that we all need a past in full literary fashion, or that one is much useful in the end. But a small one doesn't hurt.

Frank Bascombe, then—and more to the point his creator, Ford—is very much aware of those pasts in "full literary fashion," the "burden" of such pasts, and of proud, storied families such as Faulkner's Compsons. He expresses affection for his newly found cousin, "the salt of the earth," but all the while Ford is parodying, very skillfully, the high Faulknerian sense of past and family. (Frank's cousin bears the name of Buster Bascombe: a long way from the high-sounding Jason Lycurgus and Quentin Maclachan Compson of Faulkner's fictional world—who were anything but "salt of the earth.") He must have known that Bascomb was the family name of Quentin Compson's mother; a reader of Faulkner, he surely knew that *The Sound and the Fury*, like his own novel, takes place on Easter weekend, and that the two novels have other similarities. But unlike Styron in *Lie Down in Darkness*, Ford isn't duplicating Faulkner—he is having fun with him.

The subject of race is hardly absent from Ford's fiction either—Frank Bascombe rents a room to "a six-foot-five-inch Negro," an African seminary student who lives in his attic and in whose presence he feels a certain reassurance—but race is not predominant, as it also is not in most other contemporary southern fiction, at least that written by whites. African American writers, both those such as Ernest Gaines and Alice Walker who came of age in the 1940s and 1950s and those who are much younger, can hardly avoid the subject, and for good reason: they *know* that the South, and the nation, is a long way from having fully come up from racism. A more compelling theme among many white southern writers over the past decade or two has been class—or, in some cases, that treacherous intersection of class *and* race. Southerners from William Byrd through the nineteenth century Southwest Humorists and on to Faulkner and Erskine Caldwell have always been interested in social class, but in most cases before the late twentieth century and beyond, at least among white writers, southerners of privilege presumed to speak *for* southern poor whites. What is different in the past fifteen or twenty years is that many southerners of what generally would have been called poor backgrounds—Tim McLaurin, Dorothy Allison, Larry Brown, and Rick Bragg among others (and Harry Crews before any of them)—have begun to speak for themselves, in memoirs as well as in fiction.

To speak of "southern literature" in the traditional sense is especially difficult at the outset of the twenty-first century, simply because "the South" itself is such a fluid and amorphous construct. Multiculturalism is more than theory with respect to the contemporary South: the old black-white binary that had defined both southern life and southern literature has broken down and other shades, cultures, and traditions must be figured in. As the contributors to *South to the Future* (2002) point out, southern writers now depict Vietnamese in Louisiana, Puerto Ricans in Georgia, Latinos and Latinas in south Florida, and Hispanic farmworkers in North Carolina. And many of the finest contemporary scholars, when they consider what was once Dixie, now consider it not in relation to "the North," focusing on its differences, but rather see it in relation to Central and South America and to the Caribbean, cultures with which it has always had many historical and economic parallels, not the least of which is the legacy of slavery. Southern literature is hardly the same as it was because the South is hardly the same, but I do not expect for that reason to see any diminishment in the writing produced by the inhabitants, old and new, of that geographical region between—in Mencken's words—the Potomac mudflats and the Gulf. If anything, the resulting product will be richer and more varied, and that cannot but be for the best.

Suggested Readings

Andrews, William L., ed. *Literature of the American South: A Norton Anthology*. New York: W. W. Norton, 1998.

Hobson, Fred. *But Now I See: The White Southern Racial Conversion Narrative*. Baton Rouge: Louisiana State University Press, 1999.

———. *Tell about the South: The Southern Rage to Explain*. Baton Rouge: Louisiana State University Press, 1983.

Jenkins, McKay. *The South in Black and White: Race, Sex, and Literature in the 1940s*. Chapel Hill: University of North Carolina Press, 1999.

O'Brien, Michael. *The Idea of the American South, 1920–1941*. Baltimore: Johns Hopkins University Press, 1979.

Rubin, Louis D., Jr. *Writers of the Modern South: The Faraway Country*. Seattle: University of Washington Press, 1996.

Simpson, Lewis P. *The Fable of the Southern Writer*. Baton Rouge: Louisiana State University Press, 1994.

Wyatt-Brown, Bertram. *The Literary Percys: Family History, Gender, and the Southern Imagination*. Athens: University of Georgia Press, 1994.

Yaeger, Patricia. *Dirt and Desire: Reconstructing Southern Women's Writing, 1939–1990*. Chicago: University of Chicago Press, 2000.

DAVID STRICKLIN

Singing Songs about the Southland

Reaching across Lines Meant to Keep People Apart

During the Academy Awards ceremony back in the spring of 2003, a year when the musical *Chicago* garnered numerous Oscars, including Best Picture, many of the figures who worked on the film thanked various people who had helped make it possible. No one, however, bothered to thank some important people who helped make the story itself possible, the people who built the roadbeds north, such as the one that became the famous U.S. Highway 61 and the Illinois Central Railroad. There would be no story to tell today because there would not have been jazz in Chicago if it had not been for the migration to that city of vast numbers of African Americans from the South. Some went up the Mississippi River, and jazz spread to St. Louis and Davenport, Iowa, and other places likely and unlikely because of the great inland river-highway.

But most went overland, and most of the most important ones in jazz history, sooner or later, ended up in Chicago.

Chicago acted as a great magnet for black southerners, people seeking a new start, a better climate of race relations, just possibly, a chance to get out from under the debts and the threats. They went up Highway 61 from New Orleans, through the Mississippi Delta, through Memphis, on through such towns as Davenport, the home of jazz legend Bix Beiderbecke, a town that has not only the Mississippi River but also Highway 61. Partly on that storied road and partly on the IC Railroad and other routes, they made it northward, up to Chicago.

They made it to countless other places as well, either in person or symbolically, as their music not only reached the North but the rest of the United States and much of the rest of the world. They made it also in many of the ways refugees make the hard trip to strange lands of promise, fleeing trouble, seeking hope, taking what they could of their culture and imagining, even en route, ways they might transplant parts of that culture to their new homes. Think of that famous scene in the 1949 movie *The Third Man*, in which Harry Lime, the Orson Welles character, comparing unfavorably, and perhaps unfairly, Italy under the Borgias, with its chaos, intrigue, and violence, to Switzerland with its peace and tranquility, points out how the Swiss managed to produce one thing with all that calm, the cuckoo clock, and how in the midst of all that mayhem the Italians created the Renaissance. In a way, the twentieth-century South was like Italy under the Borgias, at least with regard to music. Music in the South during this time is an exemplar of that historical phenomenon wherein the most turbulent times often produce the most creative artistic expression.

In the first third of the century, African Americans were threatened continually by lynching, tenant farmers both black and white were mired in debt peonage, and religious/cultural intolerance and uneasiness were expressed in Klan activity, fundamentalism, and xenophobia. In the first decades of the century, however, southerners created or continued to develop ragtime, blues, jazz, hillbilly music, and swing. In the middle third of the century, they groaned under the burden of the Great Depression in peculiar regional ways, absorbed the amazing changes wrought by World War II, and underwent the transformative experiences of the civil rights era. At the same time, southerners played a central role in further realizing the possibilities of swing music, created its spin-off, western swing, and contributed mightily to the creation of bebop, bluegrass, country and western, rhythm and blues, rock 'n' roll, soul, and a large part of the music of the urban folk revival. In the last third of the century, as they went through the worst years of the United States' involvement in Vietnam, the loss of national confidence in the wake of that conflict and the Watergate mess, and the amazing return of the South to political prominence on the national stage, southerners participated in the full realization of country music, rock, pop, disco, punk, and even rap.

That the terms change with each passing segment of the twentieth century—"southerners . . . created," then "played central roles in creating," then "participated in the full realization of"—suggests another central fact about southern music. As the century wore on, more and more people from other parts of the country, other parts of the world, became cocreators of music with southern roots, which meant that they became cocreators of the music of the United States. Southerners did not disappear from the process; they just got a great many cocreators from other places. In this way, as well as in others, southern music essentially became during the twentieth century the music of the United States, just as, at the same time, the South became somewhat more like the rest of the country and the country became a great deal more like the South, changes brought about in part because of music. In a land where change and continuity vied throughout the century, therefore, southern music both reflected events and helped bring them to pass, in some typical and some surprising ways.

For one thing, as southerners became more affluent, they were able to pay for the music they wanted to hear and the equipment necessary to play it. And the styles of music they bought varied widely. In the early part of the century, phonograph machines were extremely popular. Early-day record players were the size of small refrigerators today. The machines were most often sold in furniture stores, which also sold the records to play on them. Because of the novelty of recordings and the fact that at the time marketing was still fairly undeveloped, people bought quite a variety of music styles. The vast popularity of Enrico Caruso in the big cities, for instance, meant that stores carried his records in towns where people had never heard opera or Caruso, for that matter. But they bought the records anyway, even if the music sounded funny to them, because it was something to listen to. These same people bought recordings of John Philip Sousa, perhaps because the town band played his marches.

Just a few years earlier, at the close of the nineteenth century and start of the twentieth, having a piano was something of a social requirement for just about any respectable family that could afford one, and increasing numbers of southern families were able to do just that. When phonograph recordings became available, many southerners bought recordings of Gene Austin, for instance, because they had copies of the sheet music of his sentimental love songs on the piano in their parlors. But some of them also bought the Carter Family and Jimmie Rodgers and learned that there was a new phenomenon out there, commercially recorded "old-time" music, some of which fed the stream that became country music, and that performers were getting paid, presumably, to sing songs like those that listeners had sung around the house for generations, sometimes the very same songs. They bought Mamie Smith and W. C. Handy and learned that many different kinds of music they might have heard or sung around town were being recorded and marketed, even if they had no idea that people were starting to call some of that music "blues" and that the recordings were part of a new wave of marketing called "race" music.

Southern music also preserved many attributes of southern culture, from its deep embrace of the folk forces that shaped common life in the South to the powerful truth that the largely biracial South was always a region of borrowing across the lines that supposedly separated the two ethnic groups that made up most of its population. "Separate" was never "equal," of course, in political, economic, or social terms, but in musical terms "separate" was essentially irrelevant. There is a special significance to the fact that during the 1920s and 1930s, the "father" of country music, Jimmie Rodgers, was famous for his stylized blues tunes known as "blue yodels." And in the 1950s and 1960s, at least, the "king" of rock 'n' roll, Elvis Presley, was also known for combining musical influences from the white and black communities. His first hit record, "That's All Right, Mama," was a cover of a song by an African American artist, Arthur "Big Boy" Cruddup, and had on its flip side a cover of "Blue Moon of Kentucky," a tune by the "father" of bluegrass, Bill Monroe. Bluegrass was supposedly one of the "whitest" forms of music, but if one actually listened to the "blue" notes in its instrumental solos, the phrasing of many of its vocals, and the lyrics of many of its songs, one realized the debt bluegrass owed to blues. Western swing, with the cowboy dress of many of its performers as well as its cowboy imagery, was grounded in a love for the blues that burned within its greatest purveyor, Bob Wills, who grew up playing fiddle in string bands at ranch dances in west Texas but who idolized the great blues singer Bessie Smith. Wills's own musical contributions to the work of his band, the Texas Playboys, featured high-pitched vocals in which he tried to imitate Smith and the "breakdown" fiddling of Anglo-Celtic folk musicians whose tunes many members of his family played and taught him as a young boy as well as fiddling that evoked the blues.

Countless southerners both famous and unknown had similar experiences in the twentieth century. They played and sang music that came out of their own folk traditions. But they blended it with traditions of people often very different from themselves. They borrowed what they liked, what worked artistically, creatively, without regard for the cultural symbolism, political suitability, or social conventions that usually prevented people from reaching across lines intended to divide them.

Such borrowing put the lie to one part of what many people intended to be the permanent separateness of black and white southerners and occurred across more than just ethnic lines within the nation. Southern musicians drew from the jazz performed by the great Belgian gypsy guitarist Django Reinhardt and his French violinist partner, Stephane Grappelly, just as Reinhardt and Grappelly drew from the recordings of the U.S. jazz and blues artists of the 1920s, 1930s, and 1940s. Borrowing continued across the decades as well, evidenced by the British invasion of the 1960s, whereby white middle-class musicians from the United Kingdom "gave" young Americans blues music they had lost track of or, more likely, had never heard of in the first place. American youth were not necessarily shamed by the fact that Keith Richards of the Rolling Stones knew more about John Lee Hooker and Howlin' Wolf than they did, but many of them bought the records of the great Mississippi Delta blues artists and others because of the Stones, who had taken their name from a blues tune. Many of them discovered Robert Johnson because of another English artist, Eric Clapton, whose signal realization as a young boy was the painful fact that he could never be a black blues musician in the southern United States. His recasting of Johnson's "Crossroads Blues" with his group Cream, a live performance of which can be found on the 1968 album *Wheels of Fire*, with its searing guitar solos, driving rhythm provided by Jack Bruce and Ginger Baker, and biting vocals by Clapton wrapped the tension and urgency of the times in Johnson's haunting depiction of the seemingly simple, yet potentially dangerous events associated with a particular crossroads.

Probably no one at the time asked, and likely few have since either, what some English guy was doing reinterpreting the legendary Johnson. Most people who heard the recording thought it was just a good rock song or, if they thought a little more deeply, that it showed the logical transition from blues to rock. Possibly a little more deeply than that, some might have realized that it represented the power of blues and rock to speak across insidious dividing lines and yank out of people's hearts the things they have in common, especially the hopes and fears that bespeak their deepest humanity. In the 1991 film adaptation of Roddy Doyle's fine novel *The Commitments*, the first of his trilogy set in the disadvantaged Barrytown section of Dublin, one of the characters is musing about the apparent anomaly of a soul band from Ireland. His explanation is that the Irish are the blacks of Europe, Dubliners are the

blacks of Ireland, and the people of Barrytown are the blacks of Dublin, and thus the idea of an Irish soul band from Ireland makes perfect sense. The harsh and often perilous life experiences, the indomitable and often generous spirit with which they met those experiences, and the richly evocative ways they expressed that spirit gave the music of southern African Americans a worldwide appeal, partly because it spoke to the timeless truths of people who suffer, who triumph, hurt, survive, weep, and rejoice, whether they live in Ireland or in Alabama.

Musical borrowing on an international scale went beyond the bounds of English-speaking nations, though, as rock groups sprang up in Japan and bluegrass bands appeared in Austria. There is a great story about the internationalization of southern music concerning the Viennese bluegrass group that found it necessary for a long while to carry a set of drums around with them. No club owner in Austria could imagine a band without drums, which, of course, are nonexistent in orthodox bluegrass. Setting up drums on the stage of a bluegrass festival in the United States would be about as good an idea as inviting a voodoo priestess to deliver the principal sermon at the annual Southern Baptist convention. But in Austria, a vernacular musical group had to have drums, so the band would set them up, apologize to the club owner and the understanding club patrons that their poor drummer was sick, offer to try to struggle on without the drums, and then tear into "Foggy Mountain Breakdown" or some other such (drum-free) bluegrass standard. As the story goes, the fans always went wild, of course, because of the power and appeal of the southern-based music. Back home, the fact that the highest quality bluegrass was performed at the end of the twentieth century by Union Station, a group led by Illinois native Alison Krauss and featuring lead singer Dan Tyminski, a native of Vermont, bothered fans not at all.

Southern music also showed how other kinds of boundaries could be crossed. While "old-time" music kept alive the attributes and yearnings of low-income rural white southerners, especially those in the upland South (people who were often thought of as culturally and socially conservative), old-time music also captivated political progressives, including many academics. Some of the better-known academics who collected old-time southern (white folk) music had no overt political reasons for doing so. Such was the case with the nineteenth-century Harvard musicologist Francis James Child, who lent his name to the famous categorization of more than three hundred British ballads he collected mainly in the Appalachian Mountains. Twentieth-century collectors followed in his footsteps, some hoping to find links to the European past, some hoping to make a name for themselves, some simply hoping to preserve something precious in the face of possible extinction through urbanization, mobility, and social fragmentation. They often found what they were looking for, namely, people who knew some old songs who would sit down with the collectors and set about singing as many tunes as they could. To find these people, the collectors—most notably the Lomax family who scoured the South, Vance Randolph the Ozarks, and John Quincy Wolf Arkansas, Tennessee, and Mississippi—tramped the hills and hollers, looking and listening for old music and new variations on it. In these ways, scholars and "plain folk" came together through the music of the South, though not always for the best of reasons.

Some of the people who loved the Child ballads and the other songs these cultural scouts heard, transcribed onto paper, and recorded on disks thought of the music as a window onto a simple time, saw it as hearkening back to what they saw as the nobility of Elizabethan England. Indeed, the Child ballads fairly drip with archaic vocabulary and syntax and British stories, place names, and historic personages. For instance, more than two dozen of them deal with the Robin Hood story. No one denies that these song-stories were present in the subculture of white, rural southerners of modest means. But for political and other reasons, some collectors and promoters of folk music tried to use that fact in the twentieth century for ill. Some had high intentions organized around the notion of "uplift," such as the rural southern equivalents of the northern urban settlement-house movement, most famously exhibited in Chicago by Jane Addams and Hull House and replicated in the South by settlement schools in rural, especially upland, areas. Settlement workers tried to use folk music to give poor mountain folk a point of pride and broaden their horizons by giving them forums where they could perform their music and help lift themselves out of backwardness.

Unfortunately, some of the well-to-do twentieth-century patrons and promoters of such events wanted to use the music, and its supposed links to a golden past of "pure" Anglo-Saxon ethnicity, to highlight what they perceived as the need to prevent racial intermarriage and other practices they saw as banes of modern life. They viewed the communities in which the old songs persisted as islands of pure British culture where something priceless had been transported intact from the misty past, and quick-frozen at the time of Shakespeare. The music had been kept alive, virtually unaltered, by the happy accident that the people who sang the songs were too poor to go anywhere else and too isolated and backward to attract any outsiders to marry. The fact that these elites needed to view southern folk music as pristine said much more about them than it did about the music or the musicians, but it did not deter or inhibit their heavy-handedness, or what one would have to call racism. They exhibited their patronizing attitude toward the people who had kept the music alive for generations in part by telling them that it was fine to broaden their horizons but that they should entertain no ideas of changing their social setting. Helping mountain folks escape poverty, either by getting them out of the uplands or by upgrading the economy of the area, was not a worthy enough outcome to the elite promoters to risk upsetting the pristine setting of the music. They needed to keep alive the romantic hope that white values could prevail over the social upheaval and race mixing that they imagined was ruining the South and the United States as much as they needed to keep alive the ballads of Bonny Barbara Allen and Sir Patrick Spens.

As David Whisnant shows in his brilliant book *All That Is Native and Fine: The Politics of Culture in an American Region*, these "cultural interventionists" accomplished many good things by making the broader public aware of southern folk music, but everything they did was colored by a simplistic, paternalistic, racist viewpoint that corrupted the very thing they were trying to preserve. That the people most closely identified with this behavior, John Powell and Annabel Morris Buchanan, founded an annual Virginia mountain festival in 1931 and named it "White Top" said as much about their methods and their mentality as it did about local place names.

Vast numbers of people who listened to the old-time white music saw matters differently. They overlooked the presumed backwardness and racism of some of the performers. They celebrated the ways the music spoke to the trials and dreams of poor whites in much the same manner that blues did for southern African Americans. They even heard the potential for social protest in some of the tunes. In these ways, going against the tendency of some romanticizers of bygone and supposed white southern ethnic purity, some mostly northern academics and progressives imposed their own agendas on old-time music, exhibiting a patronizing attitude that was just as insensitive as that of the people who wanted to use the music to celebrate white supremacy. But many nonsouthern progressives—Pete Seeger is the most famous example—befriended southern performers, played and sang their music, made some of them famous and some of them a little more affluent, gave their art to the world, and showed how it called forth the tribulations and the hopefulness of the southern people who created and sustained the music. Though it could hardly be said that all of them had progressive views, one of the manifestations of this phenomenon was the preponderance of amateur bluegrass bands that sprang up around the country whose membership was composed of college professors.

Southerners exhibited another trend that characterized much of vernacular culture during the twentieth century, the rising importance of mass communications media in spreading musical styles. This was especially important before marketing systems made recordings widely available and before phonograph machines were cheap enough for many people. Though folklore purists insisted that only direct, person-to-person, word-of-mouth transmission of folk music was worthy of the term, the "folk" thought otherwise. Common singers and players who did not know or care that scholars denied the authenticity of their music sang and played music they learned from records and radio broadcasts anyway. Thus, radio and other mass media became elements in the "folk" process. People who could never imagine actually setting foot in the front door of a fancy hotel could listen to the great swing bands, broadcasting live just about any Saturday night from the glamorous ballrooms of the most famous hotels of the day, including some in southern cities, such as the Roosevelt Hotel in New Orleans. Even though swing made up most of the live music on the nighttime feeds, listeners learned a bit about jazz from those broadcasts. The bands played jazzy arrangements of swing tunes, which had in any case grown out of jazz, and announcers spoke of jazz traditions and the great musicians of the South.

Powerful clear-channel stations broadcast all over North America, including the famous WSM-Nashville with its Grand Ole Opry, the equally famous WLS-Chicago with its National Barn Dance, and the "X-stations" operating just out of reach of U.S. law on the Mexican side of the Texas border through which vast numbers of people became familiar with the Carter Family. Many fans of old-time and country music who never got to hear Uncle Dave Macon or Roy Acuff in person or western swing fans who longed to go to a Bob Wills dance or mainstream swing fans who knew that most of the popular bands were northern-led but that many featured southern singers and instrumentalists felt that they knew these people because the artists visited their homes by means of radio. Among those listeners were countless would-be musicians who got ideas and inspiration from those broadcasts. Smaller radio stations made southerners aware of the growing presence of gospel music. Many well-known performers had a regular time in their broadcasts when they sang a daily or weekly "sacred number," but in the small-town radio stations of the South local church musicians regularly soothed the sin-sick and brightened otherwise dark days for numberless shut-ins, travelers, and inmates. Gospel-music performers, especially under the encouragement of Tennessee native James D. Vaughan, promoted appearances at local and regional revival meetings, told people where to buy records, and built a loyal fan base that made religious music in the South one of the biggest-selling genres in vernacular song.

In this way, radio created a new community. On the surface, it bore little resemblance to the old communities in which folk music and other traditions were passed down through the generations of people who knew and cared for each other. But, really, it was the same principle—an electronic mass medium brought the music of the nation, of the South, to the masses of people who never would have had a chance to hear it otherwise. Thus, in some surprising ways, the South became not only a seedbed of music for the modern United States but also for a cultural diversity that many people in the majority culture accepted musically before they accepted it in other areas of their lives. Not all of them followed the example of "Willie and Laura Mae Jones," a song about an interracial friendship by Louisiana native Tony Joe White on his tellingly titled 1968 album *Black and White*. But at least they had the example because many thousands of southerners bought the hit record.

This is not to suggest that all was sweetness and light in southern music in the twentieth century. At times defiant and aggressive, even belligerent, writers and performers of southern music asserted the desires of many in the region for independence (for example, in the song from which this chapter's title comes), ironically but perhaps not coincidentally, at the very time it was becoming more like the United States than ever before. Most of the most famous expressions of nonconformity with the century's changing social tides were pretty harmless, though some raised old concerns about the South's

The Grand Ole Opry House, Ryman Auditorium, 116 Fifth Avenue North, Nashville, Tennessee. Library of Congress, Prints & Photographs Division, HABS [or HAER], Washington, D.C., reproduction number HABS, TENN, 19 NASH, 20.

commitment to equality for African Americans. The Confederate/rebel imagery of several successful tunes suggested perhaps more a resistance to modern ways than a longing for the racial hierarchy of the Old South. Charlie Daniels had several hit songs that suggested such nonconformity, ranging from mild associations with marijuana usage, in "Uneasy Rider" and "Long-Haired Country Boy," to his celebration of southern music in "The South's Gonna Do It Again," which featured the refrain "be proud you're a rebel." Hank Williams Jr. had several songs that referred to the independence and uncompromising nature of southern and rural values and that made unflattering comparisons to urban/northern ways, most notably "A Country Boy Can Survive." In that song, the central character expresses a desire to shoot the murderer of his friend, and the song strongly suggests that the perpetrator of the deed was black. Daniels and Williams both employed Confederate flags in their marketing imagery but stopped short of open appeals to racist sentiments. Still, it was never possible to evoke Confederate symbolism without raising at least a little concern that the individuals evoking it were suggesting a return to the old days of southern race relations.

A defiant southern perspective that avoided sinking into overt support for returning to the pre–civil rights days came from Lynryd Skynyrd, especially in their hit "Sweet Home, Alabama," which offered at least ambivalent regard for prosegregation governor George Wallace and contempt for Neil Young, whose songs "Southern Man" and "Alabama" had criticized southern race relations, most pointedly in Wallace's home state. In the song, Lynryd Skynyrd paid tribute to the community of southern rock musicians, especially their penchant for "singing songs about the Southland," but clearly invited Young, and presumably other busybodies, to stay out of the affairs of southerners.

Singing songs about the Southland had been a preoccupation of performers from the time before the United States came into existence. The habit persisted and intensified during the nineteenth century, especially with the popularity of minstrelsy and its often grotesque caricatures of southern, especially African American, life. Songwriters in the New York City district known as Tin Pan Alley wrote often wildly romantic songs about the South, usually without the benefit of ever having visited the region. "That's the Good Old Sunny South" is a good example of such a tune, written by New Yorkers Jack Yellen and Milton Ager. Few southerners cared that some of their favorite songs about the South came from northern composers, perhaps because they exhibited more strongly than people from other regions of the United States the desire to hear and sing songs that mentioned their homeland.

Blues singers were some of the first and most numerous southerners to refer to the South in their songs, offering countless southern towns a measure of immortality by mentioning them. On practically any list of blues tunes, one will find place names abounding, from the "Memphis Blues" and "Yellow-Dog Blues" by W. C. Handy, the latter referring to a famous Mississippi Delta railroad line, to the "Deep Ellum Blues" by Blind Lemon Jefferson, referring to the nightlife district of East Dallas, to the "Statesboro Blues" written by Blind Willie McTell and recorded by various artists, black and white, including the Allman Brothers Band. Old-time country artists as well as modern-day country and western musicians added vast numbers of songs about, set in, or making reference to the South, from Jimmie Rodgers's "Blue Yodel Number 1" ("T for Texas, T for Tennessee") to Loretta Lynn's "Coal Miner's Daughter" to Ray Charles's "What'd I Say," with its oft-quoted reference to sending his sweetheart "back to Arkansas."

Many songwriters wrote about the experiences of transplanted southerners who left the South during the 1950s and 1960s to find work in northern industrial cities or California and wrote about the South in such tunes as Bobby Bare's hit, written by Mel Tillis and Danny Dill, "Detroit City." Merle Haggard, Buck Owens, and Dwight Yoakam spoke in numerous songs of the remarkable subculture of transplanted southerners in California dating to the Great Depression–era migration of Okies and Arkies. Urban blues and jazz musicians less often referred to place names of any sort, southern or otherwise, owing perhaps to the tendency of urban dwellers to be less conscious of their own sense of place, especially compared to sentimental rural lovers. Southerners who were forced to leave the old place, or even southern migrants who eagerly sought a chance to get away, often longed to hear about their old home. Such songs powerfully affected southern African American and white workers alike who pursued factory work and other more lucrative jobs outside the South from World War I until fairly long after World War II.

Another example of changes wrought in large part by music appeared as different kinds of southerners, including people who had considered each other beyond redemption, came to realize they liked much of the same music and started looking for ways to get along with each other. Some of this peacemaking had to do with the overall lessening of tensions after the turbulent 1960s and some with the fact that many white music lovers during the decade had been finding their way to R&B shows and revues for years and had expressed a deep love of soul music, helping make such artists as Sam and Dave and Otis Redding household names, helping to dissipate white racism. As post-1960s tensions abated, cross-racial musical popularity contributed to better relations among whites and African Americans in the South. But another kind of tension eased in the United States because of changes in southern music. It may seem somewhat trivial at first glance, but it was hardly that. It concerned relations between "longhairs" and "rednecks."

In the 1960s, country music was in a phase of serious devotion to Nashville's prescriptions for commercial success. The themes of country songs might be cheating, drinking, and fighting, but the decision makers and music producers in Nashville viewed themselves, and the music they produced, as being in touch with normal, God-fearing, hard-working America, especially its southern reaches. Partly because southerners had often served in military conflicts out of proportion to their numbers in overall U.S. society, southerners created many patriotic or prowar songs, tapping especially the old tradition of the "event song." Texan Johnny Horton excelled at this, making hits in 1959 of "The Battle of New Orleans" and in 1960 of "Sink the Bismarck," though Horton was not above altering history for commercial purposes. After "The Battle of New Orleans" was banned in Britain, for instance, he recorded a second version of the song for release there in which the British won the famous battle of January 8, 1815!

A few years later, most southerners found themselves supporting U.S. involvement in the war in Vietnam. Staff Sergeant Barry Sadler's quintessential pro–Vietnam War song, "The Ballad of the Green Berets," was not a country song per se, but the 1966 hit appeared on an album of country tunes he recorded and got an enormous amount of play on country stations. Merle Haggard's famous pair of songs "Okie from Muskogee" and "Fightin' Side of Me" expressed a message of support for patriotic values, which precluded burning one's draft card or defying authority figures such as college deans. Haggard's many fans were so busy buying his records that they didn't take the time to point out that he had had rocky relations with authority figures at various points in his life and that the body of his work included quite a few odes to misbehavior. At the time, though, Haggard's own appearance mirrored to a great extent the one whose virtues he extolled in "Okie from Muskogee," in which he says, "We don't let our hair grow long and shaggy, like the hippies out in San Francisco do."

As the 1960s gave way to the 1970s, country music fans became militant, to the point that various national newspaper and magazine articles referred to the dangers of country's prowar, progun, antifeminist, anti-intellectual ethos. Ironically, though, just about the time national observers were becoming aware that country music had a huge following, and not just in the South, its militancy toward longhairs and countercultural types softened, largely because of the appeal of a musical instrument, the electric guitar.

Scarcely a decade after Haggard recorded his famous lines about how a good, patriotic American male's hair ought to look, he had let his own hair grow and acquired quite a scruffy-looking beard. Furthermore, if one looked at the cover art on many country albums, one would find that beginning in the 1970s vast numbers of country stars looked indistinguishable from the rock stars they had formerly discounted. Some even began to confuse the categorizers, and sometimes the public, by appealing to people on both sides of the rock/country divide. Charlie Daniels's song "Uneasy Rider," for instance, borrowed its name from the iconic counterculture film that represented in graphic terms the hostility between longhairs and rednecks, yet the song exhibited a sense of humor about long hair, commies, and rednecks with green teeth that appealed to country and rock audiences alike. This was only possible because from the 1960s on bands from the Rolling Stones to the Flying Burrito Brothers to Crosby, Stills, Nash, and Young (yes, *that* Young!) combined country music motifs with rock-flavored instrumentals and vocals. Later, country musicians such as Dwight Yoakam, Garth Brooks, and Mary Chapin Carpenter used rock motifs and increasingly relied on rock-type guitar solos.

Indeed, the electric guitar's importance as a defining instrument came to be felt as much in country as it had in rock, in some ways more. Power-chord pyrotechnics and solos played at ear-splitting volumes came to dominate heavy metal bands in the 1970s. Punk rock began to rely on hitherto strange chord progressions, sound effects, and electronic instruments. Disco threatened the very foundations of western civilization, and not just because it scarcely had need of electric guitars. Someone who wanted to play rhythm and solos like those of Chuck Berry—not incidentally, an African American artist who drew heavily from country music styles to create his own—almost had to leave rock to find work. Many of those players did so by finding their way into country bands. If they had never played country music before, they certainly knew about the examples of Gram Parsons and Crosby, Stills, Nash, and Young— who himself recorded a solo number about his desire to get "Back to the Country" that probably galled some of his old southern critics but probably tickled as many of them who thought that southern/country values might have won over the Canadian expatriate hippie songwriter. (Heck, he isn't even an American, let alone a Yankee, and here he is doing something that sounds like country music!) When those guitarists got into country bands, they took their long hair with them. By 1990 a long-haired country star named Travis Tritt celebrated this transformation when he recorded a song commending country music's amalgamation with rock, "Put Some Drive in Your Country."

When African American R&B stylist Ray Charles recorded an album of country songs, and when white country star Willie Nelson recorded an album of pop standards, they were demonstrating what southern musicians literally made into an art form in the twentieth century. They reached across lines to create the music they wanted to perform because they knew it was music people wanted to hear. They might employ traditional southern themes and images, or they might create new ones that people came to associate with the South simply because the vernacular music of the United States was so deeply rooted in the South. Whether they or their many counterparts actually were singing songs about the Southland or not, they were speaking quite directly to some of the most powerful forces of the twentieth century, both in the South and in the United States.

Suggested Readings

Cantwell, Robert. *Bluegrass Breakdown: The Making of the Old Southern Sound.* Urbana: University of Illinois Press, 1984.

————. *When We Were Young: The Folk Revival.* Cambridge, Mass.: Harvard University Press, 1996.

Giddens, Gary. *Visions of Jazz: The First Century.* New York: Oxford University Press, 1993.

Goff, James. *Close Harmony: A History of Southern Gospel.* Chapel Hill: University of North Carolina Press, 2002.

Malone, Bill C. *Country Music, U.S.A.* Rev. ed. Austin: University of Texas Press, 2002.

Malone, Bill C., and David Stricklin. *Southern Music/American Music.* Rev. ed. Lexington: University Press of Kentucky, 2003.

Palmer, Robert. *Rock & Roll: An Unruly History.* New York: Harmony Books, 1995.

Shaw, Arnold. *The World of Soul.* New York: Paperback Library, 1971.

Southern, Eileen. *The Music of Black Americans: A History.* New York: W. W. Norton, 1971.

Titon, Jeff. *Early Downhome Blues: A Musical and Cultural Analysis.* Urbana: University of Illinois Press, 1977.

ANDREW DOYLE

On the Cusp of Modernity

The Southern Sporting World in
the Twentieth Century

At the turn of the twenty-first century, southern professional sports franchises
and intercollegiate programs are classed among the leaders in their fields.
Southern college football programs are perennially ranked among the best
in the nation, and the South is currently home to seven National Football
League franchises. The Atlanta Braves finally brought home a World Series
championship in 1995, and Tobacco Road in North Carolina is one of the most
prestigious addresses in the nation for both men's basketball and women's
soccer. To the consternation of hockey purists, there are as many National
Hockey League franchises in the former Confederacy as there are in Canada.
While NASCAR has transcended its southern roots, most of its fans, drivers,

and traditions are still southern. Backed by a fiery spirit of civic boosterism, a first-rate organizing committee, and an abundance of corporate money, Atlanta hosted the 1996 Olympics, the crown jewel of international athletic competition. Professional and big-time intercollegiate sports in the South are a fully integrated element of the global entertainment industry, wired by electronic media to consumers around the world.

Such a scenario would have been utterly unfathomable a century earlier. Even the most giddily optimistic of southern boosters would have been loath to predict such an embarrassment of riches. Mass-market spectator sports and the modern athletic ideology existed only in vestigial form in the South prior to 1900. The social, economic, and cultural conditions necessary for modern sporting competition simply did not exist in the South. Like all forms of commercial entertainment, professional sports (including big-time college sports) require the concentrated population, transportation nexus, and media network that are found only in cities. They also require consumers with sufficiently high levels of disposable income who are accustomed to purchasing entertainment in the marketplace.

The South lacked a critical mass of all of these elements prior to the 1890s. Also, relatively few southerners had adopted the social and cultural values that underpin the modern sporting ideology. Modern sports demand a commitment to equality of opportunity—the metaphorical level playing field. While the vast majority of white Americans honored this concept in the breach with regard to race, postbellum southerners were slow to internalize the meritocratic ethos that is central to modern sporting competition. Southerners were also slow to adopt certain other prerequisites for modern sports. Sporting competition requires a rationalized system of administration, coaching, and player development, and leagues require functional bureaucracies to ensure that competing teams can succeed collectively. Horse racing in New Orleans and Louisville is a partial exception to this rule, but the sport was inefficiently administered and only sporadically profitable prior to the turn of the century.

The South of the latter years of the nineteenth century stood poised on the cusp of modernity, and twentieth-century southern sports can fairly be said to have begun around 1890. Minor league baseball came to the South in 1885, when civic boosters, buoyed by the spirit of the New South ideology, established the Southern League. Yet even to speak of a Southern League as a well-defined organization is misleading, as the league repeatedly collapsed in disarray, completing its entire schedule in only four of its first fifteen seasons. Sporting entrepreneurs and urban boosters gamely reconstituted it following each failure. In 1900, as the South recovered from the depression of the 1890s, the Southern Association was organized to replace the ill-fated Southern

League. While it struggled in its early years, it began to prosper by the 1910s and operated continuously for more than sixty years.

Professional baseball benefited from the new urban society that was taking shape in the South. Middle-class professionals could afford fifty-cent box seats, and many workers could splurge on a ten-cent bleacher seat. New electric streetcars efficiently transported crowds numbering in the thousands to and from newly constructed ballparks. With its growing middle class that touted its position on the cutting edge of southern progress, Atlanta was a logical site for a successful minor league baseball franchise. The *Atlanta Constitution* and the rival *Journal* were each among the first southern newspapers to dedicate a separate section to sports, doing so shortly after the turn of the century. This provided crucial free publicity for all spectator sports, including the Atlanta Crackers. With solid popular support, a growing economy, and a ballpark built in 1903 that could accommodate nine thousand spectators, the Crackers thrived. Their strongest rivals were the Birmingham Barons, which were supported by that city's booming industrial economy and the desire of civic leaders to keep pace with Atlanta. Millionaire industrialist A. H. "Rick" Woodward bought the team in 1910 and built Rickwood Field, the first concrete-and-steel stadium in the South and the only one in the minor leagues at that time. Buoyed by steady revenue streams from strong attendance, the Barons and the Crackers were the most successful franchises in the Southern Association, together winning twenty-nine championships in the league's sixty-three-year existence.

Dozens of additional minor leagues sprang up and died out with regularity throughout the century, especially in the decades prior to World War II. Like the Southern Association, the Texas League was eventually accorded Double-A status by organized baseball. Baseball insiders regarded it as having a talent level equal to or slightly below that of the Southern Association. Many other leagues, ranging from Single-A to Class D, have come and gone over the decades. Industrial-league baseball arose around the turn of the century, and in its heyday in the 1920s and 1930s, its quality of play was roughly comparable to a Class B minor league. Industrial teams in Birmingham became known for their high level of athletic talent, but the textile leagues of the Carolinas occupy an especially prominent place in southern sports lore. Residents of the rapidly expanding mill villages formed loosely organized town teams during the 1890s, and these teams gradually formed institutional links with textile mills around the turn of the century. By the 1920s, the mill leagues had become a key element of the social life and communal identity of mill towns. Established players often received easy work assignments in the mills, and the stipend from a single game could double or triple an average weekly salary.

Over eighty major leaguers began their careers on Carolina mill teams, the most notable of whom is the legendary Shoeless Joe Jackson. He began work at Greenville's Brandon Mill at age six as a sweeper and never attended school regularly. He earned a starting spot on the mill's team at thirteen, and he was soon dazzling upstate fans. Signed by the Philadelphia Athletics at nineteen, he compiled the third-highest career batting average in major league history. Banned from baseball for his role in the 1919 Black Sox Scandal, Jackson embodies aspects of the complex dialectic between regional and national identity that characterized southern sports for much of the twentieth century. He had to go north to find an arena commensurate with his talent, yet he was heckled by opposing fans as an illiterate southern bumpkin and was ill at ease in the fast-paced atmosphere of major league baseball. Many baseball historians have attributed his complicity in the conspiracy to his lack of sophistication. He apparently was not eager to participate in the fix, but he could not say no when his teammates pressured him. After his banishment from baseball, Jackson lived the remainder of his life in Greenville, where he owned a liquor store and played and managed in the textile leagues into his fifties. Ty Cobb's baseball talent was arguably superior to that of Jackson, but his link with southern identity is more prosaic, as it was primarily manifested in his virulent racism.

Baseball became recognized as the "national pastime" in the late nineteenth century, and southerners' adoption of baseball thus represents their willingness to accept sectional reconciliation on northern terms. Sports, however, have virtually no intrinsic cultural meaning. A sport's cultural text is established in a complex interplay between the interpretation advanced by its promoters as conveyed by the media and the response to those ideas by the public at large. Baseball and football were strongly linked in the public mind to progress, bourgeois values, industrial capitalism, and science and technology. Northern newspapers and opinion journals hailed football, and, to a lesser extent, baseball as "scientific" sports that embodied the progressive mentality of the new century. Their southern counterparts consistently followed their lead, indicating the hegemonic authority possessed by the northeastern elite. Historian Michael Oriard has described how American football was considered to be especially scientific in nature. It was regularly called "scientific football" to distinguish it from soccer, and "machine" was sportspage boilerplate for a football team. With its hierarchical command structure, increasingly sophisticated game strategy, set plays requiring precision timing, and on-field division of labor, football's creators believed that it replicated the form and function of an industrial corporation. It was thus conceived as a means of inculcating Machine Age habits and attitudes into the elite young men who would one day become the owners and managers of industrial corporations. Football violence, while obviously not regarded as "scientific," was a means of instilling the masculine aggressiveness necessary to compete in the Darwinian world of corporate capitalism. This interpretation of football's cultural text was disseminated by socially powerful northeasterners who published their ideas in books and publications generally accepted as authoritative. Theodore Roosevelt, Henry Cabot Lodge, Harvard professor Dudley Sargent, Yale president Francis Walker, and Walter Camp were among the many Ivy Leaguers who promoted this interpretation of football and modern sports generally.

The progressive southerners who supported the diffusion of football to the region thus regarded it as a means of teaching the meritocratic and technocratic values of modernity to southerners. In addition to these perceived ideological and instrumental benefits, football gave southerners something that baseball could not—major league status. Until the 1960s, southern baseball was strictly minor league. In contrast, some southern football teams began to schedule intersectional games against the most powerful teams from outside the region as early as the 1890s, and almost every major southern program played at least one such game annually by the early 1920s. Despite the loss of nearly every one of these games, often by humiliating margins, southern sports fans were almost deliriously happy even to take the field against big-time competition. Southern newspapers invariably hailed every such defeat as a "defense of southern honor," and students flocked to train stations to greet the vanquished warriors on their return home.

Lack of money was the central cause of the deficiencies of virtually every social institution of the early-twentieth-century South, and football programs were no exception. For example, the Yale football program generated over fifty thousand dollars in 1903, a sum roughly equivalent to the entire operating budget of Alabama Polytechnic Institute (Auburn). Most southern universities could afford to employ only second- or third-rate coaches, and they lacked systematized and rationalized methods of recruiting and training athletes. Only a minority of public high schools had organized sports programs prior to the 1920s, and many rural areas had no public high schools at all, let alone high school sports. Colleges played games for two decades on roped-off sections of city parks or on campus parade grounds, and crowds regularly disrupted games by pouring onto the field. Municipalities and universities began to construct athletic fields with wooden bleachers by the 1910s, but these paled in comparison to the luxurious concrete-and-steel stadiums in the Northeast and Midwest. Aggregate southern wealth grew steadily during the Progressive Era, which benefited both minor league baseball and university athletic programs. However, the developmental gap was too large to be overcome in such a short time.

The 1920s witnessed the proverbial great leap forward, for both southern sports and the urban middle class that was its mainstay. The industrial, financial, and service sectors boomed, creating rising real incomes and shorter working weeks. As was the case in the nation as a whole, the southern market for commercial sports expanded dramatically, and many observers have called the 1920s "the golden age of sports." College football grew particularly rapidly. Nationally, attendance at college football games doubled and gate receipts tripled during the decade, and the corresponding increases in the South were likely even greater. Appropriations for universities rose proportionately with tax revenues, providing greater institutional support for athletic programs. Growth in the numbers and aggregate wealth of alumni created a stronger athletic booster network, although this also engendered problems for university administrators attempting to gain a greater degree of control over increasingly powerful athletic programs. The athletic talent pool expanded, as a much greater proportion of the white agrarian and working classes now attended high school. High school sports programs proliferated, and the now-familiar pride that southern communities take in their local school teams became a significant social phenomenon. Southern universities began systematically to recruit athletes of modest financial means and subsidize their expenses, even though athletic scholarships remained illegal until the early 1950s. Sports coverage in daily newspapers intensified, and the novel medium of radio added a major new dimension to sports coverage. The South crossed many crucial developmental milestones during the 1920s, and the sporting world was only one of many sectors of southern society that achieved both qualitative and quantitative growth.

The transformation of southern college football during the 1920s is exemplified by the decline of Vanderbilt and the rise of the University of Alabama. As shocking as it may seem to today's fans, Vanderbilt had the dominant football program in the South during the first two decades of the twentieth century. Virginia, North Carolina, Auburn, and Georgia Tech (which benefited from the coaching skills and public relations savvy of John Heisman) also had strong programs. Vanderbilt's competitive edge lay in the high proportion of private prep school students who attended the university. Sewanee (formally the University of the South) likewise had a surprisingly good program prior to 1920 despite its small enrollment. Since football was primarily an elite sport prior to the 1920s, prep schools generally had good football programs. As the talent pool began to include more athletes from poor backgrounds, the public universities' aggressive booster networks and lower admissions and academic standards erased the advantages previously held by schools like Vanderbilt and Sewanee.

Like many of his contemporaries, University of Alabama President George Denny used football as a public relations vehicle to increase enrollment and reduce the hostility of those who regarded the university as a playground for spoiled rich kids. Denny instituted a more extensive system of subsidizing athletes and hired Wallace Wade and several full-time assistant coaches in 1923. Working sixteen-hour days, Wade introduced year-round training and sponsored summer courses for high school coaches that extended Alabama's recruitment network. These efforts paid off in an undefeated 1925 season and an invitation to become the first southern team to play in the Rose Bowl. Alabama rallied for a stunning come-from-behind victory over the Washington Huskies and claimed the first of its many national championships. In the wake of the upset victory, joyous crowds poured into the streets of Montgomery and Birmingham, and newspapers across the South splashed banner headlines across page one. Politicians and civic leaders crowed that this proved that southerners were as vigorous, competent, and deserving of respect as any Yankee. Even Auburn students cheered Alabama's victory. Other southern teams soon rose to the pinnacle of national prominence.

Georgia Tech defeated Michigan in the 1929 Rose Bowl to claim another national championship for the South, and in the same year, Georgia inaugurated its new campus stadium with a victory over mighty Yale. Southern football fans were no longer Dickensian orphans peering through the window at the wealthy family enjoying a holiday feast. In college football, if not in more substantive social and economic categories, they were among the elite. Southerners had invented a tradition of victory and inclusion that at least partially countered a mentality grounded in alienation and lost causes.

Men's college basketball also grew significantly during the 1920s, but this rate of growth was magnified by its marginal status prior to then. Southerners were slow to adopt the game after its invention in 1891. The YMCA, YMHA, Amateur Athletic Union (AAU), and ethnic clubs were mainstays of basketball in the Northeast, but these were less well developed in the South. Also, many northeasterners played basketball year round because urban population density left little open space for football or baseball. Not until about 1910 did southern intercollegiate basketball competition acquire even rudimentary levels of organization. Most sports fans and even many players generally regarded it merely as filler between football and baseball seasons. Also, basketball had become the most popular competitive sport among women, giving it a "sissy" image to young men steeped in a culture of aggressive masculinity.

The 1926 Rose Bowl in Pasadena, where the undefeated University of Alabama beat the Washington Huskies (20-19) and became the 1925 college football national champions. Courtesy of the Paul W. Bryant Museum, University of Alabama.

As was the case with men's sports, women's college basketball developed more slowly in the South. Southern women had to overcome the same social and cultural barriers that impeded the growth of men's sports, and like their northern sisters, they had to fight against the still-powerful legacy of Victorian gender conventions. But they also faced additional restrictions imposed by the social ideal of the southern lady. They persevered anyway, and their affinity for basketball was emblematic of their desire to push the limits of socially sanctioned gender roles. Southern women took to basketball even more quickly than men, mostly because men had so many other sporting options. Clara Baer, a professor at Newcomb College in New Orleans, was one of the early proponents of women's basketball. She created a separate set of rules for women in 1895 and gave it the dainty-sounding name of "basquette." Operating carefully within the strictures of contemporary gender roles, Baer stressed that her game cultivated poise and grace rather than competitiveness. In apparel that seems overly restrictive and even silly to the modern eye, female players wore long dresses and bloomers through the 1910s. Yet these outfits offered more freedom than the corsets, petticoats, and capacious skirts that respectable women had long been expected to wear. Male spectators were almost always banned from women's games, and even female spectators were sometimes banned. When women were permitted to attend games, they often could not cheer, as some deemed this to be unladylike.

Most Americans, including most women, also saw overt competitiveness as unladylike as well. Female physical educators throughout the nation generally discouraged intercollegiate competition along the male model, instead promoting intramural sports and "play days" that emphasized social activities almost as much as athletic competition. They also promoted calisthenics, walking, and bicycle riding as alternatives to competitive sports. Golf, tennis, and archery were often deemed to be acceptable sports for respectable ladies because they were seen as intrinsically graceful and because of their association with the country club set. While many of the restrictions placed on female athletes seem grossly unjust to twenty-first-century sensibilities, one of the motivations may appear less unreasonable in retrospect. Many female physical educators were aghast at how men's athletics emphasized elite athletes at the expense of fitness for all, stressed a win-at-all-cost mentality, and had become commercialized. In response, the women's physical education establishment successfully de-emphasized varsity competition in most colleges throughout the nation. Women's intercollegiate athletics generally hewed to this less competitive model from the 1920s until it was energized by the feminist movement of the latter third of the century.

African American and working-class white women were less bound by the social conventions that circumscribed the sporting choices of white collegians. As was the case with college women, basketball was their preferred sport. Community, industrial, and AAU teams were beyond the control of the elite-dominated physical education establishment, and they achieved a relatively high degree of popularity throughout the South from the 1920s through the 1950s. Such teams generally played a vigorously competitive brand of basketball and often flouted the collegians' more conservative dress code by wearing dazzling satin uniforms. They often drew large crowds and attracted widespread community support. While somewhat more beholden to both bourgeois norms and the wishes of the physical educators, southern high schools and historically black colleges often sponsored highly competitive varsity basketball programs as well. Pamela Grundy notes that the all-black North Carolina Athletic Conference often sponsored a girls' state high school championship tournament in the 1930s and 1940s, and the historically black colleges in the state formed the North Carolina Women's Intercollegiate Athletic Association in the mid-1930s to promote varsity competition.

The Great Depression was a major setback for the growth of football and baseball, bound as they were to the commercial economy. Minor league baseball was particularly hard hit, and many marginal franchises that had survived in the boom years went under after the bubble burst. Attendance at college football games fell precipitously between 1929 and 1934, but rebounded somewhat in the latter years of the decade. Hard times did not hinder the steady advance of southern football toward competitive parity, however. Alabama continued its dominance, winning Rose Bowls and national championships in the 1930 and 1934 seasons. The rise of southwestern universities to national prominence was a significant development as well, as LSU, Texas, Texas A&M, TCU, and SMU each claimed national titles in at least one of the half-dozen or so annual football polls between 1930 and 1941. Under head coach Robert Neyland, the University of Tennessee rose from also-ran to national power during the 1930s, claiming national titles in 1938 and 1940. Neyland, an active-duty Army general during much of his tenure, symbolizes the growing identification of football with the military. While military themes had long been a part of football's cultural text, this had intensified during and after World War I. This was one aspect of football's increasing identification with social and political conservatism, which hastened the transfer of the center of football gravity from the Northeast to the Midwest and South.

The proliferation of bowl games during the 1930s created yet another link between college football and the ubiquitous spirit of southern civic boosterism. On New Year's Day 1935, Miami inaugurated the Orange Bowl and New Orleans the Sugar Bowl, and Dallas established the Cotton Bowl two years later. These games generally featured a marquee southern team against one from outside the region, effectively guaranteeing intensive national newspaper and radio coverage. While bowl games raised money for charitable causes, urban boosterism was the prime motivational factor in their creation. Civic leaders used them as a means of promoting tourism and enhancing the name recognition of their cities. They wined and dined the teams and their large traveling parties, and they provided an especially warm welcome to journalists. Extravagant parades and halftime shows were a hallmark of these games, especially the Orange Bowl. Heeding the truism that sex sells when cotton won't, promoters shamelessly employed cheesecake to attract media attention. The promotional photo of a hulking football player in full pads standing surrounded by a bevy of bathing beauties was a public relations staple, and parades and halftime shows featured hundreds of cheerleaders, majorettes, and dancers.

Bowl games also highlighted the race issue in southern sports. It had rarely arisen prior to the 1920s, when organized baseball and all southern universities were segregated and very few nonsouthern universities recruited African American football players. However, a handful began doing so during that decade, and that number grew during the 1930s. When southern coaches and administrators demanded that their northern counterparts bench black players in intersectional games, the latter almost always did so. Charles Martin has identified dozens of occasions between the 1920s and the 1940s in which northerners capitulated in this fashion, a practice referred to as the Gentleman's Agreement. It reflects the growing social conservatism of the coaching fraternity, as well as the lure of sizable gate receipts generated by high-profile intersectional games.

A number of great African American athletes were born in the South but emigrated to other regions as part of the massive black exodus that took place between 1910 and 1970. Two in particular became especially noteworthy during the 1930s. Both heavyweight champion Joe Louis and Olympic sprinter Jesse Owens were born in Alabama and moved with their families as young children to Detroit and Cleveland, respectively. Owens's record four gold medals at the 1936 Berlin Olympics and Louis's victory over German heavyweight Max Schmeling were hailed as a powerful symbolic counterpoint to the totalitarianism of Nazi Germany. Each achieved iconic status among African Americans, especially Louis. However, only a few mainstream pundits noted the uncomfortable reality that both men had been driven from the South by a system of racial oppression that was benign only in comparison to the horrors of Nazi Germany.

The war against Nazi racism provided a major impetus to the civil rights movement, which in turn had a dramatic impact on the sporting world. Georgia-born Jackie Robinson, who had moved to southern California at age two and became a four-sport athlete at UCLA, breached the color line in organized baseball when he signed a minor league contract in 1946. The Dodgers assigned Robinson to their International League affiliate in Montreal specifically so he would not have to play minor league games in the South. Robinson's hugely successful rookie season with the Dodgers in 1947 and the gradual desegregation of other major league teams affected spring training in Florida. A few towns cancelled games rather than let Robinson or other African Americans play there. However, in a pattern that would become increasingly common as the civil rights movement intensified, most city leaders refused to defend segregation when doing so would cost them money or bring negative national publicity. The Dodgers also broke the athletic color line in exhibition games outside of Florida, including a three-game series in Atlanta between the Crackers and the Dodgers in April 1949 that was held in defiance of threats from a local Klan leader. Savvy civic leaders understood how crucial Atlanta's well-cultivated image of racial moderation was to its continued economic growth, and they characteristically used these games to bolster that image.

A disproportionate number of the lower-level minor leagues were located in the South, precipitating a lengthy conflict between the increasingly biracial baseball world and the Jim Crow system. The barriers tumbled haltingly and grudgingly. Many southern minor league franchises eventually signed African American players, and most of their competitors accepted interracial competition rather than quit their leagues. Several franchises signed black players during the 1951 season, and several more, including the Dallas Eagles of the Texas League, did so in 1952. The first African Americans played in the South Atlantic League the following year, including Jacksonville's nineteen-year-old second baseman, Mobile native Henry Aaron. Yet if a relative handful of African Americans were finally receiving equality of opportunity on the field, southern society still treated them miserably. They generally stayed at all-black hotels or in private homes, ate in kitchens or on buses while their teammates ate in restaurant dining rooms, and endured relentless abuse from fans. Progress in college football came even more slowly. Southern universities resisted the integration of their student bodies, let alone their athletic teams. However, as northerners began to repudiate the Gentleman's Agreement, many universities grudgingly accepted interracial competition as the price they had to pay for playing in the big time. In 1947, the University of Virginia became the first southern university to permit interracial competition on its campus, and SMU played an integrated Penn State team in the 1948 Cotton Bowl.

This partial thaw in the racial dynamics of the southern sporting world lost momentum when, in the wake of the *Brown* decision, white southerners adopted the strategy of massive resistance. In that year, the Atlanta Crackers bowed to pressure from other Southern Association franchises, notably the Birmingham Barons, and demoted their first black player after only four games. A now infamous Birmingham city ordinance codified the "unwritten law" against interracial sports, criminalizing even a game of checkers. An attempt by two racially moderate city commissioners to repeal it was defeated by a resounding three-to-one margin in a referendum held six months after the *Brown* decision was announced. A year later, Georgia governor Marvin Griffin attempted to prevent Georgia Tech from playing a racially integrated University of Pittsburgh team in the 1956 Sugar Bowl. He melodramatically stated that this game posed a grave threat to civilization. "The South stands at Armageddon. The Battle is joined. We cannot make the slightest concession to the enemy in this dark and lamentable struggle," he intoned. Yet the desire of Tech officials and Atlanta civic leaders to avoid a public relations nightmare, not to mention the southern passion for football, overwhelmed Griffin's opposition. Tech played in (and won) the game. The Mississippi State men's basketball team was denied the opportunity to compete in the NCAA tournament in 1959, 1961, and 1962, but it literally sneaked out of the state to play in the tournament the following year.

While increasing numbers of southern universities became willing to defy the proscription of interracial competition, desegregation of their own teams was several orders of magnitude more difficult. The championship game of the 1966 NCAA basketball tournament provided a symbolically potent boost to desegregation efforts and hastened the demise of the white supremacist order in southern sports. In that game, a team from Texas Western College with five African American starters upset an all-white University of Kentucky team coached by Adolph Rupp, a well-known opponent of racial integration. Rupp's status as the leader in career victories by an NCAA basketball coach and the prominence of the University of Kentucky basketball program only added to the magnitude of the victory.

Ironically, desegregation precipitated the demise of Negro League baseball, as it lost many of its best players and much of its fan base to the major leagues. While African American semipro teams had been playing since the late nineteenth century, organized professional leagues did not exist in either the North or the South until the 1920s. However, teams generally were not financially stable, and the leagues suffered from a chronic lack of organization. Teams generally barnstormed around the country, playing a majority of their games against semipro competition. League schedules were haphazard at best. These problems were irrelevant to African American fans, who regarded Negro League baseball as a cornerstone of black sporting identity. As was the case with white baseball, the most powerful and profitable franchises were located in the Northeast and Midwest. Still, every southern city of any size had either a professional or semipro African American team. The Birmingham Black Barons, which had sprung from the rich pool of industrial league talent in Birmingham, were generally regarded as the best southern franchise. The Black Barons more than held their own against the best northern competition, especially during the 1940s, when they appeared three times in the Negro World Series.

Men's athletics at historically black colleges served as a focal point of pride and identification for African Americans as well, but they generally appealed to a higher social stratum. Black college football in particular became a significant part of southern middle-class black social life. In contrast to Negro League baseball, black college sports survived desegregation due to institutional support and a loyal fan base among students and alumni. However, the competitive quality declined when big-time football programs in the North began to recruit southern African American players in earnest in the 1960s

The Birmingham Black Barons Base Ball Club and their team bus. Courtesy of the Negro Leagues Baseball Museum, Kansas City, Mo.

The Black Atlanta Crackers. Courtesy of the Negro Leagues Baseball Museum, Kansas City, Mo.

and southern programs began to do the same a decade later. While their white counterparts remained bound by the taboo against strenuous competition, African American women's intercollegiate sports also gained ground after World War II. The women's track team at Tennessee State University performed brilliantly on the biggest stage in the world, winning over a score of Olympic medals between 1956 and 1976.

Men's college basketball improved across the South after World War II, but the true quantum leap was made in North Carolina. Sports once again served to diminish the cultural distance between the South and the rest of the nation, as two northern coaches were instrumental in creating a southern sporting tradition in what had been regarded as a northern game. Everett Case of Indiana became head coach at North Carolina State in 1946, and New Yorker Frank McGuire came to the University of North Carolina in 1952. Each employed a fast-paced style of play pioneered by white and black northeasterners in the 1930s that emphasized team speed, fast breaks, and the one-handed jump shot. The composition of McGuire's teams might have been expected to upset southern sensibilities, as most of his star players were Catholics and Jews from the New York City area. However, no complaints were heard on Tobacco Road when McGuire's "Southern Yankees" won the NCAA tournament in 1957. While it does nothing to diminish the legitimacy of the emotion that several generations of fans have invested in it, the fact is that the vaunted North Carolina and Atlantic Coast Conference basketball tradition is only half a century old and was begun by men from outside the region. By the 1980s, the Southeastern and Southwestern conferences were nationally competitive, and most observers regarded the ACC as the best in the nation. North Carolina State won national titles in 1974 and 1983, and North Carolina did the same under longtime coach Dean Smith in 1982 and 1993. (The 1982 team was led by a skinny guard from Wilmington named Michael Jordan.) Duke University won a national title in 1991, and followed it with three more over the next decade.

Football, of course, had deeper southern roots than basketball, and by the postwar years, southern prowess in the sport had eliminated virtually all traces of its Yankee origins. Alabama, Auburn, Tennessee, Georgia Tech, LSU, Texas, Ole Miss, Georgia, and Arkansas each ranked first in at least one end-of-season poll between 1946 and 1965. Desegregation finally began during this period as well. Southern universities all admitted African American students for the first time in the early 1960s, and the desegregation of their athletic programs generally followed several years later. The basketball teams usually were the first to recruit black athletes, because blacks comprised a larger proportion of the best players and because white southerners generally were more emotionally invested in football programs. But the barriers inevitably fell. The University of Houston was the first team in the Southwest Conference with an African American varsity football player, and the University of Kentucky was the first in the Southeastern Conference. By 1972, all of the major southern football and men's basketball programs had been desegregated.

Paul "Bear" Bryant became head coach at Alabama in 1958, and he won national championships in 1961, 1964, and 1965. He symbolized the complex and often contradictory world of the postwar South. Born into rural poverty and embodying the traditional masculine virtues of the agrarian South, Bryant rose to fame and wealth without losing his folksy demeanor. He was personally a racial moderate who negotiated with archsegregationist governor John Patterson to enable Alabama to break the "unwritten law" and compete against a racially integrated Penn State team in his first season at Alabama. Yet he won his first three national titles with teams composed of undersized white boys who became a symbol of sectional pride to white southerners buffeted not only by the historical legacy of poverty and defeat, but also by their status as national pariahs during the civil rights era. Alabama was also one of the last teams to desegregate—no African American wore an Alabama varsity uniform until 1971. Yet Alabama's teams of the 1970s came to symbolize the new regional paradigm of harmonious race relations so fervently promoted by the newly moderate business and political leadership, partly due to their on-field success. The Alabama program during the 1970s was one of the most dominant in college football history, and Bryant broke the record for career wins by a head coach in 1981.

The confluence of race and sports has generated torrents of analysis by journalists, pundits, and historians. Many have come to the facile conclusion that interracial sports have been a panacea for American and southern racial ills. They reason that white and black teammates working together toward a common goal, clasping hands in a huddle, or hugging one another in either triumph or defeat somehow obviate the racial divisions that still exist in contemporary society. Yet while racial controversies spring up in the headlines with regularity, the new racial dynamics of the southern sporting world have helped to shape a more inclusive southern society. It is indeed significant that interracial teams represent tradition-bound southern universities and that young athletes learn the lessons of cooperation and competition in a multiracial environment. Many injustices remain to be redressed—the shockingly low proportion of African American coaches and athletic administrators is a glaring example. Also, a case can be made that African American athletes are merely updated versions of the singers and dancers who have historically been given license to entertain whites. Yet contemporary southern society is fundamentally different from the one in which an interracial game of checkers was impermissible.

The popularity of women's sports grew significantly over the last quarter of the twentieth century, but as was increasingly the case, the South merely mirrored national trends. The feminist movement removed many of the social and cultural barriers that had discouraged female participation in competitive sports, and Title IX of the Educational Amendments Act of 1972 acted as a powerful stimulus to the development of female sports at the high school and collegiate levels. The South's general slowness to adapt to social change and the lingering attachment to the ideal of the southern lady has hindered the expansion of women's sports to an extent. However, southern schools' propensity to link institutional identity to athletic success has been beneficial to women's athletic programs. If a school identifies itself as a "winner," it tends not to tolerate marginal athletic programs, regardless of the gender of the athletes. High school and college women's teams attract much of the same local and regional loyalty as their male counterparts, but like the men, the success of certain programs enables them to attract a national following. The most salient example of this is the women's soccer program at the University of North Carolina, which has built a dynasty rivaled only by that of the Yale football program in that late nineteenth century. By winning an amazing seventeen national titles between 1981 and 2001 and supplying many of the stars of the United States national team, the Carolina soccer team has transcended regional and even national identity. They serve as a symbol of athletic achievement for women and girls around the world. The continuing growth of competitive women's sports will be one of the most significant developments in twenty-first-century sports.

The postwar economic boom, coupled with the demise of legal segregation, opened the door to the expansion of professional sports in the South. Seeking to expand markets during the boom years of the 1960s, major league baseball and the National Football League were the first to recognize that the South was fertile ground for expansion. Less troubled by racial problems than southeastern cities, Dallas obtained the Cowboys in 1960 and Houston acquired the Colt .45s (later the Astros) in 1962. In a bravura display of Atlanta's unabashed boosterism, Mayor Ivan Allen personally convinced the owners of the Milwaukee Braves to relocate their franchise to Atlanta in 1966. The floodgates soon opened, as over two dozen additional professional franchises popped up in southern cities over the next three decades. Southern cities aggressively sought these teams as markers of big-league status. By 2000, nearly one-quarter of the franchises in the "big four" professional sports were located in the South: five in Major League Baseball, six in the National Hockey League, eight in the National Basketball Association, and nine in the National Football League. A recent ESPN survey found, to no one's surprise, that football is the South's most popular and profitable professional sport. However, this is also true of the nation as a whole, and the South differs only by the degree of its devotion to the sport. Regional variations in sporting preferences still exist, but they have declined as the commercial entertainment market has become increasingly homogenized.

Professional franchises have become much less dependent on grassroots fan support over the past two decades, but again, there is no substantial regional variation in this area. The economic fortunes of all professional teams depend to a great extent on corporate and taxpayer support. Taxpayer-funded stadiums and arenas, national television contracts, sponsorship deals, and the sale of luxury boxes, season tickets, and personal seat licenses to businesses form the economic foundation of professional sports teams. Big-time men's college sports still depend to a greater extent on traditional networks of alumni and regional fan support, and the ESPN survey found that southerners are generally more supportive of college football than fans in any other region. Fans in North Carolina and Kentucky display a stronger affinity for college basketball than those in any other region except the Northeast and Indiana. This continuing attachment to local college teams is a vestige of a period earlier in the century when sectional and local identity were much more powerful determinants of sporting preferences. College teams are among the last of the "local heroes" in the big-time sporting world, both in the South and in the nation. The southern affinity for high school sports, especially football, remains strong as well. H. G. Bissinger's best-selling *Friday Night Lights* describes the fervent devotion to football felt by residents of Odessa, Texas, and similar books could be written about hundreds of other southern towns and cities.

Perhaps more than any other sport, stock car racing continues to embody the complex dialectic between regional and national identity. The National Association for Stock Car Auto Racing (NASCAR) has carefully cultivated the idea that the early years of southern automobile racing were dominated by moonshine runners who had honed their driving skills outrunning lawmen on the back roads of Appalachia. Like most widely believed myths, there is a certain degree of truth behind the image. Junior Johnson of North Carolina, the most celebrated of the early drivers, raced on the early NASCAR circuit while still operating his family moonshine business. His luck ran out in 1956, when he was finally convicted and served eleven months of a two-year sentence. Tom Wolfe burnished Johnson's image as a modern-day social bandit in a 1965 *Esquire* profile, which also introduced the phrase "good old boy" into the national lexicon.

Yet automobile racing was introduced to the South at the turn of the century by the same urban progressives who promoted football, baseball, and other modern sports. They did so in the service of civic boosterism and a desire to break the bonds of provincialism and link the region more fully with the mainstream of American culture. Racing was especially attractive to local leaders given the automobile's strong popular association with technological sophistication as well as the ability of races to generate favorable national press coverage. Historian Randal L. Hall notes that the urban elites of Savannah, New Orleans, Galveston, Atlanta, and numerous other southern cities sponsored road races in the years prior to World War I to showcase the progressivism and sophistication of their cities. Daytona Beach, Florida, hosted a number of early automobile races partly because its hard sand beaches were so suited to racing, but also because local leaders believed that such races would enhance the local tourism industry. Urban boosters lost interest in sponsoring road races after World War I, and the popularity of these early racing spectacles did not readily translate into a sustainable racing circuit with a centralized governing body. By the 1930s, short tracks dotted the South, but racing was generally characterized by low revenues, often-unscrupulous promoters, and a limited fan base.

William G. "Big Bill" France of Daytona founded NASCAR in 1948 and quickly began to rationalize the business side of the sport. He oversaw the growth of a symbiotic relationship with the Big Three automakers and negotiated sponsorship deals with oil companies and auto-parts manufacturers. He moved his races from dirt tracks to paved ones, and in 1959 he built the first superspeedway in Daytona. Over the next twelve years, others were built in Charlotte, Atlanta, and Talladega, Alabama. From the beginning, France also marketed NASCAR throughout the nation. He held races in the Northeast, Midwest, and California, even though many of his southern drivers could not afford to travel there to race. France intuitively understood that the nascent "southernization" of American culture could enable him to sell a cultural form strongly linked to the South to whites around the country. He built the "NASCAR Nation" on a solid southern base, and he skillfully incorporated the same working- and lower-middle-class northerners who made country music a nationally popular art form and who voted in large numbers for George Wallace for president in 1968 and 1972.

NASCAR experienced phenomenal growth from the 1970s through the 1990s, and it was the only major sport to enjoy increased television ratings during the 1990s. Increased corporate sponsorship of NASCAR and its driving teams reflected the growing power of corporate money in sports. In 1971, Junior Johnson personally brokered a deal by which R. J. Reynolds became a primary sponsor of NASCAR. Cars that had once borne the logos of a few automotive brands became 210-mile-per-hour billboards, sporting the logos of a myriad of consumer products. Many of these, notably Tide detergent, are marketed primarily to women. While the testosterone-laden world of auto racing may not seem to be very welcoming to women and families, women comprise a sizable proportion of contemporary NASCAR fans. NASCAR fandom remains virtually all white however, despite some recent efforts to market the sport to African Americans and Hispanics. The class status of race fans has risen significantly in recent decades, mirroring the increasing aggregate wealth of the South. Luxury boxes at the superspeedways often come with six-figure price tags. Yet the outlaw image of its roots remains a central element of NASCAR mythology and is arguably is a key reason for its growing popularity.

The social and economic transformation that has propelled the South to the center of the sporting world has also had a dramatic effect on hunting and fishing. Due to its abundant wildlife and the many millions of southerners who have hunted and fished for subsistence, outdoor sports have been regarded as particularly "southern" since the colonial era. The wealthy planter who displayed his mastery by bagging hundreds of birds or a fearsome wild boar or bear, as well as the yeoman or slave who supplemented his family's diet with fish and game, made hunting and fishing a part of the social fabric and domestic economy of the South. Yet while many poor southerners still hunt and fish for subsistence, outdoor sports have undergone the same process of professionalization and rationalization that have transformed all other major sports. Hunters and fishers now must procure state licenses, adhere to seasonal restrictions and bag limits, and respect property rights. Many hunters now pay hefty dues to join hunt clubs for access to good hunting land. While many still fish from riverbanks, bridges, or piers, many others do so from boats that cost as much as some small homes. Quantification and regulated competition characterize hunting and fishing tournaments, a disproportionate number of which are held in the South. Like virtually every other aspect of modern American life, southern hunting and fishing can reasonably be described as commodified activities marketed primarily to the middle class.

Since the late nineteenth century, sports have reflected the blurring of regional lines and the increasing incorporation of the South into the national social and cultural mainstream. When Hank Aaron hit his 715th home run, the fact that he was a native of Alabama playing on a team from Atlanta mattered less than the sheer magnitude of his breaking the most sacrosanct record in American sports, and in no small measure, that an African American was the one to break it. More people around the world associate Michael Jordan with Nike than with his hometown of Wilmington or the University of North Carolina. And are the Miami Hurricanes or the Dallas Stars truly "southern" in any meaningful sense of the word? While Alabamians are fanatically devoted to Alabama and Auburn, working-class Pittsburghers' attachment to the Steelers, New Englanders' tragic (at least until 2004) love affair with the Red Sox, or Nebraskans' loyalty to Big Red football demonstrate that southerners have no monopoly on devotion to sports teams. Boilerplate rhetoric positing football as a southern religion was probably overblown to begin with, and partisan devotion to any local team becomes more outdated as the South becomes increasingly integrated into a postmodern world. The southern sporting world, like the rest of southern society, is not radically different from that of any other region in an era of globalization and the transformative power of big money. However, southerners probably still possess a bit more of the visceral emotional attachment to their local heroes than residents of any other region. Vestiges of an earlier era in which sectionalism and devotion to tradition were still strong will continue to linger in the southern sporting world until well into the twenty-first century.

Suggested Readings

Dean, Pamela. "'Dear Sisters' and 'Hated Rivals': Athletics and Gender at Two New South Women's Colleges." *Journal of Sport History* 24 (Fall 1997): 341–57.

Doyle, Andrew. "Fighting Whiskey and Immorality at Auburn: The Politics of Southern Football, 1919–1927." *Southern Cultures* 10 (Fall 2004): 6–30.

———. "Foolish and Useless Sport: The Southern Evangelical Crusade against Intercollegiate Football." *Journal of Sport History* 24 (Fall 1997): 317–40.

Grundy, Pamela. *Learning to Win: Sports, Education, and Social Change in Twentieth-Century North Carolina*. Chapel Hill: University of North Carolina Press, 2001.

Hall, Randal L. "Before NASCAR: The Corporate and Civic Promotion of Automobile Racing in the American South, 1903–1927." *Journal of Southern History* 68 (August 2002): 629–68.

Lanctot, Neil. *Negro League Baseball: The Rise and Ruin of an American Institution*. Philadelphia: University of Pennsylvania Press, 2004.

Martin, Charles. "The Rise and Fall of Jim Crow in Southern College Sports: The Case of the Atlantic Coast Conference." *North Carolina Historical Review* 76 (July 1999): 253–84.

Miller, Patrick B. "The Manly, the Moral, and the Proficient: College Sport in the New South." *Journal of Sport History* 24 (Fall 1997): 285–316.

O'Neal, Bill. *The Southern League: Baseball in Dixie, 1885–1994*. Austin, Tex.: Eakin Press, 1994.

Ownby, Ted. *Subduing Satan: Religion, Recreation, and Manhood in the Rural South, 1865–1920*. Chapel Hill: University of North Carolina Press, 1990.

CHARLES REAGAN WILSON

Making the South

Religion in a Twentieth-Century Region

The evangelical religion that had grown to prominence on the nineteenth-century southern frontier still dominated the region at the dawn of the twentieth century. The Reverend H. C. Morrison, of Asbury College, could not imagine another place "where there is a stronger, better faith in the Bible, where the Sabbath is better observed, where a larger percent of the people attend church, and where virtue in womanhood and honesty in manhood are more common and command a better premium." This high self-evaluation among one of the southern faithful was typical. The region's churches had survived the defeat of the Confederacy, the dramatic racial division of the region's Christians after the war, and a postwar poverty of spirit and goods that might have destroyed lesser institutions. The churches' self-satisfied attitudes reflected their power within southern culture and also their ease within that culture, not challenging its fundamental assumptions.

Religion provided a pronounced sense of regional mission and identity for white southerners. Victor I. Masters, South Carolina–born preacher, writer, and editor of a Baptist newspaper for over two decades, saw the South as the nation's—indeed, the world's—last best hope for an evangelical empire of righteousness. "Evangelical faith has had here its best chance in the world to show what it can do for a civilization," he wrote in 1918. Because of the South's material deprivation after the Civil War, it had developed "a great gentleness of spirit which was worth more than all the billions we have now gained." Because of the postwar suffering it endured and the qualities of spirit it developed as a result, the South had "a peculiar responsibility" to show its moral and spiritual superiority. The region's "consciousness of its own pains and sorrows, of the gallantry and chivalry of its sons, of its mistakes and sufferings, of its superiority to the worst calamities which came of it, of its ability to build a civilization out of ashes, makes the present South worth far more both to the nation and to itself." Failure to live up to this responsibility would "mean farewell to the best traditions of the South, and to the high and sacred destiny for which our noblest and best have prayed the South should be made fit."

Turn-of-the-century southern churches were pillars of regional life, as important to understanding the South as Jim Crow and rural-influenced values. Evangelical religion was a hegemonic force in southern life, and religion came to shape the institutions, values, and outlooks of the modern South. In 1900, 3.5 million whites out of 6.2 million church members belonged to the three historically southern denominations—the Southern Baptist Convention (SBC), the Methodist Episcopal Church, South, and the (Southern) Presbyterian Church in the United States. An interdenominational, biracial, evangelical Protestant religion dominated the region as in no other society in the Western world. In Alabama in 1900, for example, 97 percent of people who belonged to churches were Protestant. In Georgia in 1906, 43 percent of the state's people were church members, 92 percent of whom were either Baptist or Methodist. Church affiliations with like-minded Protestants outside the region were rare (the Episcopalians and Lutherans were an exception— their relatively small numbers in the South encouraged them to make outside connections). Churches thus provided regionally insulated institutions that nurtured southern identity.

African Americans established independent churches after the Civil War, sometimes withdrawing their membership from biracial churches, and, in any event, combining evangelical denominational traditions with the distinctive folk religion generated in the slave quarters. Those churches grew in the late nineteenth century, becoming institutions of southern black identity, but also reinforcing the general evangelical hegemony in regional religion. In Alabama, for example, black Baptists were the largest single religious group, constituting 30.8 percent of the state's church membership, compared with 20.6 percent for Southern Baptists, and black Baptists outnumbered whites in Arkansas, Mississippi, and other Deep South states. African American churches offered fellowship, social services, a political training ground, and a general sanctuary in a hostile world.

The predominant southern white denominations had come to cultural hegemony in the mid-nineteenth century, and the sectionalism of that era remained, as southern evangelicalism became a main support for regional sociocultural values and norms. They continued to preach the religion of the Lost Cause at the turn of the century and afterward, sacralizing the Confederacy. White churches legitimated an even more fundamental anchor of the southern way of life, racial segregation. Methodist bishops at their 1886 General Conference outlined the abiding orthodoxy, decrying "sentimental extravagance in the direction of the discolored current of social equality," while the Mississippi Baptist Convention in 1891 insisted that blacks "are distinct" and to claim otherwise was "to inflict an evil on them and to raise an insurmountable barrier to success." Historian Rufus B. Spain noted that at the turn of the century "theories of race were as much a part of Southern Baptist thinking as the Virgin Birth or the Second Coming."

The evangelical Protestant dominance could obscure, though, the considerable diversity that characterized religious life in the region, from the early twentieth century to midcentury, when change became more palpable. Sectarians were prominent in the southern religious landscape. Evangelicals began as sectarian in the early nineteenth century, and new sectarian groups emerged at the turn the twentieth century as well. The "isms" that conservative southerners identified with other parts of the nation, whether Mormonism or Transcendentalism, did not take easy root in the region—although colonies of Shakers and Christian socialists did emerge briefly in the early part of the century. But Baptists alone represented a variety of traditions, and it made considerable difference to those involved whether one was a Primitive, Free Will, Missionary, or Independent Baptist.

Sectarian groups that grew out of other existing faiths also proliferated at the turn of the century. The Churches of Christ split off, for example, from the Disciples of Christ, both groups tracing their ancestry back to the Presbyterians on the frontier. They were both Restorationist churches, with deep theological and ecclesiastical commitments to New Testament traditions and local church autonomy, but members of the Churches of Christ did not believe in using musical instruments in worship or in organized missionary work. Such divisions often had social causes as well. In this case, the division was sectional and rural-urban. The Churches of Christ emerged in middle and west Tennessee, and in every city except Nashville, the Disciples gained more members than the Churches of Christ.

Holiness churches grew out of Methodism and energized the region's spiritual life at the turn of the twentieth century. Holiness advocates saw John Wesley's belief in a postconversion second infusion of grace as a central doctrine, leading to perfectionism, and they formed state associations and camp meeting sites. Methodist bishops eventually denounced the idea that Holiness was a separate faith but welcomed its adherents to remain within the folds of the church, which some did. Other believers, however, split off to form new Holiness sects.

Pentecostalism, in turn, emerged in the early twentieth century from a radical wing of Holiness through the sharpened awareness and practice of such gifts of the spirit as the baptism of the Holy Spirit, speaking in tongues, and faith healing. This was a national phenomenon, but Cleveland, Tennessee, became a center for it. A. J. Tomlinson, who had led a group of Holiness believers in western North Carolina and eastern Tennessee, served for two decades as General Overseer for the Church of God, one of the most significant Pentecostal groups. The Deep South produced another leading denomination, the Church of God in Christ, founded in Memphis in 1906 by Mississippian Charles Harrison Mason.

Pentecostalism often appealed to the disfranchised and politically powerless but also to the upstanding working class as well. It relied on charismatic leaders, a rigid conservatism with respect to doctrine, and strict personal morality. Sectarians in general often embraced schism because of the intensity of their beliefs. The Church of God split, for example, in 1923—Tomlinson left the church and took with him about a third of the membership to form the new Church of God of Prophecy. Grady R. Kent would later lead other disaffected faithful out of that group to form the Church of God (Jerusalem Acres), which centered on the concept of "New Testament Judaism."

Despite the differences among such churches, they shared a fundamental conservative outlook on much doctrine. "The theology of the South is the same in its broad essentials among all the religious groups," wrote Edwin McNeill Poteat Jr. in 1934. If you were to "scratch any sectarian back," you would see that "the same orthodox blood flows." This insight is true enough, but it underplays the broader significance of sectarianism in the South. Many southerners, black and white, were trapped in a culture of poverty through much of the twentieth century, and religion reflected this reality. Sectarian groups offered empowerment in a society that disfranchised, segregated, economically exploited, and generally abused too many of its people. Urban churches and leading denominations were among the region's most powerful institutions, parts of an establishment whose members had close ties to other leaders in politics, economics, and education, but smaller sects, urban churches of the poor, and rural churches were a different matter altogether. They provided moral support, the limited social services that helped meet the crises of life and death, and even political organization for social protest at times.

Sociologist Will Herberg once identified Protestantism, Catholicism, and Judaism as the dominant American faiths, not just in numbers but in terms of sociocultural influence as well, and the role of Catholics and Jews in the overwhelmingly evangelical Protestant modern South provided a distinctive twist on his observation. Catholics were a real cultural force in south Louisiana and along the Gulf Coast, but elsewhere they were small in numbers. They suffered from nativist opposition in the four decades after 1890, which limited their political involvement. The church's policies promoted a separatism designed to help Catholicism take root in a sometimes hostile region. Devotional societies, recreational agencies, recruitment of native southern priests, and above all, parochial schools enabled Catholics to preserve their identity in the Protestant South. At the same time, the church made accommodations to the South's social and cultural system, instituting, for example, its own version of segregation in the 1890s.

Jewish southerners have a long history in the region—synagogues there date back to the colonial era. Mostly German and eastern European in background, southern Jews experienced the ethnic tensions often found in American society, but living in the South made for special demands. Anti-Semitism was at its worst in the decades from 1890 to 1930 and again during the civil rights years after World War II. The lynching of Leo Frank in 1915 symbolized the dangers of living in a sometimes violent society, and in this same era, Jews who had long held political office throughout the region faced limited political opportunities. Jews in the South practiced their religion but often did not emphasize their cultural and ethnic distinctiveness. This attitude helped them accommodate themselves to the society dominated by their evangelical brethren. They built temples as signs of their devotion to God, and Protestant southerners often saw Jews as being like the Old Testament figures so familiar to them from their knowledge of the Bible. Southern Protestantism stressed piety, and they respected Jewish devotion to the faith. Jewish accommodationism promoted a preference for Reform Judaism, and "temple" in the South could seem familiar to Protestant eyes. Jews might not attend the temple services so often, but their children would likely be in (Jewish) Sunday school on the first day of the week. Jewish southerners often chose to honor the Sabbath at home, even if with nonkosher meals. Food, in fact, is often seen as a sacrament of the blended Jewish-southern identity, as in Eli Evans's reference to kosher grits and a Louisiana cookbook's recipe for matzo ball gumbo. Although a small minority in the South, Jews have a long historical presence in the region and were integral parts of the religious life of small towns and later urban areas.

Catholics and Jews in the South lived ever within the boundaries of an evangelically dominated world. Conservative, proselytizing Protestantism marked the landscape. William Faulkner once noted that religion played a prominent role in his fiction because he grew up in Mississippi with it all around him. "It's just there," he said, and indeed it was "just there" throughout the South. Just as White and Colored signs were visual icons of the southern way of life, so were Jesus Saves and Get Right with God signs. Evangelicalism encouraged witnessing, testifying, preaching, and converting, all of which meant an openness about one's religion that made it a public affair. Southerners became used to street preachers, invitations from neighbors to attend Sunday school, and visits to newcomers to welcome them to the religious life of the community. This religious tradition valued piety, and religious people wore their religion on their sleeves—and everywhere else, too.

Evangelistic campaigns were among the major rhythms of southern life. A prime season for revivalism was summer, during July and August, when the crops were laid by. Frank Dixon, a northern observer of southern religion in 1900, noted that southern Baptists regarded "evangelism as the be-all and end-all of religion." Typical was the participant in a Macon, Georgia, revival in 1900 who wrote that "it looked as if the entire community had professed conversion." Georgia evangelist Samuel Porter Jones lived until 1907, the most famous preacher in the region and nationally influential. He stressed the importance of moral behavior and helped make preaching on Prohibition a key feature of the southern pulpit. If anything, mass revivals became even more popular in the 1920s, when southerners heard such traveling preachers as Billy Sunday and Mordecai Ham and such lesser-knowns as J. C. Bishop, the "Yodeling Cowboy Evangelist." After World War II, Billy Graham would introduce revivalism into new national and international venues.

Revivalism stood at the center of southern religious life, suggesting its orientation toward the conversion of the lost in the essential evangelical dynamic of sin and salvation. This focus militated against concern for a social gospel. Prohibition was the supreme social movement of early-twentieth-century evangelicals in the South, broadly conceived as a reform effort to preserve the family and fight disease. Ministers generally preferred to preach on soul salvation and individual personal morality, and the deeply entrenched

A religious sign along a Georgia road in 1937. Library of Congress,
Prints & Photographs Division, Washington, D.C., reproduction number
LC-USF34-017234-E.

doctrine of the "spirituality of the church" tended to discourage churches from
taking a lead in fundamental questioning of society's justness. This did not
mean that individuals and agencies did not witness for a social gospel, because
they surely did so. Episcopal minister Edgar Gardner Murphy worked with
textile workers in Montgomery and led successful efforts in Alabama to pass a
child labor law, and Will W. Alexander, a former clergyman, helped found the
Commission on Interracial Cooperation in 1919 in Atlanta and directed it for
a quarter century, bringing a religious zeal to efforts for racial reconciliation.
Isa-Beall Neel became the first woman elected a vice president of the SBC
in 1931, and she was a state chair of the Association of Southern Women
for the Prevention of Lynching, a region-wide organization headquartered
in Atlanta. The Methodist Commission on Social Service Movements, the

Baptist Christian Life Commission, and innumerable agencies within the African American churches encouraged the development of an authentic social gospel tradition in the South, even if the growth of such a tradition was limited by lack of funds and lack of interest on the part of the larger denominational concerns.

The efforts of some of the region's religious leaders to engage social issues were part of religion's role in the South's long struggle to come to terms with modernity. Well before the twentieth century, the clergy had accepted the benefits of material prosperity, despite its threats to spiritual life. Ministers gladly accepted major donations from the well off, and these helped fuel southern evangelical growth. Coca-Cola magnate Asa Candler's 1914 donation to set up the Candler School of Theology at Emory University was especially notable, given that his brother Warren was a major figure in the Methodist Episcopal Church, South. The southern denominations came to embrace the bureaucracy and large-scale organization that are a part of modernization, and they made major contributions to building the modern South's infrastructure through hospitals, orphanages, homes for the aged, and schools and colleges. Professionalization of the clergy soon required educational levels well beyond what it took to answer the simple call to preach that had animated generations of earlier southern preachers.

Modern thought, however, generated profound anxieties in a region that rested often in traditional ways and worried that those new ideas would upset the region's peculiar system of race relations. In the early twentieth century, modernism appeared mostly as an exterior threat in the South, as advocates of higher criticism of the Scriptures and scientific evolutionism had been effectively removed earlier from positions of influence. Southern religious leaders tended to identify religious "freethinking" with the North. One preacher lambasted the University of Chicago, for example, as a "satanic institution" for its encouragement of the higher criticism that nurtured "infidelity, atheism, rationalism, and materialism." He concluded it was a "slaughterhouse of faith." A writer in the Baptist *Religious Herald* noted that Southern Baptists believed that modernists had conquered the North, and that God's truth there lay under "piles of rubbish."

The southern faithful worked to maintain not just orthodox thought but proper social behavior as well. Georgia in the 1920s was one of six states, for example, that required daily Bible reading in public schools, reflecting the reliance on the Scriptures as the ultimate anchor against free thought. Birmingham outlawed dancing in public places in the same decade. Opposition to the teaching of evolution in schools became a broader movement that galvanized the southern faithful. The Scopes Trial in 1925 symbolized

The Reverend J. M. Hendley conducting a revival in Inman Park, Atlanta, in 1939.
Courtesy of the Kenan Research Center at the Atlanta History Center.

the conflict between modernism and traditional religious faith, a dramatic trial that fostered across the nation the image of the South as a backward, benighted Bible Belt. H. L. Mencken claimed that no local citizen of Dayton, Tennessee, where the trial took place, doubted "so much as the typographical errors in Holy Writ," and he observed that saying someone was a religious skeptic was tantamount "to accusing him of cannibalism." With the ridicule of fundamentalism in the Scopes Trial, though, and its ineffectiveness in stemming the teaching of evolution, and with the repeal of Prohibition in 1933, fundamentalist forces retreated, working in different venues, such as private schools and colleges, independent associations, and interdenominational groups, to keep their views alive.

Southern religion faced one of its most dramatic challenges with the rise of a new activist civil rights movement after World War II. African American churches produced such leaders of the call for justice as Martin Luther King Jr., Fred Shuttlesworth, and Ralph David Abernathy. Local churches and lay religious leaders were crucial in animating protest in grassroots efforts that made the movement a true region-wide protest. The protests grew out of Gandhian nonviolent principles, Christian teachings on social justice, and the traditions of the southern black church. Dr. King came out of the black Atlanta middle-class church world, and his eloquence drew from the long heritage of rural religion that had anchored black communities under the harshest Jim Crow regimes.

The civil rights movement turned the cause of social change into a powerful moral challenge for the white South. White ministers faced difficult choices. Those who supported racial changes often lost their pulpits and left the region. To avoid preaching about the issue was to ignore the great moral question of the era. Some ministers used old biblical arguments going back to slavery times to justify white supremacy. Most religious leaders simply counseled moderation, goodwill, and opposed violence, but all too few came out against the Jim Crow system until the price of not doing so became clear in the mid-1960s.

The end of legal segregation did not directly affect the churches as private institutions. Although blacks and whites shared traditions of worship, denominations associated with each race maintained their separate identities. Still, religious leaders have been among the leading advocates of racial reconciliation in recent decades, usually working together in community groups that apply principles of Christian fellowship to activities outside the boundaries of formal church life.

The South's struggle with social change came at the same time as increased modernization after World War II, during which increased prosperity, a diversified economy, urban anonymity, mass culture, consumerism, corporate business, and social diversity began to challenge the traditional southern way of life. Prosperity surely affected churches, with much of the wealth of the rising middle class going into an ecclesiastical building boom. Respectable churches came to have carpeted sanctuaries, social halls, extensive educational space, and large parking lots. The bigger congregations soon supported gymnasiums, game rooms, reducing salons, and kitchens to cook evening meals. Managing the growing congregations required new paid staff, such as associate pastors, ministers of education and music, radio and television ministries, musical productions, and ambitious youth programs.

The institutional church has accommodated itself to an increasingly secular society. The churches of the middle class coexist especially easily with the comforts of modern life. Secularization, moreover, prevents as tight a hold on public morals as before. Megachurches are independent congregations that have taken root in southern suburbs and cities, representing a new form of middle-class religious expression that tries to make a place for a relatively undemanding religion among people who may have strayed from denominational homes. They are housed in massive glass-and-steel structures and support thousands of worshipers. These Wal-Mart superstores of churches are modeled more on the California Crystal Cathedral of television evangelist Robert Schuller than on anything from the old brush arbor. Their offerings to the spirit are sermons aimed at the busy middle class, who expect only to attend worship and not commit to other, ongoing church activities. Like earlier southern evangelicals, they aim to influence society by individual conversions and the example of changed lives. Atlanta, befitting its status as the hearth for the newest South, is a breeding ground for megachurches, including the World Changers Ministries Christian Center, Inc., with its founding pastor, the Reverend Creflo A. Dollar Jr.

The South's traditional denominations have continued, nonetheless, to dominate the region's spiritual life in a period of enormous change. America in the 1950s experienced a large increase in church membership, and the South was no exception. In 1936, for example, about 43 percent of Georgians were church members, about the same rate as in 1906, but about 60 percent of the state's population by 1971. Throughout the region, the Baptists, Methodists, and Presbyterians persisted as the three largest denominations. The fate of the SBC in recent times is especially revealing of the ongoing conflicts between traditional regional religion and a modernized world. Dating back to the 1840s, the SBC is a southern folk institution, and no denomination was more important in preserving the sense of a southern identity over such an extensive time period. Since the late 1970s, though, its members have engaged in internecine warfare, leading to a fundamentalist takeover and a loss of much of its membership and a division of churches and institutions.

During World War II, the convention decided to seek members outside of its traditional southern territory, resulting in the SBC now having congregations in all fifty states, with a decided westward tilt, in fact. The SBC traditionally stressed the mission of converting the world, but the new SBC wants to make the world behave better and think more like the SBC. It has a more pronounced creedal emphasis, reflecting the abiding fundamentalist commitment to the faithful affirming the essentials of the faith. A tension within the convention had always existed between, on the one hand, fundamentalists who favored an inerrant interpretation of the Scriptures, moralism, doctrinal rigidity, and political crusades against liquor and evolution, and, on the other hand, the pietists who stressed the centrality of individual grace and salvation from sin. The traditional importance of the Word in the southern faith, the Biblicism that has united Protestant believers, has become even more significant in the new SBC, as its members stress its inerrancy. When Jimmy Carter recently resigned from the SBC, he accused it of investing such authority in the Bible that it had become an icon for southern Baptists, a telling argument to make against a Protestant church that rejects icons.

The conservative religious right political movement is kin to the strict fundamentalist theology of the new leaders of the SBC. It reflects an effort to impose on society and church institutions a discipline that believers see as having once existed in the small towns and rural society of the earlier South that then became besieged, according to its advocates, in the era of dramatic social change in the 1960s. The religious right aims to anchor the nation's politics in a moral outlook grounded in the Bible. It has been a national movement, but with many southern leaders such as Jerry Falwell, Pat Robertson, and Ralph Reed. Southerners responded to the goals of groups like the Moral Majority, the Religious Roundtable, and the Christian Coalition, whose agenda self-consciously touted "traditional values," especially related to family. The religious right has been concerned with abortion, pornography, homosexuality, and prayers in schools, and before its defeat, the equal rights amendment. Concern for prohibition of the sale, or even consumption, of alcoholic beverages, however, is not a part of this political agenda, a major departure from traditional southern ethics of the churches. The new items represent, though, a continued belief that the churches have to impose their moral code on a society in need of discipline.

Despite these efforts to impose an orthodox Protestant religious attitude, rooted in a traditional fundamentalist-evangelical outlook, on the contemporary South, change continues unabated. The new immigration of Hispanics into the South has dramatically increased the presence of Roman Catholics in the region, and northerners moving south have also brought to the region denominations and traditions once unknown there. The Mormons, Seventh-day Adventists, and Unitarians all have a significant, growing presence in the region. Moreover, the secularized society still nurtures the need for transcendence. An impersonal and bureaucratic world, based in the capitalist economy, has triumphed, bringing spiritual as well as material relief to the generations of southerners who endured endemic poverty, but this new modern world has lost the old sense of community and personalism that suffused evangelical religion as not just a church force but a societal one. The sense of place and stability, based in kin and religion, had long been central to the southern value system, but more impersonal ways now characterize the modern South, engendering alienation. Flannery O'Connor breathes satire when she has an advice columnist in her novel *Wise Blood* (1952) suggest to a troubled man that he should "try out" religion. "A religious experience can be a beautiful addition to living if you put it in the proper perspective and do not let it dominate your life." The fictional columnist adds that the man's problem was one of "adjustment to the modern world."

O'Connor, the devout Roman Catholic, admired the southern faithful who still took religion seriously, despite the allures of the superficialities of modern life, and the South still does take religion seriously. The Get Right with God signs, even though they are now manufactured rather than handmade, still speak to an authentic religious passion. V. S. Naipaul, the well-traveled novelist, visited the South in the 1990s and observed that he had never met people "so driven by the idea of good behavior and the good religious life." He captured the continuity that persists within the enormous changes in the South of the new millennium.

Suggested Readings

Bailey, Kenneth K. *Southern White Protestantism in the Twentieth Century.* New York: Harper and Row, 1964.

Bauman, Mark K., and Berkley Kalin, eds. *The Quiet Voices: Southern Rabbis and Black Civil Rights, 1880s to 1990s.* Tuscaloosa: University of Alabama Press, 1998.

Boles, John B. *The Great Revival: Beginnings of the Bible Belt.* Lexington: University Press of Kentucky, 1996.

Harvey, Paul. *Freedom's Coming: Religious Culture and the Shaping of the South from the Civil War through the Civil Rights Era.* Chapel Hill: University of North Carolina Press, 2004.

Hill, Samuel S. *Encyclopedia of Religion in the South.* Macon, Ga.: Mercer University Press, 1984.

Lincoln, C. Eric, and Lawrence Mamiya. *The Black Church in the African American Experience*. Durham: Duke University Press, 1990.

Schweiger, Beth Barton, and Donald G. Mathews, eds. *Religion in the American South: Protestants and Others in History and Culture*. Chapel Hill: University of North Carolina Press, 2004.

Changing Power Structures and Relations

ALEXANDER P. LAMIS

The Emergence of a Two-Party System

Southern Politics in the Twentieth Century

Politics in the American South during the first six decades of the twentieth century was dominated by a one-party system rooted in the desire of white southerners to maintain segregation and second-class status for African Americans. The consequences of this odd political structure were many, not the least being that the region's political development occurred apart from the national mainstream. When the nation resolved its racial dilemma in the mid-1960s, the South proceeded during the last thirty-five years of the century to create a fascinating two-party system that has had far-reaching political results both for the South and the nation.

The one-party Democratic South took hold during the last decades of the nineteenth century. The Republican Party, identified with Abraham Lincoln and the prosecution of the Civil War and Reconstruction, had difficulty taking root in the defeated region, apart from a few mountain strongholds of anti-secessionist sentiment. Instead, by the dawn of the twentieth century whites throughout the region rallied to the Democratic Party in an effort to preserve white supremacy. The argument was simple: if whites divided their votes between two parties, blacks would hold the balance of power and could bargain for concessions that could eradicate their inferior status.

The result of white unity within the Democratic Party meant that, for the first six and a half decades of the century, politics in most of the South was conducted within an odd one-party framework. Just as this unusual system was starting to unravel in midcentury, V. O. Key Jr. published a brilliant analysis of the one-party South in *Southern Politics in State and Nation*, which remains the best guide to this now vanished political edifice.

The destruction of the underlying support for the one-party Democratic South began in the late 1940s and proceeded in an uneven fashion until the critical events of the mid-1960s, the passage of the Civil Rights Act of 1964 and the Voting Rights Act of 1965, both sponsored by national Democratic leaders. The "betrayal" of the white South on civil rights—which began with President Harry S. Truman prior to the 1948 election and was completed momentously by President Lyndon B. Johnson in the mid-1960s—precipitated the death of the one-party system.

A measure of precision in analyzing these developments is provided by figure 1, which traces the demise of the one-party South. The solid line in the figure charts Democratic Party strength in the South from 1932 to 2002 as measured by a composite of the Democratic vote percentages for three key offices—governor, U.S. senator, and U.S. representative. The measure, devised by Paul T. David and appropriately called David's Index, is calculated every two years with each of the three offices counting a third. In figure 1, David's index of Democratic Party strength (the solid line) is plotted along with the Democratic vote for president (the dotted line)—showing the presidential percentages alongside the composite percentages enables one to see the degree of complexity involved in the process of overall partisan change, which quadrennial presidential voting percentages on their own don't reflect.

The presidential trend line in figure 1 confirms that huge Democratic presidential majorities in the region disappeared in 1948. In that year President Truman moved the party off of dead center on the question of civil rights for African Americans. Or, as Minnesota's Hubert H. Humphrey phrased it during a floor debate at the 1948 Democratic National Convention: "[It is time] for the Democratic Party to get out of the shadow of states' rights and to walk forthrightly into the bright sunshine of human rights." Truman's initiatives coupled with the strong platform language on the issue at the 1948

FIGURE 1

Democratic Party Strength in the South, 1932–2002 (percent)

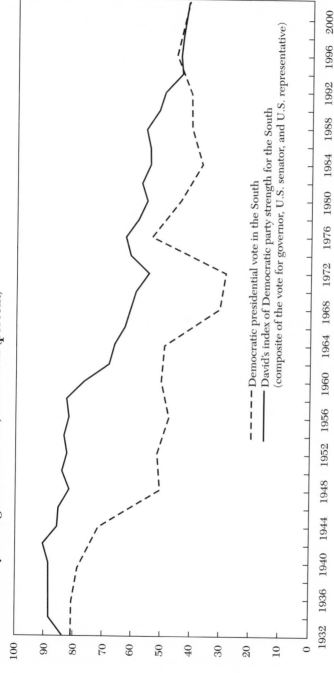

- - - - Democratic presidential vote in the South
——— David's index of Democratic party strength for the South
(composite of the vote for governor, U.S. senator, and U.S. representative)

Source: Paul T. David, *Party Strength in the United States, 1872–1970* (Charlottesville: University Press of Virginia, 1972). Updates for figures 1 and 2 by the author and Andrew M. Lucker of Case Western Reserve University. William Claggett of Florida State University supplied updated figures through 1994 with the permission of the Inter-university Consortium for Political and Social Research. To have a figure for governor and senator every two years, David averaged the preceding and following elections whenever no election occurred. Thus, the figures for the most recent election are only tentative. For the regional figure, state figures have been weighted roughly according to population using the number of members of the U.S. House each state is allotted, a weight that changes every ten years. The South is defined as the eleven states of the former Confederacy.

convention precipitated the Dixiecrat presidential candidacy of South Carolina Governor Strom Thurmond, which denied the victorious Truman the electoral votes of several southern states.

At the state level, the one-party Democratic monolith did not begin to crack until the late 1950s, as illustrated in figure 1. The 1954 U.S. Supreme Court decision declaring public school segregation unconstitutional foreshadowed big changes, as did the birth of the southern civil rights movement in the latter half of the 1950s. But white southern resistance both to the high court's rulings and to the protestors' demands stymied action until the 1960s. Likewise, throughout the 1950s southern Democrats in Congress blocked meaningful civil rights legislation. And because a Republican, Dwight D. Eisenhower, was in the White House during much of the 1950s, the Democratic Party avoided confronting its bitter regional cleavage, a situation that abruptly changed with the election of John F. Kennedy, a Massachusetts Democrat, as president in 1960.

Despite a cautious beginning, President Kennedy employed the power of the federal government in 1962 and 1963 to enforce court-ordered integration at several southern universities and to assist civil rights workers. Then, in mid-1963 he introduced a sweeping civil rights bill that would, among other things, outlaw racial discrimination in public accommodations and employment. After Kennedy's assassination, President Johnson grabbed the mantle of civil rights and skillfully guided landmark legislation to passage in 1964 despite a last-ditch southern filibuster in the Senate. The next year strong federal voting rights protections were enacted into law. The end result of these momentous developments for southern politics—a second Reconstruction—cannot be emphasized enough. In short, the rationale for the one-party Democratic South collapsed.

These events unleashed a torrent of Republican activity in the South. In Mississippi, Republican candidates in 1963 burst forth on the ballot under the slogan K.O. the Kennedys. In the 1964 presidential election, the Republican Party nominated U.S. senator Barry Goldwater of Arizona, who had stood with the southerners against the civil rights bill. Goldwater was buried in that year's national landslide for President Johnson, but the Republican standard-bearer carried five southern states. During the fall campaign, Thurmond dramatically switched to what he called "the Goldwater Republican Party." Throughout Dixie in the mid-1960s southerners suddenly found a new political party struggling to get established. Figure 1 graphically displays the result of this partisan turmoil. From its 83.0 percent perch in 1958, Democratic Party strength in Dixie plummeted to 63.4 percent by 1966 and bottomed out at 55.0 percent in 1972.

The Republican Party's growth was propelled in these early years of the two-party South by two key factors. The first was white southern resentment against the Kennedy-Johnson-Humphrey national Democratic integrationists. Southern Republicans sought to ride this resentment to power by tying their state Democratic opponents to the national Democratic Party at every turn, a dubious strategy given the impeccable segregationist credentials, at least in the early years, of a host of southern Democrats.

The second factor propelling the Republican Party in the South revolved around conservative economic issues tied to a restrictive view of the role of government. Since the New Deal, the two major parties outside of the South have fought over a series of economic-class and role-of-government issues. Because the South had just one party, the New Deal conflicts had to be played out within it. Thus, southern economic conservatives in the 1930s, 1940s, and 1950s often found themselves in agreement with the national policies of the anti–New Deal Republican Party even though they retained their Democratic affiliation for regional purposes. In the 1960s, with the one-party rationale shattered, it was now possible for southern conservatives to build a Republican Party along the lines of those in, for example, Pennsylvania or Ohio. And, it is this aspect of the GOP's party-building strategy that Republicans prefer to emphasize today while downplaying the racial element. In the heat of the partisan struggle, in fact, the twin factors of race and economics often merged.

As the Republican Party began to build at the state level, propelled by the white reaction to the end of segregation, it made its most faithful converts among those attracted by its conservative position on New Deal–type economic-class issues. But it also picked up substantial support from white Democrats angered by their national party's "betrayal" on the race issue. Mixed into the situation was the logical compatibility of conservative economic-class Republicanism and the anti–civil rights protest. The GOP, as the party philosophically opposed to an activist federal government in economic matters, gained adherents also from those who objected to federal intervention in the racial affairs of the states. The two streams of protest could not be easily separated in the political arena, and the Republican candidates, who recognized that they were beneficiaries of both prongs of reaction, rarely made the effort.

The best exposition of the subtle merger of these twin forces was offered by South Carolinian Lee Atwater eight years before he became chairman of the Republican National Committee after serving as the architect of George Bush's 1988 presidential election victory. It came during a 1981 interview while he was a member of President Ronald Reagan's White House political staff:

ATWATER: As to the whole Southern strategy that Harry Dent and others put together in 1968, opposition to the Voting Rights Act would have been a central part of keeping the South. Now [the new Southern strategy of Ronald Reagan] doesn't have to do that. All you have to do to keep the South is for Reagan to run in place on the issues he's campaigned on since 1964 . . . and that's fiscal conservatism, balancing the budget, cut taxes, you know, the whole cluster. . . .

QUESTIONER: But the fact is, isn't it, that Reagan does get to the Wallace voter and to the racist side of the Wallace voter by doing away with Legal Services, by cutting down on food stamps?

ATWATER: You start out in 1954 by saying "Nigger, nigger, nigger." By 1968 you can't say "nigger"—that hurts you. Backfires. So you say stuff like forced busing, states' rights, and all that stuff. You're getting so abstract now [that] you're talking about cutting taxes, and all these things you're talking about are totally economic things and a by-product of them is [that] blacks get hurt worse than whites. And subconsciously maybe that is part of it. I'm not saying that. But I'm saying that if it is getting that abstract, and that coded, that we are doing away with the racial problem one way or the other. You follow me—because obviously sitting around saying, "we want to cut this," is much more abstract than even the busing thing *and* a hell of a lot more abstract than "Nigger, nigger."

The strategies of the nascent southern Republican Party are only part of the story. Perhaps of greater significance for the first decades of two-party competition was the remarkable transformation that came to the southern Democratic Party in the aftermath of the traumatic events of the mid-1960s. With federal protection, African Americans entered the electorate in large numbers, and they did so as Democrats. Of course, it was natural enough that they should affiliate with the Democratic Party since the party's national leaders were the force behind the Second Reconstruction. And, while it was ironic that southern blacks would became part of the former party of segregation, the potential of this large new source of votes was not lost on white southern Democratic politicians as they assessed their altered situation in the latter half of the 1960s.

These leaders—Jimmy Carter in Georgia in 1970 was one of the pioneers—proceeded in the 1970s and 1980s to assemble potent coalitions of nearly all blacks and those whites who had weathered the integration crisis with their Democratic voting inclinations intact. These ideologically diverse, black-white Democratic coalitions became a central feature of the South's politics in the post–civil rights era. They were a key element in blunting the Republican surge, as the challenging Republicans well understood. Here's how the chairman of the Georgia Republican Party in 1974, Robert Shaw of Atlanta, described the diverse Democratic coalition that was demolishing GOP statewide challenges in the Peach State: "So what catches us is that you find the [white] conservative rural vote going in voting the straight party ticket, and by the same token you find the urban blacks voting the straight party ticket. And they'd be considered a liberal element, with the South Georgia farmer voting conservative. And yet they're voting hand in hand, and when they do, they're squeezing the lives out of us. And yet there's no tie-in between the two at all. Ideologically, they're as far apart as night and day."

To keep these diverse Democratic coalitions together required considerable political skill, and the white moderate Democratic leaders who arose in state after state provided it. They included, in addition to Carter, Sam Nunn of Georgia, James B. (Jim) Hunt Jr. of North Carolina, Lawton Chiles of Florida, William Winter of Mississippi, Dale Bumpers of Arkansas, and Richard Riley of South Carolina, to name only a few. They were aided by the benefits that accrued to the Democrats by virtue of their near monopoly on public office through the 1950s—namely a strong Democratic voting tradition (the famous "Yellow Dog" Democrats who, legend has it, would vote for a canine over a Republican) coupled with a storehouse of ambitious, experienced candidates who were already in office. Further, they had a stroke of luck when one of their own, Georgia's Carter, was elected president in 1976. And, of course, the Watergate scandal, that national Republican disaster, hurt the GOP in the South as well.

As figure 1 demonstrates, Democratic Party strength reversed its downward movement in 1974, rising to 61.4 percent in that year and going up to 63.0 percent two years later when Carter won the White House. It dropped to 59.0 percent in 1978 and then stabilized around the mid-50s for the next ten years, registering 56.4 percent in 1988. Although there was considerable variation from state to state, the regional figures underscore the fact that in the first two decades of two-party competition in Dixie, the revitalized and restructured post–civil rights era southern Democratic Party was not an easy target for the South's rising Republicans. The 1990s were to be quite different.

In the 1990s the South entered a strikingly new phase in its thirty-year experience with two-party politics. During the first two-thirds of the decade, the Republican Party made stunning advances, achieving majority status for the first time. The development is captured in figure 2, which, in contrast to figure 1, plots Republican growth directly for three key categories of offices.

Imagine for a moment that figure 2 stops at 1990. After the 1990 balloting, the GOP controlled 10 of the region's 33 top statewide offices (11 governorships and 22 U.S. Senate seats), or 30.3 percent. In the 1990 elections, Republicans won 33.6 percent of the region's seats in the U.S. House, or 39

FIGURE 2

The Growth of the Republican Party in the South, 1960–2002 (percent)

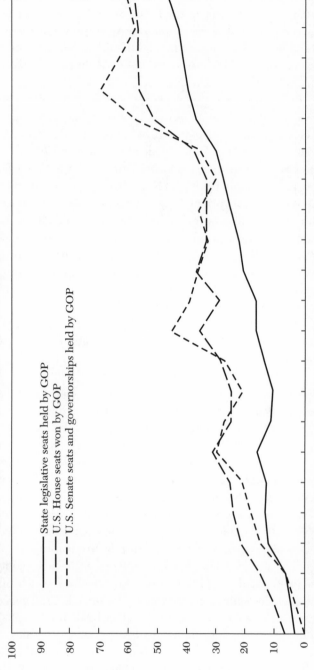

State legislative seats held by GOP
U.S. House seats won by GOP
U.S. Senate seats and governorships held by GOP

of the 116 seats allotted to the eleven states after the 1980 census. Finally, at the state legislative level, the Republicans controlled 27.8 percent of the seats after the 1990 elections. Progress in all three categories since 1960 had been remarkable, but, as the new decade began, the GOP fell far short of majority status in the region.

Now, consider the astonishing Republican leap represented in the mid-1990s portion of figure 2. After the 1996 elections the GOP in Dixie held 23 of the 33 governorships and U.S. Senate seats, a stunning 69.7 percent. In the 1996 elections the Republicans won 56.8 percent of the South's U.S. House seats, or 71 of the 125 seats assigned the region after the 1990 census. Even at the state legislative level the GOP reached 40.0 percent of the seats after the 1996 voting, and more than a score of party switchers plus a dozen or so special and odd-year election victories pushed the figure up to 41.5 percent by 1998. How did this breakthrough occur? What were its causes and what does it mean for southern politics in the twenty-first century?

Southern voting patterns need to be placed within the national context. With the exception of Jimmy Carter in 1976, Democratic presidential candidates lost heavily in the South from 1968 through 1988. For example, Governor Michael Dukakis of Massachusetts, the Democratic standard-bearer in 1988, received only 40.9 percent of the southern vote to George Bush's 58.3 percent; this compares to Dukakis's nationwide vote of 45.6 percent to Bush's 53.4 percent. These Democratic nominees (Carter in 1976—but not in 1980—is again the exception)—Hubert Humphrey in 1968, George Mc-Govern in 1972, Walter Mondale in 1984, and Dukakis—were losers outside of the South as well. At the core of these Democratic losses was a nationwide difficulty in attracting the white working class to the party.

Bill Clinton, the savvy, nationally oriented, veteran Democratic governor of Arkansas, thoroughly comprehended his party's presidential weakness. At a May 1991 gathering of the Democratic Leadership Council, a group of centrist Democrats, he declared: "Too many of the people who used to vote for us, the very burdened middle class we're talking about, have not trusted us in national elections to defend our national interests abroad, to put their values in our social policy at home or to take their tax money and spend it with discipline. We've got to turn these perceptions around, or we can't continue as a national party."

After securing the 1992 Democratic presidential nomination and picking a fellow southerner, Senator Al Gore Jr. of Tennessee, as his vice presidential running mate, Clinton stuck to his "new Democrat" theme in a brilliant national campaign. One of the Democratic ticket's first television commercials described the two southerners as follows: "They are a new generation of

Official White House photograph of President Bill Clinton with Vice President Albert Gore, on left, and Attorney General Janet Reno, on right. Library of Congress, Prints & Photographs Division, Washington, D.C., reproduction number LC-USZ62-113158.

Democrats, Bill Clinton and Al Gore. And they don't think the way the old Democratic Party did. They've called for an end to welfare as we know it, so welfare can be a second chance, not a way of life. They've sent a strong signal to criminals by supporting the death penalty. And they've rejected the old tax and spend politics."

There was, of course, considerably more to the 1992 presidential election besides Clinton's much-highlighted "new Democrat" shift to the center. President Bush's popularity had plummeted by early 1992 as the economy remained in the mild recession it had entered over a year earlier. With his single-minded focus on economic issues, Clinton benefited from the lingering recession and a general uneasiness about the country's economic direction. And, then there was Ross Perot, who attacked both parties for their joint responsibility in expanding the national debt by running huge budget deficits year after year.

While the Clinton-Gore electoral strategy was built on the 1988 base of nonsouthern states Dukakis carried or ran well in, the national Democratic candidates made a strong effort in several southern states beyond their home states. Although Clinton's victory with 43.0 percent of the vote to Bush's 37.4

percent was based on states outside of the South, the Arkansan did considerably better in the South than any Democratic standard-bearer since Carter. He carried four of the eleven southern states—Georgia and Louisiana, plus the ticket's home states of Arkansas and Tennessee. The Democratic presidential percentage in the region was 41.2 percent compared to Bush's 42.6 percent, quite a turnaround from 1988. Perot had a regional average of 15.8 percent compared to his national percentage of 18.9 percent. (Incidentally, the number of African Americans in Congress from the South more than tripled in the 1992 elections as the result of the creation of twelve new black-majority districts to go with the five existing districts.)

The 39 southern electoral votes the Clinton-Gore ticket won (out of 147 allotted to the old Confederacy) were not critical to the Democrats' electoral college victory with 370 votes, 100 more than the required 270 majority. But this strong national Democratic showing in the South (albeit by two Southern Baptists) is noteworthy. As figure 2 shows, southern Republicans gained in all nonpresidential categories in 1992, although their successes were modest compared with what would come in 1994. Also, David's index of Democratic Party strength declined a few more percentage points in 1992, registering a

Official White House photograph of President George H. W. Bush. Library of Congress, Prints & Photographs Division, Washington, D.C., reproduction number LC-USZ62-98302.

fraction above 50 percent, which, in retrospect, appears to be a fitting poetic pause at the precipice (see figure 1).

The 1994 midterm elections took place against a backdrop of rising voter disenchantment and pessimism. A late October *New York Times* article based on interviews with party strategists and election analysts described an "anti-Clinton, anti-Government sentiment" that had Democrats more than a little concerned. The article noted that "professionals in both parties said they had never seen so many factors breaking the Republicans' way."

When the votes came in on election night, it became clear that the Republican Party had achieved a smashing national victory, capturing the U.S. House for the first time in forty years with a gain of 55 seats, retaking the Senate with 8 new seats, and winning a dozen new governorships. The southern component of this GOP sweep was historic in its own right because, after the election, the party held a majority of the South's U.S. House and Senate seats and governorships for the first time since Reconstruction. Brief consideration is in order as to how President Clinton, the energetic "new Democrat," ended up in just twenty-two months leading his party to such a huge national defeat.

Clinton himself serves as an excellent witness. Addressing a Democratic dinner in Washington in late September 1994, he said, to quote from a *New York Times* account, that "his efforts to reduce the Federal deficit, increase global trade and rewrite foreign policy had not yet restored optimism about the future—and about his Presidency—because their very nature is to make the future less predictable." Calling this fear of change wrong and irrational, he said the Democratic Party had to tackle the issue head-on.

Missing from Clinton's fall speeches was any mention of the major domestic initiative of his presidency up to then: the ambitious, failed effort to restructure the nation's health care system to provide affordable access to care for all Americans. As an Iowa Democratic senator observed: "You can't say the health care reform package he sent up here to Congress is centrist." And therein lies a key ambivalence that permeated Clinton's first two years and worked to his political disadvantage. His health care initiative was an important effort to accomplish a major goal on the national Democratic agenda since the New Deal, a scheme that would necessitate heavy government involvement in a large segment of the American economy. Its failure—and Clinton's poor political management of the reform was chiefly responsible for its failure—dashed the hopes of those who believed in the goal he so eloquently proclaimed, and at the same time it gave ammunition to his enemies, who were able to claim that Clinton, despite his rhetoric, was indeed a "big government" liberal. Clinton wanted it both ways—to be a "new Democrat" and to be the champion of "those who have less," who frequently can be aided only by effective governmental action. The performance left him vulnerable, and Republicans rarely missed their target in 1994.

"We're prepared to place our trust in the people to reshape the government. Our liberal friends place their trust in the government to reshape the people." That's the way Georgia's Newt Gingrich, the architect of the House triumph, put the GOP argument in one of his milder formulations of it. Proclaiming his goal to "renew American civilization," Gingrich placed the blame for society's ills on the "counterculture," which, he said, "permeates this administration." "It is impossible to maintain a civilization with twelve-year-olds having babies, fifteen-year-olds killing each other, seventeen-year-olds dying of AIDS and eighteen-year-olds getting diplomas they can't read." When asked at a news conference the morning after his election triumph what his opponents' biggest mistake in the campaign was, he reiterated his chief themes: "The Democrats adopted a McGovernite view of foreign policy and military power, Lyndon Johnson's Great Society structure of the welfare state, and counterculture values. And those three things are so destructive that until the Democratic Party weans itself of those and gets back to the basic fundamentals of American civilization, it is going to have a virtually impossible time governing successfully."

Figure 2 captures the unprecedented 1994 GOP gains in the South. The party picked up 16 U.S. House seats to give it 51.2 percent of the region's seats (64 of 125). Republicans won both U.S. Senate seats in Tennessee and retained another it had captured in a special election in Texas in 1993. At the gubernatorial level, Republicans made a net gain of 2 in 1994, icing to the cake of a Republican victory in Virginia the previous year. In Texas Republican George W. Bush, the son of the former president, defeated Democratic Governor Ann Richards's bid for reelection. A Republican congressman replaced a retiring Democratic governor in Tennessee. A recent Democratic convert held the South Carolina governorship for the Republican Party. In Alabama a former Democratic governor won the governorship running as a Republican. Altogether the 1994 results gave the Republicans 6 of the South's 11 governorships. These results were reflected in a plunge in David's index of Democratic strength in the region from 50.1 percent in 1992 to 44.6 percent in 1994.

The combined category of GOP governorships and U.S. Senate seats, which totaled 18 on election night, grew to 19 the next day when Senator Richard Shelby of Alabama, a conservative Democrat, announced he was switching to the Republican Party. Thus, after all the election winners were sworn in, the GOP controlled 19 of the top 33 elective offices in the region, or 57.6

percent. At the state legislative level, Republicans in 1994 made their largest gains since 1966, advancing 6.7 percentage points, leaving them in control of 37.0 percent of the region's legislative seats. With the Republicans now in control of Congress, five conservative Democratic members of the U.S. House chose in 1995 to switch to the GOP. The 1994 GOP breakthroughs in the region occurred as a result of a combination of two forces: a national electoral tide in which the South contributed at least its share but not much more, and the continuation of the settling-in of two-party competition.

On the national scene, familiar major players dominated 1996 elections. However, those who were riding high after the November 1994 elections and through much of 1995, namely, Speaker Gingrich and the other leaders of the Republican-controlled 104th Congress, were put on the defensive by the negative public reaction to the partial shutdowns of the government in late 1995 and early 1996, which resulted from bitter budget disagreements. President Clinton bounced back from the midterm election defeat and found his political footing partly by skillfully adopting portions of the Republican agenda. For example, in his January 1996 State of the Union address, he brought forth thunderous cheers from the Republican congressional ranks when he declared the "era of big government is over." In a postelection conversation with reporters, Clinton, in the words of one news account, argued that "the policies enacted in his first two years in office, like his deficit reduction plan and his anti-crime legislation, had come to be appreciated only in 1996. And he cited his ability to work with Congress at the end of the [1996] legislative session as 'the thing that sealed all this.'" And, of course, the economy remained strong in 1996.

Despite a vigorous campaign, Senator Bob Dole of Kansas, the former Senate majority leader and the 1996 Republican presidential standard-bearer, trailed Clinton in the polls throughout 1996. Clinton was reelected with 49.2 percent of the popular vote nationwide, amassing 379 electoral votes, to Dole's 40.7 percent and 159 electoral votes. Ross Perot received only 8.4 percent. Clinton again carried four southern states, including three he had won in 1992—Arkansas, Tennessee, and Louisiana. This time he lost Georgia narrowly but added electoral vote–rich Florida, which he won handily, 48.0 percent to Dole's 42.3 percent. Even with a total of 51 electoral votes from Dixie, Clinton's southern vote was again not decisive. However, Clinton ran well enough even in the southern states he lost to score a not inconsiderable twenty-year Democratic first in Dixie: Clinton's total popular vote in the South was just under 25,000 votes more than Dole's—46.2 percent for Clinton to 46.1 percent for Dole.

The GOP retained control of Congress in 1996, a feat the party had not accomplished since the 1920s. The Republicans gained 2 seats in the Senate, giving them a 55-to-45 margin. In the House they lost 10 seats, reducing their numbers to 226 compared to the Democrats' 208.

Despite a weak presidential candidate and a national congressional outcome that, at best, could be called a stalemate, the southern GOP continued its forward progress. Republicans captured 2 open Democratic U.S. Senate seats: one in Alabama and the other in Arkansas. In 1995 a Republican (who had been a Democrat right up to the filing deadline) won the Louisiana governorship. And when Democratic Governor Jim Guy Tucker of Arkansas was convicted of Whitewater-related crimes and resigned in July 1996, the Republican lieutenant governor, Mike Huckabee, became governor, giving the GOP a net 1996 increase of 4 in the category of major statewide offices, boosting its record 1994 total to a staggering 69.7 percent in 1996. Republican U.S. House seats in the South increased by 7 to 71, or 56.8 percent. The number of GOP state legislative seats continued to increase as well. There is no question that the GOP's 1996 momentum in Dixie was primarily the result of intraregional dynamics since there was no national tide to share the credit as in 1994.

In the 1998 elections southern Democrats made their best showing since 1990, recapturing the governorship in South Carolina and Alabama and picking up a Republican-held U.S. Senate seat in North Carolina. Despite the Republican gain of the Florida governorship, which was won by Jeb Bush, another son of former President Bush, Democrats were still able in 1998 to cut back on the high percentage of the South's top elected offices occupied by the Republican Party after the 1996 elections. With a net Democratic gain of 2 seats, the Republicans controlled 63.6 percent of the 33 highest-profile elected positions after the 1998 balloting. The battle for the region's U.S. House seats ended in a stalemate in 1998; Republicans continued to occupy 71 seats as they had in 1996. The steady GOP growth at the state legislative level halted in 1998. Republicans gained 10 seats in southern lower houses but lost nearly an equal number in upper houses to remain at 41.5 percent of the region's 1,782 state legislative seats.

In the 2000 elections the South played a crucial role in the victory of the Republican presidential standard-bearer, Governor Bush of Texas, providing him all of its electoral votes, which amounted to over half of the electoral votes he needed to win—147 of the 271 he secured in his razor-thin victory over Vice President Gore of Tennessee. With the exception of Florida, Bush had substantial victory margins in most of the other ten Southern states. The margin was so close in the Sunshine State, however, that it took seven weeks after Election Day and a narrow five-to-four decision by the U.S. Supreme Court to tip the result to the GOP. Despite the disputed nature of the outcome, there was no disputing the importance of the region to the Republican presidential victory. In over half of the southern states, Gore ran only marginally stronger than Dukakis did in 1988.

The other results in 2000 were consistent with recent patterns showing the settling-in of two-party competition in the region. For example, Republicans advanced their percentage of state legislative seats by 1.5 percentage points, reaching 43.0 percent after the 2000 elections (see figure 2). Democratic Party strength in the region, as measured by David's index in figure 1, declined only slightly to 43.7 percent from the 44 percent range it remained at through the latter half of the 1990s. In 2000 the GOP again won 71 of the region's 125 U.S. House seats, as the party narrowly retained its majority in that national body for the third straight election. On the other hand, Democrats continued to make small gains in the category of major statewide offices. In 1999 Democrat Ronnie Musgrove won the Mississippi governorship, which had been held by a term-limited Republican, and in 2000 Democrats won U.S. Senate seats in Florida and Georgia that had been previously held by Republicans, although they lost one in Virginia. Thus, after the 2000 balloting, Republicans controlled 19 of the top 33 positions, or 57.6 percent, a return to the percentage the party had first attained in 1994.

Boosted by President Bush's aggressive campaigning, the Republican Party had a remarkably strong performance in the 2002 midterm elections, regaining narrow control of the U.S. Senate and adding seats to the party's majority in the U.S. House. Capitalizing on high public approval of his leadership in response to the terrorist attacks on September 11, 2001, the president invested his prestige in scores of close races around the nation, achieving notable success. GOP victories in the South in 2002 played an important role in the Republican Party's national advance.

Southern Republicans gained 3 seats in the U.S. House in 2002, not counting a former Democrat-turned-independent from Virginia who had joined the GOP caucus in 2000 and who won reelection in 2002 as a Republican. After the 2000 census, the eleven southern states were allocated 131 U.S. House seats, a net increase of 6. Republicans won 76 of these, or 58.0 percent, counting the Virginia party switcher. In percentage terms, the total represents only a modest increase over the 56.8 percent (71 of the then-allocated 125 seats) that the southern GOP won in each of the three elections from 1996 to 2000. But, in the current era with a narrowly divided U.S. House, those 3 additional seats made up half of the historic 6-seat gain achieved by the Republicans nationwide in 2002. It is extremely rare for the party of the president to gain seats in a midterm House election as the Republicans did in 2002; in fact, in the twentieth century the president's party lost House seats in all but the 1934 and 1998 off-year elections.

In the major statewide elections of 2002, Republicans defeated incumbent first-term governors in South Carolina, Georgia, and Alabama, captured a U.S. Senate seat from a Democrat in Georgia, and held U.S. Senate seats being vacated by Republicans in South Carolina, Tennessee, North Carolina, and Texas. Southern Democrats defeated a Republican U.S. senator in Arkansas and won the governorship of Tennessee, which had been held by a term-limited Republican. In a high-visibility runoff in Louisiana a month after the November general election, a Democratic U.S. senator, Mary Landrieu, turned back a well-financed Republican challenge by Suzanne Haik Terrell, the state's elections commissioner, with 51.6 percent of the vote to Terrell's 48.4 percent. While the GOP did not gain a U.S. Senate seat from the South in 2002, the party's ability to hold 4 of its own open seats in the region cannot be discounted.

After factoring in the 2001 Democratic capture of the Virginia governorship, which had been held by a term-limited Republican, Dixie's GOP in 2002 increased by 1, from 19 to 20, the number of the region's 33 governorships and U.S. Senate seats the party controlled, or 60.6 percent. Further, at the state legislative level, the GOP made sizable gains in 2002, advancing 3.7 percentage points to control 46.7 percent of the South's state legislative seats, or 833 of 1,782 seats. The 66-seat increase represented a third of the 200 state legislative seats the party gained nationwide in 2002 (see figure 2).

The Republican successes of 2002 can be further measured by reference to David's index of Democratic strength, which registered 42.2 percent in 2002. This represents a decline of 1.5 percentage points in the index since 2000 and marks a new post-Reconstruction low for the South's once-dominant Democratic Party.

In contrast to the overall trend, there was considerable diversity among the southern states. Democratic strength actually increased in five of the eleven—Alabama, Arkansas, Tennessee, Texas, and Louisiana. In four of the other six, the Democratic decline was modest, that is, comparable in size to the increases measured in the party's five strongest states. In the other two—Mississippi and Virginia—the slide was in double-digit figures, reflecting the failure of the Democrats to run a candidate against two long-term Republican senators, Thad Cochran of Mississippi and John W. Warner of Virginia.

Apart from the numbers, the results of these recent elections from 1998 through 2002 reveal a rich complexity present in the southern partisan reality as the twentieth century gave way to the twenty-first. Key dynamic elements in the current partisan mix offer a glimpse into the future of southern politics.

Everywhere in Dixie the advancing Republican Party divided between adherents who were motivated primarily by economic conservatism and those, commonly labeled the Christian or religious right, who were more interested in an array of conservative social and cultural issues. The two groups coexist uneasily. For example, a prominent mainstream Georgia Republican, Johnny Isakson, expressed his frustration with the Peach State GOP's religious right in a 1996 interview: "They're not always wrong, but if you don't always agree with them, you're always wrong." Despite the tension, the religious right has contributed significant organizational might to the GOP.

Further, the southern Republican Party has benefited significantly from its ability to present itself as the party of reform. For example, Glen T. Broach and Lee Brady examined recent South Carolina politics and concluded: "The story of the [South Carolina] GOP's rise . . . is in part a tale of youth, strategic savvy and organizational energy that enabled the Republicans to position themselves as the party of the future. By contrast, the complacency and organizational ineptitude of the Democrats prevented them from shaking their image as the party of the past and 'good ol' boy' corruption." Similar patterns can be found in other southern states.

Turning to the issue of race in southern politics at the turn of the century, one confronts a complex of issues that entangles both parties in a variety of subtle and not-so-subtle ways. The pervasiveness of the issue was aptly characterized as "the moose on the table" by North Carolina's white former Democratic secretary of state, Janice Faulkner: "The moose comes in and sits on the table with every conversation. If we are really looking into gaining insight into what is happening, we need to get the moose off the table— the resentments of whites from the days of integration of the schools, the competition for scarce economic development dollars, the increasing cost of entitlement programs." Southern blacks might well accept the analogy, but their list of resentments would be different, flowing as it would from being on the receiving end of discrimination in the era of segregation and earlier. Such is the historical legacy that Dixie's current political system confronts.

Black-white relations in the southern party system fall into two related categories: those between the two parties and those within the biracial Democratic Party coalition. On the former, Jack Hawke, a one-time North Carolina GOP chair, observed: "One of the disturbing factors is that the parties racially are becoming more polarized to a degree that has hurt the Democrats in terms of white flight. But as the Democratic Party shrinks in size and numbers, percentage-wise it becomes more black-dominated. Republicans have not been successful for a variety of reasons in attracting enough black support to offset the notion that the Democratic Party is becoming the party of minorities and the Republican Party is becoming the party of white folks." A retired former Democratic official in Alabama, Pete Mathews, put the issue more bluntly: "[Many Republicans] do not like black people. I don't give a [expletive] who tells you they do. I'm telling you they don't. And that's who they perceive as controlling the Democratic Party and they're right."

Such comments like Hawke's and Mathews's have on occasion led to the prediction that eventually the South will have a nearly all-black Democratic Party to go with its nearly all-white Republican Party. In my view, this is not going to happen. Certainly racial tension between the two parties is unlikely to end any time soon, probably not until many more blacks participate in politics through the Republican Party, which will eventually happen. In the meantime, the bulwark to a racially polarized party system is the continued existence of the black-white southern Democratic coalition. That biracial alliance is clearly under considerable pressure and undergoing change in the face of the rapid Republican rise since the early 1990s. But, in terms of the region as a whole, the biracial Democratic coalition is very much alive, even as it confronts its own set of intraparty racial tensions.

Black-white tensions surface from time to time in the southern Democratic Party. The diverse black-white Democratic coalition that took hold in the South in the post–civil rights era has grappled with those tensions for several decades. The coalition, however, is far from collapse either at the voter or leadership level.

The southern Democratic Party in the last decade is epitomized by leaders like former Governor Jim Hunt of North Carolina and Senator Zell Miller of Georgia. They are moderate coalition-builders with good instincts for issues with broad popular appeal, such as former Governor Miller's lottery-based HOPE Scholarship program in Georgia. These southern Democratic leaders stress fiscal responsibility, support public education, favor welfare reform, and promote efforts to fight crime. They shy away from the unpopular "tax-and-spend liberal" label associated with their party's losing presidential nominees of the 1980s. The next generation of Democratic leaders will likely follow the successful moderate course adopted by Hunt, Miller, and others.

Consider the Democratic coalition's fate in 2000. After Georgia's Miller was appointed in July 2000 to the U.S. Senate on the death of Republican senator Paul Coverdell, he held the seat in the November 2000 general election with 55.9 percent of the vote to the 40.2 percent of his Republican opponent, Mack Mattingly. Exit polls indicated that Miller won 92 percent of the votes of Georgia's African Americans along with 45 percent of the state's white vote. By contrast, Gore, in losing Georgia's electoral votes to Bush (43.2 percent to 55.0 percent), received only 26 percent of the votes of Georgia's whites; like

Miller, Gore won 92 percent of the African American voters. If the black-white Democratic coalition virtually collapsed at the presidential level in the South in 2000, it obviously remained in place for Miller as well as other southern Democrats.

The 2002 elections exhibited mixed results for the coalition. While it held strong in states like Arkansas, Louisiana, and Tennessee, it unraveled in the gubernatorial elections in South Carolina, Alabama, and Georgia, where first-term Democratic governors were all defeated. The result in Georgia drew special attention because the black-white Democratic coalition had won the governorship throughout the new era of two-party competition, remaining the only state in Dixie not to elect a Republican governor. That changed dramatically on November 5, 2002, when Republican Sonny Perdue, having successfully attracted large numbers of rural white voters, stunned the Georgia political establishment by defeating Governor Roy Barnes. One Atlanta political consultant called the result "a meltdown" for the Democrats in rural areas.

A variety of factors were offered after the election to explain how the well-financed Barnes, who led in all the preelection opinion polls, lost to state senator Perdue, a Democrat until 1998, including opposition from public school teachers angered at the Democrat's education policies. Frequently cited was Barnes's successful effort to shrink the Confederate battle emblem on the Georgia flag, a change that was designed to appeal to African Americans but was not popular among rural whites. In the days immediately following the election, Perdue convinced several Democratic state senators to switch to the Republican Party, giving the GOP control of the upper house for the first time since Reconstruction. The Georgia partisan legislative shifts were similar to those that had occurred in neighboring South Carolina eight years earlier following another breakthrough election. Despite these Republican gains, Georgia Democrats in 2002 easily retained a sizable majority in the lower house, won two additional U.S. House seats, and were elected to all statewide constitutional offices below the governor, including that of attorney general and labor commissioner (both posts being held by African Americans). Thus, despite a good election outcome in 2002 for the rising GOP in Dixie, the South's partisanship remained, for the time being at least, dominated by dynamic elements that have been present in the region for several decades.

As we await the start of the next phase of southern politics, it is clear that the arrival of the mature years of southern partisan competition in the last decade or so has had an important impact on national politics: it has given the country its first genuinely national party system since the middle 1850s. The implications of this development for the country's political institutions are only now coming to be fully understood. For Dixie, one result of this nationalizing trend is the promise that national forces are likely to influence the South's future partisan direction at least as much as regional forces. However, this nationalization of southern politics doesn't mean that differences between the North and the South have evaporated. For example, white southerners tend to be more conservative overall on social and cultural issues than white northerners, although on economic and role-of-government issues whites in the South and North divide about the same.

As the South's full political reintegration into the Union proceeds, it is important to recognize that the region already accomplished a remarkable feat by the end of the twentieth century: by installing a fully functioning, mature system of two-party competition, the South advanced the cause of democracy for all its citizens. How far we have come in the South is best conveyed by quoting Professor Key's 1949 assessment of the impact of the one-party system on the region's political life in his famous midcentury classic:

> Consistent and unquestioning attachment, by overwhelming majorities, to the Democratic party . . . has meant that the politics within southern states—the election of governors, of state legislators, and the settlement of public issues generally—has had to be conducted without the benefit of political parties. As institutions, parties enjoy a general disrepute, yet most of the democratic world finds them indispensable as instruments of self-government, as means for the organization and expression of competing viewpoints on public policy. Nevertheless, over a tremendous area—the South—no such competing institutions exist.

Along these same lines, Key wrote to his chief associate, Alexander Heard, in 1947 while researching *Southern Politics*:

> In those moments between going to bed and to sleep I've been speculating a little on our general strategy. One night I had the bright notion that maybe the thing to do was to set out our prejudices at the beginning (as a warning to one and all) and say that our purpose in talking cold turkey is to promote these ends. . . . We believe in a brawling, fighting, arguing, contentious democracy, not because it promotes good government but because it insures popular government. . . . Hence, we believe that popular government redounds to the good of all by keeping the top dogs on their toes, by encouraging the ablest woods colts to earn the position to which their inheritance entitles them, and by weeding out those of incompetence who presume to position.

Over fifty years later, no one can deny that Key's hope for a "brawling, fighting, arguing, contentious" democratic South has been realized in the current, competitive two-party system firmly in place throughout Dixie, a system that does provide the "means for the organization and expression of competing viewpoints on public policy" and that can—given intelligent and imaginative leaders—cope with the South's problems.

Suggested Reading

Bartley, Numan V. *The New South, 1945–1980*. Baton Rouge: Louisiana State University Press, 1995.

Bartley, Numan V., and Hugh D. Graham. *Southern Politics and the Second Reconstruction*. Baltimore: Johns Hopkins University Press, 1975.

Black, Earle, and Merle Black. *Politics and Society in the South*. Cambridge, Mass.: Harvard University Press, 1987.

———. *The Rise of Southern Republicans*. Cambridge, Mass.: Harvard University Press, 2002.

Carter, Dan T. *The Politics of Rage: George Wallace, the Origins of the New Conservatism, and the Transformation of American Politics*. New York: Simon and Schuster, 1995.

Grantham, Dewey W. *The South in Modern America: A Region at Odds*. New York: HarperCollins Publishers, 1995.

Key, V. O., Jr., with the assistance of Alexander Heard. *Southern Politics in State and Nation*. New York: Alfred A. Knopf, 1949.

Lamis, Alexander P. "Southern Politics in the Twentieth Century." *Atlanta History: A Journal of Georgia and the South* (Winter 2001): 28–41.

———. *The Two-Party South*. 2nd expanded ed. New York: Oxford University Press, 1990.

———, ed. *Southern Politics in the 1990s*. Baton Rouge: Louisiana State University Press, 1999.

Tindall, George Brown. *The Emergence of the New South, 1913–1945*. Baton Rouge: Louisiana State University Press, 1967.

Woodward, C. Vann. *Origins of the New South, 1877–1913*. Baton Rouge: Louisiana State University Press, 1951.

CHARLES S. BULLOCK III

JANNA DEITZ

Transforming the South

The Role of the Federal Government

South Carolina governor Strom Thurmond adopted "states' rights" as the rallying cry when he sought the presidency in 1948. The official title of the party under whose banner Thurmond ran was the States' Rights Party, which, because it focused its efforts in the South, became popularly known as the Dixiecrat Party. Thurmond recognized the potential that the federal government had to change race relations in the South, and he, along with most white southerners at that time, opposed any such efforts. He boasted that the military force of the national government would be impotent against southern commitment to white supremacy. Well before Thurmond's forty-eight years

The authors would like to thank Joan Kirchner in Senator Sam Nunn's office for help in tracking down some of the federal revenue and expenditure data.

in the U.S. Senate ended in 2002, however, federal pressure had pushed the South further toward racial equality than the Dixiecrats could have imagined.

The federal government's carrot-and-stick approach in the South resulted in dramatic changes in race relations, but the influence of the national government in the region extended far beyond race. Federal dollars induced the South to institute changes that it would have otherwise opposed, and rules and regulations in federal programs coerced transformations that money could not buy. Court orders forced the closing of antiquated jails, largely eliminated prayers from classrooms and football fields, and improved treatment of the mentally ill. The infusion of federal dollars created jobs and helped develop the highways, airports, and other pieces of infrastructure that in turn enabled the South to attract private investment. Public and private funding has gone far toward erasing the South's distinctive features.

The array of federal programs and the ways that they have affected the South are far too extensive to explore fully in this brief essay, so the materials presented here, arranged by three types of public policy (regulatory, redistributive, and distributive), should be viewed as illustrative rather than comprehensive. It is not hyperbole, however, to assert that the South would be much like a third-world area but for the demands of and assistance provided by the national government.

Rather than examining the many areas in which federal regulations have forced changes in southern public policy, we restrict our efforts to three facets of civil rights for African Americans—public accommodations, public schools, and voting rights. This approach is not only justified by considerations of space but also by the central role that efforts to extend equal opportunities played in the life of the South after World War II.

Although federal policy ultimately forced a transformation in southern race relations, for generations national policy condoned the racial separation that was the cornerstone of the southern way of life. After 1896, when the Supreme Court in *Plessy v. Ferguson* interpreted the Fourteenth Amendment's equal protection clause to permit "separate but equal" facilities for blacks and whites, racial separation became the rule in the South. Virtually all public accommodations were racially segregated as white southerners fully embraced separation, even if equal treatment of blacks usually came up short. Whites saw racial separation and white supremacy as core values.

During the days of "separate but equal," virtually every aspect of southern life was segregated. Some institutions, like public schools and private clubs, were rigidly separated. In facilities patronized by both blacks and whites, the races would be separated within those facilities. Members of both races could attend sporting events or the movie theater, but African Americans were relegated to outfield bleachers and theater balconies. Other private facilities, such as restaurants, refused to seat blacks although they might be served from the back door. Public services, such as buses and railroads, had separate waiting areas and seating reserved for each race.

The first flash point in the civil rights movement, the Montgomery bus boycott led by Martin Luther King Jr., involved public accommodations but was conducted without federal involvement. The boycott in Alabama's capital city ultimately brought the bus company to the brink of financial ruin and prompted it to eliminate segregated seating.

In the early 1960s, direct action carried out by black college students challenged the racial seating practices in many restaurants across the South. The sit-in effort, which got its start in Greensboro, North Carolina, used economic muscle to pressure owners to serve both races. Sit-in participants encountered both the wrath of business owners whose facilities were targeted and frequently the local police, who arrested the protestors for disturbing the peace. At times the arrests came only after the absence of police allowed whites to attack the peaceful protesters. As with challenges to segregated schools and discriminatory voting practices, the protestors turned to the federal government for relief.

By the 1960s, leaders of the civil rights movement, such as Martin Luther King Jr. and John Lewis (a member of Congress from Georgia since 1987), had learned how to mobilize the national media to publicize their demands. Courts had interpreted the interstate commerce clause of the Constitution to protect the rights of African Americans traveling from state to state. Segregated seating and separate facilities, while still permissible for intrastate travel, had been prohibited on any public vehicles traveling across state lines. However, like the equal aspect of "separate but equal," this was another guarantee honored more often in the breach than in the observance. To point up this failure to enforce constitutional guarantees and in an attempt to secure even broader federal involvement, a handful of carefully chosen and trained protestors set out from Washington, D.C., by bus to test racial tolerance across the South. As dramatically told by Representative John Lewis in his autobiography *Walking with the Wind*, the Freedom Riders made it to Anniston, Alabama, where white thugs beat them and burned their bus.

Another Alabama event that contributed to the pressure for enactment of public accommodations protections was Birmingham's notorious police chief Bull Connor's use of police dogs and water cannons against civil rights protesters, many of whom were schoolchildren. The viciousness of the official response in Birmingham, a community so marked by the frequent use of dynamite by white racists against black civil rights activists that it had earned the label "Bombingham," played out on national television and sparked support outside the region for President Johnson's 1964 Civil Rights Act.

Portions of this legislation guaranteed the right of minorities to patronize not only public facilities but also private ones that purported to be open to the public. Henceforth, African Americans would be spared the indignity of being turned away from a restaurant. When traveling, they could use restrooms in filling stations and need not have carefully identified in advance the hotels and motels where they could stay.

Beginning in the 1930s, the Supreme Court began to scrutinize the implementation of "separate but equal" in higher education. The court explored whether southern jurisdictions provided equal resources for higher education. Southern states failed to offer advanced degrees at black schools comparable to those found at white universities. The Supreme Court first took notice of this disparity in a Missouri case in 1938. The pace accelerated after World War II as the court deemed inadequate the southern practice of paying out-of-state tuition to send black students to northern states to pursue degrees not available at in-state black schools. In response to these court challenges, South Carolina and Texas created black law schools. An African American denied admission to the University of Texas Law School brought suit asserting that the black law school failed to match up with the white school in the caliber of its faculty, the holdings of its library, and the intellectual stimulation of its student body. The Supreme Court concluded that this new entity was not the equal of the University of Texas Law School.

The Texas law school case set the stage for the frontal attack on the "separate" aspect of the *Plessy v. Ferguson* phrase. A series of cases from South Carolina, Virginia, Kansas, and Delaware reached the Supreme Court as *Brown v. Board of Education*. In each instance, the funding and resulting education differed dramatically between black and white schools. For example, at about the time that Clarendon County, South Carolina, became a defendant in one of the lawsuits, expenditures for black students averaged only $43 per year, less than a quarter of the $179 spent on each white child. In *Brown v. Board of Education*, the Supreme Court went beyond the spending disparities and ruled that "separate but equal" could not be squared with the requirements of the equal protection clause. Relying on Kenneth and Mamie Clark's research that linked segregation with negative self-image, the court concluded that racial separation left an indelible, harmful mark on African American children. In coming to that conclusion, the Court rejected the *Plessy* logic that as long as facilities were equal, no harm stemmed from racial separation.

While more astute southerners had seen this decision looming, it took much of the region by surprise. The Supreme Court recognized the potential opposition to *Brown* and took the extraordinary step of scheduling another hearing. It invited states not parties to the initial litigation to submit amicus briefs to help the court fashion a ruling for implementing desegregation. In 1955 in what came to be known as *Brown II*, the court used broad, vague language to guide school districts and lower courts when confronted with demands for desegregation. Rather than ordering an immediate end to racial separation, the court set a nonspecific deadline of ending it with "all deliberate speed." A second shortcoming of *Brown II* was its failure to spell out what constituted desegregation. Would it be sufficient for jurisdictions to cease requiring segregation? Or would integration be necessary? Did *Brown* really mean the end of all racial separation? The Supreme Court gave no guidance.

Congress finally took steps to support what had been exclusively a judicial initiative when it included three sections that dealt with school desegregation in the 1964 Civil Rights Act. This legislation provided an administrative remedy that could deny federal school aid to segregated districts. While the threatened loss of federal dollars, which became far more plentiful with the passage of the Elementary and Secondary Education Act in 1965, prompted some districts to desegregate, others willingly gave up federal aid to maintain segregation. These resistant districts ultimately came into compliance when federal judges threatened to enjoin state funds and hold the local school officials in contempt.

Most southern communities focused on the "all deliberate speed" phrase and took no steps toward desegregation. While a few jurisdictions in west Texas and other areas of the peripheral South where black populations were small dismantled their segregated systems, not even token changes occurred in the Deep South. In jurisdiction after jurisdiction, litigation challenged the unwillingness of local school authorities to change their racial policies. And in jurisdiction after jurisdiction court orders ultimately required at least token desegregation whereby the plaintiffs were admitted to what had been all-white schools. Scores of lawsuits were filed before the Supreme Court finally ruled in 1968 in *Green v. County School Board of New Kent County* that there should be no white schools and no black schools—just schools.

The *Green* decision seemingly mandated racial balance among the schools within each school district, although a degree of racial imbalance persisted in most urban districts. In small districts, however, *Green* answered definitively the question of what needed to be done to comply with *Brown*. Token desegregation was inadequate and full integration of students and faculty was required. The final step toward desegregating southern schools came in *Swann v. Charlotte-Mecklenburg*, which authorized busing to move children throughout an urban district to promote racial balance.

In 1969 the Supreme Court clarified the time frame of "all deliberate speed." In a Mississippi case the court stated that the time for deliberate speed had passed and that school districts in that state must desegregate immediately. The noncompliant districts were told to integrate when students returned from the Christmas holidays.

With the ambiguity of *Brown* eliminated and federal pressure continuing unabated, school desegregation spread across the South. By 1970, schools in the South were less segregated than those in other sections of the country.

While the federal government became deeply involved in eliminating separate but equal practices and desegregating schools, hospitals, and other public facilities, the question of political rights took on even greater significance. As with desegregation, southern states showed little interest in voluntarily taking steps toward extending equal suffrage to African Americans on their own. Federal court orders eliminated the white primary and the grandfather clause as a loophole for whites who could not pass literacy tests. Until the white primary was ruled unconstitutional in 1944, African Americans had been excluded from Democratic primaries on the grounds that the party was a private organization that could determine conditions for membership. Since two-party competition was nonexistent in southern states, the only meaningful elections occurred in the Democratic primaries and runoffs. The one barrier to black political participation that most southern states removed on their own was the poll tax, which affected the poor of all races, although four states continued to collect the tax until the mid-1960s when the Twenty-fourth Amendment to the Constitution and a Supreme Court decision barred the practice.

African Americans, who had risked their lives fighting to restore political sovereignty in Asia and Europe, challenged the Jim Crow rules governing voter registration at home. Especially in urban areas, the return of these patriots coupled with the demise of the white primary swelled the ranks of black voters and resulted in the election of a handful of African Americans to public office. The story, however, was far different in rural areas, where challenges to white political hegemony were rebuffed so harshly that few, if any, African Americans even made it onto the voter rolls.

In 1956, on the eve of the enactment of the first modern federal legislation aimed at protecting black suffrage, only about one-quarter of the South's African American population of voting age was registered to vote. While this proportion had doubled over the previous decade, it revealed the persistent disparity in black and white participation rates in electoral politics. Potential black voters continued to face literacy tests in most of the region. In states where the testing process was most onerous, applicants had to demonstrate their ability to read, write, and interpret passages of the state or federal constitution to the satisfaction of local registrars. The United States Civil Rights Commission documented numerous examples of registrars discriminating against black applicants or simply refusing to allow African Americans to register. A few states required that prospective voters demonstrate their good character, but since only registered voters could vouch for prospective voters, it was difficult if not impossible for African Americans to meet this requirement.

White southerners used coercion to fight requirements imposed by law. Night riders shot into the homes of civil rights activists, burned churches that hosted voting rallies, beat demonstrators, and even killed some of those who dared register or help others register. This violence, which typically went unpunished by local authorities, dissuaded all but the bravest in rural communities from even attempting to register. In addition to physical intimidation, white opponents employed economic intimidation. Those who challenged the all-white electoral system risked having loans called in by white-owned banks or not being permitted to gin their cotton at white-run gins. Tenant farmers might be turned out by their white landlords. White school boards refused to renew the contracts of black teachers active in the civil rights movement.

The federal government hesitantly began to assert itself in 1957 after Congress enacted the first civil rights law since Reconstruction. The 1957 Civil Rights Act authorized the U.S. attorney general to sue local officials who discriminated against prospective black voters. The federal government provided the attorneys and research necessary to prosecute, thereby overcoming obstacles to challenging local voter discrimination, such as finding an attorney to take the suit and raising the money to cover expenses associated with litigation. The 1957 act also eliminated the need to find an individual to serve as the plaintiff. Since the United States prosecuted the case, no local individual would be named plaintiff and thus become a target for physical and economic intimidation.

Federal legislation slowly worked to expand black registration. By 1964, more than 40 percent of age-eligible southern blacks had registered and their votes provided the margin of victory for Lyndon Johnson in several southern states, where, for the first time, most whites cast ballots for a Republican, Barry Goldwater, one of the few nonsouthern senators to oppose the wide-ranging 1964 Civil Rights Act.

In 1965, President Johnson goaded Congress to go still further to protect black political rights in the South. The new legislation focused on jurisdictions that had the clearest records of impeding black political participation. States and counties that employed tests or devices as prerequisites to registering, like a literacy test, and in which fewer than half of the voting age population had voted in the 1964 presidential election or was registered to vote that year were singled out for attention. In these jurisdictions, the U.S. attorney general could supplant local authority and send in federal officials empowered to sign up qualified voters turned away by racist registrars. Moreover, federal officials could be sent to monitor election-day activities to see whether newly registered blacks faced obstacles when trying to vote. These powers, along with the banning of registration tests and devices in the covered jurisdictions, were expected to eliminate the obstacles that had kept southern blacks out of the political arena. To ensure that inventive racist officials did not design new barriers to black participation, section 5 of the Voting Rights Act required that the covered jurisdictions submit all changes in electoral laws for approval by representatives of the federal government before they could be implemented. Two routes for achieving clearance existed: (1) the administrative route, which involved submitting the new statute to the attorney general of the United States; or (2) the judicial route, whereby a suit was brought in the district court of the District of Columbia to obtain a declaratory judgment that the new statute did not discriminate on the basis of race.

To make the threat of federal involvement real, immediately after signing the legislation into law, President Johnson dispatched federal voting examiners to Alabama, Louisiana, and Mississippi. When southern officials saw that the federal government was prepared to supplant local authority, they came into compliance. The ranks of African Americans registered to vote swelled rapidly so that by 1970 two-thirds of African Americans of voting age had registered. Even in the most recalcitrant states, increases in black registration came quickly and impressively. Prior to the 1965 Voting Rights Act, only 6.7 percent of the voting age blacks in Mississippi and 19.3 percent of those in Alabama had managed to register. Within four years, the ranks of the registered in Alabama included a majority of the African Americans and in Mississippi the figure had swelled to almost 60 percent.

By the 1980s, the disparities in registration and turnout rates between blacks and whites had largely disappeared. Some research suggests that to the extent that black and white participation rates differ, the explanation is not discrimination but instead the primary correlate of turnout—socioeconomic differences. In predominantly black communities, such as Atlanta and New Orleans, black turnout often exceeds white. Following passage of the federal motor voter law, which permits registration at a wide variety of public offices including drivers' license bureaus and also allows for downloading voter registration forms off of the Internet, racial barriers to registration have been eliminated.

Once federal law knocked down barriers to registration and voting, the emphasis of the civil rights movement shifted from ensuring access to the polling booth to promoting the attainment of public office. Two developments led to an increase in the number of black elected officials, and both involved federal support. One was the rewriting of section 2 of the Voting Rights Act in 1982 to replace an intent test with a results test when courts assessed whether political rules disadvantaged minorities. If minorities had fewer opportunities than whites to win public office, federal courts now stood ready to invalidate the existing system. Activists in many communities filed section 2 lawsuits in the 1980s seeking to replace at-large elections for local governing bodies with single-member district plans in which one or more districts would be majority-minority. The other path involved the application of the section 5 federal oversight provision to redistricting plans. Unlike in the past when the Justice Department only objected if the political position of minorities was weakened by a districting plan, in the early 1990s it demanded that majority-minority districts be created when possible. These two initiatives greatly increased the ranks of minority officeholders.

When the Voting Rights Act was first enacted in 1965, only about one hundred African Americans held elective office in the South and most of these served in small, rural towns that had few white residents. At the outset of the twenty-first century, blacks held statewide offices, serving as attorney general and labor commissioner in Georgia, state auditor in North Carolina, a member of the powerful Texas Railroad Commission, and judges on appellate courts in most southern states. While no state currently has an African American governor, Doug Wilder served as Virginia's chief executive from 1990 until 1994. In 2003 every southern state except Arkansas had at least one African American in Congress and Georgia had four. The region as a whole had seventeen African Americans serving in Congress. In addition, thousands of African Americans serve in the region's state legislatures and local governments—Mississippi leads the list with almost nine hundred. The presence of blacks in government councils might not guarantee that their policy preferences will be enacted, but they can see to it that options are at least presented for consideration.

Black elected officials are not alone in being responsive to the concerns of African Americans. White Democrats, many of whom owe their success to strong support among black voters, have been increasingly attentive to African American policy requests. White politicians who courted black support have offered in return a share of public benefits, including government jobs. On entering a southern state or local government facility prior to the mid-1960s, rarely did one encounter an African American in any but the most menial of positions. All of those responsible for implementing policy decisions were white. Today, African Americans help shape and implement policy and, as a result, they have access to better-paying positions. Also, prior to the mid-1960s, one could often recognize a black section of a community because so few roads were paved. Now public services tend to be distributed evenly throughout a community.

Black involvement in the political process also changed the rhetoric of politics. George Wallace vowed "segregation today, segregation tomorrow, segregation forever" when taking the oath as Alabama's governor in 1963. A few months later, he dramatically stood in front of federal marshals as they sought to enroll black students at the University of Alabama. Not that many years later, while still governor, Wallace crowned a black homecoming queen at the same university and observed, "We're all God's children. All God's children are equal." Andrew Young (D-Ga.), who in 1972 was the first African American (along with Barbara Jordan [D-Tex.]) to be elected to Congress from the South in the twentieth century, summed up the impact of growing black political influence as follows:

> It used to be Southern politics was just, "nigger" politics, who could "outnigger" the other—then you registered 10 to 15 percent in the community and folks would start saying, "Nigra," and then you get 35 to 40 percent registered and it's amazing how quick they learn how to say "Nee-gro," and now we've got 50, 60, 70 percent of the black votes registered in the South, everybody's proud to be associated with their black brothers and sisters.

To some extent, these programs addressed long-standing problems. Losing a war is economically disastrous, both in terms of the drain of resources from the fighting itself as well as from a destroyed infrastructure. After the South lost the Civil War, it not only had to confront these problems but also had to deal with the fact that it had lost much of its wealth, which had been invested in slaves. Following the war, increased property taxes resulted in land-poor families losing their holdings. The relationship of the South to the North was much like that of a colony to an industrialized nation. The South provided raw materials but generated little industrial output. Despite the success of Sun Belt cities such as Atlanta, Charlotte, Dallas, Houston, and Nashville in the latter half of the twentieth century, it is not hyperbole to say that parts of the rural South have yet to recover from losing the Civil War.

Because of its poverty, the South benefited disproportionately from federal redistributive programs beginning with the New Deal. In the desperately poor South, the Works Progress Administration (WPA) and the Civilian Conservation Corps provided much-needed jobs to some of the unemployed. These

Governor George C. Wallace trying to block the integration of the University of Alabama in 1963. Library of Congress, Prints & Photographs Division, Washington, D.C., reproduction number LC-U9-9930-20.

1930s programs also opened the way for rural migration to southern cities. As William Faulkner's brother John chronicles in *Men Working*, those who left cotton fields for the WPA made numerous missteps as they sought to move up the economic ladder, but their lives as sharecroppers had ended.

Because southern states have provided a less extensive safety net than states in the Northeast and Midwest and on the West Coast, the poor in the South have depended heavily on federal aid. Medicaid made it possible for many poor southerners to get regular health care for the first time in their lives. Federal efforts, such as the distribution of surplus commodities during the Depression, have fed many southerners. Some of the poorest counties in the country are in the South, where large numbers of families have relied on food stamps to survive since the advent of the Great Society. The South's greater dependence on food stamps is evident in the region's share of the national budget for this program, which stood at 34 percent in 2001. The South contains 30 percent of the nation's population and receives more than a third of the budget for the federal government's primary food program.

As a major beneficiary of these and other programs, it is not surprising that for many years the South received more federal dollars than it paid in federal taxes. Even though the urban centers in the South have become economic powerhouses, the imbalance between taxes paid to Washington and benefits received has not been eliminated and grew in some states as the twentieth century drew to a close. Despite economic gains in parts of the South, table 1 shows that in 1984 eight of the states in the region got more back in federal spending than they contributed in federal taxes. Mississippi, the poorest state in the nation, got the biggest bang for its buck, receiving $1.66 back from Washington for every tax dollar paid. A decade later, in the early days of the nation's longest period of economic expansion, seven states had a more favorable balance of payments than in 1984, and nine states got back more than they contributed. The most recent available figures from 2001 show that every southern state except Texas receives back more than it pays in taxes. Mississippi continues to lead the region with a return of $1.78 per dollar paid in federal taxes. On a per capita basis, Virginia ranks second nationally in fiscal 2001 with federal dollars going to the state at a rate of $10,720 per person. Alabama, Florida, Mississippi, and Tennessee also ranked above the national average of $6,875 per person.

Federal dollars have made substantial contributions to the development of the South's infrastructure. To some extent these benefits are the result of the power of the region's senior legislators, who have frequently chaired key congressional committees. While most of these benefits have been available nationwide, one significant program had a regional focus. The Tennessee

TABLE 1

Federal Expenditures per Dollar of Federal Taxes Paid

	1984	1994	2001
Alabama	1.28	1.37	1.53
Arkansas	1.23	1.26	1.45
Florida	1.05	1.03	1.05
Georgia	1.09	1.04	1.01
Louisiana	0.89	1.33	1.42
Mississippi	1.66	1.69	1.78
North Carolina	0.93	0.98	1.06
South Carolina	1.24	1.25	1.30
Tennessee	1.18	1.12	1.20
Texas	0.78	0.97	0.92
Virginia	1.42	1.39	1.45

Source: Patrick Fleenor, ed., *Facts and Figures on Government Finance* (Washington, D.C.: Tax Foundation, 1984, 1994, 2001).

Valley Authority (TVA), created during the New Deal, brought flood control to the watersheds of the Tennessee and Cumberland Rivers by building dams that would also generate electricity. In time, as Philip Selznick describes in his classic study *TVA and the Grass Roots*, the emphasis shifted to permit development of the lands bordering on the TVA lakes for recreation, spawning a lucrative industry.

TVA provided electricity to rural stretches of Tennessee, Virginia, North Carolina, Georgia, and Alabama that private suppliers found economically unattractive. For many years TVA power was cheaper than private power, which helped lure industry into the river basins, thereby promoting economic development. The construction of the TVA dams provided jobs, and new industries helped families escape poverty. We can trace the impact of the TVA in popular culture. "Song of the South," a country song recorded by the group Alabama in the late 1980s, for example, tells the story of a father who got a job with the TVA, enabling the family to move to town and buy a washing machine and then a Chevrolet. Elsewhere in the South, power came over lines strung by the federal Rural Electrification Administration, bringing lights and the radio to farm families.

The South also benefited from national programs that helped the region catch up with more affluent parts of the country. These programs included the interstate highway system. More recently, federal dollars have improved urban rapid transit in the region. The construction of Atlanta's mass transit train, for example, depended heavily on federal assistance.

Southern farmers benefited from the subsidies provided under the Agriculture Assistance Act and crop supports. Southerners on the House Agriculture Committee frequently chaired subcommittees that specialized in crops grown in their region—cotton, tobacco, and rice—and promoted these crops while protecting other southern products such as sugar and peanuts from foreign competition.

Federal crop payments enriched large landholders, including Senator James Eastland (D-Miss.), but little of this money found its way into the overalls of sharecroppers and small farmers. Federal agriculture dollars enabled land barons to mechanize their operations, resulting in thousands of hands being turned off the land. Even as recently as 2001, after millions of acres had been taken out of production for homes and shopping centers, 28 percent of the national agriculture assistance budget found its way south.

The United States entry into World War II necessitated construction of military facilities for the training of tens of thousands of personnel to fight the Axis powers. Many of these new bases were located in the South. Over the following six decades, the South continued to be the home for a dispropor-

Workers at the TVA's Watts Bar Dam construction site in 1942. Library of Congress, Prints & Photographs Division, Washington, D.C., reproduction number LC-USW3-003370-D.

tionate share of military facilities. While location was important, southerners who chaired the Senate or House Armed Services Committee contributed to the South's surfeit of military bases. Georgia, home to the Third Army at Fort McPherson, Fort Benning, Hunter Air Field, Warner Robins Air Force Base, Dobbins Air Force Base, the Ranger School, the East Coast Nuclear Submarine Base at King's Bay, Fort Stewart, and Fort Gordon, has provided two chairs of the Senate Armed Services Committee (Richard Russell, 1949–53, 1955–69, and Sam Nunn, 1987–93) and a chair of the House Armed Services Committee (Carl Vinson, 1949–53, 1955–65). When Mendel Rivers (D-S.C.) and Edward Hebert (D-La.) chaired the House Armed Services Committee, their states also flourished. California, which has not provided leadership to the key military committees, has seen several large bases closed.

While Georgia has done especially well when it comes to acquiring and maintaining military bases, it is not alone. Thirty-eight percent of the national defense budget in the fiscal year 2000 found its way to the South. Even after rounds of base closings, the South is home to eighty-five military bases, 40 percent of all bases in the nation. Six of the ten locations with the largest number of personnel are in the South, led by Fort Bragg in North Carolina and Fort Hood in Texas, each of which had more than forty-four thousand active duty and civilian personnel in 2000. The top-ten United States military locations based on number of personnel include Camp Lejeune in North Carolina; Arlington, Virginia; Norfolk, Virginia; and Fort Benning, all of which had at least twenty-three thousand active duty and civilian personnel in the community. In 2000 almost half (47.7 percent) of all active duty personnel were stationed in the South. The overrepresentation of civilian workers was less extraordinary, but the South housed 39.8 percent of these individuals, well above the 29.9 percent of all Americans living in Dixie in 2000.

Half of the top-ten locations ranked by military expenditures are in the South, and a sixth is Washington, D.C. Southern cities in which military expenditures topped $2.25 billion in 2000 were Fort Worth; Norfolk; Arlington; Marietta, Georgia; and Huntsville, Alabama. The eleven-state region received 51.8 percent of the federal dollars distributed in the prime military contracts in fiscal 2000, a substantial increase from six years earlier, when the South's share stood at 32.3 percent. The largest beneficiaries of this dramatic rise in defense dollars were Texas and Virginia, which saw increases of at least 50 percent. The benefits of federal spending on military bases and contractors extended throughout the immediate community and far beyond, generating profits for car dealerships, appliance stores, the real estate market, entertainment, and so forth.

The federal government deserves much of the credit for transforming race relations and the economic situation in the South. While the prominence of southern Republicans in Congress has led some commentators to speak of the "southernization" of the United States, in fact the South has been losing its uniqueness. Without federal demands and dollars, the region would have remained far more distinctive. Only the power of the national government could overcome the region's intransigence in the sphere of race relations and the magnitude of its economic deprivation. Left to their own devices, southerners would have been much slower to challenge their caste system. Left to its own resources, the South would have remained shackled to an agrarian economic system far longer.

Federal pressure was also necessary to force the South to eradicate its deeply rooted practices of racial separation. The South took no voluntary steps to desegregate schools or to integrate public accommodations until the federal government applied pressure. Had the federal government remained on the sidelines as it had for generations, it is hard to believe that race relations in the South would have evolved to anywhere close to the stage they have today.

Perhaps the most extraordinary federal action was its circumscribing the authority of states and localities in conducting elections. The obdurate South finally gave in to an even more committed federal government that supplanted state authority to register voters, draw new legislative districts, and regulate elections. These interventions constituted significant restrictions on states' rights and were necessitated by regional unwillingness to make changes on its own. Without this extraordinary federal involvement, the South would be a far different region from what we know today.

Suggested Readings

Ball, Howard, Dale Krane, and Thomas P. Lauth. *Compromised Compliance: Implementation of the 1965 Voting Rights Act*. Westport, Conn.: Greenwood Press, 1982.

Bass, Jack, and Walter de Vries. *The Transformation of Southern Politics: Social Change and Political Consequence since 1945*. New York: Basic Books, 1976.

Bullock, Charles S., III, and Mark J. Rozell, eds. *The New Politics of the Old South*. 2nd ed. Lanham, Md.: Rowman and Littlefield, 2003.

Davidson, Chandler, and Bernard Grofman, eds. *Quiet Revolution in the South: The Impact of the Voting Rights Act, 1965–1990*. Princeton: Princeton University Press, 1994.

Green, Elna C., ed. *Before the New Deal: Social Welfare in the South, 1830–1930*. Athens: University of Georgia Press, 1999.

Grofman, Bernard, ed. *Legacies of the 1964 Civil Rights Act*. Charlottesville: University Press of Virginia, 2000.

Kluger, Richard. *Simple Justice: The History of Brown v. Board of Education and Black America's Struggle for Equality*. New York: Knopf, 1976.

Landsberg, Brian K. *Enforcing Civil Rights: Race, Discrimination and the Department of Justice*. Lawrence: University Press Kansas, 1997.

Mann, Robert. *The Walls of Jericho: Lyndon Johnson, Hubert Humphrey, Richard Russell, and the Struggle for Civil Rights*. New York: Harcourt Brace, 1996.

Rodgers, Harrell R., Jr., and Charles S. Bullock III. *Coercion to Compliance*. Lexington, Mass.: Lexington Books, 1976.

———. *Law and Social Change: Civil Rights Laws and Their Consequences*. New York: McGraw-Hill, 1972.

JAMES D. ANDERSON

On the Meaning of Reform

African American Education in the
Twentieth-Century South

The focus of this essay is on the meaning of African American education in the twentieth-century South, both its significance within the African American community and in the context of the broader development of public education throughout the region. It examines the history of African American education in the South through the lens of a series of reform (grassroots campaigns for equality and justice) and counterreform (state-sponsored campaigns to preserve segregation and inequality) movements that date back to the colonial era, although the focus is on those that emerged in the twentieth century.

Slaves, free persons of color, ex-slaves, black citizens, white populists (to some extent), and civil rights activists headed up reform movements that were liberal in their efforts to achieve civil and political equality and fought for universal democratic education while slaveholders, planters, and white supremacists led counterreform movements that were conservative in their resistance to even the slightest movement toward racial equality or democratic expansion of universal public schooling and that sought to shape educational opportunity to serve the interest of slavery, sharecropping, and/or racial segregation until well into the twentieth century. To be sure, there is more to the history of southern education than the history of African American education, but the latter plays a leading role in it. The history of southern education from the colonial era to the late twentieth century is largely characterized by this pattern of grassroots reform and state-dominated counterreform movements precisely because the African American experience is at the center of it. In so many ways, the African American presence has defined the shape and character of education in the South—the expansion of literacy in the colonial era, the origin of state school systems in the postbellum period, the southern education movement of the Progressive Era, desegregation and the massive resistance to it during the 1950s and early 1960s, the civil rights movement of the late 1960s, and the "No Child Left Behind" reform movement of today all owe to that presence.

In the late eighteenth century African Americans began a significant campaign to achieve literacy under slavery, and perhaps the first educational reform movement in the region, at least the first to threaten the established social order, began formally with the creation of the first known school for African Americans at Goose Creek Parish in Charleston, South Carolina, in 1695. This small initial effort to make slaves literate expanded during the middle of the eighteenth century. During the 1740s, believing literacy to be a prerequisite for baptism, the Society for the Propagation of the Gospel trained slaves in Christian principles and taught them to read and write in Virginia, Maryland, and South Carolina, colonies that contained about 90 percent of slaves in British America during the mid-eighteenth century. A school for slaves was opened in South Carolina in 1743 and by 1747 had graduated forty scholars. By 1755 seventy African American children were enrolled in the South Carolina school. Literate slaves were, to be sure, a small minority of the whole. Slaves, as well as free persons of color, who could read and write numbered in the tens or hundreds while the slave populations of Virginia, Maryland, and South Carolina numbered in the tens of thousands. Still, historians of slave literacy estimate that by the beginning of the nineteenth century approximately 10 percent of slaves acquired the ability to read and write on a basic level.

The South's dramatic reaction to the spread of literacy during the early national and antebellum periods cannot be understood apart from efforts by slaves and free persons of color to seize a good deal more education than they were offered under slavery. This countermovement to the spread of literacy among slaves and free persons of color began in the eighteenth century. As early as 1740, South Carolina enacted a law prohibiting any person from teaching or causing a slave to be taught to read or write. In 1770 the Georgia Colony enacted legislation forbidding the teaching of slaves to read as well as to write. The laws against teaching slaves to read and write grew out of a variety of fears and concerns, the simplest of which concerned the use of literacy as a means to freedom (through the forging of passes by potential runaways). The argument against African American literacy expressed with the greatest degree of agitation concerned the dangers of incendiary literature. Even in colonial times powerful opposition to slave literacy arose among slaveholders in an attempt not only to prevent the forging of passes but also to head off insurrection or at least to weaken any prospective insurrectionary leadership.

Restrictions against African American literacy grew tighter over time. Local ordinances supplemented state laws; in some places it became a crime merely to sell writing materials to slaves. The slave revolts led by Gabriel Prosser in 1800, Denmark Vesey in 1822, and Nat Turner in 1830 resulted in antiliteracy laws being passed throughout the Lower South and even influenced the Upper South as well. In 1829 Georgia began to fine, whip, or imprison anyone teaching slaves to read and write. In 1830, Louisiana and North Carolina followed suit with antiliteracy laws that stated that literacy tended to excite dissatisfaction and insurrectionary emotions in slaves. In its 1830–31 legislative session, Virginia provided penalties for teaching slaves to read or write. Alabama's harsh legislation grew directly out of the postinsurrectionary panic of 1831–32. South Carolina, revising its 1740 ban on slave literacy, passed in 1834 the most sweeping law against teaching slaves and free persons of color to read or write. In Arkansas and Tennessee the legislatures resisted the exponents of legal repression, but public opinion against African American literacy had so hardened that the actual opportunities for slaves and free persons of color to learn withered as much as in states where illiteracy was legally mandated. Kentucky also refused to enact an antiliteracy law, but Missouri, admitted to the Union in 1821, caught up with other southern states in the late 1840s.

The passage of restrictive laws against slaves and free persons of color learning to read or write constituted the first massive counterreform movement by southern states against the expansion of educational opportunities and resulted in a decline of literacy rates among African Americans during the antebellum era. Carter G. Woodson estimated that black literacy rates declined by half during the period 1830–60, but more recent studies, relying on evidence from the Federal Writers Project slave narratives, indicate that more slaves learned to read after 1825 than Woodson could have known about. Nonetheless, there can be little doubt that the slaveholders' reaction against the spread of literacy among African Americans not only put the brakes on the literacy campaign but also caused a significant decline in the rate of literacy. At any rate, African Americans emerged from slavery with an illiteracy rate of approximately 90 percent.

Although the powerful opposition of slaveholders to slave literacy succeeded in keeping the vast majority of African Americans illiterate, it did not prevent the forging of a literate leadership that was extremely important to the second major reform movement, the campaign for universal public education in the immediate postemancipation period. Many African Americans leaders in education, government, ministry, and community during Reconstruction were men and women who first became literate under slavery. Their ideas about the value and purpose of literacy and formal schooling took shape during the slave experience and reflected a consciousness of literacy as a means of resistance as well as a concrete knowledge of antiliteracy laws and customs as mechanisms of control and oppression. Postwar African American educators and political leaders tended to view literacy and formal education as means to liberation and their frames of reference sparked the drive for universal schooling in the South after slavery.

Ex-slaves' most fundamental challenge to the planter-dominated ideology and structure of educational opportunity manifested itself in post–Civil War campaigns for universal, state-supported public education. African American educational leaders and politicians joined with Republicans and southern whites (known as scalawags) in southern constitutional conventions to legalize public education in the constitutions of the former Confederate states. By 1870, every southern state had specific provisions in its constitution to ensure a public school system financed by a state fund. Even when white southerners regained control of state governments, they kept the central features of educational governance and finance created by the ex-slave-Republican coalition. In vital respects, ex-slaves led a campaign to revolutionize the South's position regarding the right of ordinary citizens to "free" (tax-supported) universal public education.

A convergence of circumstances made the postwar educational-reform movement possible, but chief among them was the acquisition of citizenship and the right to vote under the Fourteenth and Fifteenth Amendments to the Constitution. As long as African Americans voted and were able to hold office in southern state and local governments, their social and educational

Illustration in *Harper's Weekly* of the Zion school for African American children in post–Civil War Charleston, South Carolina. Library of Congress, Prints & Photographs Division, Washington, D.C., reproduction number LC-USZ62-117666.

interests could not be easily ignored. In 1870 African Americans constituted the majority of the total population in the states of Louisiana, Mississippi, and South Carolina. African Americans comprised more than 40 percent of the state population in Alabama (48 percent), Florida (49 percent), Georgia (46 percent), and Virginia (42 percent). Black children fared well educationally from the moment of enfranchisement during Reconstruction to the era of disenfranchisement in the late nineteenth and early twentieth centuries because African Americans constituted a powerful and ever-growing voting bloc.

African American sociologist and historian Horace Mann Bond was among the first scholars to document the dramatic shift in black public education from relative equality during the era of political empowerment to gross inequality following the disenfranchisement campaigns of the late nineteenth century. As late as 1890 African American children, who constituted 44 percent of the total school-age population in Alabama, received 44 percent of the school money appropriated in the entire state. Similarly, in North Carolina the per capita expenditure for black children in 1890 was equal to that for white children in the state. In Alabama and Mississippi, African American children enjoyed relatively equal benefits from the school funds from Reconstruction until 1890.

The relative equality achieved primarily through the combination of grass-roots school campaigns and the use of newly acquired political power to accrue educational benefits paid handsome dividends between 1870 and 1900. It enabled African Americans in the South to close the largest achievement gap in its history, the literacy gap. By 1900 slightly more than half of southern blacks claimed to be literate, a remarkable accomplishment in light of conditions a generation earlier when the ex-slave population was approximately 90 percent illiterate. The postbellum decline in rates of illiteracy was larger among blacks than whites. Even this portrayal does not tell the full story of the remarkable and rapid decline of the illiteracy rate among black southerners. The overall rate remained high because large numbers of older African Americans (virtually all of whom had been enslaved at birth) were illiterate during the immediate postbellum period and many of them stayed illiterate. The literacy rate in 1900 for black males aged ten to fourteen was 64 percent and for black females aged ten to fourteen the rate was 71 percent. Hence, whereas the high rates of illiteracy imposed by slavery continued to remain high among adults (in 1900, 64 percent of black men aged forty-five to fifty-four were illiterate), African American children were becoming literate at a very fast pace. The spread of literacy among black southerners was a consequence of the acquisition of literacy by the young through school attendance. Because high rates of illiteracy among African American adults persisted into the twentieth century, it seems apparent that the majority of black children did not learn to read and write at home. Rather, illiteracy rates declined rapidly among the young as school attendance rates rose over time. In 1900, about 65 percent of African American children aged ten to fourteen attended schools, although only 36 percent of the five-to-fourteen age group attended school.

At the dawn of the twentieth century African Americans only needed a decent system of public education to attain higher levels of educational advancement. It was at this point that the dominant white South mounted a region-wide counterreform movement, a campaign of massive resistance to the educational progress of black southerners. Indeed, the postemancipation reform movement bred a counterreform movement that produced the greatest racial inequalities in education in southern history. To be sure, whites in the post–Civil War South responded to the idea of public education for all children in a variety of ways depending on their class backgrounds and political and social interests. While rural white planters in general staunchly resisted universal public education for black children, white urban industrialists supported a system of universal public schooling with clearly prescribed racial and class limitations. Further, there were some white southerners who supported black public education without wanting to prescribe a special kind of curriculum for African American children. However, throughout the dominant white South the most pervasive view of universal schooling for all children was that educating black children would revolutionize the region's economic and social order in a way that was not in its interest. Neither the racially moderate views of particular southern white industrialists nor the support of a few white liberals could counterbalance the opposition of the planter-dominated South. Their views carried the day and were reflected in the policies and actions of state and county governments. During the first half of the twentieth century the dominant white South would use state power to repress the development of black public education, a process of repression so severe that it continued to affect the shape and character of educational opportunities for African American students throughout the twentieth century.

The trend down from equality began in particular states in the late 1880s. Mississippi was the first; in 1886 its legislature passed a law that enabled local boards to set teacher salaries on the basis of the certificate held by the teacher. This law was so framed that a school board could give an African American teacher the minimum monthly pay of twenty-five dollars and a white teacher of the same level the maximum monthly pay of fifty-five dollars. Similarly, South Carolina in its Constitution of 1895 gave the local school boards the power to discriminate in allocating the school funds between the races. Alabama changed its law in 1890, substituting for the old system of relative equality one that allowed common school funds to be spent by local school boards as they saw fit. By 1930 African American children in Alabama, then 40 percent of the school-age population, received 11 percent of the school funds, a major downward slide from 1890. The pattern was the same in other southern states. For example, in Mississippi the African American proportion of the total school-age population (60 percent) received about 20 percent of the annual state school appropriation in 1910. The black-to-white ratio of per pupil expenditures declined in every southern state between 1890 and 1910. In some states (Florida, Mississippi, Virginia, Louisiana), expenditures per black pupil actually fell in constant dollars. In other states, expenditures per black pupil grew at a much slower rate than spending per white pupil. No longer having to reckon seriously with the voting and political power of black communities, white state governments pushed aside the educational aspirations of African American parents and students and created for them a racially separate and grossly unequal system of public schools. The nature and structure of that counterreform reveal much about the South that was coming to maturity during the first half of the twentieth century.

The heightened resistance to the educational progress of African Americans greatly modified and distorted the concept of public education in southern state governments. Ever since the common school crusades of the 1830s, public education was understood to be a state-sponsored institution dedicated to the education of all children and to diffusing virtue and knowledge. To achieve these goals, the schools were to be made free to rich and poor alike. The free school system was to be financed by a tax on property, and all property owners, irrespective of whether they had children attending the public schools, were to pay a school tax because everyone, it was presumed, derived political, civil, social, and economic benefits from the existence of free schools. The counterreform movements by southern states in the early twentieth century inverted this democratic theory of public education, taking the position that the state should pledge itself to the education of white children, even going so far as to suggest that the portion of the school funds paid by African Americans should be diverted to white schools. The obvious corollary of this policy was that black southerners, despite being taxed for public education, would have to find other means to provide universal schooling for their children or else, as many white southerners preferred, have virtually no schooling at all.

The upshot of the diversion of public taxes to support schools for white children was that throughout the first half of the twentieth century black schools had largely to depend on private philanthropy and what African Americans called "double taxation," the practice of paying for their schools through voluntary contributions of land, labor, and money. In 1915, for example, of the more than one thousand schoolhouses for African American children in Alabama's "Black Belt," approximately 60 percent were privately owned. More than twenty years later, not much changed in this respect. Of more than twenty-four hundred school buildings for African American children in Alabama in 1938, 70 percent were privately owned. The vast majority of schools for African American children were held in churches or in buildings that were privately owned. Other southern states followed a similar policy of relegating public education for African American children to the quasi-private realm. In 1940, roughly half of all black common schools in Mississippi still met in tenant cabins, lodges, churches, and stores—privately owned structures that under state law could not be improved with public funds. There were also some ninety black high schools in Mississippi, most of them either privately owned by African Americans or built through grants from northern foundations. Sunflower County, Mississippi, a Delta county with a sizable black majority, maintained no publicly owned school buildings for African American children in 1940.

The movement to close the attendance gap at the elementary school level by funding education for African Americans in significant part with voluntary contributions from ordinary citizens and private philanthropy was the third major reform movement by African Americans, but the first in the twentieth century. Between 1914 and 1932, ordinary African American citizens, despite living and working in cash-poor economies, raised over $4.7 million to help construct nearly five thousand Rosenwald schools, primarily for the education of elementary school children. This total does not include the additional voluntary contributions they made in the form of land, labor, and materials. Moreover, in addition to the initial contributions to construct school buildings, African Americans raised thousands of dollars annually to pay for the maintenance and improvement of grounds and buildings.

The Rosenwald building program radically transformed the structure of black common schools in the rural South and school attendance rose rapidly as schools became available. Rosenwald schools were built in 66 percent of the 1,327 southern counties. They were located in 95 percent of the counties in South Carolina, 90 percent in Alabama, 86 percent in Louisiana, Maryland, and North Carolina, and 75 percent in Virginia. Rosenwald schools were spread throughout the South and particularly in counties with large African American populations. In 1935, enough elementary schools had been constructed to accommodate the majority of young African Americans. In 1900, 36 percent of black children of elementary school age (five to fourteen) attended school in the South, compared to 55 percent of white children. The early-twentieth-century campaign to improve educational opportunities for the youngest of African American school children resulted in the closing of the elementary school attendance gap. By the time the Rosenwald school campaigns ended in the early 1930s, 90 percent of blacks aged five to fourteen were attending school compared to 91 percent of white children of the same age. This remarkable achievement rested squarely with African American communities and their willingness to invest private dollars to build "public" schools.

The campaign to improve educational opportunities at the secondary level took longer and was more difficult. Throughout the first half of the twentieth century African American youth in the South were largely excluded from public secondary education. For instance, the number of four-year public high schools for white students in Georgia increased from 4 in 1904 to 122 in 1916. At that time Georgia had no four-year public high schools for its African American students, who constituted 46 percent of the state's secondary school–age population. This was not merely an isolated instance of inequality; a complex system of racial subordination extended throughout the South. Thus in 1916, Mississippi, South Carolina, Louisiana, and North Carolina had no four-year public high schools for African American children. African American children constituted 57 percent of Mississippi's secondary school population, 57 percent of South Carolina's, 44 percent of Louisiana's, and 33 percent of the high school–age population in North Carolina. The states of Florida, Maryland, and Delaware each had only one public high school for African American students in 1916. Needless to say, access was extremely limited, depending on location and public means of transportation, something that was seldom provided for African American children prior to the *Brown v. Board of Education* decision in 1954.

This pattern continued into midcentury. On the eve of World War II, 77 percent of the high school–age black population in the South was not even enrolled in public secondary schools and of those who were enrolled, very few attended on a regular basis. The extent of the subordination was even more dramatic in states with the largest proportion of African American students. In Alabama, Arkansas, Georgia, and Louisiana, more than 80 percent of the black high school–age populations were not enrolled in public secondary schools in 1940. More than 90 percent of Mississippi's black high school–age population was not enrolled in public secondary schools at the onset of World War II. The war naturally made the situation worse. From 1940 to 1946 the enrollment of African American students in public secondary schools in the South decreased by over 30 percent. By 1948 enrollment began again to increase, but more than two-thirds of African American high school–age students in the 1950s were not enrolled in public high schools. As late as 1957, Sunflower County, Mississippi, had no public high schools for black students.

By the mid-twentieth century, the mounting importance of a high school education to economic success made this system of inequality progressively more repressive for African American youth. By 1950 public secondary schooling had become a central part of American life and culture and perceived by parents as vital to their children's future. The transformation of the public secondary education system during the first third of the twentieth century symbolized the extent to which schooling had become a strategic part of the national experience. From about 1890 to 1935 the American high school was transformed from an elite, private institution into a public one attended by white children en masse. It was a time of expanding educational opportunities in which publicly and privately supported schemes to locate the talented burgeoned and in which scholarship and loan programs for those students were provided with equal enthusiasm. African Americans knew they were being cheated out of their right to access the new educational opportunities. As the public high school, only marginally a factor in American life at the dawn of the twentieth century, became the "people's college" by midcentury, the extent of African American exclusion from it testified to the existence of a larger system of racial subordination that dated back to the white supremacy movements of the late nineteenth century.

In certain respects, by 1950 the racial inequality in high school graduation rates had deepened since 1900, when very few Americans of any race or gender attended high schools, and high school completion was only marginally a factor in national economic and social life. In 1940, for example, only 12 percent of African Americans aged twenty-five to twenty-nine were high school graduates, compared to 41 percent for whites in the same age category. As African Americans recognized a growing gap in educational opportunities at the secondary level, they launched campaigns seeking better educational opportunities for their children, campaigns that became a central plank in the larger platform for civil and political equality. Lacking access, for the most part, to voting power, political offices, finance, and the higher reaches of industry, parents, ordinary citizens, and community leaders across the South made the right to equal educational opportunity the centerpiece of the larger crusade for justice and equality. Ultimately, attaining equal opportunity at the secondary level compelled ordinary citizens to challenge Jim Crow and other legal and customary forms of racial subordination.

The major "victory" came with the U.S. Supreme Court ruling in *Brown v. Board of Education* in 1954. This decision not only represented the symbolic end of Jim Crow schooling but also sparked a new and more invigorated grassroots campaign for educational equality at all levels. The crusades for equal educational opportunity that began in South Carolina, Kansas, Virginia, Delaware, Washington, D.C., and later in Little Rock, Arkansas, spread across the nation, giving renewed hope to long-standing movements for justice and equality in the field of education. The struggle for racial equality escalated in the years immediately following the *Brown* decision. African American parents and their children began to petition and file lawsuits across the South, requesting admission to hitherto white schools. In Georgia, Charlayne Hunter and Hamilton Holmes pressed for and finally won admission to the University of Georgia in 1961. James Meredith confronted "Ole Miss" in 1961 and entered in 1962 amid rioting that again brought federal troops to enforce the law of the land. His matriculation precipitated a race riot in which two persons were killed. Then, in the fall of 1963, Governor George Wallace stood at the entrance door to the University of Alabama promising to maintain racial segregation and seeking to prevent Vivian Malone and James Hood from en-

Vivian Malone, one of the first African Americans to attend the University of Alabama at Tuscaloosa in 1963. Library of Congress, Prints & Photographs Division, Washington, D.C., reproduction number LC-DIG-ppmsca-05542.

rolling. On the schoolhouse steps federal authorities pushed aside Governor Wallace and, symbolically, the proponents of equal educational opportunity had won a major victory against Jim Crow.

The white South countered with yet another reform strategy to maintain traditional limitations on educational opportunities for African Americans. As historian Marcia Synnott has demonstrated, even before the *Brown* decision was handed down, two strategies of counterreform were emerging in the South: "moderation" and "massive resistance." Both were equally committed in principle to a defense of segregation, but they employed different strategies. The more liberal segment of the white South considered moderation to be a wise tactic of self-reformation, at once conservative in its scheme to preserve the Jim Crow social order and moderate in its flexible response to the new demands created by the *Brown* decision. The tactic of moderation, through token compliance and school equalization programs, sought to avoid or at least delay sweeping federal interventions and to put off answering black demands for widespread desegregation. The "massive resistance" strategy, constructed by reactionaries who insisted that any change would set in motion the forces of dissolution, trumpeted defiance. In 1949, Alabama, for example, adopted the moderation plan of its Governor's Committee on

Higher Education for Negroes to provide for the black youth parallel educational opportunities that would be fully comparable to those opportunities provided in the state institutions for white students. However, the bond issue to finance the recommendations was not approved owing to the forces of massive resistance. In South Carolina, whites opposed to desegregation maneuvered within the law first to postpone implementation of *Brown* and then to determine the minimum amount of desegregation that African Americans would accept. South Carolina's main delay tactic was to offer blacks money to equalize school facilities, hoping to hold on to the racially separate side of *Plessy* by making good on the long-standing promise to equalize facilities. To secure African American support for its efforts to avoid racially desegregated schools, South Carolina allocated between 1951 and 1954 about $120 million, of which 61 percent was spent on school construction for black children, who were just under 44 percent of the state's total school enrollment. Whether southern states practiced "moderation" or "massive resistance," all seemed to realize that either compliance with or resistance to desegregation would require them to make improvements in public education for black children. The grassroots demands for change could no longer be ignored given *Brown v. Board of Education*. Consequently, over the next two decades public schools, especially at the secondary level, were improved throughout the southern states.

The improvements paid dividends in terms of increased educational attainment at the secondary level, progress that was impossible under the pre-*Brown* systems of racial subordination in which high schools were frequently unavailable to African American students. In 1960, the eighth grade was the terminal grade for the vast majority of the South's African American school children. Mississippi, with over 80 percent of its black population having completed fewer than nine years of school, ranked first in the nation in the denial of educational opportunities to African American children. South Carolina and Georgia, with 79 and 75 percent, respectively, followed. By 1970, however, 31 percent of African Americans twenty-five years old and over had graduated from high school and among younger persons (twenty to twenty-four years old) 62 percent were high school graduates. By 1997, 86 percent of African Americans ages twenty-five to twenty-nine were high school graduates Indeed, between 1987 and 1997, the gap in high school completion between African Americans and whites in the twenty-five- to twenty-nine-year-old age group narrowed to the point where there was no statistical difference in 1997. This also represented a remarkable achievement. As high school achievement grew during the post-*Brown* years, civil rights activists turned their attention even more sharply to higher education, to which African American access had been stiffly resisted by southern state governments ever since Reconstruction.

The southern states effectively resisted tax-supported higher education for African Americans during the nineteenth century. Prior to 1900, of the seventeen states mandating racially segregated education, only Virginia, Alabama, North Carolina, and Maryland went beyond what was required to meet the terms of the 1890 Morrill-McComas Act and made any efforts to establish tax-supported institutions for African Americans. Moreover, even in these four states, tax-supported "higher education" for African Americans was limited to normal school education, despite the fact that in some instances (e.g., Alabama) these institutions were called "universities." Further, fourteen of the seventeen southern states simply refused to establish land-grant colleges that permitted blacks to attend until induced to make some provision for their education in order to receive the funds. Within a decade of the passage of the Morrill-McComas Act, the seventeen southern states acceded to the "nondiscrimination" provisions of the statute by agreeing to designate or establish land-grant colleges for blacks. But these institutions, like the state normal schools, were colleges in name only. They also were forced by the states to function primarily as precollegiate teacher training institutes. Not one of them met the land-grant requirement to teach agriculture, mechanic arts, and liberal education on a collegiate level. In vital respects, black southerners entered the twentieth century without any viable state-supported institutions of higher education.

By World War I, this pattern of racial discrimination in public higher education had not changed significantly. A major government document produced during the World War I era emphasized the poor state of black higher education in the seventeen southern states. Thomas Jesse Jones of the Bureau of Education (Department of the Interior) conducted a massive survey of higher education for African Americans in the southern states. In 1916, there were sixteen land-grant colleges and seven state-controlled colleges for African Americans in the South. Although land-grant colleges enrolled approximately one-third of the nation's white college students in 1916, the sixteen black land-grant colleges had virtually no students enrolled in college-level curricula. Only Florida Agricultural and Mechanical College enrolled students in college-level curricula. The seven state (as opposed to land-grant) colleges were reported as having no students at the collegiate level. Thus, in 1916, of the twenty-three black public colleges in seventeen southern states, only one was making a serious effort to become a legitimate college.

Persistent efforts to repress the development of black public higher education characterized the South during the pre- and post-*Brown* eras. In 1904,

Governor James K. Vardaman vetoed the appropriation for the state normal school for blacks in Holly Springs, Mississippi, arguing that higher education was "spoiling" African American agricultural and domestic laborers. Consequently, the Holly Springs Normal School, which had trained two thousand public school teachers since opening in 1873, was forced to close in 1904.

In 1919 Alabama State Teachers College and Alabama A&M were placed under the governance of Alabama's board of education. The board promptly demoted both institutions to junior college status, which meant that the state maintained no institutions in which blacks could secure a four-year college education. During much of the period from 1900 to 1950, therefore, and especially up until the 1930s, most of the students enrolled in black public colleges were enrolled at the elementary and secondary level, with a few in junior college courses. Of the 7,535 students enrolled in the twenty-three black public colleges in 1916, 4,061 were classified as elementary level students, 3,400 were considered secondary or high school level students, and the remaining 74 were distributed between the categories of "unclassified" and "collegiate."

Until 1938, Alabama maintained one public college for African Americans and no graduate and professional schools while maintaining seven public colleges for whites, including several graduate and professional schools. Mississippi supported only one college for blacks, Alcorn, the land-grant college, but it supported six colleges for whites, including two graduate schools. The state of South Carolina supported one college for blacks and six for whites; Louisiana had one state-supported land-grant college for blacks but four state-supported institutions of higher education for whites. In 1930, African Americans were 35.7 percent of the total population in Alabama, 36.9 percent in Louisiana, 50.2 percent in Mississippi, and 45.6 percent in South Carolina. Thus the four states with the largest proportions of blacks supported four public institutions of higher education for them while maintaining twenty-three public colleges for whites. Moreover, none of these states provided graduate and professional educational opportunities for African Americans.

This pattern continued until the *Gaines* decision forced southern states to at least acknowledge the "separate but equal" principle of *Plessy* by making some improvements in public historically black colleges and universities. On December 12, 1938, the Supreme Court of the United States handed down its decision in the case of Lloyd Gaines against the University of Missouri (*State of Missouri EX REL. Gaines v. Canada*, 305 U.S. 337). The Court ruled that Gaines must either be admitted to the law school of the University of Missouri or that the state must, at some place within its borders, provide for the applicant's legal education on a parity with that offered any other citizen of Missouri at state expense. This decision represented the most significant reiteration of "separate but equal" since the Supreme Court handed down *Plessy v. Ferguson* in 1896. It fell like a bomb into the very center of the southern states' resistance to black public higher education. Although it did little to soften southern resistance to higher education for African Americans, it did force southern states to invest modest amounts in black colleges as they attempted to meet the "spirit" of *Gaines v. Canada* without complying fully with African American demands for equal facilities and resources. In 1938, very few southern states provided within their borders any graduate and professional opportunities for their black citizens. Some made legal provisions for out-of-state scholarships to be awarded to African Americans for graduate and professional education, but most simply refused to address the question. Work that was listed as being on the graduate level in 1938 was offered within state borders by the state colleges for blacks in Texas and Virginia. Six other states, Kentucky, Maryland, Missouri, Oklahoma, Tennessee, and West Virginia, provided out-of-state scholarships for African American students to go elsewhere to pursue graduate and professional courses similar to those offered white students at publicly supported, racially segregated, in-state institutions. Nine southern states made no provisions for the education of African Americans on the graduate and professional level. These states were Alabama, Arkansas, Delaware, Florida, Georgia, Louisiana, Mississippi, North Carolina, and South Carolina.

Hence, the *Gaines* decision posed a new challenge to southern states with respect to graduate and professional training in particular and higher education for blacks in general. In Mississippi, Jackson College, which had been run as a private church school for sixty-three years by the American Baptist Home Mission Society, became a state teachers' college by an act of the state legislature in 1940. In Alabama, the board of education restored the status of Alabama A&M, the land-grant college for blacks, as a four-year college in 1940, it having been demoted to a junior college in 1919. In Louisiana, Southern University was quickly authorized to offer graduate majors in animal husbandry, botany, chemistry, comparative literature, economics, German, education, engineering of mechanics, English, French, geology, government, history, home economics, mathematics, music, psychology, and zoology. While the department of education of Louisiana approved this, Southern University was not accredited by the regional accrediting agency, the Southern Association of Secondary Schools and Colleges. In 1947 South Carolina appropriated only sixty thousand dollars to cover the cost of graduate training and training in medicine, law, and pharmacy for its African American graduate and professional students. In contrast, it appropriated more than three hundred thousand dollars for the study of pharmacy and medicine alone for white youth. Throughout the South, the typical response was one of subterfuge, a nod to the *Gaines* decision without making genuine efforts to equalize educational facilities for African American students in publicly supported colleges.

Clearly, the most direct effect of the *Gaines* decision was the rapid increase in makeshift graduate and professional work offered by black colleges. And this was particularly true of black public colleges, which were ordered to offer such work by white state officials to meet the requirements of the *Gaines* decision within the segregated framework. In the fall of 1938, just before the *Gaines* decision was handed down, only seven black colleges (five private and two public) with a total enrollment of 478 students (30 of whom were enrolled in the publicly supported institutions) offered graduate work. Ten years later, sixteen black colleges were offering graduate work. Ten of these sixteen schools were public colleges with 70 percent of the total enrollment of 1,140 African American graduate students in the regular term. The black public colleges also had 54 percent of the total enrollment of the 5,067 African American graduate students enrolled in summer terms. By 1953, of the seventeen public and private institutions offering graduate work, the ten black public colleges enrolled 65 percent of the 2,321 African American students doing graduate work during the regular term and 76 percent of the 6,929 enrolled in summer school.

The unfortunate aspect of this mushroom growth of graduate work, especially in the state institutions, was that the overwhelming majority of them were unprepared to teach graduate-level courses. In fact, as late as 1957, three-fifths of the black state colleges offering graduate work to over half of the graduate students in black colleges were not fully approved by the Southern Association of Secondary Schools and Colleges, their regional accrediting agency. And to make matters worse, under the pressure of the *Sweatt, Sipuel,* and *McLaurin* decisions, some of these same institutions were forced to add professional work, especially law, to their offerings. In so doing, despite some improvements, the southern states made a mockery of graduate and professional work in black public colleges. Institutions that were barely colleges were transformed almost overnight into graduate and professional schools. Long after this period black public colleges found themselves struggling to overcome the legacy of state-imposed mediocrity and be received as academically sound institutions.

Ironically, in many instances, southern state governments used their historical underdevelopment of black public colleges as a rationale for not improving them during the post-*Gaines* and post-*Brown* eras. When the *Gaines* decision demanded an equalization of facilities, the southern states responded by arguing that the high cost of graduate work and the extensive facilities required made the establishment of graduate and professional work in black public colleges impractical and an impossible financial burden. Indeed, it was a significant financial burden, but primarily because southern states had repressed the development of black public colleges throughout the late nineteenth and twentieth centuries.

Instead of responding to the *Gaines* decision by equalizing facilities and resources in public institutions, many southern states merely allocated to black private colleges modest funds for the graduate and professional training of African Americans. In 1958, for example, the largest black graduate and professional faculty reported was eighty-seven at Tuskegee Institute, a private college, and the smallest number at Jackson State College, a public college, where there were two. This pattern of development further retarded the growth of black public colleges and fostered a public perception of them as limited, provincial, and inferior institutions. Southern states not only reinforced the public image of black colleges as mediocre institutions, but they also passed up an excellent opportunity to rectify decades of discrimination against the adequate development of black public colleges with their vindictive response to the *Gaines* decision.

The failure to compensate for decades of discrimination in the post-*Gaines* era extended the underdevelopment of black public colleges into the twenty-first century. In 1992 the federal district court in *Knight v. Alabama* and the United States Supreme Court in *Ayers v. Mississippi* ruled that vestiges of the separate and unequal system remained in the South's state policies. The most recent federal efforts to desegregate southern state systems of public higher education date to 1969, when the Department of Health, Education, and Welfare ordered ten states to develop college desegregation plans. A total of nineteen states were eventually ordered by either the department or the federal courts to come up with desegregation plans. After more than two decades these battles made their way to the United States Supreme Court in the case of *Ayers v. Mississippi* in 1992. Ten years later, a U.S. district judge signed off on a million-dollar settlement plan to end Mississippi's twenty-seven-year-old college desegregation battle (the case was filed by the late Jake Ayers Sr. in 1975). Still, some were dissatisfied with the settlement, arguing that it did not address such issues as faculty pay and admissions inequities. Also, the settlement designated Jackson State University as a "comprehensive university," but failed to back up the designation with sufficient funds and programs. Moreover, the *Ayers* case promised a settlement only for Mississippi, that is, to end state policies or practices or remnants traceable to prior segregation in that state only. It does not force other southern states to comply with it, although the ruling may help to guide other states. Therefore, the struggle to gain equality in public higher education continues into the twentieth-first century and promises to be long and hard. Although there is nothing that legally prohibits southern states from going beyond the *Ayers* settlement in developing historically black institutions of higher education and thereby rectifying more than a century of racial discrimination in public higher education, history suggests that there will be little progress without court-ordered remedies.

The reform and counterreform movements left feelings of ambivalence, resentment, and disappointment on the jubilee anniversary of *Brown v. Board of Education*. The modern era of school desegregation, like so many previous educational reform movements in the South, crystallized the different and conflicting cultural norms, economic interests, and political ideologies undergirding southern life. In vital respects, counterreform efforts designed to stifle compliance with *Brown* took their toll on African American communities. Precisely at the moment that black southerners acquired access to universal k–12 education, southern states proceeded systematically to dismantle the basic infrastructure that had been traditionally responsible for African American educational achievement. In 1968, after years of resistance, desegregation came suddenly to the South. The large majority of historically black public schools were shut down during the initial stage of school desegregation in the late 1960s and early 1970s. Throughout the region school desegregation eliminated an entire generation of black principals, and the impact on guidance counselors and other administrative staff at historically black schools was very similar. More important, as Mildred J. Hudson and Barbara J. Holmes demonstrated, an estimated 38,000 black teachers and administrators lost their jobs in seventeen southern and border states between 1954 and 1964. Further, another 21,515 African American teachers lost their jobs between 1984 and 1989. David S. Cecelski demonstrated that in North Carolina, from 1963 to 1970, the number of African American principals in the state's elementary schools plunged from 620 to only 170. Even more striking, 209 African American principals headed high schools in 1963, but less than 10 did in 1970. By 1973, only 3 black principals had survived the process of wholesale displacement. The cumulative impact of such changes seriously damaged the basic infrastructure of African American education in the South. Many communities faced the daunting task of coping without traditional systems of support while transitioning into new systems of desegregation that were poorly organized and even resistant to the aspirations of African American children. The nature of this transition was not inevitable. Rather, it reflected the thoughtless manner in which states and localities prepared for desegregation and also the continuing resistance to educational progress in African American communities. In many places desegregation was never attempted with a serious effort to make it work and represented a haphazard and even counterreform strategy to the mandate of *Brown v. Board of Education*.

Few if any African Americans were prepared for the mass closing of historically black schools that, along with churches, were the most cherished social institutions in their communities. Black principals, teachers, parents, students and ordinary citizens knew that their schools were the setting of many of their most important social and cultural events, and that black principals and teachers were among the most important voices and role models in their communities. This had been the case since Reconstruction, and after more than a century of tradition black southerners had undoubtedly come to take much of their heritage for granted.

Black southerners approached desegregation with different aspirations, cultural values, and political assumptions. Most of these, of course, were related to the desire to limit white power and control over education, since they had come to view white control as the essence of racial segregation. African Americans wanted desegregation to be a two-way street and a process whereby blacks and whites shared power and control over education. They resisted attempts by local school boards to close all of the black schools and force African American students to attend the formerly all-white schools. They wanted assurances that black principals, teachers, and service workers would not lose their jobs during school desegregation. They wanted to be able to sit on school boards and have some control over curriculum decisions, extracurricular activities, and issues related to discipline and suspension. Finally, they wanted promises that African American children would not be "tracked" into lower-level classes, which could be a means of sustaining racial segregation and subordination within "desegregated" schools. As a consequence of the form in which desegregation was ultimately implemented, black southerners came to a fuller understanding of the fact that racial subordination (not racial separatism) marked the essence of Jim Crow society. In other words, African American children could be subordinated in desegregated contexts albeit in different ways from the way they had been subordinated in segregated settings. The oft-repeated fears of social intermingling and mongrelization notwithstanding, the single greatest impediment to better African American schools was, as Neil R. McMillen has argued, white fear of the revolutionary political and economic implications of educating a population that had long served as the cushion for the southern economy. Whites protected themselves by attempting to maintain firm control over all aspects of the educational process both during segregation and desegregation. Thus, within African American communities white domination and control came to symbolize the continuing effects of Jim Crow in the post–civil rights era. Likewise, the sharing of power and control over educational institutions has come to symbolize the end of earlier systems of racial injustice.

The last reform movement of the twentieth century, one that has extended into the twenty-first century, remains a mystery. It is a paradox within itself. For the first time in southern history state governments pledged educational equality for all citizens irrespective of race and class and promised to leave no child behind. Indeed, southern regional and national leaders, from Jimmy Carter to George Bush, have garnered wide recognition for their support of educational reforms and are known nationally for leading the recent state-mandated reforms to improve the quality of education for all children. Bill Clinton, Richard Wilson Riley, Lamar Alexander, and George W. Bush all became during their tenure as governor of their respective states among the best-known leaders of statewide accountability systems based on standards and aligned assessments that used sanctions and rewards as a means of getting districts and schools to comply. At least on the surface it's a top-down progressive movement that seeks educational equality for all children in the region irrespective of race. Still, this top-down reform movement seems unaware of the historical context in which it unfolds.

The South is a region that has inherited ambivalent and contradictory values regarding public education. During the antebellum and post–Civil War periods, as the region attempted to pass laws and enacted policies fostering public responsibility for education among portions of its white population, it also passed laws and created customs that made literacy a crime among its African American population. During the postbellum period, as schools were built and teachers were held in high esteem in some instances, schools were burned and teachers were ostracized and even lynched in other instances. As one set of experiences reflected the formation and development of values that promoted a system of universal public education for all children, the opposing tendencies fostered opposition to public education for all children and promoted a racially qualified system of separate and unequal education. This set of conflicting values possessed an inertia and staying power that in most settings permitted its survival into our own present. As the South moved toward the close of the twentieth century this tension had modified, even softened in vital respects, but it remained a fundamental part of the region's heritage. As the federal courts continue to find, many standards and policies in southern public education today are not only traceable to the Jim Crow system and were originally adopted for a racially discriminatory purpose, but they also represent the continuing effects of past systems of racial discrimination. Today, the rhetoric of southern educational reform fits nicely into a widely held and often-repeated story about standards, accountability, and a commitment to leaving no child behind in pursuit of higher academic achievement. One can witness firsthand the interweaving of southern history into the grand narrative of progress and commitment to equality and justice. To do so, however, is to ignore the region's long history of resistance to educational progress for all citizens and its entrenched norms of inequality and racial subordination.

Thus, as John Charles Boger has argued, if accountability reforms are imposed on school systems characterized by decades of racial segregation and inequality, they could exacerbate the isolation of schools that are disproportionately filled with black and other minority children from low-income families—the students will disproportionately fail state accountability tests, thereby entrenching broad patterns of grade retention and demoralization, and middle-class and white parents, along with better-trained, more highly-qualified teachers, will abandon those schools. In view of previous reform movements this would constitute a most unfortunate result. All previous grassroots reform movements in the region have resulted in remarkable educational progress among the region's most downtrodden children. Doubtless, the latest reformers have no appreciation of the big shoes they are trying to fill if they truly mean to leave no child behind. Is this movement the final battle in a long war to achieve racial equality in southern public education or another top-down counterreform movement to preserve privilege and inequality?

Suggested Readings

Anderson, James D. *The Education of Blacks in the South, 1860–1935*. Chapel Hill: University of North Carolina Press, 1988.

Belknap, Michael R., ed. *Civil Rights, the White House, and the Justice Department, 1945–1968: Desegregation of Public Education*. New York: Garland Publishing, 1991.

Chirhart, Ann Short. *Torches of Light: Georgia Teachers and the Coming of the Modern South*. Athens: University of Georgia Press, 2005.

Patterson, James T. *Brown v. Board of Education: A Civil Rights Milestone and Its Troubled Legacy*. New York: Oxford University Press, 2001.

Plank, David N., and Rick Ginsberg, eds. *Southern Cities, Southern Schools: Public Education in the Urban South*. Westport, Conn.: Greenwood Press, 1990.

Urban, Wayne J., ed. *Essays in Twentieth-Century Southern Education: Exceptionalism and Its Limits*. New York: Garland Publishing, 1998.

THOMAS G. DYER

A New Face on Southern Higher Education

Dimensions of Quality and Access
at the End of the Twentieth Century

When Edwin Slosson, scientist and journalist, published his book on *Great American Universities* in 1910, he did not have to set foot in the South. The fourteen chapters of the book, published serially in the American magazine *The Independent* during 1909 and 1910, recounted week-long visits Slosson made to each of the universities named by the Carnegie Foundation for the Advancement of Teaching, which ranked universities according to how much they spent on instruction. Slosson, who held a Ph.D. and who also had a solid reputation as a journalist, sought to flesh out the Carnegie rankings by including facets pertaining to enrollments, teaching practices, living arrangements, and physical plants. He visited nine prominent "endowed" institutions: Harvard, Columbia, Chicago, Yale, Cornell, Princeton, Penn, Stanford, and Johns Hopkins and five state universities: Michigan, Minnesota, Wisconsin, California, and Illinois. The only time that he ventured south of the Mason-Dixon Line was when he traveled to Johns Hopkins, perhaps the least "southern" of any university below that fabled line.

During the late nineteenth and early twentieth centuries, the Northeast, the Midwest, and, to a lesser extent, the West experienced a university-building mania as state governments joined wealthy philanthropists to erect massive (by early-twentieth-century standards) institutions with thousands of students, hundreds of faculty members, and annual budgets that defied imagination and opened the era of the American university. At a time when exploding national wealth made possible the rise of American universities, southern "universities" remained essentially liberal arts colleges and tiny ones at that. Southern higher education in the early twentieth century was poor, fragmented, and almost completely focused on undergraduate education. Some southern colleges and universities were among the oldest in the United States and had been relatively stable, and a few even prosperous, before the Civil War. In the antebellum South, plans for modern universities with graduate and professional study enjoyed a brief popularity before the war intervened and ultimately eliminated those dreams. But in the postwar period and well into the twentieth century, southern institutions struggled just to stay alive, as both state-sponsored and denominationally sponsored colleges fought each other for public favor during a prolonged period of retrenchment and reaction in southern life.

The differences between the universities that Slosson visited in 1910 and southern universities could hardly have been greater. Regional poverty and southern indifference to higher education combined to keep its institutions of higher learning incredibly poor during the late nineteenth century and unable, for the most part, to experiment with university-level education. If there were massive quality gaps, there were also substantial differences in size and access to university education. In 1909 when Harvard reached a total enrollment of more than four thousand students, the University of Georgia enrolled slightly over five hundred, about the average size for state universities in the South at that time.

During the first two decades of the twentieth century, however, a handful of southern state universities sought to remake themselves so as to draw more support from the states in which they were located, to serve more students, and to move away from collegiate norms toward university standards. As Michael Dennis has shown, progressive leaders at the University of Virginia, University of Tennessee, University of Georgia, and University of South

The Rotunda at the University of Virginia. Holsinger Studio Collection (#9862), Special Collections, University of Virginia Library.

Carolina looked with interest at the ways in which the University of Wisconsin had forged a new identity by linking itself more closely to the government and the people of the state through a program of public service and outreach. Focusing in the main on enhancing the social sciences, agriculture, engineering, teacher training, and business, and relying in part on federal extension and experiment-station funds, these southern state universities struggled to transform themselves and achieved some limited success. Throughout the interwar era, however, they lost momentum, partially because they had to fight with a variety of new public institutions often founded largely for political reasons and barely funded by the states that founded them.

There were bright spots. During the 1920s and 1930s, another handful of southern universities showed an interest in moving toward national norms in higher education. The University of Virginia, the only southern member of the Association of American Universities, continued on a positive track, and other southern universities with growing aspirations were not far behind. By 1922, the University of North Carolina had achieved AAU membership, joined by Texas seven years later. There were also stirrings of growth at Vanderbilt and Emory, which had received large benefactions in the 1910s. But by far the most impressive endowment of a southern university was made to Trinity College—later renamed Duke University—in North Carolina on which the tobacco magnate James B. Duke had conferred nearly sixty million dollars by the time of his death in 1925.

By the onset of the agricultural depression of the 1920s and the Great Depression of the 1930s, southern higher education had overexpanded to the point that reforms had to be undertaken to streamline emergent state systems, which resulted in draconian cuts in the limited state funds that had been appropriated to support state institutions as well as to the demise of a number of them. Some relief came via the New Deal. Under the aegis of the Works Progress Administration and other New Deal agencies, many buildings were added to southern campuses and the National Youth Administration provided student assistance. Some southern campuses found their physical plants doubled in size as a result of the New Deal. Programs of the federal government, sometimes roundly condemned in the states of the old Confederacy, financed physical facilities on southern campuses that the states themselves had refused to provide.

By and large, however, objective observers found little to commend with respect to southern universities or in the overall picture of southern higher education. Edwin Embree, an official of the Rosenwald Fund, declared in 1935 that no southern university could claim scholarly eminence. "A great university in the South is the insistent need in American scholarship today," Embree asserted. The year before, the American Council on Education found that graduate education in the South ranked dismally, noting that only two southern programs could be considered eminent among the two-hundred thirty or so with a national standing. Most damning perhaps were the judgments of Howard Odum, the southern scholar of regionalism, who offered a particularly bleak picture of the South's universities in 1936. Odum wrote that "for the most part, the educational South appears not only unwilling to face" certain facts about southern higher education but also is "resentful of their presentation."

> It is not only that the region has no university of the first ranking but that it lacks college and university scholars and administrators of topmost distinction, measured by the usual standards of achievement and recognition. . . . [I]t lacks a reasonable number of endowed institutions sufficiently free from state or church dominance to function independently in the best manner of university standards and sufficiently well endowed to set the pace for other regional universities and to keep interregional and national influences and participation constantly on the scene. . . . The region has no educational administrative leaders who participate freely in the nation's councils of learning or who have access to its larger sources of endowment and support.

Further, during the Depression years, local and state governments made a number of overt intrusions into the affairs of southern universities that showed how vulnerable colleges and universities could be to the political whims of southern leaders. In Depression-era Texas, Mississippi, South Carolina, and Georgia, politicians led attacks on individual universities or entire systems. Perhaps the worst of these, and the one with the most enduring effects, was Governor Eugene Talmadge's peremptory firing of nine faculty members and employees of the state university system on trumped-up charges mostly relating to accusations that academicians were promoting race mixing or condoning other violations of the repressive policies of the Talmadge era in Georgia politics, which threw the entire system into chaos. Talmadge was particularly fond of railing against the "furriners" who had invaded Georgia colleges and universities and had brought alien ideologies with them. His and his cronies' interference in the academic affairs of the state became so egregious and so oppressive that the Southern Association of Colleges and Schools withdrew accreditation from all units of the University System of Georgia except the historically black schools, which the association did not accredit in any event. The Talmadge affair had an indirect salutary effect in Georgia where an outraged citizenry rejected Talmadge's bid for reelection and adopted a set of reforms designed to create conditions of academic freedom in the public system, thus laying the foundation for the emergence of a progressive system of higher education in the state. On the other hand, the Talmadge affair did incalculable harm by creating a highly negative image of southern universities and colleges as weak, insular institutions powerless to resist the intrusions of a demagogue like Talmadge. As World War II began, southern colleges and universities were at low ebb.

As the historian Clarence L. Mohr has shown, the war and its aftermath dramatically altered the picture of southern higher education. Mohr has pointed to the presence of federal programs on the wartime campuses as one way in which southern institutions both benefited from the war and became culturally more diverse. Military programs established on the campuses brought thousands of soldiers, sailors, and airmen to study in southern institutions. At Texas A&M University alone, more than forty thousand students took part in wartime training and related educational programs.

Southern institutions benefited in a variety of ways from the military presence on campus. The War Department financed construction and renovation of numerous buildings on southern campuses during the war, which it later (after the war or when the programs were finished) usually turned over to the host institutions. Thus, New Deal construction and federally financed wartime construction modernized and expanded some southern colleges and

The University Arch and the entrance to the University of Georgia campus.
Courtesy of Georgia Photographic Services.

university campuses, giving them far better facilities and transforming their decrepit physical plants into adequately functioning ones.

In many ways, World War II itself was prelude to a tremendous expansion in southern higher education that would be driven by the GI Bill and an expansive national science policy that gradually brought southern institutions into phase with a national research agenda that had been built on "big science" during the war. The postwar influence of federally sponsored contracts and grants drove many southern institutions toward full participation in the national science system that emerged in these years and toward self-assessments that were grounded in national, not regional, standards. And the GI Bill was a major force in making southern universities accessible. Enrollment grew dramatically, often doubling from prewar levels. As Mohr concludes, even when "due allowance is made for southern higher education's gender and racial inequities, the Second World War must still be regarded as the catalyst for an unprecedented drive toward education democratization."

The single greatest force in freeing southern higher education to pursue both expanded access and enhanced quality came when civil rights activists and attorneys forced reluctant, often recalcitrant, southern universities to open their doors to African Americans. The roots of such activity ran to the late 1930s but began to gather real strength in the late 1950s, culminating in the sometimes violent desegregation of key state universities in Georgia, Alabama, and Mississippi. Other state universities followed suit with the private universities generally not undertaking meaningful desegregation until the publics had begun the process. Once the civil rights advocates had won the battles, it allowed many of the universities to give voice to less repressive, more liberal sentiments that had been suppressed for decades by the force of the white southern cultural and political consensus on segregation. Desegregation proceeded at an uneven pace across the region, but there is little doubt that the great cultural and political transformation that accompanied it had a liberating effect on institutions of higher learning that, for decades, had lived with the hypocrisy of advocating free inquiry while denying free access.

A more liberal political climate gave rise to a group of New South governors, like Carl Sanders of Georgia and William Winter of Mississippi, who, recognizing its cultural as well as its economic benefits, were eager to invest in higher education. But dramatic infusions of state funds in the mid- and late 1960s as well as the salutary impact of desegregation took a while to produce results. In 1965, at a time when southern states were becoming fully alive to the need for investment in public higher education and when economic growth in the region was accelerating rapidly, Allan M. Cartter of the American Council on Education assayed the state of southern universities. He argued that the South had historically placed too much value on the "social aspects of higher education (social aspects which themselves have been redefined at various times) and has undervalued the economic benefits." As a result, the region had a poor record of investment in higher education, which had led to "retarded economic development" and made the South a "net importer of most specialized talents."

Cartter focused especially on graduate education, particularly at the doctoral level, because of the level of specialization involved and because of its importance to the economy and the further development of higher education. He pointed to some startling historical facts concerning doctoral education in the South. Prior to 1900, only six southern universities were included among the forty-four universities in the United States that awarded doctoral degrees. Twenty-one more American universities joined the elite forty-four before 1920, but only four of these were in the South. By 1965, thirty-five southern universities made some effort at doctoral education but almost half of those did not award their first doctoral degree until after 1945. Of the more than 50,000 doctoral degrees awarded in the United States in the five years from 1958 through 1962, fewer than 6,000 were awarded in the entire South, amounting to less than 12 percent of the national total. Still, that represented nearly a threefold increase over the total number of doctoral degrees awarded in the region for the period from 1926 to 1947 when southern universities collectively granted 2,461 doctoral degrees or 4.8 percent of the national total.

Cartter also showed how badly faculty compensation lagged behind that in other regions, with southern universities paying faculty members a full 25 percent less than the top national universities. Similar disparities existed in state appropriations, library resources, income from contract research, and quality of graduate students who attended southern institutions. In the end, he concluded that in 1965, the region "cannot as yet boast of a single outstanding institution on the national scene." Moreover, although the region had "a fair share of good universities," it also had "more than its share of poor ones." In a time of increasing national competition "for faculty, students, foundation support and government contracts," Cartter stated, "southern higher education must become quality conscious or be left behind."

In the forty years since Cartter's report, the growth in size and quality of southern higher education and particularly the university sector has been extraordinary. Many factors account for the improvement: a far healthier economy than in the earlier part of the twentieth century; the gradual (if often grudging) demise of segregation; the availability of federal funds for bricks and mortar programs; the emphasis by a group of post–World War II southern political leaders on addressing the inadequacies of public higher education; and the enhancement of an indigenous southern philanthropic establishment with the means to support the development of a small number of distinguished private universities. Most important was the rolling of unprecedented large sums of tax money into public higher education from the late 1950s into the 1990s, in complete contrast to the pattern earlier in the century. Until roughly midcentury, southern legislatures had been penurious in the extreme when it came to funding state universities and other elements of the public higher education system.

With greater resources and improving reputations came the opportunity to build better faculties. Southern universities increasingly became able to attract faculty researchers in the sciences, social sciences, and other areas who could bring in substantial outside funding and who might have had little interest in working for southern universities earlier in the century. And while no studies have been done of the migration of scholars and scientists to southern universities, it seems likely that over the last forty years, faculties have become far more diverse in terms of geographic origin. It is also likely that southern universities have been able to reverse the brain drain that long plagued the region. A new breed of faculty member working with a new breed of savvy administrator enabled southern universities to become aggressive and successful in competing on a national basis for external research dollars and for dollars to support outreach, teaching, and professional development. By the end of the twentieth century, many southern universities had budgets that matched those of sizable corporations. For example, the annual budget of the University of Georgia, which stood at only five hundred thousand dollars in 1945, surpassed the billion-dollar mark in the late 1990s. Southern universities, like American universities generally, began to resemble corporations in other ways as well. Much more entrepreneurial, far more focused on raising external funds, and much more competitive than in earlier times, they lost some of the relaxed ways of the ivory tower as they entered the competitive wars of the new academy.

Southern universities have also seemingly lost much of their collective identity. Indeed, during the last forty years, the study of southern universities and colleges as a group has waned, as has the regular drawing of interregional comparisons like those undertaken by Edwin Embree and Allan Cartter. The result has been that we have very little to go on when generalizing about the dimensions of quality and reputational growth among southern institutions. One of the few systematic commentaries available came from the Vanderbilt historian Paul K. Conkin in 1985, twenty years after Cartter's article. Conkin studied the qualitative dimensions of American universities and surprised some observers when he included the University of North Carolina and the University of Texas among the top ten public universities in the United States and the University of Virginia and the University of Georgia in the top twenty. He did not include any southern institutions among the top ten private universities, but he did place Duke, Emory, Rice, and Vanderbilt in the second ten.

Now, of course, we have the much praised (when you're up) and much excoriated (when you're down) rankings of American colleges and universities as published by the national news magazine *U.S. News and World Report*. The *U.S. News* rankings have been pilloried and condemned on every methodological ground imaginable, but virtually every American college and university as well as virtually every graduate program gives careful, close, and hopeful attention to the rankings when they appear annually. They then use their position in the rankings as one more arrow (a very large one indeed) in the institutional public relations and marketing quiver. As American higher education becomes ever more commercialized and oriented toward market forces, such rankings mean much.

While the rankings have been minutely scrutinized, few, if any, analyses have been done with an eye to the comparative strengths of higher education across regional boundaries. A none-too-scientific look at the most recent *U.S. News* ranking (2005) presents an interesting profile of regional strengths in higher education as measured by the news magazine's survey. Southern universities are most prominent in that segment of the rankings that focuses on "Top Public National Universities," essentially a rating of state universities, which conforms to the historical pattern—state schools have long been the most high profile of southern institutions of higher learning and also the most visible.

Four of the top ten state universities are southern institutions—Virginia, North Carolina, William and Mary, and Georgia Tech (the last of which, incidentally, usually enjoys a top-five rating among all American engineering schools). From year to year Virginia usually grapples with Cal-Berkeley for the first spot in the *U.S. News* rankings of public universities, although in the most recent rankings, Mr. Jefferson's university slipped into a second place tie with Michigan, Berkeley having taken over the top spot unchallenged. The second ten among the public nationals includes three more southern institutions: the University of Texas, the University of Florida, and the University of Georgia.

Several aspects of these rankings deserve comment. First, two regions collectively dominate the rankings of state universities: the South with seven of the top twenty and the West, which also has seven. The ranked southern schools are well dispersed over the region; the western schools are concentrated in California: of the seven in the West, the only non-California

The Old Well and South Building (ca. 1943) at the University of North Carolina at Chapel Hill. North Carolina Collection, University of North Carolina Library at Chapel Hill.

institution is the University of Washington. Midwestern state universities, historically viewed as the strongest state universities, have only four of the twenty spots, while the Middle Atlantic states have three. New England, the plains region, the Rocky Mountain states, and the Southwest have no public universities in the top twenty.

Southern states also do well within the category of "National Universities: Top Schools." This listing probably gets the most attention from the higher education community and from prospective consumers of higher education (parents and students). The top twenty schools in this category are all private institutions, "endowed" universities as they would have been styled by E. E. Slosson in 1910, and are considered the crème de la crème of American universities. The history of American higher education suggests that this group should be dominated by the great private universities of the Northeast, and that is clearly the case as far as the very top of the list goes, which comprises Harvard, Princeton, Yale, and Penn, in that order. But fifth place goes to Duke, a southern interloper. Further, the top twenty institutions in this listing are regionally much more diverse than the top five. Six institutions from New England occupy slots among the twenty, but three other regions (Middle Atlantic, South, and Middle West) have four each while the West (California in this case) has two. The southern institutions included in the "National Universities: Top Schools" category are Duke, Rice, Emory, and Vanderbilt.

Among the top thirty institutions in this category, we find that seven are located in New England and, surprisingly perhaps, seven are in the South. Five of the seven southern institutions are private (Duke, Rice, Vanderbilt, Emory, Wake Forest) and two are public (Virginia and the University of North Carolina). Across the top thirty, there is a relatively even regional distribution. In addition to the seven universities each from New England and the South, the Middle Atlantic states account for six of the top thirty, and five each are located in the West (all California schools) and the Middle West. Nationally, only five public universities crack the top thirty, Cal-Berkeley, Michigan, and UCLA, in addition to the two southern universities, Virginia and North Carolina. No top thirty universities can be found in the vast area (encompassing several American regions) between the Mississippi River and the California border except for Washington University in St. Louis.

If all of this sounds a little too much like discussion of the NCAA Bowl Championship Series among football fans, it's intended only to make one fairly simple point and that is the following: if there had been similar rankings of American universities in 1965 when Allan Cartter wrote his article, it's highly unlikely that any southern university would have cracked the top twenty in either the list of the top national universities or the top public national universities. And, if one were able to project reputational rankings further back into the twentieth century, it's even less likely that southern schools would have been included. Put simply, the standing of southern universities as measured by the *U.S. News* rankings would have seemed pure fantasy to any of the higher education experts who studied such matters in the first sixty years of the twentieth century.

What Clarence Mohr categorized as an "unprecedented drive toward education democratization" in the post–World War II South has resulted in greatly increased access to higher education throughout the region. Population growth and accelerated development of higher education in the region have steadily increased the region's share of national enrollment in higher education from 20 percent in 1920 to 25 percent in 1947 to 31.6 percent in 2001. In 2001, more than five million students attended college in the South (defined here as the member states of the Southern Regional Education Board) of nearly sixteen million who attended colleges and universities in the United States. Much of the higher enrollment can be traced not to the growth of universities, however, but to growth in the region's two-year colleges. The development of these institutions accelerated in the 1960s, and enrollments have grown to the point that by 2001, 31.5 percent of all students attending two-year colleges in the United States were enrolled in southern institutions. Regional rates of recent high school graduates attending college also improved, although southern rates trailed the national average slightly. In the fall of 2000, 55.3 percent of that year's high school graduates enrolled in college compared to 57.6 percent nationally. Among southern states, Mississippi, at 62.5 percent, had the highest rate regionally of recent high school graduates who were college bound.

The region's colleges and universities have, of course, faced numerous challenges in the last forty years. Concerns persist about the difficulties African Americans face in pursuing degrees in higher education. A study by the Atlanta-based Southern Education Foundation, which focused on nineteen southern and border states, pointed out that while the numbers of African Americans attending college has grown substantially since the 1970s, their percentage among first-year college students has increased only 2 percent, from 15 percent in 1976 to 17 percent in 1996. Improved access to two- and four-year colleges in some states enabled statewide systems to enroll African Americans in proportions that approached the percentages of blacks in the general population, but in the public capstone institutions, the number of African American enrollments often fell far short of the percentage of the state's population of African Americans. As the new century opened, ethnic diversity in southern higher education seemed certain to increase across the region. What had been essentially a black and white system was poised to change to one that was multiethnic, owing to the growing presence of more ethnic groups in the region including, in particular, large numbers of Spanish-speaking immigrants and newly transplanted Asians.

Many questions remain concerning the future of southern higher education, and many unanswered questions about its past exist as well. Indeed, for much of the twentieth century, southern higher education labored not only under tremendous fiscal and political disadvantages, it also suffered from widespread public perception that it was inferior in virtually every way to higher education outside the region. For the first six decades of the twentieth century, such perceptions had substantial validity. But one suspects even then that negative perceptions of southern culture in general had much to do with less-than-favorable attitudes toward southern colleges and universities. Dismissive, sometimes sneering, attitudes toward southern colleges and universities dominated elite academic circles in the United States for most of the twentieth century, and remnants survive into the twenty-first. It is not uncommon for academics who work in southern universities and colleges to encounter colleagues from other regions who happily share highly negative views of southern institutions, views that associate broader regional stereotypes of the South with its colleges and universities. Also available to such devotees of southern inferiority is the none-too-inaccurate stereotype of southern universities as football factories, institutions where passions for intercollegiate athletics outrun passions for the life of the mind. Football factories notwithstanding, most contemporary negative attitudes toward southern universities seem rooted in old-fashioned regional prejudice, the expression of which arouses very few complaints outside the South.

Southern history is studied far more intensively than the history of any other American region, but scholars have not given much attention to the evolution of higher learning in the South. The appearance of a few strong histories of individual colleges and universities during the past twenty years and a surge in studies dealing with desegregation are hopeful signs for the future. One of the questions that seems most likely to attract scholars has to do with just how *southern* southern higher education is. Paul Conkin, who also wrote a history of Vanderbilt University, laid out a number of ways in which that institution might be understood with respect to its reflection of the region's past and contemporary cultures. Writing in 1985, Conkin concluded that regional self-consciousness remained an important part of Vanderbilt's identity and could be seen in patterns of speech, a slower pace than other excellent universities in other regions, and in "class and religious homogeneity." He also noted that

Vanderbilt had historically been characterized by "a notable lack of insistent, rigorous intellectuality" compared to some American universities.

The ways in which southern colleges and universities can be studied historically against the backdrop of southern culture are legion. An important question will be whether the drive toward enhanced national status and the presence of more cosmopolitan faculties and student bodies has resulted in those institutions becoming less southern. On the other hand, attachments to other elements of regional culture, the passion for football, for example, seem to suggest that southern colleges and universities are not yet willing to give up all aspects of regional identity. Frequent and repeated athletic scandals as well as a worrisome concentration of institutional power in the hands of what have recently been described as *überboosters* do not augur well for the future and recall the sort of untoward external influence in the affairs of universities that was a part of the regional culture in the early and mid-twentieth century. And neither does a recent trend of budget cuts in higher education by state legislatures offer much hope for the future. Following a national trend, some states across the region (notably Virginia) give glimpses into a future where distinguished southern state universities may be almost entirely shorn of state support and end up becoming more private than public, with all that implies for more restricted access and the survival of publicly supported higher education. From that perspective, the period of expansive growth and enthusiasm for higher education in the South from 1960 until 2000 may turn out to be an anomaly in the broader history of higher learning in the region.

Suggested Readings

Cartter, Allan M. "Qualitative Aspects of Southern University Education." *Southern Economic Journal* 32 (July 1965): 39–69. Suppl. no. 1, pt. 2, "Education and the Southern Economy."

Conkin, Paul K. *Gone with the Ivy: A Biography of Vanderbilt University*. Nashville: Vanderbilt University Press, 1985.

Durden, Robert F. *The Launching of Duke University, 1925–1949*. Durham: Duke University Press, 1993.

Dyer, Thomas G. "Higher Education in the South Since the Civil War: Historiographical Issues and Trends." In *The Web of Southern Social Relations*, edited by Walter J. Fraser and Jon Wakelyn, 127–45. Athens: University of Georgia Press, 1986.

———. *The University of Georgia: A Bicentennial History, 1785–1985*. Athens: University of Georgia Press, 1985.

Geiger, Roger L., ed. "Southern Higher Education in the 20th Century." Special issue of *History of Higher Education Annual* 19 (1999).

Mohr, Clarence L. "World War II and the Transformation of Southern Higher Education." In *Remaking Dixie: The Impact of World War II on the American South*, edited by Neil R. McMillen, 33–55, 166–72. Jackson: University Press of Mississippi, 1996.

Mohr, Clarence L., and Joseph E. Gordon. *Tulane: The Emergence of a Modern University, 1945–1980*. Baton Rouge: Louisiana State University Press, 2001.

Pratt, Robert A. *We Shall Not Be Moved: The Desegregation of the University of Georgia*. Athens: University of Georgia Press, 2002.

Slosson, Edwin E. *Great American Universities*. New York: Macmillan, 1910.

Thelin, John R. *A History of American Higher Education*. Baltimore: Johns Hopkins University Press, 2004.

Contributors

James D. Anderson is head of the Department of Educational Policy Studies and Gurgsell Professor of Educational Policy Studies at the University of Illinois at Urbana-Champaign. He is the author of *The Education of Blacks in the South, 1860–1935* (1988). Anderson served as president of the History of Education Society in 1992. His new book, *Racial Desegregation in Higher Education*, is forthcoming from Teachers College Press.

Julia Kirk Blackwelder is associate dean of the College of Liberal Arts and professor of history at Texas A&M University, College Station. Her books include *Styling Jim Crow: African American Beauty Education in the Segregation Era* (2003), *Now Hiring: The Feminization of Work in the United States, 1900 to 1995* (1997), and *Women of the Depression: Caste and Culture in San Antonio, 1929–1939* (1984).

Charles S. Bullock III is the Richard B. Russell Professor of Political Science and the Josiah Meigs Distinguished Teaching Professor at the University of Georgia. His recent books include *Elections to Open Seats in the U.S. House* (2000), which he coauthored with Keith Gaddie, the second edition of *The New Politics of the Old South* (2003), coedited with Mark Rozell, and *Runoff Elections in the United States* (1992), which he coauthored with Loch Johnson. The last book won the V. O. Key Award presented by the Southern Political Science Association as the best book on southern politics published in 1992. Bullock has served as president of the Georgia and Southern Political Science Associations and as chair of the Legislative Studies Group. He has served as an American Political Science Association Congressional Fellow and a Brookings Institution Guest Scholar.

David L. Carlton is an associate professor of history at Vanderbilt University. He is the author, most notably, of *Mill and Town in South Carolina* (1982) and, with Peter A. Coclanis, *The South, the Nation, and the World: Perspectives on Southern Economic Development* (2003).

James C. Cobb is Spalding Distinguished Professor of History at the University of Georgia. Some of his publications include *Redefining Southern Culture:*

Mind and Identity in the Modern South (1999), *Georgia Odyssey* (1997), *The Mississippi Delta and the World: The Memoirs of David L. Cohn* (1995), *The Selling of The South: The Southern Crusade for Industrial Development, 1936–1990* (1993), *The Most Southern Place on Earth: The Mississippi Delta and the Roots of Regional Identity* (1992), and *Industrialization and Southern Society, 1877–1984* (1984). His most recent book is *Away Down South: A History of Southern Identity* (2005). Cobb served as president of the Southern Historical Association in 1999.

Pete Daniel is a curator at the Smithsonian's National Museum of American History. He has written six books including *Lost Revolutions: The South in the 1950s* (2000), winner of the Elliott Rudwick Prize from the Organization of American Historians; *Breaking the Land: The Transformation of Cotton, Tobacco, and Rice Cultures since 1880* (1985), winner of the Charles S. Sydnor Prize from the Southern Historical Association and the Herbert Feis Award from the American Historical Association; and the forthcoming *Toxic Drift: Pesticides and Health in the Post–World War II South*. He is a past president of the Agricultural History Society and will become president of the Southern Historical Association in November 2005.

Janna Deitz is an assistant professor of political science at Western Illinois University. She received her Ph.D. from the University of Georgia in 2004 and has presented research on women candidates in southern elections at the Citadel Symposium on Southern Politics. Her research interests include legislative behavior, congressional elections, and campaign finance.

Andrew Doyle is an associate professor of history at Winthrop University in Rock Hill, South Carolina. He is currently working on a manuscript titled "Causes Won, Not Lost: College Football and Southern Culture, 1888–1917." He has published numerous articles on southern sports in the *Journal of Sport History*, *Southern Cultures*, and the *International Journal of the History of Sport*.

Thomas G. Dyer is University Professor and director of the Institute of Higher Education at the University of Georgia. He is the author of *Secret Yankees: The Union Circle in Confederate Atlanta* (2001), *The University of Georgia: A Bicentennial History, 1785–1985* (1985), *To Raise Myself a Little: The Diaries and Letters of Jennie, a Georgia Teacher, 1851–1886* (1982), and *Theodore Roosevelt and the Idea of Race* (1980). Dyer was editor of the *Georgia Historical Quarterly* from 1982 to 1989, chairman of the editorial board of *The New*

Georgia Guide (1996), a senior consultant for the *Encyclopedia of Southern Culture*, and chair of the editorial board of the University of Georgia Press for three terms.

David Goldfield is Robert Lee Bailey Professor of History at the University of North Carolina at Charlotte. Currently, he is conducting research for a book titled "Rebirth of a Nation: America during the Civil War Era." His publications include *Southern Histories: Public, Private, and Sacred* (2003), *Still Fighting the Civil War: The American South and Southern History* (2002), *Region, Race, and Cities: Interpreting the Urban South* (1997), *Black, White, and Southern: Race Relations and Southern Culture* (1990), *Cotton Fields and Skyscrapers: Southern City and Region, 1607–1980* (1982), and *Urban Growth in the Age of Sectionalism: Virginia, 1847–1861* (1977). His professional activities include serving as editor in chief of the *Journal of Urban History* (1990–present), president of the Urban History Association (1996–97), and consultant to the U.S. Department of Justice, Civil Rights Division, on voting rights cases.

Grace Elizabeth Hale is an associate professor of history at the University of Virginia. She is the author of *Making Whiteness: The Culture of Segregation in the South, 1890–1940* (1998). She has published numerous articles in journals and edited collections and has also served as a consultant for film and video documentaries on the segregated South.

Fred Hobson is Lineberger Professor in the Humanities at the University of North Carolina at Chapel Hill and editor of the *Southern Literary Journal*. A winner of the Lillian Smith Award and the Jules Landry Award in southern studies, he is the author of a number of books, including *Tell about the South: The Southern Rage to Explain* (1983), *Mencken: A Life* (1995), and, most recently, *The Silencing of Emily Mullen and Other Essays* (2005). He has published essays and reviews in a number of magazines and journals, including the *Atlantic Monthly*, the *New York Times Book Review*, the *Times Literary Supplement*, the *Southern Review*, and the *Virginia Quarterly Review*.

Alexander P. Lamis is an associate professor of political science at Case Western Reserve University in Cleveland. He is the author of *The Two Party South*, 2nd exp. ed. (1984) and editor of *Southern Politics in the 1990s* (1999) and *Ohio Politics* (1994; 2nd ed. forthcoming, 2006). He received a Ph.D. in political science from Vanderbilt University and a J.D. from the University of Maryland Law School.

John Shelton Reed is William Rand Kenan Jr. Professor Emeritus of sociology at the University of North Carolina, Chapel Hill, where he was director of the Howard Odum Institute for Research in Social Sciences and helped to found the university's Center for the Study of the American South. He has written or edited over a dozen books, including *Minding the South* (2003), *1001 Things Everyone Should Know about the South*, written with his wife, Dale Volberg Reed (1996), *Kicking Back: Further Dispatches from the South* (1995), *Surveying the South: Studies in Regional Sociology* (1993), *"My Tears Spoiled My Aim" and Other Reflections on Southern Culture* (1994), *Whistling Dixie: Dispatches from the South* (1992), *Southern Folk, Plain and Fancy: Native White Social Types* (1986), *Southerners: The Social Psychology of Sectionalism* (1983), *One South: An Ethnic Approach to Regional Culture* (1982), and *The Enduring South: Subcultural Persistence in Mass Society* (1975). He was a founding coeditor of the quarterly *Southern Cultures*. He has been president of the Southern Sociological Society and the Southern Association for Public Opinion Research and was appointed by President Reagan to the council of the National Endowment for the Humanities.

David Stricklin is the director of the Butler Center for Arkansas Studies in Little Rock and a former associate professor and chair of the Humanities Division at Lyon College. He was awarded the 1999 CASE/Carnegie Arkansas Professor of the Year and is a former chair of the board of directors of the Arkansas Humanities Council. He is a coauthor with Bill C. Malone of *Southern Music/American Music* (2003) and author of *A Genealogy of Dissent: Southern Baptist Protest in the Twentieth Century* (1999).

Dana F. White is Goodrich C. White Professor in the Graduate Institute of the Liberal Arts at Emory University. He is author of *The Urbanists, 1865–1915* (1989) and coeditor of *Olmsted South: Old South Critic/New South Planner* (1979). White has served as consultant for exhibitions at the Atlanta History Center, the Ivan Allen Jr. Braves Museum, and Emory's Woodruff Library. Together with fellow urban historian Tim Crimmins, he conceptualized, wrote, and narrated the award-winning eight-part documentary series *The Making of Modern Atlanta*. He is currently working on a study of segregated filmgoing in Atlanta with film historian Matthew Bernstein and an analysis of Greater Atlanta with urban geographer Truman Hartshorn.

Charles Reagan Wilson is the director of the Center for the Study of Southern Culture and a professor of history at the University of Mississippi. His books include *Judgment and Grace in Dixie: Southern Faiths from Faulkner to*

Elvis (1995) and *Baptized in Blood: The Religion of the Lost Cause, 1865–1920* (1980). He coedited with William Ferris the *Encyclopedia of Southern Culture* (1989) and edited *The South and the Caribbean* (2000), *Religion and the American Civil War* (1998), *The New Regionalism* (1997), and *Religion in the South* (1985). Wilson is also editor of a new University of North Carolina Press book series entitled New Directions in Southern Studies, the first title of which will be published in 2006.

Gavin Wright is the William Robertson Coe Professor of American Economic History at Stanford University. He received his Ph.D. in economics from Yale University in 1969 and taught at the University of Michigan from 1972 until 1982. His publications include *The Political Economy of the Cotton South* (1978) and *Old South, New South: Revolutions in the Southern Economy since the Civil War* (1986). Wright is past president of the Economic History Association and the Agricultural History Society.

Index

Aaron, Henry (Hank), 199, 207
Abernathy, Ralph David, 60, 218
Absalom, Absalom! (W. Faulkner), 158–59, 166
African Americans: economic interests of, 5, 28–29, 48, 83; employment of, 45–46, 57, 95–96, 98, 102–3, 281–82; literacy rates of, 264–68; migration of, 8–9, 57, 82, 88, 135, 198, 256–57; political influence of, 88–90, 89t, 230, 255–56; socioreligious engagement of, 216, 218; as southerners, 9, 88, 147
Agee, James, 163
Agnes Scott College, 47
Agricultural Stabilization and Conservation Service (ASCS), 103
agriculture: and federal assistance for agribusiness, 4, 92–105, 118, 259; and land/labor ratios, 79; modernization of, 56, 81, 92–99, 104–5, 139, 259; and out-migration, 56, 82; and ratio of black/white farmers, 102–3; synthetic chemicals in, 99–102
Alabama, 6, 26, 32–33, 35, 66, 129; Anniston, 249; Birmingham, 6, 64, 68, 70, 109, 113, 165, 249–50; Huntsville, 122, 261; Montgomery, 59–60, 62, 249; Selma, 88, 165
Alabama A&M College, 277–78
Alabama Governor's Committee on Higher Education for Negroes, 275–76
Alabama State Teachers College, 277
Alcorn College, 277
Alexander, Lamar, 283
Alexander, Will W., 214
Allen, Ivan, 83, 204
All God's Dangers (Rosengarten), 94
All the King's Men (Warren), 161

American Council on Education, 288, 291
Ames, Jessie Daniel, 25, 48, 54
Anderson, James D., 12
Anderson, Sherwood, 165
Applebome, Peter, 88
Arkansas, 6, 83, 86, 93, 265
Arnall, Ellis, 117
Asbury College, 209
Ash, Mary Kay, 54
Asian Americans, 26, 53, 147
As I Lay Dying (W. Faulkner), 158
Assimilation, American Style (Salins), 34
Association of American Universities (AAU), 287
Association of Southern Women for the Prevention of Lynching, 25, 48, 215
Atlanta, Ga.: economic development of, 5, 95–96, 106–7, 120; sociopolitical development of, 82–83, 87, 89–90, 136, 144–45
Atlanta Crackers (baseball team), 190, 199
Atlanta Journal-Constitution, 12, 44, 67, 145, 190
Atlanta Student Movement, 63
Atlanta University Center, 57
Atwater, Lee, 229
Auburn University, 193
Autobiography of an Ex-coloured Man (J. W. Johnson), 156
Awakening, The (Chopin), 155
Ayers, Edward, 66
Ayers, Jake, Sr., 280
Ayers v. Mississippi, 280

Bacote, Clarence, 134
Baer, Clara, 195–96
Baldwin, James, 132
Baptists, 11, 152, 211, 216, 219–20, 278

Barnes, Roy, 244
Bartley, Numan, 81
Beckwith, Byron De La, 6
Benson, Ezra Taft, 97
Bethune, Mary McLeod, 48
Big Woods (W. Faulkner), 94
Bird, James, 70
Birmingham Barons (baseball team), 190, 199
Birmingham Black Barons (baseball team), 100
birthrate, 34, 41–42, 47, 79, 151
Bishop, J. C., 214
Bissinger, H. G., 205
Black, Jim, 30
Black Boy (R. Wright), 161
blacks. *See* African Americans
Blackwelder, Cora Kay, 47
Blackwelder, Julia Kirk, 3, 14
Bleikasten, Andre, 160
Boger, John Charles, 284
Bond, Horace Mann, 267
Bond, Julian, 62, 71
Borjas, George, 34
Bowers, Sam, 71
Boyd, William, 86
Bradley, Mamie, 58
Brady, Lee, 242
Brady, Tom, 71
Branch, Taylor, 60
Briggs, Asa, 130
Broach, Glen T., 242
Brooks, Clayton McClure, 72
Brotherhood of Sleeping Car Porters, 60
Brown, Mrs. Homer L., 96
Brownell, Blaine A., 138
Brown v. Board of Education (1954): and black aspirations, 282–83; and *Brown II* (1955), 251; and collapse of one-party system, 228; overturns *Plessy*, 58, 250; paves the way for the Sun Belt, 51; resistance to, 70, 103, 199, 272–75, 281–82. *See also* U.S. Supreme Court
Bryant, Paul "Bear," 203
Bullock, Charles S., 4, 13
Bureau of Education, 276

Bush, George H. W., 233
Bush, George W., 66, 237, 239, 283
Byrd, William, 170

Cabell, James Branch, 155, 157
Caldwell, Erskine, 94, 158
Calhoun, John C., 4
Candler School of Theology, 216
Cane (Toomer), 156
Carlton, David, 4, 6, 13
Carnegie Foundation for the Advancement of Teaching, 285–86
Carson, Rachel, 102
Carter, Jimmy, 7, 220, 230–31
Carter family, 152
Cartter, Allan M., 291, 293, 296
Case, Everett, 202
Cash, W. J., 2, 148, 150, 156, 162; *The Mind of the South*, 147, 163
Catholics/Catholicism, 22, 34–36, 213, 221
Cecelski, David S., 281
Cell, John, 2
Chaney, James, 70
Chappell, Fred, 168
Charlotte College, 48, 50
Chesnutt, Charles W., 155
Chicago, Ill., 56, 130
Chicago School of Sociology, 130
Childhood (Crews), 94
Chiles, Lawton, 231
Chopin, Kate, 155
Christian Coalition, 220
churches. *See* religion; *and specific denominations*
Churches of Christ, 211
Church of God, 212
Civilian Conservation Corps, 256
Civil Rights Act (1964), 6–7, 64–65, 83–84, 226, 250–51, 262
civil rights movement: catalysts for, 198; direct action campaigns of, 6, 59–65, 70, 248–49; and economic development, 82–83; under Johnson, Lyndon B., 226; and women's rights, 52
Clark, Jim, 6

Clark, Kenneth and Mamie, 250
Clark, Septima, 51
Clark, Victor, 110
Clark Atlanta University, 57
Clinton, Bill, 7, 48, 233–38, 283
Cobb, James C., 81, 118
Cobb, Ned, 94
Cobb, Ty, 191
Cochran, Thad, 241
Cone, Bonnie, 48
Confederacy (geographical area), 87, 108, 144, 211
Confessions of Nat Turner, The (Styron), 166
Congressional Hispanic Caucus, 30
Congress of Racial Equality (CORE), 62, 64
Conkin, Paul K., 293, 298
Connor, T. Eugene "Bull," 6, 71, 249
Coogler, J. Gordon, 154
Cooperative State Research Service, 103
Cotton States and International Exposition (1895), 144
Cowley, Malcolm, 160
Cranford, Alfred, 67
Crews, Harry, 94
cultural distinctives: and commercial sports, 10, 188–89, 191, 205; and economic distinctives, 84–85; of the New South, 10, 54–58, 78–79, 138, 149–52, 248; racial, 9, 12, 30, 36, 72–73, 88, 147; religious, 35–36, 209–11, 214, 219–20; and southern culture industry, 151, 207; and southern way of life, 88, 138, 214, 248

Daimler-Benz AG, 8
Daniel, Pete, 3, 13
David, Paul T. (David's Index), 226, 227t, 235, 241
Davidson, Donald, 156–57, 161
Davis, Thadious, 9
Deitz, Janna, 4, 13
Delta Air Service/Lines, 100–101
Delta Wedding (Welty), 164
Denmark, Leila, 48, 54
Dennis, Michael, 286

Denny, George, 193
desegregation. *See* integration
Dexter Avenue Baptist Church, 60–61
Dirt and Desire (Yaeger), 164–65
Disciples of Christ, 211
Dixie, 82, 144, 165, 256–57
Dixon, Frank, 214
Dixon, Thomas, 155
Dole, Bob, 238
Dollar, Creflo A., Jr., 219
Douglass, Frederick, 155
Doyle, Andy, 10–11
Du Bois, W. E. B., 13
Duke, David, 32
Duke, James Buchanan, 118, 288
Duke University, 121, 202, 287
Durr, Clifford, 60
Dust Tracks on a Road (Hurston), 161
Dyer, Thomas G., 12

Eagle Forum, 52
East Coast Nuclear Submarine Base (Ga.), 260
Eastland, James, 259
economic growth and development: and cheap labor, 80, 112–13; after Civil Rights Act, 82; and civil rights legislation, 83–84; decline of, 79, 109–12; federal assistance for, 4, 92–97, 122, 258–61, 289; and financial institutions, 111; and globalization, 8, 107, 125; and political economy, 5–6, 86–87, 95, 229; and portability, 119–22; regional, 13, 79, 109–10; versus southern distinctiveness, 10, 77, 79, 84–90, 109–12; and sports, 192, 197–98, 206–7; after World War II, 4–5, 40, 50, 106–7, 121. *See also* federal government; industrial development
Edge City (Garreau), 136
Edgerton, Clyde, 168
Edmonds, Richard H., 22
education: and Elementary and Secondary Education Act (1965), 251; extension services for, 92, 103; graduate and professional, 47, 277–81,

Frank, Leo, 22, 67–68
Franklin, Jimmy Lewis, 147
Franklin, John Hope, 148
Franklin, Shirley, 52
Freedom Riders, 64, 249
Frey, William H., 88
Friday Night Lights (Bissinger), 205
Fulton Bag factory, 44

Gaines, Ernest J., 11, 168, 170
Gaines decision, 277–78
Garreau, Joel, 136
General Electric Company, 118
General Motors Corporation, 120, 124
Georgia: Albany, 129; Baker County, 129, 137; Catawba County, 33; Cherokee County, 137; Dobbins Air Force Base, 260; Fort Benning, 57, 260–61; Fort Gordon, 260; Fort McPherson, 122, 259–60; Fort Stewart, 260; Gwinnett County, 26; and HOPE scholarship program, 243; Hunter Air Field, 260; Marietta, 261; Newton, 33, 129; as representative of the South, 144–45; as two entities, 137; Warner Robins Air Force Base, 260. *See also* Atlanta, Ga.
Georgia College for Women, 47
Georgia College of Medicine, 48
Georgia Institute of Technology, 47, 194, 199, 294
Gibbons, Kaye, 168
Gingrich, Newt, 237–38
Glasgow, Ellen, 155, 157
Glenn, Norval, 149
God's Little Acre (Caldwell), 94, 158
Goldfield, David, 12
Goldwater, Barry, 7, 228, 253
Gone with the Wind (Mitchell), 3, 43
Goodman, Andrew, 70
Gordon, Caroline, 164–65
Grady, Henry W., 2, 8, 108
Graham, Billy, 214
Grand Ole Opry, 99, 152
Graves, Anna, 50
Gray, Fred, 60
Great Depression, 3, 96–98, 196–97

Great Migration (1916–20), 3, 118, 135
Green, Paula, 157
Green Index ratings, 87
Griffith, Marvin, 199
Grundy, Pamela, 193, 196

Hackney, Sheldon, 148
Hale, Grace Elizabeth, 3, 12
Haley, Alex, 24, 147
Hall, Randal L., 206
Ham, Mordecai, 214
Hamer, Fannie Lou, 52, 54, 71
Hamlet, The (W. Faulkner), 160
Handlin, Oscar, 134
Hannah, Barry, 167–68
Harding, Vincent, 57
Harris, Eddie, 147
Harris, Joel Chandler, 52
Hartsfield, William, 68
Hawke, Jack, 242–43
Heard, Alexander, 226
Heberle, Rudolph, 131
Hebert, Edward, 260
Heckman, James, 83
Heisman, John, 193
Herberg, Will, 213
Hiatt, John, 146
Hiring the Black Worker (Minchin), 84
Hispanics, 12, 26–37, 53, 147, 221
Hodges, Luther, 121
Holiness churches, 212
Holly Farms, 86
Holly Springs (Miss.) Normal School, 277
Holmes, Barbara J., 281
Holmes, Hamilton, 273
Hood, James, 273
Hope, Lugenia Burns, 42
Hose, Sam, 67
Houston Astros (baseball team), 204
Houston Chronicle, 30
Huckabee, Mike, 239
Hudson, Mildred J., 281
human capital. *See* labor force
Humphrey, Hubert H., 226
Humphreys, Josephine, 167–68
Hunt, James B. "Jim," Jr., 231, 243

Hunter-Gault, Charlayne, 147, 273
Hurston, Zora Neale, 24, 161–62; *Dust Tracks on a Road*, 161; *Their Eyes Were Watching God*, 161
Hutchison, Kay Bailey, 52

illiteracy. *See* literacy
I'll Take My Stand (Ransom), 148, 152, 156–57, 161
immigration/immigrants, 3–4, 20–22, 29, 32–35, 50, 256–57
In Country (B. A. Mason), 168–69
industrial development, 5, 45–47; and automotive industry, 5, 8, 124–25; exemplified by football, 191–92; globalization threats to, 125; history of, 6, 45, 81–84, 106–12; inducements for, 118–20; and manufacturing, 94–95, 110–11, 120; modernization of, 117–19; recruitment for, 86–87; and Silicon Forest Phenomenon, 85–86; in the Southeast, 144; and southern culture industry, 151; strategies for, 13, 113–17, 119–26; and technology and stagnation, 79–80; textiles as case study of, 122–23. *See also* economic growth and development; textiles industry
Ingalls shipyards, 122
integration: black/white views of, 65; of collegiate sports, 202–3; and economic development, 6; as impossible, 65, 70–72; of public schools, 251–52, 274–75
International Harvester Company, 98
Interstate Commerce Commission (ICC), 64, 111, 249
Invisible Man (Ellison), 166–67
Isakson, Johnny, 242

Jackson, Maynard, 52
Jackson, Shoeless Joe, 191
Jackson College/State University, 278, 280
Jacoway, Elizabeth, 83
Jefferson, Thomas, 148
Jet magazine, 58, 64

Jews/Judaism, 20–25, 35, 68, 147, 213–14
Jim Crow system, 134; after *Brown* decision, 70, 274–75, 281–83; literary depictions of, 161; and multiculturalism, 65–66; and professional sports, 198–99; as southern distinctive, 40; after World War II, 5, 35, 252
Johnson, Charles S., 144; *Patterns of Negro Segregation*, 132; *Statistical Atlas of Southern Counties*, 129
Johnson, Claudia Alta (Lady Bird), 52
Johnson, Gerald W., 156
Johnson, James Weldon, 156
Johnson, Junior, 54, 205–6
Johnson, Lyndon B., 226, 228, 253
Johnston, Olin D., 116
Jones, Lu Ann, 95
Jones, Samuel Porter, 214
Jones, Thomas Jesse, 276
Jordan, Barbara, 48, 52, 54, 256
Jordan, Michael, 202, 208

Kartiganer, Donald, 160
Kelley, Camille, 48
Kenan, Randall, 147
Kennedy, John F., 7, 64, 228
Kent, Grady R., 212
Kentucky, 14, 50, 265, 278; Middlesborough, 109
Key, V. O., Jr., 226, 245
Killers of the Dream (Lillian Smith), 162
King, Lonnie C., 63, 71
King, Martin Luther, Jr., 6, 59–60, 64, 70–71, 145, 147, 218, 249
Kirby, Jack, 88
Knight v. Alabama, 280
Ku Klux Klan, 6, 24, 32, 43, 63, 66

labor force: children in, 115; in Great Depression, 98; as illiterate, 124; kinship networks among, 53, 114–15; and labor-intensive industries, 87, 114; out-migration of, 135; productivity levels of, 84; racial segregation of, 82; regionalism of, 79; as unskilled, 8, 80, 111, 113; women in, 44–45; work ethic of, 95

labor unions, 60, 115–17
Lamis, Alexander P., 3, 13
Landrieu, Mary, 241
Lane Poultry, 86
Lanier, Bob, 28
Lanterns on the Levee (Percy), 164, 167
Last Gentleman, The (Percy), 167
Latinos/Latinas. *See* Hispanics
Lee, William States, 118
Let Us Now Praise Famous Men (Agee), 163
Lewis, John, 249
Lie Down in Darkness (Styron), 166, 169
Light in August (W. Faulkner), 158
literacy, 65–66, 124, 129, 252–53, 264, 266–68
literary criticism, 160, 165
literary movements and genres: autobiography, 163–64; black traditions, 11, 161–62; Harlem Renaissance, 11; New Criticism, 160; slave narratives, 155; southern canon, 164–67; Southern Literary Renaissance, 155–57; southern motifs, 11, 94, 155–57, 165, 167–70, 221; Southern Regionalists, 157; Southwest Humorists, 160, 170
literature of the South, 127–29, 137, 146–48, 152–69, 205, 221, 249, 257
Lockheed-Georgia aircraft plant, 122
Lodge, Henry Cabot, 192
Look Homeward, Angel (Thomas Wolfe), 157
Louis, Joe, 198
Louisiana, 254, 267, 277; New Orleans, 20, 22, 26, 130; Tallulah, 100; West Feliciana Parish, 129
Louisiana State University, 197
Loury, Glenn, 147
Lumpkin, Katharine Du Pre, 164
Lutherans, 210
lynching, 22, 58, 66–68, 213

Making of a Southerner, The (Lumpkin), 164
Malone, Vivian, 273

Man in Full, A (Tom Wolfe), 2, 26, 127–29
Mansion, The (W. Faulkner), 160
Married Ladies' Social Club, 42
Marrs, Suzanne, 165
Marshall, Thurgood, 58, 70–71
Mary Kay, Inc., 54
Maryland, xiv, 264–65, 272, 276–78
Mason, Bobbie Ann, 168–69
Mason, Charles Harrison, 212
Masters, Victor I., 11, 24, 35, 149, 209–10
Mathews, Pete, 243
Matthews, John T., 160
Mattingly, Matt, 243
McCorkle, Jill, 168
McCormick, Cyrus, 110
McCullers, Carson, 165
McGuire, Frank, 202
McMillen, Neil R., 282
media: and civil rights action, 57–59, 62–65, 99, 190, 249; magazines, 10, 58, 135, 162, 164, 285
Memphis Office for Multicultural and Religious Affairs, 31
Mencken, H. L., 154–55, 218; "Sahara of the Bozart," 154
Men Working (John Faulkner), 257
Meredith, James, 273
Methodist Commission on Social Service Movements, 215
Methodist Episcopal Church, South, 210–12, 216, 219
Miller, Zell, 243
Miller Brewing Company, 124
Milliken and Company, 123
Minchin, Timothy, 84
Mind of the South, The (Cash), 147, 163
Mississippi, 143–44, 161, 254, 267, 269, 275–77, 289; and *Ayers* decision, 280–81; Bayou Mound, 90; Clarksdale, 98; Duck Hill, 68; Lamar County, 129; Money, 58; Philadelphia, 70, 165; Port Gibson, 24; Sunflower, 272; Woodville, 24
Mississippi State University, 199–200, 273

Missouri, xiv, 265, 277–78
Mitchell, Margaret, 3, 43
Mohr, Clarence L., 289, 291, 297
Montgomery Improvement Association, 60–61
Moore, Harry T., 68
Moral Majority, 220
Morehouse College, 47, 57
Mormons, 221
Morrill Act (1862), 92
Morrill-McComas Act (1890), 276
Morris, Willie, 166
Morris Brown College, 47
Morrison, H. C., 209
Moviegoer, The (Percy), 167
multiculturalism, 65–66, 146–47, 151, 170
Murphy, Edgar Gardner, 214
Murray, Albert, 147
Murray, Lurline Stokes, 94
Musgrove, Ronnie, 240
music, 11, 99, 212, 259
Myrick, Sue, 52

NAACP (National Association for the Advancement of Colored People), 6, 25, 57–58
Naipaul, V. S., 148, 221
Nash, Diane, 64, 71
National American Woman Suffrage Association, 43
National Association of Colored Women's Clubs, 48
National Beauty Culturists League, 45
National Cancer Institute, 102
National Civil Rights Museum, 152
National Council of Jewish Women, 25
National Youth Administration, 256–57, 288
Native Americans, 36
Native Son (R. Wright), 161
nativism, 36
Neel, Isa-Beall, 215
Negroes with Guns (R. F. Williams), 70
Negro League (baseball), 200
Neighborhood Union (Atlanta), 42

Newcomb College (New Orleans), 195–96
New Deal: Agricultural Adjustment Administration (AAA), 4, 92, 95–98, 259; Agricultural Research Service (ARS), 100–101; and agriculture, 93, 95–105, 118, 259; Federal Writers Project, 266; and higher-education assistance, 288; and military spending, 4, 122, 289; National Youth Administration, 256–57, 288; political coalitions of, 95; Rural Electrification Administration (REA), 118, 259; Tennessee Valley Authority (TVA), 228; Works Progress Administration (WPA), 256–57, 288
Newman, Frances, 156–57
Newport News shipyards, 122
New South: as an American counter-point, 149; in antebellum period, 108–9, 111; as the Bible Belt, 218; change and continuity in, 10–11, 85–90, 149–51; as conservative and postindustrial, 54; development strategies in, 119–26; economic development of (*see* industrial development); Green Index ratings of, 87; health care in, 55, 257; immigration patterns in, 20, 26, 50; infrastructure development in, 117–19, 138, 216, 258–59; as multiracial, 12, 28–29, 37, 52–53, 90, 132, 146–47, 297–98; as "Nation's No. 1 economic problem," 144; and population shifts, 7, 82, 88, 256–57, 267; sociocultural changes in, 54–55, 57–58; socioeconomic development of, 30–31, 92, 94; and southernization of America, 150–51; as sports mecca, 151, 188–89, 192–94; as the Sun Belt, 165; urban/rural, compared, 130–31; voting patterns in, 233; women's role in, 50, 150
New York City, 136
Neyland, Robert, 197
Nixon, E. D., 60, 71
nonviolence, as strategy versus way of life, 70, 218

North Carolina: Bessemer City, 109; Camp Lejeune, 261; Catholicism in, 35; Charlotte, 35, 42, 88, 117, 120; Eden, 124; Fort Bragg, 261; Gaston County, 109; Greensboro, 62, 88, 249; Greenville, 191; Hispanics in, 30, 32–35; as part of the South, xiv; Raleigh-Durham, 88; Research Triangle Park, 62, 121–25

North Carolina A&T College, 62

North Carolina Athletic Conference, 193, 196

North Carolina State University, 121, 202

North Carolina Women's Intercollegiate Athletic Association, 193, 196

Nunn, Sam, 231, 260

O'Connor, Flannery, 164–65; *Wise Blood*, 221

Odum, Howard W., 146, 157

Odum Institute's Southern Focus Poll, 144

Office of Multicultural and Religious Affairs, 31

Ohio, 130

Oklahoma, xiv, 278

Old South, 52

OneGeorgia Authority, 137–38

One South (J. S. Reed), 147

Oriard, Michael, 191

Owens, Jesse, 198

Page, Thomas Nelson, 155

Parks, Rosa, 58, 60, 71

Patterns of Negro Segregation (C. S. Johnson), 132

Patterson, John, 203

Patterson, Orlando, 30–31, 72, 90

Peer, Ralph, 150

Pentecostals, 34–35, 212

Percy, William Alexander, 11, 165; *Lanterns on the Levee*, 164, 167; *The Last Gentleman*, 167; *The Moviegoer*, 167

Perdue, Sonny, 244

Perot, Ross, 234–35, 238

Perry, Rick, 30

pesticides, 99–102

Phagan, Mary, 23

pharmaceuticals, and Research Triangle Park, 122

Piece of My Heart, A (Ford), 168

Pigford v. Glickman, 103

Plessy v. Ferguson, 5, 58, 60, 248, 250, 277–78

Poe, Edgar Allan, 155

political development, 5, 7, 30, 82–84, 145, 228–32, 235–36, 242–43; Atlanta model of, 90; of blacks, 89, 89t; of conservatism, 197, 220, 229–30, 242–43; and Democratic Leadership Council, 233; and Democratic Party, 4, 57, 144, 151, 225–28, 231–37, 241–44, 252, 255–56; and Dixiecrat Party, 6, 228, 247; and Freedom Democratic Party, 64; after modernization, 81, 95–97; and National Woman's Party, 43; and New Right agenda, 70; and partisanship, 244–45; and regionalism, 79, 87, 149; and Republican Party, 28–29, 52, 225–26, 229–30, 236–43; and States' Rights Party, 6, 247

Pollack, Harriet, 165

Pope, Rosalyn, 62

Porter, Katherine Anne, 164

Poteat, Edwin McNeill, Jr., 212

Potter, David, 149

poultry production, as regional industry, 86

poverty in the South, 107–8, 129, 137, 212–13, 257

Powell, Lew, 145

Powell, Padgett, 167

Prairie View A&M College (Tex.), 47

Presbyterian Church in the United States (Southern), 210–11, 219

Price, Reynolds, 166

Prohibition movement, 42, 214, 218, 220

Prosser, Gabriel, 265

Rabinowitz, Howard, 108

race relations: in fiction, 10–11, 161–63, 170; fostered by federal government,

race relations (*continued*)
248, 250–54, 261; as impossible history to write, 56–57, 65, 70–72; and public policy, 248; religious views of, 168; use of term, 72

racial/ethnic tensions: between blacks and Hispanics, 12, 32–34; and class, 32–33, 54, 95–96, 170, 193, 196, 206; on education issues, 282–84; and integration, 65–66; between political parties, 242–43; in rural areas, 32–33, 95–96

racial segregation: and civil rights movement, 64–65; in employment, 82–83; epithets for, 134–35; fostered by women's organizations, 43; and franchise laws, 5, 59, 66, 80, 252–53; in higher education, 47, 193–94; and industrial recruitment, 82–83; as literary motif, 168; maintenance of, 58–59, 132; in the New South, 132, 229–30; nostalgia for, 88; as political agenda, 70, 230; public/private, 59–60, 248–49; rituals of, 58–59; and self-image, 12, 250; of social/religious institutions, 53, 92, 103, 211; socioeconomic impact of, 40, 51, 70–71; in sports, 193–94, 197–98; and urbanization, 22, 132, 138; violent support of, 66–67; after World War II, 50, 57

Randolph, A. Philip, 60

Ransom, John Crowe, 148, 152, 156–57, 161

Ray, Celeste, 37

Reagan, Ronald, 230

Red Hills and Cotton (B. Robertson), 164

Reed, John Shelton, 9–10; *The Enduring South*, 79; *One South*, 147

Reed, Ralph, 220

regionalism: and economic development, 13, 78–79, 109–10; persistence of, 87, 90, 143–44, 149; and the political economy, 85–87; and urban-rural balance, 130

religion: as basic to southern life, 11, 24, 35, 149, 209–10; and black churches,
210–11; and church and state as indistinguishable, 35; and church attendance, 210, 213–14, 219–20; and clergy, 216, 218; and fundamentalism, 219–21; in literature, 165; as political factor, 242; as regionally insulated, 210; and revivalism, 214–15; and sectarianism, 211; secularization of, 8, 218–21; social engagement of, 216; women's role in, 54. *See also specific denominations*

Religious Roundtable, 220

Republican Party. *See* political development: and Republican Party

Restorationist movement, 211

Rice University, 296

Rich's Department Store, 63

Rickwood Field baseball stadium, 190

Riis, Jacob, 22

Riley, Richard Wilson, 283

Rivers, Eugene, 147

Rivers, Mendel, 260

R. J. Reynolds Company, 206

Roberts, Elizabeth Maddox, 156

Robertson, Ben, 164

Robertson, Pat, 220

Robinson, Jackie, 198

Robinson, Jo Ann, 60

Rock Springs (Ford), 167

Rodgers, Jimmie, 150

Roosevelt, Eleanor, 5

Roosevelt, Franklin D., 4, 129, 144

Roosevelt, Theodore, 192

Rork, Jonathan, 87

Rose Hill–Magnolia Elementary School, 32

Rosengarten, Theodore, 94

Rubin, Louis D., Jr., 23–24, 166

Rupp, Adolph, 200

Russell, H. J., and Company, 89

Russell, Richard, 260

Rust Belt, 136

Rust Brothers, 98

"Sahara of the Bozart" (Mencken), 154

Salins, Peter, 34

Sanchez, Tony, 30

Stricklin, David, 10–11
Student Nonviolent Coordinating
	Committee (SNCC), 62
Styron, William: *The Confessions of Nat
	Turner*, 166; *Lie Down in Darkness*,
	166, 169
Sullivan, Herschelle, 63
Summons to Memphis (Taylor), 146
Sun Belt: development of, 50–51,
	132, 136–37; epithets for, 28, 136;
	in-migration to, 82; use of term, 28,
	39, 165; women's contribution to
	growth of, 42
Sundquist, Eric, 160
Supreme Court. *See* U.S. Supreme
	Court
Swann v. Charlotte-Mecklenburg, 251
Synnott, Marcia, 274

Tait, Lenora, 63
Talmadge, Eugene, 288
Talmadge, Herman, 71
Tate, Allen, 155–57; *The Fathers*, 161
Taylor, Peter, 146
telecommunications, and Research
	Triangle Park, 122
Temple Synagogue (Atlanta), 68
Tennessee: Bristol, 151; Cleveland,
	212; Dayton, 157, 218; Graceland
	(Memphis), 152; Henning, 25;
	Memphis, 31–32, 120, 152; Nashville,
	64, 152, 155–56; as representative of
	the South, 151–52; South Pittsburgh,
	109; Spring Hill, 124
Tennessee State University, 202
Tennessee Valley Authority (TVA), 118,
	259
Terrell, Suzanne Haik, 241
Texas: Austin, 26; Dallas, 26; Dallas
	Cowboys, 204; Dallas–Fort Worth,
	120, 122; farmsteads in, 91; Fort
	Hood, 261; Fort Worth, 261; and
	gubernatorial election, 14, 237;
	Hispanics in, 28, 30; Houston, 20,
	28, 136; Jackson County, 129; Jasper,
	70; Kelly Field, 50; Odessa, 205; San
	Antonio, 36, 130; Santa Fe, 35

Texas A&M University, 197, 289
Texas Christian University, 197
Texas League (baseball), 190
Texas Southern University, 48
Texas Western College, 200
textiles industry: baseball teams of,
	190–91; and child labor law, 214;
	and cut-and-sew operations, 119,
	124; decline of, 81, 107; foreign
	competition with, 116; and garment
	factories, 45; and General Textile
	Strike, 117; industrial weakness
	of, 122–24; integration of, 83–84;
	maturation and portability of, 112–13;
	as prototypical southern industry,
	116–17; women in, 44–45
Their Eyes Were Watching God
	(Hurston), 161
Thurmond, Strom, 228, 247
Till, Emmett, 58
Tillman, Ben, 71
Time of Man, The (Roberts), 156
Tindall, George B., 37, 151
Tobacco Road (Caldwell), 94, 158
Tocqueville, Alexis de, 148
Tomlinson, A. J., 212
Toomer, Jean, 156
Town, The (W. Faulkner), 160
trade, 20–21, 109–11
trade unions, 60, 115–17
Trans-Mississippi region, 145
transportation, 110–11, 117, 135–36,
	145, 259, 272
Trinity College (Duke), 287
Truman, Harry S., 51, 57, 226, 228
Tucker, Cynthia, 12
Tucker, Jim Guy, 239
Turner, Nat, 265
Tuskegee Institute, 280
Twain, Mark, 155, 160
Tyson Foods, 86

Unitarians, 221
United Daughters of the Confederacy
	(UDC), 43, 54
University of Alabama, 193, 197, 273
University of Florida, 294

University of Georgia, 273, 286, 293–94
University of Houston, 202
University of Kentucky, 200
University of Missouri, 277–78
University of North Carolina, 202, 204, 287; academic rankings of, 294, 296; Chapel Hill, 121, 157–58; Charlotte, 50; Institute for Research in Social Science, 129–30; Odum Institute's Southern Focus Poll, 144
University of South Carolina, 286–87
University of Tennessee, 197, 286
University of Texas, 197, 287, 294
University of Texas Law School, 250
University of Virginia, 193, 199, 286–87, 294, 296
urban areas: contrasted with rural areas, 130–31, 213; edge cities of, 136–37; as essential for professional sports, 190; ethnic tensions in, 32; growth and development of, 13, 40, 130, 134–40; as impossible to integrate, 70–71; in the New Economy, 85; pollution in, 55; racial segregation in, 71, 132–34; rural migration to, 56, 256–57; sprawl versus smart growth of, 14, 137–38; of the Sun Belt, 136; as unattractive to immigrants, 22
Urban South, The, 129–31
U.S. Commission on Civil Rights, 103, 253
U.S. Congress, 231–33, 237–39, 260
U.S. Constitution, Nineteenth Amendment, 50–51
U.S. Department of Agriculture (USDA), 92–98, 102, 103, 118, 259
U.S. Department of Defense, 135
U.S. Department of Health, Education, and Welfare, 280
U.S. Department of Interior, Bureau of Education, 276
U.S. government. *See* federal government
U.S. military, 4, 51, 122, 259–61, 289–91
U.S. News and World Report, 294
U.S. Supreme Court: *Ayers v. Mississippi*, 280; *Plessy v. Ferguson*,

5, 58, 60, 248, 250, 277–78; *State of Missouri EX REL. Gaines v. Canada*, 277–78. See also *Brown v. Board of Education* (1954)

Vance, Rupert, 145–46
Vanderbilt University, 193, 287, 296, 298–99
Vandiver, Ernest, 63
Vardaman, James K., 276–77
Velasquez, Jose, 32
Vesey, Denmark, 265
veterans, 6, 68
Vietnamese immigrants, 147
Vinson, Carl, 260
violence, 66–71, 213, 253, 273
Virginia: Arlington, 261; black population of, 267; Jamestown, 130; military facilities in, 122, 261; Norfolk, 261
voting: and black elected officials, 89–90; and civil rights movement, 248; and disfranchisement, 5, 59, 66, 80, 252–53, 267; by emigrant southerners, 4; influence of race on, 13; and motor voter law, 254; and Reconstruction franchise laws, 66, 266–67; and redistricting, 234, 255; and southern partisan trends, 226, 227t, 233–34; and voter registration, 64, 252–53; and white primary laws, 5, 58
Voting Rights Act (1965): effect of, on Democratic Party, 226; enforcement/implementation of, 253–55; immediate impact of, 6–7, 64–65, 89, 252; restricts states' rights, 262

Waccamaw Sioux, 36
Wachovia Bank and Trust Company, 117
Wade, Wallace, 194
Wagner Act (1935), 167
Wake Forest University, 296
Walker, Alice, 11, 170
Walker, Francis, 192
Walker, Margaret, 147
Walking with the Wind (Lewis), 249

Wall, Bennett H., 131
Wallace, George, 71, 256, 273
Wallace, Joe, 71
Wall Street Journal, 145
Wal-Mart, 92
Walser, Aliene, 42
Walton, Anthony, 147
Warner, John W., 241
Warner, Sam Bass, Jr., 129
Warren, Robert Penn, 15, 156, 160–61
Washington, Booker T., 72
Washington Post, 136
Watson, Tom, 71
Watts, Michael, 86
Weems, Robert E., Jr., 89
Welty, Eudora, 164–65, 167
West, Michael R., 72
West Virginia, xiv
White, Dana, 13
whites: and citizens' councils, 6; in
    collegiate sports, 203; and Democratic
    Party, 225–26, 242; and desegregation,
    62, 66–69; and integration, 65,
    70–72; as NASCAR fans, 206;
    out-migration of, 96–98, 103–4;
    reactions of, to *Brown* decision,
    282–83; regional differences among,
    149; religious/cultural hegemony of,
    211; segregation of, 12, 248; solidarity
    of, 22; on universal public education,
    268–69
William and Mary College, 294
Williams, Robert F., 70
Williams, Wayne, 68
Wilson, Charles, 11
Wilson, Woodrow, 71
Winesburg, Ohio (S. Anderson), 165
Winter, William, 231, 291
Winthrop Normal and Industrial
    College, 47
Wise Blood (O'Connor), 221
Wolfe, Thomas, 157–58

Wolfe, Tom, 134, 136–37, 205; *A Man in
    Full*, 2, 26, 127–29
Woman's Christian Temperance Union
    (WCTU), 42
women: and Civil Rights Act (1954),
    51–52; education of, 47–48, 53, 204;
    expanding career opportunities for, 14;
    as members of the Ku Klux Klan, 43;
    as middle class, 53–54; occupations of,
    5, 44–47, 55, 215; as political leaders,
    52; role of, in the South, 14, 39–42,
    150; as southern writers, 164–65;
    and sports, 11, 195–96, 202, 204,
    206
Women's Political Council, 60
Woodson, Carter G., 265
Woodward, A. H. "Rick," 190
Woodward, C. Vann, 7, 10, 109, 148–49
Woolworth Stores, 63
Works Progress Administration (WPA),
    256–57, 288
World Changers Ministries Christian
    Center, Inc., 219
World War II: effect of, on Jim Crow
    system, 198, 289; effect of, on the
    South, 4–5, 35, 97; and reconfiguration
    of the United States, 14, 42, 45–47,
    135, 291
Wright, Gavin, 4, 13, 118
Wright, Richard, 3, 130, 161–62; *Black
    Boy*, 161; *Native Son*, 161

Yaeger, Patricia, 164–65
Yoder, Edwin M., Jr., 1
Young, Andrew, 147, 256
Young Ladies' Independent Social Club,
    42
Young Married Ladies' Club, 42
YWCA (Young Women's Christian
    Association), 42

Zinn, Howard, 149